AF531491

Health and Wellness Tourism

Health and Wellness Tourism

Jung Bahadur Gupta

RANDOM PUBLICATIONS
NEW DELHI (INDIA)

Health and Wellness Tourism

ISBN 978-93-5111-545-8

Published in 2015 in India by

RANDOM PUBLICATIONS

4376-A/4B, Gali Murari Lal, Ansari Road
New Delhi-110 002
Phone : +9111-43580356, 011-23289044, 011-43142548
e-mail: sales@randompublications.com,
info@randompublications.com, randomexports@gmail.com

Type Setting by : Friends Media, Delhi-110089
Printed at : Thomson Press (India) Ltd

Preface

Health and Wellness tourism is the travel of people to another country for the purpose of obtaining medical treatment in that country. Traditionally, people would travel from less developed countries to major medical centers in highly developed countries for medical treatment that was unavailable in their own communities, The recent trend is for people to travel from developed countries to third world countries for medical treatments because of cost consideration, though the traditional pattern still continues. Another reason for travel for medical treatment is because some treatments may not be legal in the home country, such as some fertility procedures. Some people travel to obtain medical surgeries or other treatments. Some people go abroad for dental tourism or fertility tourism. People with rare genetic disorders may travel to another country where treatment of these conditions is better understood. However, virtually every type of health care, including psychiatry, alternative treatments, convalescent care and even burial services are available. Medical tourists are subject to a variety of risks, which may include deep vein thrombosis, tuberculosis, amoebic dysentery, paratyphoid, poor post-operative care, and/or others. The first recorded instance of people travelling to obtain medical treatment dates back thousands of years to when Greek pilgrims traveled from all over the Mediterranean to the small territory in the Saronic Gulf called Epidauria. This territory was the sanctuary of the healing god Asklepios. Spa towns and sanitariums may be considered an early form of medical tourism. In 18th century England, for example, patients visited spas because they were places with supposedly health-giving mineral waters, treating diseases from gout to liver disorders and bronchitis.

I would like to thank my team for standing beside me throughout my career and writing this book. My special thanks go to "Random Publications" who have published the book.

– Jung Bahadur Gupta

Contents

1

Health Planning: Impacts on Tourism

Since the Second World War, governments in Western industrialised countries have engaged in the planning of health services (Rodwin 1984). Health planning institutions and approaches have varied, but they have shared a common range of concerns. These include:

- How should health needs be assessed and met?
- How should a health system be organised and financed?
- What is the appropriate role and scale of hospitals? and
- What are the appropriate responsibilities for public health programmes?

Over the years the focus of health planning effort has changed. Health planning has evolved from the post-war expansionary phase to issues of cost containment and now to a concern with accountability and health outcomes. The early successes of creating a 'medical–industrial complex' have led, ironically, to a need to critically examine issues of effectiveness, efficiency and equity.

This chapter introduces the main theoretical issues and debates pertaining to planning in general and health planning specifically. It describes the different ways in which planning is conceived and practised. Definitions of key terms are provided. The fundamental dilemma of planning — whether to plan for health services or to plan for health improvement — is also raised.

WHAT IS PLANNING?

Planning can be thought of in numerous ways and is applicable to numerous activities. Most people try to arrange ahead many of the events of life. Budget planning is concerned with the allocation of limited and finite financial resources. Town planning is concerned with the control of influence on the future pattern of urban development and urban services. Most countries — at the national, state or local levels — engage in national security planning, economic planning, social planning, environmental planning and regional development planning. Dictionaries typically define the verb 'to plan' as meaning 'to arrange the parts of', 'to realise the achievement of' or 'to intend'. In the colloquial sense, then, 'planning' is concerned with deliberately achieving some objective by assembling actions into some orderly sequence. Green suggests that planning, as a separate identifiable activity in organisations, emerged from three strands of development. First, the rise of modern, complex industrial organisations in the late nineteenth century required decisions about the future to be taken in a considered and explicit manner.

Second, the Russian Revolution of 1917 led to the attempt to build an economy based on nationally determined plans and, hence, to the need for formal state planning (and planning bureaucracies). Third, the shortages experienced during the Second World War led to centralised controls in many Western countries.In Western industrialised democracies, planning as a generic activity and as a profession is commonly identified as emerging in the twentieth century, particularly after the Great Depression of the 1930s. Planning evolved as an attempt to mitigate the negative consequences of a laissez-faire market economy that was characterised by unrestrained pursuit of self-interest by individuals and corporations. The idea was for the state to intervene in markets through planning instruments in order to protect the collective interest. Public planning has thus had a long association with the notion of the welfare state and it has often been seen to be in conflict with private interests.Definitions of planning often reflect a tension between the technical tasks undertaken by the profession and the end objectives to be achieved by the tasks. In a generic and technical sense, planning can be conceived of as:

- 'the process of preparing a set of decisions for action in the future, directed at achieving goals by preferable means'; or
- 'making current decisions in the light of their future effects'.

However, ways of thinking about planning have evolved with changes in society and the economy. In the 1940s, planning was concerned to set up the desired future end state in detail (that is, blueprint), but by the 1960s planning concentrated on the objectives of the plan and ways of obtaining them or systems planning. Hall suggests that, in the 1970s, planning became more heterogeneous and diffuse and it could be characterised as continuous participation in conflict. Friedmann would emphasise that planning, as the application of technical reasoning to specific problems and leading to action or policy intervention, occurs in a social and political context.

Mainstream planners typically work for the state, although increasing numbers also work within civil society. The planning profession has historically seen the discipline as 'basically a methodology, a set of procedures applicable to a variety of activities aimed at achieving selected goals by the systematic application of resources in programmed quantities and time sequences designed to alter the projected trends and redirect them towards established objectives'. Such a perspective emphasises the technical and rational aspects of planning. Taylor and Reinke expand on this perspective when they agree that 'effective planning requires stepwise application of selected multidisciplinary methods and procedures to designated programmes and projects within specified time frames'. They add that 'planning is not simply a technical exercise; it is an ongoing process of learning, adapting to change and educating'.

As planners move into positions of facilitating change, the traditional model of rational planning is inserted into, if not transformed by, political practice. The values inherent in planning are made explicit by Blum. Planning, he says, 'is devoted to directing and attaining social changes of a specific and desired nature' and is the 'preferred means of achieving deliberate change'. Friedmann also sees planning practice as linking scientific and technical knowledge to processes of societal guidance, if not social transformation.

In the 'societal guidance' model, planning is articulated through the state and is concerned with systematic change, while the political practice of system transformation becomes the focus on planning practice concerned with social transformation.

Parston suggests that planning is both an occupation and an idea. As an occupation, planning is work, a job. As an idea, planning is 'a process which is undertaken to meet some desired objective or to fulfil some purpose'. He argues they are inseparable. Forester also sees an activist role for the planner, in that planners are not only involved in problem solving; they are also concerned with problem finding or the mobilisation of attention to issues of concern.

As an activity that all organisations carry out with a greater or lesser degree of explicitness, planning involves making choices. When carried out by the public sector, planning is often conceived of as an intervention in the free market. In theory, the market allows equilibrium to be established between supply and demand as resources move in response to price signals.

State intervention is limited and 'non-market goods' are produced in a complementary public sector. Classical economists see the market as the most efficient means of operating an economy. However, certain key conditions have to be met. These include good knowledge by the purchaser (or consumer) of the goods or services on offer, buyers and suppliers operating independently and the market operating independently to the extent that a purchase by one consumer does not necessarily affect the decision by another to purchase.

Planning, as an instrument of state intervention, has been justified on a number of grounds since the second half of the twentieth century. Milton Friedman, an economist who champions the free market, supports state intervention in the presence of natural monopolies and externalities. The liberal perspective suggests that state intervention is justified in order to correct market failure, to redistribute income and to manipulate fiscal and monetary policies in order to affect aggregate demand. Structuralist critiques of the state suggest that the contradictory need to maintain the conditions for capital accumulation and to raise revenue to meet its own obligation creates the need to convey an image of pursuing common and general interests of society as a whole, allowing access to power and responding to justified demands.

Planning has also been more recently criticised for its utilitarianism. Modern statecraft has been described as 'devoted to rationalising and standardising ... a social hieroglyph into a legible and administratively more convenient format'. State planning schemes can be seen as a means of social engineering, greater regimentation of communities and daily lives and enhanced state capacity.

Different conceptions of the role of the state will drive views on the nature and extent of state intervention required. For the health sector, views on the need for and the nature of, state intervention depend on whether the state is seen as regulator, service provider, financier or policy formulator for the health sector. In relation to health planning as a form of state intervention, the promarket position argues that health planning is likely to increase administrative controls and reduce professional autonomy and consumer choice. Health services delivery systems based on a professional model or a competitive free enterprise model would be favoured. The radical critique, in contrast, would see health as a right rather than a commodity and would prefer distribution of health resources on the basis of need. A model that requires central planning and regionalisation of health resources, such as the National Health Service in England prior to the Thatcher reforms, would be favoured. A mid-way position, represented by liberals, would accept a mixed system of public and private service provision and financing and focus state intervention on criteria such as accountability, rationality and equity.

Irrespective of their ideological positions, all governments ultimately need to make allocative decisions. Given that pure markets do not exist in the Australian context and that public sector financing and provision are dominant features, the setting of health care priorities is largely determined through health planning. The question, then, is not whether health care should be planned, but what to plan, by whom, how and when.

PLANNING TRADITIONS

Friedmann classifies the intellectual traditions of planning theory according to their political ideology as well as the intended use of knowledge.

The 'policy analysis' tradition derives from organisational theory, particularly how large organisations might improve their ability to make rational decisions. It is a rational–technical approach which builds on public administration, systems analysis and welfare and social choice theory and offers no distinctive philosophical position. The 'social reform' tradition is concerned with institutionalising planning practice and making action by the state more effective. Planners within this tradition tend to advocate a strong role for the state, which has both mediating and authoritative functions. Building on institutional economics and political sociology, they are interested in planning instruments and technical tools that help to manage the economy in the public interest.

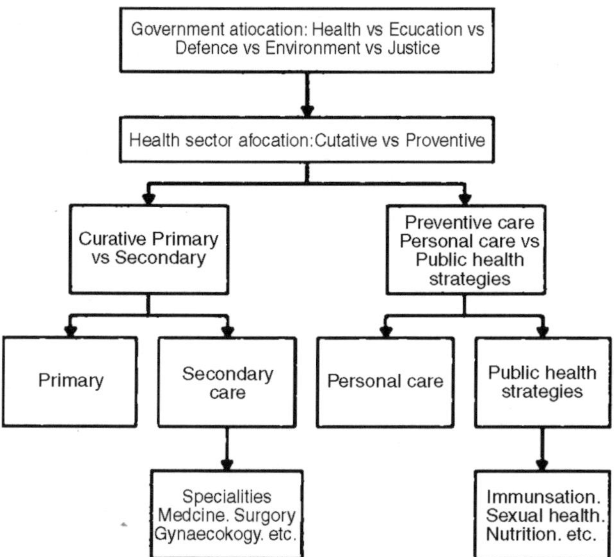

Fig. Levels of Allocative Decision Making by Government

The 'social learning' tradition is derived from organisational development approaches and focuses on the relationship between theory and practice. Rather than treating scientific knowledge as a set of building blocks for the reconstruction of society, planning is viewed as an ongoing dialectical process in which the main emphasis is on new practical undertakings.

Table. Intellectual traditions of Planning Theory.

	Political ideology	
Knowledge to action	Conservative	Radical
In societal guidance	Policy analysis	Social reform
In social transformation	Social learning	Social mobilisation

The 'social mobilisation' tradition departs from all others by asserting the primacy of direct collective action from the grassroots (that is, the community). It is an ideology of the dispossessed, is concerned with social solidarity and aims to change the status quo. All of these traditions can be found in the brief history of health planning in Australia and they continue to co-exist. The Australian health care system has historically been characterised as a publicly planned and regulated system of supply. Even in the Australian private sector, risks are pooled through insurance arrangements and both private health care and insurance are heavily subsidised. Rational-technical planning models have been a feature of decision making about resource allocation in the health system for several decades. At the same time, the Australian approach reflects strong cultural values about health care: that access should be determined by clinical need and not by the ability to pay; that people have a right to health care when they need it; and that health care is a key responsibility of government. Within this cultural context there have been significant shifts in policy, including a move away from institutional health care to community-based health services. Such policy debates and the ensuing processes of change often put planners within the social transformation mode.

Green argues that the track record of planning internationally is often not good, as plans often fail either to be implemented or to respond to the real needs of the community. He suggests that failures arise due to:

- An emphasis on the formal process of planning, leading to it becoming a bureaucratic function or an end in itself;
- Technical failure to analyse needs appropriately or to estimate resources accurately;
- Imposition of plans from the centre in a top-down fashion, without involvement of providers and communities; and/or
- Isolation from other decision-making processes (such as budgets or human resources management).

The lessons are equally relevant to Australia and other countries — planning efforts will fail if planning is constructed as a narrow notion of apparently rational procedures being applied by a small group of technocrats who are oblivious to the broader political factors.

Planning involves choices and change and, as such, will always have its opponents. Planning is neither ideology nor all powerful, but it does exist and have its effects. Understanding power structures and historical constraints, alongside the technical analysis and recognition of opportunities for action, is central to successful planning.

MODELS OF THE PLANNING PROCESS

Early planning thought is dominated by the comprehensive rational model. In this model the set of procedures essentially consists of:

- Goal setting, through identification of problems to be solved, needs to be met, opportunities to be seized and aspirations of stakeholders to be met.
- Plan formulation, through systematic analysis of alternatives, setting of criteria to choose amongst the options and examination of consequences of proposed actions.
- Plan implementation, through deploying a range of actions such as budgets, project schedules and regulatory measures.
- Monitoring and feedback, through reviewing achievements and updating the information, thus maintaining the currency of the plan.

Such understanding of the planning process implies a systems view and a systems approach. The strength of this comprehensive, rational approach is that it is analytical, information-based and allows system design to be a central concern. It also allows for the introduction of normative thinking and valuation into planning. It is a set of technocratic or analytical processes that can be applied to a range of political and social contexts. The outcomes of the planning process reflect the definition of the planning problem, the information used for planning, the governance arrangements for the planning process and the extent to which the planning process is subject to public scrutiny.

The difficulties associated with this model — recognised over time — include the fact that planners seldom start with a blank slate and often do not have access to full information. The comprehensive rational planning model essentially conceives of planning as a technical and top-down activity led by expert planners. In reality, however, planning activities tend to be iterative with various activities occurring in parallel, rather than a chronologically ordered cycle of events. Furthermore, many problems require political rather than technical solutions. Nonetheless, the essential planning skills needed to cope with complex and changing environments can still be built upon the foundation of rational planning.

An alternative approach is the mixed scanning model advocated by Etzioni. Rather than considering comprehensively the alternatives for action, mixed scanning focuses only on selected areas of interest. Once the priority areas are chosen, the analytical process hones in on the marginal changes that are possible. This model is more pragmatic than the rational comprehensive model, insofar as it is a less costly process in terms of time and information resources. The analytical process is otherwise comparable. The critique of the rational planning model rests primarily in the political nature of planning. A third and distinct model is incrementalism, or what Lindblom terms 'muddling through'. The planning process is neither cyclical nor iterative, as the model is simply one of moving from the present position to the desired objectives by acting on a series of political windows of opportunity. The essence of this model is a series of disjointed steps, in contrast with the process of pure rationalism. Its emphasis on the political dimensions more accurately reflects the real world. It is also more flexible and allows for a faster response to changing environments. However, incrementalism may serve to institutionalise existing power relations rather than encourage change, or it may lead to a lack of direction.

LEVELS OF PLANNING

Whether the model is comprehensive rationalism or mixed scanning, the analytical, problem-solving process outlined above can be applied to different levels of planning. These different levels are relevant across different fields of planning, be it health services, organisational development, urban affairs or military engagement.Dever outlines three levels of planning:

- Policy planning, which deals with what ought to be done, is the most conceptual and important in establishing system design. Planning at this level is normative and oriented towards future goals. There is also emphasis on design, on what should be rather than what is.
- Strategic planning, which deals with what can be done, is concerned with possible activities, implications for system structures and effectiveness and creation of instruments for action. The emphasis is on analysis (of need, of systems and institutions, or of stakeholders) which can lead to defining means to achieve desired goals.
- Operational planning, which deals with what will be done, is the most concrete. The focus is on specific activities to be undertaken and the resources required for implementation. The final outcome is an operational or implementation plan.

Friedmann places the levels of planning within a political and bureaucratic context. At the higher level of bureaucratic practice, planning may be focused on societal guidance and covers activities concerned with system maintenance and change. It is usually a top-down management of public affairs and incorporates policy planning and strategic planning as outlined above. The next level of bureaucratic practice is administrative planning. This involves both management of programme routines and developing processes for institutional change. It is comparable to operational planning above.

STYLES OF PLANNING

Planning at the macro level can be seen as synonymous with policy making. Planning becomes a process of strategy formulation with concerns focused on power in political systems, consensus versus conflict views of how society functions and questions about issues such as the role of government, the media, interest groups, political parties and global politics.A more instrumentalist perspective tends to inform planning as strategy development at the organisational level. Mintzberg sees strategy development in organisations as occurring in one of three ways:

- Leader-driven strategy, where the strong leader determines strategy.
- Adaptive strategy, where small (often disjointed) reactive steps are taken to resolve problems/issues (incrementalism).
- Formal planning (rationalism), where analysis is used to develop explicit strategies.

Some organisations rely on the visions and strategies of a single charismatic or powerful leader who may derive their power from expertise, position, shared values or ideas, or coercion. Such a top-down approach is likely to discourage others from being innovative and creative. Further, it does not recognise the increased effectiveness associated with collaboration with communities and stakeholders.

In contrast, adaptive or power–behavioural approaches rely on negotiation, bargaining and the importance of coalitions. This approach recognises that multiple goals can co-exist in organisations and that there is a need to constantly reflect, plan and amend strategies. Incrementalism can be a useful perspective as it provides for organisational plurality, supports an analysis of organisational power and questions whose interests will be served through a particular strategy. But it may also lead to 'muddling through' without direction.

Formal planning can provide a set of concepts, directions and procedures to help people to think and act strategically, with a view to developing a comprehensive short- and long-term agenda. Formal processes can potentially provide an organised approach to developing innovative ideas and for involving people at all levels. A plan, however, is best seen as just one building block in a series of events that determine macro-level strategy (Quinn 1991). Moreover, there is a wide variety of values and approaches to formal planning which may be more or less participatory, planned or impulse-driven, top-down or bottom-up, implicit or explicit, focused on the past or on the future, or concerned with both.

Macro-level strategic planning often involves a mixture of formal planning, incrementalist (power–political) processes and management techniques, depending on the issue and context. There may even be times when openness to new ideas, information and approaches and a strong commitment to a particular issue or goal are more important than a brilliant strategic analysis. Hall et al. suggest that when an issue has high legitimacy, feasibility and support, it is likely to become an agenda item.Insofar as planning is an activity concerned with effecting change, the planner is not a neutral technocrat. Benveniste suggests two essential approaches to planning in terms of how the planner defines his/her role:

- Advocacy planning, where planning is a means of redressing the imbalances between different groups with different power and the role of the planner is to take an active role in facilitating change.
- Apolitical planning, where planning is the use of technical knowledge to achieve political or managerial compromise.

In the classification offered by Friedmann, 'apolitical planning' is comparable to 'allocative planning', which is concerned with distribution of scare resources among competing claimants or uses. 'Advocacy planning', however, is sub-divided into 'institutional planning' and 'radical planning', with the former oriented towards facilitating institutional change and the latter attempting to draw on organised citizen power to promote social transformation. The former can also be conceived of as adopting a pluralist approach involving negotiations with key stakeholders and communities to reach an equilibrium or consensus.

The latter, on the other hand, may adopt a structuralist analysis and be based on collaboration between planners and communities in order to confront and address the determinants of inequity. Sandercock offers a typology of planning approaches based on the evolution of urban planning models. These include:

- The rational comprehensive model, where the planner is indisputably the expert.
- The advocacy planning model, where the planner represents the interests of the disadvantaged (though leaving intact the workings of plural democracy).
- The radical political economy model, where planning is an instrument of the capitalist state and the planner's role is as the revealer of contradictions and an agent of social innovation.
- The equity planning model, where the planning effort consciously seeks to redistribute power, resources or participation.
- The social learning and communicative action model, which acknowledges the value of local and experiential knowledge.
- The radical or emancipatory planning model, where the planner's allegiance is to the community rather than the state and his/her role is to work for social transformation through community-based organisations.

In examining the evolution of planning practice, Sandercock suggests some new pillars for post-modern planning:

- Greater and explicit reliance on practical wisdom;
- People-centred, as opposed to focusing on the planning document;
- Need to access multiple ways of knowing (for example, community experiences);
- Greater emphasis on community empowerment; and
- Recognition of the existence of multiple publics and developing multicultural literacy.

She stresses different sources of information and evidence for planning, with the keys being: knowledge through dialogue; knowledge from experience; learning from local knowledge; learning to read symbolic and non-verbal evidence; learning through contemplative or appreciative knowledge; and learning by doing, or action planning. The inherently value-laden nature of planning thus raises some critical questions about who should be involved in the planning process, how they should be involved and when they should be involved. The answers to these questions are often informed by an understanding of why a planning process is being undertaken. It can be asked:

- Is planning an aid or replacement to political decision making?
- Is planning a means of improving social justice?
- Is planning a means of getting some focus on the future?
- Is planning a gentle, persuasive route to turn ideas into action?

- Is planning a method for shared decision making?
- Is planning a means of improving the quality of effort applied to problem solving?
- Is planning a means of control?

Clarity about the answers to the above questions will result in different ways to resolve the issues which frequently occur in 'doing' planning, such as:

- What should be the process for developing a plan?
- Who should write the plan (for example, consultants, planners or managers)?
- What are the merits of a centralised versus decentralised approach?
- Who should be involved in the planning activities (for example, managers or consumers)?
- What should be the governance arrangement for the planning process?
- What are the merits of group consultation versus individual consultation?

Some of these questions may appear to be purely technical, yet most embody notions about the distribution of power, the winners and losers in any changes to the status quo and the legitimacy of the planning exercise as perceived by the stakeholders.

PARTICULAR FEATURES OF HEALTH PLANNING

The particular features that distinguish health planning from other forms of planning relate to the peculiarity of the health system. Palmer and Short suggest that the distinctiveness of health policy results from three broad defining factors:

- The unique role of the medical profession;
- The complexity of health care; and
- The nature of community expectations and values associated with health.

Some see that health care is distinguished by its hierarchical nature and by the dominance of the medical profession. Medical dominance is seen as being achieved through professionalism (freedom from scrutiny), authority over other health workers and professionals and by shaping social beliefs and understandings about health. Furthermore, the orientation towards curative care, including resource allocation to this area, is reinforced by the nature of the medical profession. Shortell and Kaluzney identify a number of operational features that distinguish health care organisations. While they recognise that many other organisations may possess one or more of these features, health care organisations will display a combination of these factors. Amongst these are:

- Definition and measurement of output is difficult.
- Work is variable and complex.

- Work is likely to be emergency work.
- There is little capacity for error.
- Activities require considerable coordination amongst a range of professional groups.
- Work is highly specialised.
- Workers are highly professionalised with strong allegiances to their profession.
- There is little control over doctors, yet they generate the costs.
- Dual lines of authority often operate.

Hospitals, of all health service organisations, may be particularly impervious to changes in the external environment. As 'closed systems', hospitals have what Taylor described as the hospital's 'cult of efficiency': long-established work patterns, routines, roles and power relations. The hierarchy is maintained with tight scheduling, numerous rules and regulations and control mechanisms. The rigidity, control, tight scheduling and official rules and regulations in health service institutions have long been critiqued. Health service agreements, awards, commitments and understandings also serve to mitigate against organisational change. The bureaucratic culture is determined by the accumulation of the decisions of clinicians.

In more recent times, the traditional power base of doctors may have been partly eroded in the face of health care reform, managerialism, the strengthening power base of other professions in the health field (including economists, planners, nurses, lawyers and alternative medicine), unremitting cost control and the growth of active consumer interest groups. Organisational boundaries are also being blurred with horizontal integration and collaboration between hospitals and community-based health services and between the private and public sectors. Networks of services are increasingly becoming more useful descriptions of the health system.

The complexity of promoting health in the face of increasing societal inequity and environmental degradation is challenging health professionals to work in different ways.Health planning has also been challenged by the rapid pace of change. Public sector reforms, including the introduction of purchaser–provider split models, initially raised questions about whether there is a role for state planning. Experience with formula-based output payments, however, still suggests that the state health authority has to plan for the volume and types of services to be purchased. More recently, purchasers have learned that their planning needs to be at a finer level, since the need for health services is a more specific concept than the need for health.The particular features of the health system described above have several implications.

One is the relationship between health management, health planning and clinical practice. Should health planning be an integral component of health management? Should health planning be the bridge between clinical practice, health management and the political process? Should health planning be the process by which clinical knowledge is channelled to drive health system reform? Another important issue is the relationship between health planning and health financing and accounting.

Should health planners be advocates for health and for patients? Should health planners be technicians involved in the distribution of finite health dollars? Should health planners be the decision makers who decide what to purchase in a purchaser–provider relationship? In practice, all of these roles are present in health planning to a greater or lesser extent. Health planning is thus practised in an environment where technical and bureaucratic traditions exist simultaneously with complexity and change on both technological and social dimensions.

MODELS OF HEALTH PLANNING

Health planning is essentially concerned with improving health and with improving health services delivery or system performance. These two aims, however, require somewhat different approaches to planning. A planning effort concerned with improving population health (also called population-based planning) usually employs the following iterative process:

- Select health issue(s) of concern.
- Identify risks.
- Evaluate population risk levels (at present and in future).
- Select programmes to eliminate or reduce risks.
- Compare needed programmes with existing programmes.
- Adjust resources.
- Evaluate.

A planning exercise focused on improving health services delivery (also known as institution-based or resource-based planning) is also iterative and may use similar logic but has different starting points. The general model is:

- Select health service(s) of concern.
- Determine current demand.
- Forecast potential demand.
- Compare forecast with present resource capacity.
- Adjust resources.
- Evaluate.

Despite comparable logic, there are significant differences between the two models in orientation and methodological requirements. The population-based planning model establishes resource requirements based upon assessment of the risk levels and the health status of a given population. As such, it incorporates a broader understanding of the determinants of health, particularly the social and environmental factors influencing health outcomes. Its tendency is to focus on preventive programmes and reorientate the health care system towards primary health care. It also gives recognition to the need for intersectoral collaboration and for community action in achieving health status improvement. Its main problems rest with gaining an accurate assessment of health status and risk levels and testing the capacity of the health sector to influence broader determinants of health.

The resource-based planning model can be applied to a service or a facility. It is largely an attempt to match supply with demand and its implementation is concerned with adjustments within the existing delivery system, most commonly with rationalisation of existing resources. This form of health planning is the dominant approach.

At a broader level, the differences in population-based and resource-based planning models also reflect different political interests. The resource-based approach is largely concerned with institutional growth and development and serves the dominant interests of the institutional sector. In the health sphere, the dominant institution is the hospital and the dominant interest it serves is the medical profession. The population-based approach, on the other hand, is concerned (by definition) with community and societal interests. It requires the planner (and the planning body) to address the needs of the population as the central issue in the planning process and, as such, to become an advocate for community interests.

The history of health planning is characterised by movement from facilitybased planning to a focus on health outcomes. This reflects a number of important trends. First, there has been a shift in health policy, from expansion of hospital facilities to the need to rationalise resources, through to a concern for the health return on the investment. Second, this shift in orientation itself has reflected the contest in policy space between dominant professional interests and community and consumer interests, supported by 'corporate rationalisers'. Third, there has been a shift from relegating planning to a technical analytical function, to becoming an integral part of management if not an approach to management. It can be expected, then, that the judicious combination of resource-based planning and population-based planning will be the direction for future development.

Health planning operates in a complex and changing environment. Planning can be highly technical or solely political. It can be done to help with 'muddling through' of daily decision making or with a radical envisioning of the future system. The essential problem faced by health planners is as follows. While there is general agreement among policy makers and the community that all people should enjoy good health and have access to health care, planners are not and have not been, able to specify what constitutes an optimal system of health and related services for keeping the population healthy. The challenge is not solely in the technical design of a health system. Insofar as a health system reflects societal norms and expectations as well as the resources available, planning is a political process and requires a multitude of tools for implementation. The planning predicament, then, embodies the tasks associated with leveraging support for action.

CORE HEALTH PLANNING PRINCIPLES

There are a number of planning parameters which are commonly used and essentially form the 'language' of health planning. The core health planning principles include equity, accessibility, efficiency, quality and effectiveness. Each is discussed in turn.

EQUITY

Equity in health planning is often defined as equity of access, which means that an individual will receive an equal opportunity to receive health care, irrespective of personal characteristics such as income, race, gender or place of residence. Equity may be assessed through consideration of the definition of the target group, the methods for promoting access and analysis of the geographical or locational equity.

An important alternative concept is equity of outcome, which refers to the fairness of the outcomes from a particular health care intervention or service. This approach to equity takes into account the range of sociological, economic and other factors that may mitigate against a fair distribution of health chances. Equity of outcome implies the need for redistribution such that new or additional resources are targeted to redress inequity.

ACCESSIBILITY

Access is the capacity or potential to obtain a service or benefit. Access incorporates notions of geographical access, physical/architectural access, cultural/ linguistic access, service acceptability and affordability. Service accessibility may refer to several things: geographical accessibility (for example, travel time to the service, or transport routes); cultural accessibility (for example, availability of interpreters for non-English-speaking background (NESB) immigrants, Aboriginal health workers, or the appropriateness of the environment for young people); physical accessibility (for example, ramps for disabled people or people with prams); service availability (for example, waiting times, opening hours, access for people working and so on); or financial access (that is, whether the cost of a service constitutes a barrier).

EFFICIENCY

Efficiency focuses on the maximisation of total benefits from the use of a given amount of resources. Technical efficiency, or productive efficiency, refers to maximising service or strategy outputs by using minimal inputs. In some social services, measures of efficiency are defined as being synonymous with costeffectiveness in that they relate outcome to input (such as the cost of obtaining one extra year of life). In this book, efficiency will be related to service outputs, not to outcomes.

The efficiency of a particular service or strategy can be assessed or planned for in a number of ways. One approach is to compare the service or strategy to other similar services/strategies on the basis of agreed outputs. It may be important that these output indicators be adjusted to reflect casemix, where such information is available.

Allocative efficiency is concerned with maximising the health and welfare of the community through ensuring an appropriate distribution of benefits. This is particularly important in considering the balance of investment between inpatient and community-based services, between preventive and curative services and between ongoing professional care and the self-help and support services provided by lay volunteers.

Dynamic efficiency is concerned with adaptability of the system over time. It is an economic concept that has yet to come to the fore in the health arena, but it can be expected to assume greater prominence as issues of sustainability attract greater attention.

QUALITY

Quality measures the degree to which a health care professional or service conforms to pre-set standards. Quality measures may include process measures (that is, the activities undertaken as a part of the service) or outcome measures (that is, the result). Ideally, both process and outcome measures would be used.

Information on the quality of processes can be obtained through analysing selected performance measurements (for example, casemix adjusted measures of complication errors, medication errors, transfers to higher levels of care, readmission rates, customer satisfaction, employee surveys, timeliness, waste and defects) or by generating information on a particular issue (for example, the proportion of people with acute myocardial infarction who receive streptokinase treatment within an hour of arriving at hospital).

EFFECTIVENESS/OUTCOMES

Effectiveness is the level of benefit when a service is rendered under ordinary circumstances by average practitioners for typical patients. This is distinct from the concept of efficacy (the level of benefit expected when health services are applied under ideal conditions).

A health outcome is a change in the health of individuals or a group of people or populations that can be attributed wholly or partially to a health intervention or a series of interventions. The key issue is how to identify the best indicators or measures of benefit or health gain. Health gain indicators, or 'outcome measures', should be directly relevant both to the health needs and to the health intervention. For instance, the percentage of the infant population immunised is a relevant indicator for an immunisation campaign. When the immunisation level can be attributed to the intervention (in this case, the immunisation campaign), it can constitute a 'health outcome'. When it cannot be attributed to the intervention, the percentage immunised is a 'health status' measure and not a 'health outcome' measure.

A service should ideally collect and analyse its own data on the outcomes of its interventions. If the service is provided as part of a broader treatment/care stream (for example, physiotherapy post-orthopaedic surgery), it is difficult to undertake outcome evaluation as outcome evaluation is best undertaken across a whole service intervention. Services should identify whether the target group is an individual or a population.

Consumers/communities should ideally be involved in deciding the value of the outcomes of the service/intervention. There are often difficulties in obtaining valid information about outcomes in ordinary service settings, due to differences in consumers/target groups/communities and the multiple factors that may influence outcomes.

As reflected by the core principles of health planning, most of the planner's work is concerned with the efficient and effective delivery of health care services. Does health planning actually make a difference to health status or the level of health experienced by individuals and communities? The answer to this question is complicated by differing understandings of what health is and what health planners do.

DEFINITIONS OF HEALTH

There are many definitions of health. Health can be defined by its presence or its absence and it can have individual or societal parameters. In 1946 the World Health Organisation (WHO) defined health as 'a state of complete physical, mental and social well-being and not merely the absence of disease or infirmity' (WHO 1946).

In this definition, health is defined as a positive experience rather than the absence of sickness and as a social rather than a solely individual phenomenon. Critics argue that it defines health as 'perfect health', a concept which is unable to be measured or obtained and is always future-oriented.

Definitions of health and what health planners do, however, vary according to the frames of reference used.

Doctors, administrators and consumers may view health differently and therefore have different views on how health needs should be met, what health services are needed and how they should be delivered.

Major health frames of references include biological/biomedical, clinical health sciences, population health, ecological public health, social health and everyday life. Planners typically focus on population issues, morbidity and demography.

DETERMINANTS OF HEALTH

The causes of illness are complex and the social, cultural and environmental impacts on health are now well documented. The determinants of health interact in complex ways, with diseases sharing common risk factors and risk factors clustered in socioeconomic groups.

Broad determinants of health may include socioeconomic structures, physical, human-made and ecological environments, health service access or quality, individual biology, cultural beliefs, personal behaviour and lifestyle choices. Specific determinants may include nutrition, infectious agents, trauma, congenital or inherited problems, the physical environment (sun, radiation, altitude), tobacco and alcohol consumption, age, gender, occupation, stress and social isolation. Epidemiological evidence increasingly points to the importance of social factors in explaining health status differences across populations.

Epidemiology is at the core of contemporary understanding of the distribution and causation of health and disease at the population level. Over the past 150 years, epidemiological concepts have undergone a number of shifts, from infectious disease epidemiology (based on germ theory) to the 'classic triad' (physical, genetic and environment causes), to the current interest in chronic diseases and multiple risk factors.

Contemporary public health approaches critique both the biomedical model and an 'illness-centred' focus on the physical risk factors of individuals and groups.

The more comprehensive 'web of causation' takes biological and social factors and interventions into account and may span the genetic to the societal. The central concept in the web of causation is that many variables may be related to a single effect through direct and indirect causes.

The main evidence for determinants of health comes from the prevalence of disease differences between different population sub-groups. The available data about the distribution of determinants are often poor, however and this makes planning for health (with any sophistication) difficult.

If the ultimate goal of health planning activities is to impact positively on health status, then decisions have to be taken about which of the myriad of factors/determinants are priorities for action and what can be done about them. Certainly, it is not necessary (even were it possible) to understand causal mechanisms fully in order to undertake prevention.

The knowledge of small components in the web of causation can significantly contribute to prevention or improved treatment/therapy. The Ottawa Charter suggests five core strategies for health improvement: building healthy public policy; creating supportive environments; strengthening community action; developing personal skills; and reorienting health services. The challenge in health planning is to act successfully on the social determinants of health.

HEALTH SERVICES AND THEIR IMPACT ON HEALTH STATUS

The importance of public health measures in improving health has long been recognised. The dramatic decline in mortality in the last 100 years has been widely attributed to the first public health revolution resulting in environmental improvements, including sanitation, nutrition, water supply, housing and education. These improvements led to significant overall declines in infectious diseases such as tuberculosis, typhus-typhoid, cholera, dysentery and diarrhoea, smallpox and scarlet fever. Medical and scientific advances such as the development of antibiotics, the development of the Salk and Sabin vaccines for poliomyelitis and developments in surgery contributed to reduced death rates in the 1950s; however, these only marginally improved mortality rates. The decline in population mortality in the last century has coincided with, rather than been caused by, the rise of modern medicine.

The impact of medical access on overall health status is likely to be less than the impact of improving working and living conditions. Current studies estimate that 60–80 per cent of current disease is preventable through social change. The Center for Disease Control in the United States attributed only 10 per cent of premature mortality to inadequate health care.

Despite the contention that medical interventions have a relatively marginal impact on the overall mortality levels of a community, medicine generally enjoys great community credence. Science and the scientific method is most frequently credited with having the explanations for illness and health and the 'curative' health system continues to consume the bulk of the health budget.

Nevertheless, whilst national mortality rates tend not to respond to increases in hospital and medical resources, medical care does contribute to the reduction of non-fatal diseases, disability, discomfort and distress. Health services extend life through interventions such as immunisation, accident and trauma services and cancer treatments.

Quality of life may also be improved through relief of pain, improved mobility (joint replacements) and effective treatment of many non-life-threatening conditions. The challenge for health planning is to ensure equitable access to costeffective health care while harnessing complementary strategies for health improvement.

PLANNING FOR EQUITY AND HEALTH

Equity or fairness in health has been defined as a 'focus on the distributional impact of health policies on different individuals and families'. Health inequality can be defined as differences in health status, whereas health inequity links differences in health to social injustice and implies unfairness and the need for amelioration. Equity in health, whilst often appearing in the rhetoric of plans or policies, is rarely adequately examined and is differentially understood and applied, despite being generally applauded as a planning goal.

There are (at least) three main approaches to equity in health: equity as the minimum standard equity of access; and equity of outcome.

EQUITY OF ACCESS AND EQUAL HEALTH CARE

Equity is achieved when an individual receives equal health care irrespective of personal characteristics such as income, race, gender or place of residence. This does not imply equal treatment in the sense of the same treatment. Rather, the treatment or care should be tailored to meet diverse individual needs and circumstances (for example, providing an interpreter for a patient who does not speak English). This approach has been the goal of much policy and planning in the last 30 years.

EQUITY OF OUTCOME

Equity is achieved when the outcomes from a health care intervention — regardless of whether it is intersectoral, prevention, treatment or palliation — are fairly distributed across population groups and individuals. Where the current distribution of outcomes is unfair, this approach provides for redistribution. Consistent with this view, a public health approach, for example, would define equity as 'affirmative action on any resource differentially distributed in the community — for example, housing, education, income and political power. It implies access to these resources by those with the least opportunities at present'.Key questions in health planning therefore include:

- Should plans focus solely on the health care sector, or is a broad-based multisectoral approach required?
- Should equity of outcome replace equity of access? As a corollary, should a goal be to simply maintain (but not improve) the current health standing of advantaged Australians whilst new resources are targeted to improve the health status of the most disadvantaged groups?

A BRIEF HISTORY OF HEALTH PLANNING

Health planning trends have followed the prevailing and shifting policy paradigms of the last 30 years. An initial focus on equity and access had shifted by the 1980s to a concern with equity and efficiency. By the 1990s/2000s the accelerated efficiency drive led to a concern about the quality and effectiveness of health interventions. Planning has evolved from an initial concern with developing much-needed data and information, through to developing normative planning standards which sought to define system and service inputs and then to a concern with outcomes, effectiveness and change management.

The changes in the paradigms have been complemented by ongoing tensions between community/public health services and traditional hospital and institutional approaches, between prevention and treatment, between the bureaucracy versus health providers and, inevitably and most recently, between market forces and planning. The dilemmas associated with developing a broader community-centred, consultative and ecological approach to health have also emerged.

This chapter provides an overview of health planning in Australia, concentrating on its evolution since the 1970s. Health planning practice has essentially developed in three streams. Hospital planning has focused on locational distribution and efficiency of service delivery. Community health services planning has been concerned with equity and population health need. The presence of more specialised planning practice — be it workforce or technology — has reflected policy demands. The planning skills of the health planner have increasingly moved into the corporate planning arena.

EARLY HISTORY OF HEALTH PLANNING

At the start of the twentieth century there was little other than basic population information on which to plan and there was considerable political interference in priority setting. Indeed, hospitals and health services were generally established for political gain, just prior to an election. Until the 1970s, special interest and advocacy groups (aside from medical and professional interest groups) were rare.

Hospitals were established with little detailed planning and without regard to related services. Bed numbers and roles were contrived by comparison with existing hospitals. In the major cities, hospitals were generally built in the inner city areas. In the rural areas, it was expected that each town should have its own hospital and that a town should be 'no more than a horse ride away' (fifteen minutes by motor vehicle).

Irrespective of the size of their catchment population, rural towns generally had an acute hospital that also provided nursing home type services. Hospitals, at this time, were relatively inexpensive to operate and when budgets were overspent the government simply increased the budget. There was a political view that hospital costs had to be met and there was little pressure on health administrators or politicians to contain costs.

Up to the 1970s, public health issues were largely dominated by a biomedical approach. Mass immunisations and screening had been undertaken in the post-war period to eradicate or control diseases such as tuberculosis and polio. By the 1970s, awareness had developed about the problems associated with an 'affluent society': smoking, drinking, obesity and traffic accidents.

Prior to the 1970s, governments tended to respond to concerns about health care direction or decision making by establishing commissions of enquiry or special senate task forces, comprising medical experts and politicians who would identify key recommendations for future action.

Whilst significant changes occurred in health services during these first seven decades of the last century, little formal planning was involved. Planning was effectively entwined with the political process.

COMPREHENSIVE HEALTH PLANNING DEVELOPS

A Division of Planning and Research and began to assess the equity of service provision in the state. This process highlighted the lack of health services in the west of Sydney in comparison to the inner city areas. The first comprehensive service plan was a plan for the rapidly growing south-west of Sydney, incorporating Campbelltown and Liverpool. This plan was revolutionary for its day in that it demonstrated the existing health service's locational inequities and also planned for the full range of services, including hospitals, community health, a new generalist community nurse service and mental health. A similar planning exercise was undertaken for the Mt Druitt area, where a polyclinic rather than a hospital was planned. By the late 1970s the unit had developed the first metropolitan-wide health service plan. Such plans required enormous technical effort, as there was little readily available data.

With the incoming Whitlam government a reformist agenda was introduced at the national level, with the introduction of national health insurance and the Community Health Programme (CHP) as key features. Sidney Sax moved from New South Wales to the Commonwealth to head up the newly established Hospitals and Health Services Commission (HHSC) in 1973. This body developed policies concerning the supply and distribution of health services and established a national health service planning model. The model envisaged a network of services comprised of primary care, private specialist care, hospitals, nursing homes, hostels and rehabilitation and domiciliary care. Of central importance were the primary care teams.

The Commission also developed the first national normative planning standards for health service provision, which were particularly pertinent for the development of the CHP. Amongst these standards were that a community of 6000 people should have two to three general practitioners and two community nurses and that communities with 40 000 people should have a community health centre, with facilities and services to support the primary care teams. The impact of the CHP on health planning was far-reaching, extending beyond the Commonwealth in that it required the introduction of populationbased planning into the state-based health system.

In response to the Whitlam government's policy of augmenting and upgrading hospitals, the Commonwealth HHSC undertook a national study of the needs and distribution of Australian hospitals. The survey highlighted the inequitable distribution of hospital beds between inner city areas and newly developed outer areas in several states. The report found an oversupply of beds in rural areas. The study suggested that the number of beds per 1000 population in Australia (6.3 beds per 1000) was too high. It recommended that Commonwealth financial assistance should be based on assessed need (that is, policy), rather than being merely a per capita distribution. This effectively constituted the first comprehensive national plan for health care in Australia.

However, as often occurs in health planning, the government pre-empted the report and announced capital grants for the development of Westmead Hospital in Sydney, Western Suburbs Geriatric Centre and Hospital in Melbourne and the Mt Gravatt Hospital in Brisbane.

DATA DEVELOPMENT BECOMES IMPORTANT

During the planning process the Commonwealth identified a 'serious shortage of the kind of information that is essential for the planning and evaluation of health services at all levels'. In 1973, the Commonwealth responded by providing a matched grant programme of $1.025 million a year. This comprised $500 000 to support the development of state-based health services planning and research, $500 000 to universities and colleges and $25 000 for seminars on data collection, record systems, planning and evaluation. Specific research training programmes were included in later years. These funds were to be used by the states to develop their planning and research capacities. Until this time, health services planning and research outside New South Wales was poorly developed. It was hoped that biomedical researchers would be enticed into health service planning and teach research skills to bureaucrats involved in planning. The role envisaged for research was to study need, access to services, productivity, efficiency and cost control. The role envisaged for planning was one of providing research findings to health service administrators, with the view that providing such advice might facilitate more rational policy. These grants provided an impetus for the development of health planning as a profession and for the establishment of state and regional planning functions.

In the 1970s there was little planning data other than population statistics. Annual reports of health authorities were only able to report the states' bed capacity, the average length of stay and the daily average, the number of newborn babies and the numbers who attended outpatient services. The hospital billing system provided additional basic data sets, as did hospital surveys. There was, however, no health status or diagnosis information and no patient information. Therefore, for health planning to be taken seriously by health administrators and politicians, significant technical and research effort was required. Consequently, the development of planning tools, including information systems, became an important priority for most planning units. For example, in its annual report in 1977/78, the Commonwealth's proud boast was that it had developed its 'computer based information bank. It now contains demographic and statistical information on hospitals, nursing homes and other institutions ... inappropriate levels of services can thus be identified' (Commonwealth Department of Health).

The first Hospital Morbidity Data Collection was developed in the Riverina area of New South Wales in the early 1960s. The departmental officer representing the NSW Health Commission successfully argued the case for statewide hospital morbidity collection, health surveys and perinatal statistics on the basis that it was 'reprehensible that the state knew more about its sheep than its people!'. By 1977 the completion of hospital morbidity data became mandatory in New South Wales and by 1978 this requirement was extended to private hospitals. The general and psychiatric collections were integrated at this time. This provided a prototype for data on the health status of populations. The data items included in the collection were demographic variables, diagnoses and operations. There was considerable negative reaction to the requirement to complete data returns from hospitals, as it was considered that this would take medical resources away from clinical care. There was also suspicion about how the data would be used. There was, at this time, no national agreement on definitions and approaches. The process of collecting and entering data was laborious. Data would arrive on paper and had to be transferred to punch cards. Data were all centrally processed by the Australian Bureau of Statistics.

The need for more uniform approaches to hospital capital works led to the establishment of a variety of planning bodies. In New South Wales, the Hospital Planning Advisory Council was established in 1973 to develop key capital planning parameters, undertake planning research and develop tools such as the 'hospital planning units' which provided capital planning standards relating to the size, location and general functionality of hospital and health services.

In 1975 a Household Health and Welfare Survey was conducted in the Gosford–Wyong and Illawarra areas of New South Wales by the NSW Division of Planning and Research in conjunction with the Commonwealth Bureau of Statistics. The survey aimed to assess acute and chronic health problems and the health services used by the people.

This became the pilot National Health Survey, which is now an important regular source of health status information.

Linking resource allocation issues to health planning was also recognised. In 1975, New South Wales developed a rudimentary 'resource allocation formula' based on the approach undertaken in Britain. Again, this formula provided a model for future population-based resource allocation exercises.

The 1970s witnessed significant new directions for health system development that began to require the advice of 'experts'. Planners were initially innovative researchers who had to 'order spreadsheets from central office by mail. They hand-drew column graphs and scatter charts and added up large numbers of hospital separations on pocket calculators to assess admission trends'.

With these beginnings, planning emerged as a technical support to the bureaucracy. Planners developed new data and information sources and began to develop normative planning standards which could define service and system inputs. Planners became experts in analysing hospital separation, mortality and demographic data as a means of assessing a community's health needs.

PRIORITY SETTING AS A PLANNING ROLE EMERGES

During the second half of the 1970s the economic environment began to change. In 1975 the incoming Liberal Fraser government questioned the efficiency of public hospitals and developed policies to force the states to establish cost control mechanisms. Health care costs had increased from about 5 per cent of GDP in 1963/64 to 7.7 per cent in 1975/76.

Planning remained in the service of decision makers, but the goal was to discourage hospital use. Bed planning ratios of four acute beds per 1000 people were established and in 1978 the Commonwealth–State cost-sharing agreement required that equal numbers of beds should be closed if new beds or services were to be opened.

The Fraser government instigated a range of cost control measures designed to regulate the expansion of hospital beds and services, the supply of practitioners, the development of community health and the consumer contribution to health care. The significant changes in the health policy environment meant that planning was not a means of developing comprehensive new services but a tool to assist in or to justify cost cutting. Planning became more integrated into management decision making.

PLANNING FOCUSES ON INCREASING HOSPITAL EFFICIENCY

In 1980 The Commission of Enquiry into the Efficiency and Administration of Hospitals reported that health information systems were inadequate and that hospital administration appeared to be inefficient.

It recommended a reduction in the number of hospital beds per 1000 population and that states develop comprehensive health service plans which would outline the development of all components of the health system on a regional and statewide basis.

Increasing pressure on the hospital budget, leading to greater support for non-hospital care, resulted from several factors: reduced hospital revenues arising from Medicare changes in 1981; the introduction by the Commonwealth of the '35 day rule' which limited acute hospital coverage to 35 days; increasing hospital staffing costs associated with the 38-hour week; requirements for improved health and safety; quality control procedures; and the safeguarding of patients' rights to informed consent.

Hospital cost control measures implemented at this time concentrated mainly on instruments such as patient payments to deter use and budgetary controls. In the 1970s, hospital administrators who spent in excess of their budget would be regularly 'bailed out' by the central-leveladministration, but by the 1980s this had changed (that is, 'come in on budget or your job may be on the line'). There was increased productivity in public hospitals during this time.

Hospital productivity improvements arose from a decrease in length of stay, an increase in samé day procedures (both due in large part to the development of less invasive surgical techniques and anaesthetics and improved diagnostic technologies), early and supported discharge for some types of care (especially ophthalmology and obstetrics) and an increase in non-inpatient or ambulatorycare as an alternative to admission (for example, home dialysis, community-basedpalliative care and diabetic management).

Information systems developed significantly. Planners and managers were able to question the variability between different hospitals and within a hospital: the costs of individual patient care; average length of stay; number of admissions; waiting times; numbers of operations; admissions through emergency departments and so on.

However, the hospitals invariably claimed that such variability was due to variations in the age and complexity of the patient mix.

At this time, information tools which had the capability for controlling for patient mix were being developed in the United States.

By the mid-1980s the Victorian Health Department and the South Australian Health Commission initiated studies into the usage of the US Diagnosis Related Group (DRG) classification as an approach to allocating funds to hospitals.

y the end of the 1980s the Commonwealth had introduced the Casemix Development Programme as part of its Medicare agreement with the states to establish systems and parameters for the use of casemix classification systems within Australia.

PUBLIC/PRIVATE SECTOR BLURRING

Whilst the private hospital sector had a long history in Australia, interest in public sector technical efficiency led to an increasing interest in a range of private health sector roles.

Health planners began to become involved in experimentation in providing health care in the private sector so as to develop competitive markets, improve efficiency (for example, through substitutability) and, in line with the current trends, develop ways of shifting costs from the public capped system to the private uncapped system.

Such approaches included planning for primary care treatment centres attached to public hospitals, planning for day surgeries and contracting out services such as pathology and radiology.

In the 1980s, state governments legislated for greater planning and regulatory control of private hospitals. The Private Health Establishments Act was passed in New South Wales in 1982 and proclaimed in 1988. Similar legislation was passed in Victoria in 1982.

These Acts provided for a planned development of private services. Licensing of hospitals would be subject to planning guidelines.

A DOSE OF EQUITY

In the 1980s, initially with support from the Whitlam Labour government and with the development of civil rights movements internationally, interest groups began to emerge as political and policy forces in Australia. Health interest groups concerned with mental health, ageing and disability and other particular health issues developed or moved from a charitable emphasis to become advocacy groups. Specific health services — such as Aboriginal medical services, women's health centres, community mental health and disability services, women's refuges, rape crisis centres and ethno-specific health workers and interpreters — were funded to address equity and access issues. Access and equity plans and policies designed to overcome access barriers began to be considered by Commonwealth and state bureaucracies.

INTEGRATED HEALTH SERVICES PLANNING DEVELOPS

Decentralisation was a key strategy of the 1980s to promote health services that were responsive to community needs, if not to incorporate community participation mechanisms. The effect of the regional- or area-based organisation was that planning for super-speciality services began to be undertaken at the central or national level, planning for secondary and primary care services was undertaken at the area/regional level and operational or business planning was undertaken at the local level. During this period, specialist planners were appointed at the central and regional/area tiers of administration and occasionally at the local level.

Systemic issues which began to be evaluated and addressed included: the level of integration of hospital and community care; the historical patterns of service delivery; traditional hospital management structures as compared to more 'responsive' area and regional structures; population locational access and equity issues, particularly as they related to hospital facilities; the possible range of private health sector roles; and the need for information tools to more effectively assess health service outputs. These systemic changes in health care management were accompanied later in the 1980s by interest in health care quality and in epidemiology. By the end of the 1980s the public health movement again began to have a voice and to provide a countervailing influence to the developing corporatist efficiency paradigm.

Changes in mental health, aged care and disability legislation and policy in the 1980s particularly supported deinstitutionalisation. The relatively large institutional or nursing home bed numbers were inappropriately concentrated in metropolitan areas, there was a lack of adequate community homes and hostel beds and, in general, there was a lack of appropriate assessment and community- and home-based alternatives. In mental health and disability services, the introduction of psychotropic drugs in the 1960s and 1970s had given impetus to community care. Important changes in mental health legislation and policy occurred during the 1980s, such that mental illness was legally redefined and procedures were improved for involuntary incarceration, as were mechanisms for appeal and review. This range of legislative, human rights, treatment improvement and cost consideration changes led to a considerable shift in the numbers of people being institutionalised.

There was considerable activity in service planning, variously supported by policies and programme funding designed to develop more integrated community-based service models. Questions about the level of community resources required for community-based treatment, rehabilitation, palliation and care were frequently raised.

STATES START TO ACT ON LOCATIONAL EQUITY

During the 1980s the planning processes highlighted locational inequity in many states. In some states, historical spending patterns were questioned through the use of needs-based indicators and early resource allocation formulae.

In New South Wales, for example, the Minister for Health, the Hon. Kevin Stewart, announced in 1979 the closure of 879 hospital beds in Sydney and 1200 in rural New South Wales and the redistribution of the savings to growth areas. In 1983 the NSW Minister for Health, the Hon. Laurie Brereton, further announced the closure of two medium-sized hospitals and the downgrading of the Sydney and War Memorial Hospitals in order to fund beds in Sydney's rapidly growing western suburbs. These latter changes created much greater furore than the previous closures. Such redistributions also occurred to a lesser extent in Melbourne and Adelaide and they continue today as major themes in hospital services planning.

Health planners gradually began to be involved in developing sophisticated technical approaches to forecasting needs and trends. In the mid-1980s, role delineation of services was developed as a planning process. Role delineation of health services allowed planners and managers to assess the support services, staffing profile, minimal safety standards and other requirements for each health care service and facility. Role delineation supported the provision of specific services outside of the hospital grounds in a more efficient or effective networked arrangement. Making such clinical requirements explicit provided a more consistent way of ensuring that patients received safe care in the most appropriate facility and service.

By the late 1980s, computer modelling became firmly established. In 1985 a forecasting model was used by the Western Metropolitan Health Region of New South Wales. This set the framework for the development of teaching facilities and further redistribution of hospital beds, within the region. In the early 1990s, HOSPIM, a locational optimisation model, was used for metropolitan hospital planning in South Australia; the Victorians developed HOSPLOC, a simulation model, for reconfiguring metropolitan hospital services; and New South Wales developed the APPI Planner. In Western Australia the epidemiological contribution to planning was enhanced in the mid-1990s through record linkage of six main health databases.

The increasing use of technologies and the use of high-cost drugs in the 1970s contributed to higher health costs. Unlike other industries, where technology reduces costs, most medical technology has not been labour displacing and often results in the creation of additional jobs. Health technology planning was begun in earnest by a sub-committee of the Standing Committee of Health Ministers (SCOHM), a predecessor to the Australian Health Ministers Advisory Committee (AHMAC). Planning ratios for services such as cardiac surgery, renal dialysis and computer tomography (CT) scanners were all issues of concern.

The application of these ratios at the state level was not easy, due to political lobbying for new and expansive technology. In the 1980s, Victoria put into legislation a planning approach to regulate the diffusion of CT scanners, linear accelerators, lithotripters and Magnetic Resonance Imaging (MRIs), whereby a need had to be demonstrated before licence would be granted. Enshrining technology planning into legislation was ultimately abandoned in the 1990s when placing financial limitations — either through Commonwealth payments or through national pooled funding via AHMAC — on technology diffusion became the preferred approach. Magnetic resonance imaging and transplantations (heart, liver, lung and pancreas) were the primary targets of funding restrictions during the early 1990s.

Health manpower (sic) planning began in earnest at both state and Commonwealth levels when AHMAC was asked to report on an 'oversupply' of doctors. The supply of doctors had increased in the 1970s due to the expansion of medical schools, as recommended by the Karmel report into medical education. Furthermore, from the 1960s, 'foreign doctors' or overseas-trained doctors gradually began to be licensed to practise in various states.

Since then, workforce planning has re-emerged at times when workforce issues have been characterised by tensions between specialisation and multiskilling, or due to contests between different professional groups (especially medicine and nursing), perceived tensions between equity principles such as equal employment opportunity (EEO) and the efficiency drive and an emerging concern with professional standards and quality care.

During the 1980s the medical profession regularly went to battle with various governments and the bureaucracy on issues which included pharmaceutical benefits, staffing of community health centres, health insurance, registration of alternative health care practitioners, medical fees and the differential between general practitioner and specialist charges. Medicare had resulted in declining revenues for hospitals and for some private physicians. These factors contributed to the development of a 'festering and periodically explosive doctor' dispute' from 1984 onwards.

In the 1990s the battles between the medical profession and governments resulted in medical workforce planning as a process to negotiate the supply of specialist doctors. The Australian Medical Workforce Advisory Council (AMWAC), a sub-committee of AHMAC, is the forum where representatives of the various specialities come to agreement about shortages and oversupplies and how these might be addressed.

The recruitment and retention of nurses, allied health and a number of other health disciplines also emerged as problems from time to time throughout the 1970s and 1980s. The fluctuations in these workforce categories reflected more the position of women in the economy and workforce.

The 1980s also heralded significant changes in the nursing profession. Since the Second World War, nursing had been beset with recurring labour shortages, poor remuneration, inadequate training and poor working conditions. The patient care context for nursing had significantly shifted, such that individual nurses rather than just the hospital matron (as under the Nightingale system) now had responsibility to independently solve clinical problems. This led inevitably to tensions between greater specialisation and multiskilling in nursing. During the 1980s, nurses' wages and conditions improved and the gradual transfer of nurse education from the hospital setting to the higher education sector provided for increasing professionalism. These changes also increased the overall costs of health care, since nursing labour represented about half the total costs of health care.

With involvement in workforce planning issues, planning moved beyond its role of the early 1980s when designated health planners had mainly been involved in developing service and strategic plans for the health system. By the end of the 1980s, in keeping with the rise of managerialism at that time, corporate and business plans derived from the US private sector began to be fashionable. These plans differed from previous strategic plans in that they defined goals, objectives and strategies for the whole organisation. Planning's corporate role became intimately tied up with its service planning role. The first state corporate plan was developed in Western Australia in 1986. In 1989 the Western Australia Strategic Plan for the Health Department fully integrated the previous corporate, strategic and service plans. Corporate plans were developed in the late 1980s and early 1990s in most other states.

RATIONING, EFFECTIVENESS AND OUTCOMES

In the 1990s, planning moved from a concern with inputs to a concern with outcomes. This movement signalled a change of focus, from measuring the services that are provided to measuring the health gain achieved from those services. An outcome focus in planning related to issues surrounding quality management, the establishment of national health goals and targets and an interest in outcome evaluation.

This shift was also consistent with the move of the planning role into organisational management and improving performance monitoring and accountability. Planning became increasingly concerned with resource allocation issues, or with organisational, capital or service planning which required an 'outcomes focus' or a focus on 'health improvement'.

Whilst a traditional service planning approach allowed planners to retreat to data collection, sophisticated forecasting and computer modelling, the health outcomes approach required evidence of relative need, knowledge of the best available evidence of the effectiveness of interventions and evidence of appropriate community, intersectoral and stakeholder consultation. It incorporated an economic component and required integrated planning processes.

At one level the outcomes paradigm provided a new set of principles on which to ration health care — merely another way for administrators to take control of the knife, wield it and then justify its use. At another level, in combination with improved information systems, the outcomes approach had potential to further challenge traditional practices and routines in health care and to develop more cost-effective, patient/community-centred and broad-based approaches to improving health.

The adoption of 'evidence-based medicine' began to be advocated both for clinical practice and in policy and planning. Such an approach required the planning process to take account of the findings of research and data and to develop skills in analysing effectiveness, safety and acceptability, the quality of evidence and the generalisability and local applicability of research and data. The outcomes movement contributed to increasing involvement of frontline health workers in clinical research, business planning and information gathering.

At the same time, designated planning units were often abandoned in favour of private consultants or market forces. Where planning was totally abandoned in favour of market forces, a commitment to distributional equity was also substantially abandoned.

Policy and planning documents became replete with both the language of economic rationalism and the public health and health outcomes lexicon. Tensions between public health and biomedicine, between outputs and outcomes and between planning and market forces characterised the health planning environment. Whereas in the previous decade the planning process could often be topdown, the public health approach and market assessment required a more rigorous and intersectoral approach to needs assessment and applied epidemiology. Health planning required a more eclectic approach that integrated processes which had previously been discrete and sequential, including service planning, economic appraisal and capital and asset planning. Planning was essentially concerned with change management and economics. Planning also became a skill expected of most health care managers and administrators.

THE FUTURE OF HEALTH PLANNING

The future is likely to see further cost restraint, new approaches to resource allocation, the predicted ageing of the population, the predicted ethical and financial difficulties for the health care system of delivering equitable services to the 'old old', an increase in technology and new treatments, a further blurring of the public and private components of health care and greater community and consumer involvement in health care.

Key questions for the system are whether to focus resources on improving the health of 'the many' (equity of access), or to focus resources, activities and interventions on those with the poorest health, thereby attempting to equalise their health outcomes with those of the rest of the population (equity of outcome). Questions must also arise as to whether health services and facilities remain at the forefront of health planning activity, or whether broader social and intersectoral approaches become pivotal.

Certainly, the current political, economic and scientific environment is replete with individualistic approaches to prevention and treatment issues. The march of bio-medical approaches to health care and health improvement remains strong and constant. A reductionist approach to improving health is ever more likely as scientists and the general community become increasingly fascinated with genetics, genetic manipulation and molecular approaches to improving health. Public health has been identified as being at the crossroads, with the inevitable clash of reductionist and broad visions of health. As health planning develops the change mechanisms that are consistent with prevailing outcomes policy paradigms, it is also at a crossroads, with individualistic, top-down approaches down one road and intersectoral, inclusive, health improvement and equity planning down the other.

PLANNING IN THE CONTEXT OF RESOURCE ALLOCATION

The health funding framework is a critical factor driving both the purpose and the process of health planning. As the health funding framework changes, so too does the role of health planning. Given the significant changes that have occurred in the funding of the health system over the last decade, it is not surprising that health planning has also undergone significant change. These changes reflect a move away from historic or cost-based funding towards resource allocationmode lsbased on population need or on output, or a mix of both.

This chapter outlines the main approaches to allocating health resources and the role that planners play in these contexts. It examines current and proposed health funding models for Australia. An overview of key theoretical models is presented, then recent developments and examples from different jurisdictions are provided.

Resource allocation can be defined simply as the process of moving funds or resources from the funders of health care to the providers and consumers of health care. There are a number of options for allocating resources and each can be interpreted and used in different ways to achieve political, economic and social goals. The arguments for different approaches to funding centre around issues of equity and social justice (that is, distributional issues), improving efficiency in the health care system (both productive and allocative) and the creation of incentives for the health system in general (and providers in particular) to act in ways which are seen as desirable.

Funding models reflect prevailing policies and values. Historically, Australians have accepted that services provided by general practitioners and medical specialists are and should continue to be, funded predominantly by a fee-for-service model, while services such as health promotion should not be funded on an open-ended fee for service basis. Likewise, the idea that public hospitals should be funded based on what they spent in the previous year — rather than be paid a fee for each product they produce — had been the norm until very recently. On the other hand, a different view about private hospitals has prevailed — no one has seriously suggested that private hospitals should be funded based on what they spent last year.

The various funding models in place in the Australian health care system have been of fundamental importance in shaping the way that services are planned and the way that health care is delivered. For example, a health service which has a capped budget has incentives to act in different ways to a health service whose budget is uncapped. Traditionally, for example, hospital managers in the private sector have been seen as 'successful' if they have been able to work with their doctors to increase demand and therefore volume. In contrast, managers in the public sector have been seen as 'successful' if they have been able to work with their doctors to decrease demand and therefore volume. (The rare exceptions include the waiting list programmes which are providing incentives for the public hospital sector to act like their private sector counterparts.)

Until recently, funding models for the health system have been relatively stable with one model (cost-based funding) dominating the public sector and another model (output-based funding) dominating the private sector. These funding arrangements have proved to be quite impervious to changes in national health insurance arrangements and to changes in the organisation and delivery of health care.

This is now changing and several new approaches to funding have been introduced in recent years, especially in the funding of the public hospital sector. In the main, these changes reflect a general move away from historic or costbased funding models towards funding models based on either population need or health care outputs. Significantly, these changes are bringing about some similarities in the funding of the public and private sectors as the public sector moves to introduce measures of output (as well as population need) and the private insurance sector is tentatively beginning to attempt to incorporate measures of need.

HISTORIC FUNDING APPROACHES IN THE PUBLIC SECTOR

Cost-based funding (also called expenditure-based, input formulae or historical funding) has been the predominant form of health resource allocation from funders to public health providers. Under this approach, the provider (that is, the hospital, health service or region) is funded based on the previous year's expenditure. The funder may choose to provide just a little more or perhaps a little less.

Cost-based funding has acted to perpetuate or conserve existing services and modes of treatment and it has led to a focus on the control of inputs. The way to access funds is to have received them in the past. This is the simplest approach to funding and has historically required little management or clinical information.

These models have been criticised (and in some cases abandoned) for several reasons. First, in a climate where outcomes and the outputs of health care are increasingly the focus of funding agencies, the historical funding approach has failed to provide incentives to improve the outputs or outcomes of health care.

Second, over time, cost-based approaches have led to a poor match between the needs of the local population and the available health care resources and services. For example, whilst new population growth has occurred on the outskirts of most capital cities over the last several decades, cost-based funding has ensured that available health care resources have continued to be channelled into hospital care in the more established areas of the cities, leaving the new growth areas isolated and inequitably served.

Third, cost-based approaches have historically provided an incentive for the provider to spend in order to assure the following year's revenue. This may occur in the form of one-off items or through the provision of additional tests, procedures or staffing. Thus, this approach has worked against efficiency.

Fourth, cost-based funding models are indiscriminate in that they reward providers for spending regardless of the competency of the provider. Finally, costbased funding models are regressive, because they reward those who spend the most and they have an inherent bias against new services, including communitybased care.

In summary, cost-based funding models can be characterised as being inherently simple, unfair (in that they reward spending), indiscriminate (in that they reward regardless of competency) and regressive (because they have a bias in favour of established services). They have provided no incentives for improving either the processes or the outcomes of health care. Consequently, there has been a move internationally away from cost-based funding models to either population needs-based or output-based models. These changes have been accompanied by fundamental changes in the nature and role of health planning.

PLANNING IN A NEEDS-BASED FUNDING ENVIRONMENT

Needs-based approaches to funding aim to distribute health care resources according to health needs. They can be conceived of as operating at two levels: at the level of the individual and at the level of the population.

At the individual level, needs-based approaches involve the funding agency providing funding to meet the identified needs of an individual consumer or patient. This may occur in three different ways. The first is the use of some type of 'capitation' funding, in which a funding agency translates (or attempts to translate) a person's particular health needs into a capitated funding allocation which is passed on to a health care provider. The provider is then expected to meet the person's needs within the fixed capitated funding allocation. In doing so, the provider carries the risk that the allocation is sufficient for the person's needs. This model is the basis of many US-style managed care programmes. Likewise, some health insurers in Australia are attempting to move towards this type of funding model.

The second approach involves funding agencies purchasing individualised packages of care for people with high support needs. In these approaches it is the purchaser (not the provider) who determines the services to be provided. This might include required standards of quality or outcome. Providers quote a price for the provision of the service and are engaged on that basis. Several of the coordinated care trials undertaken in Australia to date have tested this type of funding model.

The third approach involves a funding agency identifying a person's care needs and then seeking costed proposals from providers on how best to meet those needs. The funder identifies the needs, but it is the provider who designs and delivers the services required to meet the identified needs and who calculates the cost (or the price) of the services that they believe need to be provided. In accepting a particular proposal, the funder also accepts responsibility for paying the price quoted by the provider. The Department of

Ageing and Disability in New South Wales is experimenting with this type of approach for the purchase of services for people with high community support needs.

Needs-based approaches operating at the level of the individual rarely involve health planners, as opposed to financial planners. Rather, the decisionmaking process is undertaken by clinicians (as the providers of the service) and funding authorities (as the purchasers) and may also involve the consumer.

In contrast, population-level approaches to resource allocation have a strong reliance on health planning (rather than solely on clinical expertise). These approaches assume that health care resources ought to be distributed in relation to the number and the needs of defined populations. They also assume that the health budget is finite and that the key task is to distribute a fixed pool of money in an equitable way.

Different assumptions underpin the individualised and population-based approaches to needs-based funding. In the individualised approach, the task is to meet the needs of an individual without reference to issues such as population equity or to setting priorities that are designed to best meet the health needs of the community as a whole.

The focus is on absolute (rather than relative) need. Likewise, the resultant interventions are directed towards improving the health of the individual rather than the community as a whole.

One consequence is that individualistic models provide no framework for directing resources to those most in need.

Another is that population-level approaches (such as those that underpin public health and health promotion strategies) are not readily accommodated within an individualistic model.

Population-based approaches to funding start by assessing the needs of a particular population or section of the population. From a planning perspective, this needs-based approach to funding is inherently attractive as it incorporates the key concept of equity.

The formulae can change as populations change and can be used to provide a counterbalance to the demands of populations where such demand for health care is not supported by data on comparative need. The challenge, however, is in the implementation of planning ideals.

Planners working in a needs-based funding environment have two distinct roles.

Those in a funding agency are concerned with defining population need in such a way that the available (fixed) resources can be distributed between service providers in proportion to the needs of the populations they service.

Those working in a service provision agency have the task of using their population-based share of health funding to develop and provide services that best meet the needs of the service population.

The Planning Role in a Needs-based Funding Environment

The key role of the planner in a funding agency is to define and measure relative (rather than absolute) population health need. This requires the health planner to consider a range of issues. What is relative health need? Is it a demand for, or utilisation of, health care? If not, can need be measured independent of demand? How can health status be accurately measured across different population groups? How can the health needs of two very different population groups be compared?

In practice, national planning agencies (such as the Commonwealth Grants Commission) and planners in those Australian states which use resource allocation formulae (such as the Resource Distribution Formulae [RDF] in New South Wales) have assessed need using empirical parameters such as age and sex profiles, socioeconomic status, population density, standardised mortality ratios, fertility rates and so on in association with population size. Some utilisation data may also be incorporated to assess service catchments. In the current New South Wales formula, for example, measures of private hospital activity are incorporated on the assumption that residents accessing private sector services have a reduced need for public sector services.

As in any formula, the parameters in needs-based planning models are not value neutral. For example, the New South Wales RDF does not assess the impact of the non-English-speaking background (NESB) population, while the Commonwealth Grants Commission assumes that the NESB population has additional needs only for the first five years of settlement.

Another common assumption in funding formulae is that people's health needs are comparable and they prefer to use health services geographically close to their homes. For instance, the Commonwealth Grants Commission gives weight to population density and distance. When the weighting is applied, the more populous states receive less per capita than the states and territories with smaller populations on the assumption that geographic isolation requires additional health resources.

The Planning Role of the Provider in a Needs-based Funding Environment

Because population-based models provide funding on the basis of population need rather than health service outputs, providers (not funders) are responsible for planning services to meet the needs of their service catchments. Depending on organisational arrangements, this potentially gives the planner working at the level of service provision the opportunity to develop health care models which are not institutionally based.

Needs-based models provide incentives to improve health status and outcomes when health care providers are given responsibility for the health of their service population. They can create incentives to improve service outputs and quality. This approach potentially devolves responsibility to providers for the provision of an appropriate population-based range of health services. Public health, health promotion and alternative models of service provision can be comfortably accommodated within needs-based models.

On the other hand, needs-based models have sustained criticism because there is no mechanism for ensuring that the funds provided are used appropriately or efficiently. Regions with similar populations may receive equal resources, but the range, mix and quality of services they provide may be quite different. Whilst a capped budget should (in theory) encourage strategic planning to ensure cost-effectiveness, there is no direct incentive for efficiency. Thus, whilst the needs-based approach may achieve allocative efficiency, it does not necessarily create incentives for technical efficiency.

A key planning issue in needs-based funding models is that all risk is carried by the provider. The provider receives a global and fixed budget and is expected to meet the health needs of the catchment population. The provider carries the risk that the needs of the population may not match the available funds.

Under population needs-based funding models, planning has a major strategic and corporate role. Planners may be involved in redistributing resources from one hospital/area/region to another, in assessing the most effective means of using existing or future funds, in consulting communities about health improvement strategies, in assessing the likely reasons for outflows or inflows to the area and in defining and planning for capital improvements to accommodate new services.

Needs-based approaches are perceived to be ethical and fair and to encourage allocative efficiency. However, one obvious limitation of needs-based funding models is that they are only practical for geographically distinct populations. Patients, however, do not necessarily choose to access health services within their designated region of residence. The Australian Health Care Agreement attempts to compensate for this problem through states and territories paying each other for interstate patient flow.

PLANNING IN AN OUTPUT-BASED FUNDING ENVIRONMENT

Output-based funding approaches allocate resources according to what is actually produced, independent of population need. Because most of the outputs or products of the health system are patient care episodes and these are increasingly classified by way of casemix classifications, the term 'casemix-based funding' is also used.

The idea of output-based funding is fundamentally simple. It is based on the view that the outputs of the health system can be quantified and costed and that all providers should be paid the same amount for producing the same product. As a health care organisation is actually more complicated than that, all output-based models add additional rules to cover special circumstances (such as patients who are atypical and providers with unavoidable additional costs).

The key feature of output-based funding is that it promotes technical or productive efficiency by rewarding increased output and decreased costs. Payment of private medical practitioners (by way of the Commonwealth Medical Benefits Schedule) and casemix-based funding of hospitals (by way of Diagnosis Related Groups and other casemix classifications) are examples of output-based funding.

Most states and territories in Australia have now agreed that a pricing mechanism should be developed which can be used to fund both public and private hospitals using casemix as a measure of output. Indeed, the 1993–98 Medicare Agreement included an explicit agreement to move towards casemix usage in hospital funding.

Output-based funding models can increase equity between providers, create incentives for cost containment and generate good clinical information so that costs can be managed. A key issue is that output-based models create incentives and opportunities for greater clinician involvement in management and cost control. In this sense, output-based models can be used to increase the accountability of clinicians as the explicit budget holders of health resources.

The advantages and disadvantages of casemix or output-based funding were described in a 1998 audit report by the Auditor-General of Victoria. The audit concluded that 'casemix, with some qualifications, had achieved its major objectives of improving the efficiency of hospitals and introducing a fairer basis for funding hospitals. The objective of safeguarding quality of care had been less successfully met'.

In summary, output-based models are designed primarily to encourage productive efficiency. They are technically difficult because it is difficult to measure outputs.

They can also be regressive in that they fund utilisation rather than need. For these reasons, many states have taken the view that casemix is best used as a component of a broader funding model rather than as the exclusive basis for resource allocation.

The Planning Role of the Funder in an Output-based Funding Environment

The chief planning roles of the funding agency in an output-based funding environment are to determine the outputs to be purchased and to work at resolving the weaknesses implicit in an output-based funding model. One weakness is that, in the context of hospital funding, output-based funding approaches have thus far only taken patient episodes of care into any serious account. To date, output approaches have been heavily focused on the provision of acute services in hospitals, whilst ignoring broader health services and the encouragement of health outcomes. In determining what outputs to purchase, planners working in a funding agency need to recognise the distinction between demand (or utilisation) and population need. One risk is that equity may be jeopardised through exclusive use of output-based models. For example, if used as the sole basis for resource allocation, output-based models serve to promote the funding of existing services rather than promoting a flexible approach to changing needs.

A further task is to create output-based funding models that provide incentives to improve both the quality and outcome of care. This is not the case at present, as current output-based funding models have been developed based on the current average cost of care. Providers are reimbursed for each patient care episode based on the current average cost of production, irrespective of the quality, outcome or utility of the product they produce. This principle applies equally to high-utility outputs (such as cataract surgery) and low-utility outputs (such as tattoo removals).

It is possible for planners to design output-based models in ways that encourage quality, outcomes and utility. For example, it is now becoming possible to set 'best practice' rather than average prices, to pay more for some products and less for others based on an assessment of the utility of each product and to reward providers of quality care. However, for both technical and cultural reasons, the nexus between cost and price is yet to be broken.

Planners have three broad options in designing an output-based funding model. In a payment model, a provider is paid predetermined amounts for each patient care episode. In a relative share model, the available budget is distributed between providers in proportion to their casemix-adjusted workload. Finally, in a purchasing model, casemix is used as the 'purchasing currency' and the purchaser and the provider negotiate about the type of services to be purchased and the price which will be paid for those services.

Output-based Payment Models

Under a payment model, total funding changes according to the changes in the mix and volume of cases. This system is the one used by US Medicare in its Prospective Payment System. Payment models require an uncapped budget because the provider is guaranteed a payment each time they produce a product. In risk management terms, all the risk is carried by the funder. The providers' only risk is that the price may be too low.

Payment models are therefore not a viable option for the widespread funding of state-funded health services such as hospitals and community health services. Nevertheless, some states are making selective use of payment models for one-off programmes such as waiting list programmes.

They are, however, both a viable and an increasingly common payment model in the private sector. The funding agency (such as a health insurer) specifies the outputs for which it will pay a fee and specifies the rate at which the fee will be set. Once agreement is reached between the purchaser and the provider, the purchaser's main role is in product validation (processes which ensure that the output was actually delivered as specified) and in paying for the services that are delivered. In addition, some funders in such uncapped systems are attempting to reduce demand, either through providing disincentives for consumers to take up the service (such as by extending the waiting period for eligibility for particular services or by the introduction of co-payments) or by investing in prevention and early intervention programmes on the basis that these will reduce the demand for (more costly) treatment services.

Output-based Budget Share Models

Under a budget share or relative share model, the capped total budget is divided amongst providers in proportion to their casemix-adjusted workload. Providers with larger or more complicated workloads receive the largest shares of the budget. As the budget is capped, providers are not paid for each patient they treat; they are simply funded in proportion to their share of the work. In this model, all risk is carried by providers. Additional demand may well require providers to do additional work within their allocated budget.

Output-based Purchasing Models

Under a purchasing model (such as those used in Victoria, South Australia and Western Australia), contracts are negotiated between the funder (usually called the purchaser) and the provider. There are three main types of contracts in these models.

- The block contract. In a block contract, the purchaser and the provider negotiate a lump sum for services without specifying the price or the volume of any specific service. The contract simply specifies the broad range of included services. For example, the contract specifies that $2 million will be paid per annum for all emergency department services provided to residents of region X.

This model is relatively simple and can be structured to result in no sudden change. It requires only very basic information systems. In reality, block contracts are essentially a purchasing form of needs-based funding. Like needs-based funding, the risk is carried by the provider and not the purchaser.

- The price and volume contract. In a price and volume contract, the purchaser and provider negotiate on the volume and price for an agreed range of services. The contract usually specifies the services at the level of the clinical speciality or at the level of the relevant casemix classification. For example, the contract specifies services for 200 hip replacements (10per cent) at a total cost of $800 000. It includes provision for volumes falling outside this range.

Price and volume contracts require purchasers to understand the needs of the service population. They therefore require good information systems and can be relatively expensive to administer. Under a price and volume contract, the risk is potentially shared between the purchaser and the provider.

One important feature of a price and volume contract model is that it makes rationing explicit. Purchasers specify what they will purchase. By default, such contracts include statements about what will not be provided. In these models it is the purchaser (not the provider) who has explicit responsibility for setting health care priorities and for rationing. This is one of the key reasons that many jurisdictions have abandoned the purchaser–provider split model. It can quickly become politically unpalatable.

By accepting responsibility for determining the mix and range of services to be provided, purchasers have the opportunity to 'purchase for health gain' — that is, to make purchasing decisions based on an assessment of quality, outcomes and utility. In reality, factors such as the availability of the information required for such assessments, the prevailing political and social circumstances, the availability of capital stock and the views and interests of key stakeholders may mean that purchasing decisions may be based on many other factors other than 'health gain'.

The price-per-case contract. In the price-per-case contract, the purchaser and the provider negotiate on the price of specific services, but not on the volume. The contract specifies the services at the level of the relevant casemix or procedure classification. The volume is not fixed. A price per case is agreed and payment is made only for service episodes actually provided. For example, in a price-per-case contract for aged-care assessments, a price per case is agreed but no volume is stated. The provider will bill the purchaser for each assessment they perform.

The price-per-case contract requires good information systems. Like other fee-for-service models, the risk is carried by the purchaser since there can be no cap on expenditure. Like price and volume contracts, purchasers may base price-per-case contracts on 'health gain' among other criteria.

The price-per-case contract is similar in most respects to the outputbased payment model. There are, however, two important differences. First, there is a contractual agreement between the purchaser and the provider. Second, the price is negotiated between the parties, rather than mandated. Reforms under way in the private sector in Australia since the late 1990s have included both of these elements.

The Planning Role of the Provider in an Output-based Funding Environment

The chief planning role of a service provision agency in an output-based funding environment is threefold. The first is to negotiate with the purchaser and to enter into contractual agreements about the range and scope of services to be provided. The second is to plan their service delivery system so that they can deliver the outputs that have been contracted. The third role and one which needs to be shared with the purchaser, is to work at resolving the weaknesses implicit in an output-based funding model.

The financial incentives under output-based funding are to reduce the cost of producing health care. One implication is that planners may be engaged in undertaking efficiency reviews and in assessing whether a particular service can viably exist in an output-based funding environment. For example, a unit may have insufficient volume to achieve the economies of scale necessary to be able to deliver a service at a competitive price. In this case, the planning function is to assess whether volumes can be increased, whether costs can be reduced in other ways, or whether the unit would be better to close. Conversely, a unit may be able to deliver a particular service at a very competitive price. In this case, the planning function may involve exploring the opportunities to increase volumes by strategies designed to increase market share.

One of the main weaknesses of output-based models is that, if every episode of care draws a payment, incentives are created to treat people unnecessarily in order to increase revenue. Depending on the design of the system, there may also be an incentive to exaggerate the complications associated with a case so as to draw additional revenue. Planners may also be concerned that some cases genuinely require more resources than are allowed for in the standard payment. A further planning concern is how to counteract the incentive that is created when output-based funding models define the products of the health care system as individual episodes of care. In these cases, a focus on individual episodes of care may actively work against continuity of care.

SOME EXAMPLES OF RESOURCE ALLOCATION MODELS

Three examples — Western Australia, Victoria and New South Wales — serve to demonstrate the way in which the various states and territories are developing their approaches to resource allocation. The following examples do not provide a comprehensive description of their planning and funding models but merely seek to illustrate how some of the above changes are being implemented in practice.

THE PURCHASING MODEL

Western Australia introduced a purchasing model in 1997 and now issues an annual planning document ('Purchasing Intentions') outlining the health services it intends to purchase for Western Australians. The Health Department sees itself functioning as a single integrated purchaser of health services for the people of Western Australia. Its role as purchaser, while considering government priorities and strategic directions, is to 'conduct ongoing assessment of the need for services and to enter into contracts and Memoranda of Understanding (MOUs) with providers. Providers of health services include the Metropolitan Health Services Board (MHSB) created in 1997, country health services, nongovernment organisations and private sector health service providers'.

As part of its statewide purchasing and planning framework, Western Australia has also introduced locality purchasing.

'Locality purchasing' is the purchase of health services for discrete populations by the allocation of activity to achieve the appropriate range and level of health services. The aims of locality purchasing are to:

- Assess the need of local populations;
- Develop localised purchasing plans; and
- Ensure the purchase of targeted health services which achieve the optimum access, range and appropriate mix of services.

Private Investment in Public Sector Services:

Victoria developed an Infrastructure Investment Policy which set out its commitment to increasing and sustaining the participation of the private sector in the provision of the state's infrastructure facilities and services.

This approach was consistent with its then aim of increasing resource allocation efficiency by strengthening the partnership between the private and public sectors.

Potential areas of private sector involvement identified included:

- Operating or management contracts in areas such as hospital operation and maintenance of public sector assets such as rolling stock and vehicle fleet management;
- Turn-key project delivery, such as design, construction and delivery of a completed freeway extension;
- Build-operate-transfer projects and build-own-operate projects, such as privately built and operated hospitals; and
- Privatisation within industries such as energy, health, information technology and water and sewerage.

The Victorian Department of Human Services was actively moving to divest itself of service delivery and to position itself as the statewide purchaser of health care services.

By 1998 this had included the privatisation of about 600 nursing beds (out of a total of 3000 beds which were planned for transfer to the private sector) and contracting with the private sector for the construction and management of public hospital facilities using a build-own-operate model.

The policies of privatisation and private investment in public sector services, in health as well as other social policy areas, proved to be politically controversial.

With the change of government in 1999, the privatisation policy was reversed and the Infrastructure Investment Unit in the Department of Human Services was abolished.

A Mixed Funding Model

The seventeen geographically-based Area Health Services are legislatively responsible for improving the health of the local community and, to that end, for the funding and efficient management of all public hospitals and community health services within their boundaries.

Areas receive a global budget allocation specified under a population-based RDF. Areas are responsible for allocating their global budget between programmes and service types in line with identified community needs and local service development priorities. Areas determine the shares of the global budget to be allocated for each programme or service type (for example, acute inpatient, outpatient, community-based and so on) and then distribute the resources assigned to each programme between local service providers.

Known as 'episode funding' it pays a standard price per casemix-adjusted episode, but pays different prices for hospital infrastructure, depending on the size, role and configuration of the hospital. Adjustments are made for changes in expected workload and transitional grants. Non-inpatient services, teaching and research and public health/health promotion generally have negotiated budgets based on a combination of historical costs and planned or expected changes in workload.

Health Department is the funder and the Areas are both purchasers and providers. At this point no attempt has been made to separate the purchaser function from the provider function. This is a fundamentally different approach to that being pursued by all other states and territories.

INFORMATION FOR HEALTH PLANNING

Collecting, analysing and reporting health data are core skills in health planning. Planners need to be able to manage and use both qualitative and quantitative data in the course of assessing health status and health needs, analysing current patterns of service utilisation and justifying and modelling the impact of any proposed change.The difference between data and information has been defined as:

Data are raw facts and figures collected as part of the normal functioning of the organisation. Information on the other hand is defined as data that has been processed and analysed in a formal, intelligent way so that the results are directly useful to those involved in operations and management.

Six broad types of information are used in health planning:

- Demographic and socioeconomic data;
- Epidemiological data, including mortality data and morbidity data;
- Hospital and health services activity data;
- Health economic data on the costs and effectiveness of various types of health interventions;
- Qualitative data about needs, perceptions, preferences; and

- Data that provides evidence of the efficacy of various types of health interventions.

Sources of such data include the Australian Bureau of Statistics (ABS), the Australian Institute of Health and Welfare (AIHW), state Health Departments and local or regional health authorities. In the first part of this chapter, healthrelated data sources and issues are outlined. Methods for turning data into information are then discussed.

DEMOGRAPHIC AND SOCIOECONOMIC DATA

Demographic data and information from many government departments are important proxy measures of health status. The ABS is a key source of demographic data, with available data including the five-year Australian population census and data from one-off surveys.

The main sources of demographic and socioeconomic data commonly used by planners. Ideally, data systems should take account of quality of life issues, environmental health and the impact of structural factors on health status, so that targeting of intervention strategies can be more appropriate. As mentioned previously, however, the long-term impact of prevention, health promotion, or social or individual health risk factors is either poorly measured or unmeasured. In practice, there is a very little broad based population data that can be used to paint a picture of the health of Australians. However, there have been significant improvements in recent times and information is now available through surveys such as the National Health Survey, the National Disability Survey, the National Nutrition Survey and the National Mental Health Survey. States are also starting to conduct their own health surveys, often using computer-assisted telephone interview (CATI) methodology.

Available demographic and socioeconomic data from the ABS that might be useful include data on education, disability, housing, income, literacy, employment and unemployment patterns and regional labour force statistics. Population census information is available for five-year 'lifecycle groups' and includes data such as: the numbers of non-English-speaking residents; the numbers born overseas or in non-English-speaking countries; the numbers of Aboriginal people; the age structure of the population; education levels; occupation; income; method of journeying to work; local workforce profile; and marital status. The ABS frequently produces this information in a standardized format. For example, the ABS Index of Social Disadvantage provides comparative information on socioeconomic data by geographic region.

Many other authorities also produce health-related data. Car accident data are produced by the Roads and Traffic Authority (or the equivalent state department); population projections and urban development plans are produced by the Department of Planning (or equivalent); children at risk notifications are produced by the Department of Community Services (or equivalent); crime statistics (such as drug offences and drink-driving convictions) are produced by the Bureau of Crime Statistics; and information on welfare recipients (pensions and benefits) is available from the Department of Social Security.

Depending on the issues and questions under consideration, other statistics such as pollution levels in local creeks and rivers, occupational health and safety statistics and so on, may also be relevant.

EPIDEMIOLOGICAL DATA

Information about health status and health risks, particularly the incidence and prevalence of health conditions and about determinants of health is difficult to obtain. Service utilisation data are often used as a surrogate measure. Registries, surveys and sentinel surveillance become the main vehicles through which the picture of health is constructed.

Mortality Data

Mortality data are, perhaps ironically, the most commonly used measure of 'health'. When mortality data are used to describe health, 'health status' is generally described in terms of crude or standardised death rates, reasons for death, life expectancy and premature mortality. Mortality data are the most comprehensive collected data relating to health. Nevertheless, there are data quality problems associated with the coding of conditions mentioned on the death certificate and mortality data still fail to provide adequate identification of priority populations.

Mortality data are collected, analysed and reported by the ABS. As with morbidity data, mortality data need to be standardised by age and sex for comparative assessment. This statistic is known as the standardised mortality ratio (SMR). These data can be used to highlight issues such as premature deaths, leading causes of death by age group, infant mortality and perinatal births and deaths.

Morbidity Data

The ABS and AIHW contribute significantly to information on perceived health status, through national self-report surveys such as the National Health Survey, the National Disability Survey and the National Survey of Mental Health and Well-Being.

Specialised periodic surveys include the national dietary survey and the national oral health survey. AIHW also provides the national collection point for a number of specialised data sets. The national injury surveillance system provides information on the nature and causes of injury leading to contact with hospital emergency departments.

The perinatal statistics collection provides information on all hospital births, including birth weight. A biomedical risk factor survey is under development and would provide information about prevalence of a range of communicable and non-communicable diseases or risk factors.

At the state level a myriad of collected data can be accessed, mainly through the Departments of Health and many of these are transmitted to the AIHW to form a national data collection. The National Health Data Dictionary, produced under the National Health Information Agreement as a cooperative venture by all jurisdictions, sets common definitions and data standards and defines a national minimum data set.

Due to this initiative, state-based data on hospital morbidity and perinatal statistics have become comparable. Worker's compensation statistics, as measures of occupational injuries and diseases, are available through state compensation authorities and maintained nationally by the National Occupational Health and Safety Commission.

Specific disease registries maintained at the state level, either by the state health authority or through specialist agencies, include the following: notifiable diseases, cancer, immunisation, infectious diseases notification, breast screening and pap smear registries. These data sources depend on accurate notification or actual service contact. As such, they may reflect under-reporting and underutilisation. Where registries are supported through national programmes, such as immunisation and breast screening, comparable data are collected across Australia.

Epidemiological research and studies complement the type of information above. For example, community health surveys (health screenings) in Aboriginal communities provide both a sporadic health screening programme for the individual and, at the same time, represent prevalence surveys at the population level. In recent years, many states have initiated their own health surveys in order to gain a better understanding of population health issues, particularly health knowledge, attitudes and behaviour.

The NSW Health Survey and the Victorian Health Survey have adopted CATI (computer-assisted telephone interview) methodology for their survey work, whereas South Australia has developed a continuous surveillance system. Through the National Public Health Partnership, states/territories are moving towards a harmonised approach to population health surveys.

Many surveys are instigated and supported by various national public health programmes or strategies. The Longitudinal Women's Health Survey, initiated through the National Women's Health Programme, is following several cohorts of women over a twenty-year period in order to document how women experience health and health services as their lives change.

The National HIV/AIDS Strategy and the National Drug Strategy have supported important surveys on sexual health and on illicit drug usage. Likewise, the National Mental Health Strategy has supported a national survey of mental health and well-being.

Despite the variability of both data quality and availability across states, there is a consistent pattern of relationship between socioeconomic status and health status, however measured. The Social Health Atlas provides a graphic illustration of the links between health and poverty.

HOSPITAL AND HEALTH SERVICES ACTIVITY DATA

Hospital and health services data are key information sources on the morbidity of the population (indicators of expressed and comparative need) and on the availability and efficiency of health services.

Routine hospital morbidity data are collected on all admitted patients. The current national minimum data set for institutional health care includes information on age, sex, postcode, ethnicity, occupation, language, reason for admission, diagnoses, procedures and interventions and discharge status. Hospital morbidity data can thus be disaggregated by age, sex, geographical areas, time, ethnicity, Aboriginality, or by any other key question captured on the admission or discharge sheet. Whilst raw numbers may be relevant to a needs assessment, these numbers should also be standardised to allow for assessment of comparative need. Standardised Separation Rates (SSRs) are hospital separation rates that are standardised for the age and sex profile of the catchment area. Separations (that is, discharges, deaths and transfers) are used instead of admissions because the information is compiled at the end of an episode of care (at separation) rather than at admission.

Morbidity information can usually be obtained from the AIHW or from the state or territory Health Department. Often the required information has already been published. Increasingly, such information is routinely available over the Internet. and developmental disabilities hospitals. Most Departments of Health undertake a census of long-stay patients.

Information about primary medical care, specialist services, diagnostic services and pharmaceutical use is not easily obtained. The Health Insurance Commission is the central point for medicare data and for data about pharmaceutical benefits. There are many other specific health data collections which may vary between different states. Community health and ambulatory care data tend to be uneven in coverage and not comparable due to data definition issues.

Casemix

As discussed in Chapter 4, casemix data are being increasingly used to plan and purchase health care. Casemix information provides a measure of hospital utilisation or hospital morbidity. Casemix classification systems are similar to other classification systems but, as noted by Eagar and Hindle (1994a), special attention is given to two features. First, casemix classification systems have clinical meaning (patients in the same class have clinical similarities).

Second, in a casemix classification, each of the groupings is 'iso-resource' in that they are relatively homogeneous with respect to resource use (patients in the same class cost approximately the same to treat). Health services utilisation data are available for patients in long-stay institutions, such as residential aged care facilities, free-standing psychiatric hospitals. The most commonly used casemix classification is the Diagnosis Related Group. In Australia, the Australian Refined DRG (AR-DRG) system is in use as the national standard. The DRG system is designed for the classification of acute inpatient care and not for the classification of other types of health care. The DRG casemix system uses information about principal diagnosis, secondary diagnosis, surgical procedure, age, gender and type of discharge to assign each patient care episode to a casemix class. A DRG grouper is used to classify the required source data, such as diagnostic and procedure data coded using ICD-10-AM and to assign each patient episode to one — and only one — DRG.

Casemix classifications sort patient episodes into groups based on known patient-related cost drivers. Accordingly, the DRG system uses variables such as diagnoses, age and procedures to classify acute inpatient episodes, as these variables have been shown to predict cost.

However, they are not cost predictors for other types of care and, in consequence, other types of health care need to be classified using other variables that are known to drive health care costs. Such cost drivers include functional impairment and functioning in activities of daily living (ADL) in medical rehabilitation; measures of ADL function, symptom severity, social and economic circumstances and behaviour in mental health; stage of illness and measures of pain, symptoms, carer support and ADL function in palliative care; and clinical urgency in emergency department care.

Several casemix classification systems are now being developed in Australia (and elsewhere) for other types of health care using these types of variables. These new classifications are also beginning to be used as descriptors of health status. They include the Australian National Sub-Acute and Non-Acute Patient (AN-SNAP) classification for sub-acute and non-acute care, the Mental Health Classification and Service Cost Group classification for mental health and the Urgency, Disposition and Aged groups (UDAG) classification of emergency department care.

Several planning implications arise from these new classifications. A number of classifications are now available in Australia and, at present, there are no policy decisions on the interaction between them or on the way that they should be incorporated into routine health planning. A further issue is that, because of the historic focus on acute inpatient care, much of the required source data are not routinely collected by existing hospital and community information systems. Finally, implementation remains a state and territory issue that requires a planned, staged approach.

Nevertheless, for planning purposes it is important to understand not only the DRG casemix classification, but also the new classifications and their potential applications. Casemix information is an important source of information on expressed and comparative need in a needs assessment. Casemix information also provides powerful data for a range of other planning tasks including utilisation review, costing, resource allocation, quality improvement and clinical resource management. Casemix information can be used, for example, to compare services in terms of relative efficiency and to predict future patterns of service utilisation. Casemix information can also be used in workforce planning, to predict staffing requirements and for internal hospital contracting/charging for services.

However, casemix data provide, at best, a weak proxy measure of health status. Casemix information measures utilisation of and demand for, services (expressed need) rather than health status. They provide information about the health services that are provided, rather than information on the services that are actually needed. This is an important distinction to make. As already noted, use and demand for services may reflect a whole range of factors that have nothing to do with the health needs of the catchment population. These include the local supply and resourcing of health services, local health practitioner availability and practice, service accessibility and appropriateness, cultural factors, consumer preferences and so on. A further problem is that, in the absence of the ability to link patient records or of unique patient identifiers, hospital morbidity data (including casemix data) do not indicate multiple admissions for a single episode of illness. In this regard, hospital morbidity data provide little useful information on serious morbidity and chronic illness.

Data collections from primary care sources, such as GPs, community health, emergency departments and outpatient services, are either currently not available or not often used as sources of information about ill-health in the community (Commonwealth Department of Human Services and Health 1994). In the absence of information that is more comprehensive, the quantitative assessment of health status is frequently based only on hospital utilisation and thus provides a very incomplete picture.

HEALTH ECONOMIC DATA

Financial data about hospital performance are now readily available, in part because of the work on casemix. Financial data about community health services and public health, however, remain difficult to obtain. This is due in part to the relatively small portion of the health budget spent in these sub-sectors and in part to variable definitions of what is included in these services. A public health expenditure project, being undertaken by AIHW under the auspices of the National Public Health Partnership, is expected to reveal investments in various public health programmes across the jurisdictions.

Approaches to measuring the costs and benefits of health interventions, in the context of setting priorities and selecting health interventions. Key data include the results of cost–benefit analysis (CBA), costeffectiveness analysis (CEA) and cost–utility analysis (CUA). While health economists would normally undertake such work, health planners need to know how to ask the right questions and how to interpret the results.

QUALITATIVE DATA

Surveys are used to collect information in a standard format from a sample of individuals who are (ideally) representative of the community being studied. Surveys are the most widely used method of data collection. While surveys may only yield a limited insight into the complex issues of health need, they can be a useful first step in qualitative needs assessment.

Surveys should ideally be developed in collaboration with the people being surveyed. Collaboration should occur in all aspects of the survey design, implementation and analysis. Communities are effectively disempowered when experts work in isolation in assessing need and in determining priorities for action.

If a survey is to be used in a large population study, it is important to involve not just the community but also people with expertise in research. Technical expertise is required on matters such as survey design, sample size, survey implementation and analysis. It is critical that any survey uses quality methodologies and meets ethical standards.

Surveys can be mailed, conducted by telephone or conducted face-to-face. Face-to-face surveys can be structured, semi-structured or open-ended. The latter generally provide the most complex data. Indeed, the in-depth interview can provide insight into the determinants of health and the behaviours, systems and structures which contribute to health. Open-ended interviews can help provide a 'feel' for key issues and identify terms and key phrases used by target groups.

However, face-to-face surveys are expensive to conduct on a routine basis. An alternate method is the telephone survey. In a comparison of population health estimates using a face-to-face interview method and a telephone survey method, no statistically significant results were found between the two methods. Well-planned and appropriately weighted and analysed telephone surveys can be a less expensive way of obtaining information for a needs assessment.

Issues which may be important in interviewing include the gender, class, ethnicity and values of the researcher and the respondent. It may be important that women be interviewed by women or that an interpreter or bilingual interviewer be present. The stages of interviewing that are important are contact and engagement, establishing rapport and ensuring information accuracy.

Focus Groups

It is common for focus groups to follow on from surveys. A focus group is a group interview which focuses on a particular topic. Other group work techniques are also available. These include the Nominal Group and the Delphi Approach, which are described in Chapter 9. A range of specialist texts on the various group work techniques is available for planners wishing to increase expertise in these areas.

Community Forums/Public Meetings

Public forums may help in generating new ideas, articulating conflicts of opinion and collaboratively starting the process of setting priorities.

EVIDENCE AND CONFIDENCE

Health policy makers are increasingly seeking assurances about the value of investments in health services, in terms of both 'value for money' and whether real health outcomes are being achieved. This trend has been encouraged by the rise of evidence-based medicine (EBM). Health planners are therefore increasingly taking into account whether resources and services are being managed and delivered in accordance with best practice.The Cochrane Collaboration is an important source of information on the effectiveness of clinical interventions. The Cochrane Collaboration was developed to undertake systematic, up-to-date reviews of all relevant randomised controlled trials (RCTs) of health care. The importance of the Cochrane Collaboration to health planning is reflected in its origins.

The first Cochrane Centre opened in 1992 with funding from the United Kingdom's National Health Service Research and Development Programme. Its role was to collaborate with others in the UK and elsewhere and to facilitate systematic reviews of randomised controlled trials across all areas of health care. These ideas were extended when, in 1993, 'The Cochrane Collaboration' was established by researchers from eleven countries.'Evidence' (in EBM) is considered in four dimensions:

- Levels: the study design employed to evaluate an intervention.
- Quality: the methods used to minimise bias.
- Relevance: the relevance of the outcome measures and the applicability of the study results to the question for which evidence is sought.
- Strength: the magnitude, precision and reproducibility of the intervention effect and the attributability of outcomes to the intervention.

Based on the scientific principles of epidemiology, the Cochrane approach is concerned with minimising bias and thus classifies research into several levels on the basis of how the evidence is obtained..

Cochrane reviews (the principal output of the Collaboration) are published electronically in successive issues of The Cochrane Database of Systematic Reviews. Preparation and maintenance of Cochrane reviews are undertaken by international collaborative review groups. Such groups are organised and supported by a network of Cochrane centres, each of which specialises in a particular clinical field. Collaborative review groups, fields/ networks and Cochrane centres all seek input and feedback from consumers, which the Cochrane Collaboration considers essential in order to fulfil its goals.

I Systematic review of all relevant randomised controlled trials.

II At least one properly designed and randomised controlled trial.

III-1 Well-designed pseudo-randomised controlled trials.

III-2 Comparative studies with concurrent controls and allocation not randomised, case-control studies, or interrupted time series with a control group.

III-3 Comparative studies with historical control, two or more single-arm studies, or interrupted time series without a parallel control group.

IV Case series, either post-test or pre-test and post-test.

LEVELS OF DECISION MAKING AND EVIDENCE REQUIRED

Most of the literature on nature of evidence and evidence-based decision making in health care stems from clinical medicine and epidemiology. From the viewpoint of health planning, however, the higher the level of organisational aggregation, the more decisions are influenced by a complex array of factors,

Cochrane reviews are published in electronic format in the Cochrane and therefore the more complex the set of evidence that is required.

Library and theres is a Cochrane internet site. Several databases are includect:

- Cochrane Database of Systematic Reviews;
- The Cochrane Controlled Trials Register;
- The Database of Abstracts of Reviews of Effectiveness (DARE);
- The Cochrane Review Methodology Database;
- Reviewers' Handbook on the science of reviewing research.

Maps out the different types of decision making and the types of evidence needed. Besides the differences in types of decisions and types of evidence, there are also different barriers and facilitators associated with adopting evidence into decision making.

2

Health Care and Regulation: New Perspectives

HEALTH TOURISM IN INDIA

Health and medical tourism is perceived as one of the fastest growing segments in marketing 'Destination India' today. While this area has so far been relatively unexplored, we now find that not only the ministry of tourism, government of India, but also the various state tourism boards and even the private sector consisting of travel agents, tour operators, hotel companies and other accommodation providers are all eying health and medical tourism as a segment with tremendous potential for future growth.

Kerala — The Pioneer State

Kerala, or God's Own Country as its corporate slogan goes, has pioneered health and medical tourism in India. They have made a concerted effort to promote health tourism in a big way, which has resulted in a substantial increase of visitor arrivals into the state.

Kerala and Ayurveda have virtually become synonymous with each other. However, though Kerala has strongly focussed on Ayurveda and its wide array of treatments and medications, good facilities are also available in the other traditional forms of medicine as well as in modern medical treatment.

The bias towards health tourism in Kerala is so strong that Kerala Ayurveda Centres have been established at multiple locations in various metro cities, thus highlighting the advantages of Ayurveda in health management.

The health tourism focus has seen Kerala participate in various trade shows and expos wherein the advantages of this traditional form of medicine are showcased.

Kerala, India has one of the best qualified professionals in each and every field, Allopathi, Dental, Ayurveda etc and this fact has now been realized the world over. Regarding Medical facilities Kerala has the most competent doctors and world class medical facilities. With most competitive charges for treatment,

Kerala is a very lucrative destination for people wanting to undergo treatment of certain medical problems who do not need immediate emergency treatment.

Kerala offers World Class Medical Facilities, comparable with any of the western countries. Kerala, India has state of the art Hospitals and the best qualified doctors. With the best infrastructure, the best possible Medical facilities, accompanied with the most competitive prices, you can get the treatment done in Kerala, India at the lowest charges. A patient will come to Kerala India where he will undergo medical treatment and along with that we will show him the Kerala tourist and pilgrim destinations, as and when advised by the Doctors. The whole thing would save him a lot of money and he will get to discover Kerala, India at the same time. We assure that we provide the best medical and travel facilities during for you in Kerala, India.

Get your medical treatment done in Kerala at a fraction of the cost at which it is done abroad — in Europe or America. Besides providing you medical treatment, we will also show you different tourist destinations in Kerala, India. The complete package will cost you less that what you would have to pay for the medical charges alone, in other European, Middle East or American countries.

Prostitution and the Risk of Sexually Transmitted Infections

There are no routine data on the numbers of prostitutes with HIV infection or other sexually transmitted diseases in the UK. Many reports in the press assume a high rate of infection. In 1992 two major newspapers carried a report that 75 per cent of prostitutes working in the King's Cross area of London had HIV. The source of this information was the local vice squad, who reportedly keep records of the presumed HIV status of the women on the national police computer, in addition to having pictures of all the 'infected' women on their notice board (Ward and Day 1992). Women might be added to the HIV list if another person tells the police that she may be infected. The high rates reported are likely to reflect police prejudice against prostitutes rather than the true level of infection.

To counter such uninformed speculation, there are estimates of the prevalence of HIV in prostitutes from a number of research projects in the UK. In Glasgow in 1991, 2.5 per cent of women working as prostitutes were infected with HIV; in Sheffield no women were infected (1986-7) and in Edinburgh 14 per cent of prostitutes had HIV infection in 1988. The higher prevalence in Edinburgh reflects the inclusion of male sex workers in the sample and the local epidemic of HIV in injecting drug users. In our study, the small number of cases of HIV in prostitutes (1.7 per cent in 1986-8, 0.9 per cent in 1989-91) were related to either injecting drug use, or sex with a non-paying partner known to have HIV.

In the UK as elsewhere in Europe and North America, prostitute women with a history of injecting drugs are at highest risk of HIV. The overlap between injecting drug use and prostitution varies by town and sector of prostitution. In London between 8 per cent and 14 per cent of women prostitutes reported ever injecting drugs, in Edinburgh 28 per cent and in Glasgow 71 per cent. The variation is partly explained by the different ways women were recruited to the studies—the Glasgow sample was of street workers in an area where injecting was known to be common, whereas in London we recruited women working in a range of sectors of prostitution.

Prostitute women who inject drugs and share equipment are clearly at increased risk of HIV infection in the same way as other drug injectors. Prostitutes who do not inject may also be at increased risk because of their sexual contacts—either with clients or non-paying partners. This risk can be reduced by the consistent use of condoms, or by avoiding penetrative sex. Most studies in the UK have concluded that prostitutes now use condoms all or most of the time with their clients, and this is likely to be an important explanation for their relatively low rates of HIV.

In London, we found that the proportion of women reporting always using condoms with their clients for vaginal sex increased considerably over the years. In 1985 slightly less than 50 per cent of women said they used condoms with all clients for vaginal intercourse; by 1990 this had risen to 98 per cent. However, condom use with non-paying partners remained less common, and women are at risk of sexually transmitted infections from these men.

The various studies in the UK therefore suggest the following general picture in relation to HIV risk: women working as prostitutes report high levels of condom use in commercial sex, but remain at some risk of HIV from injecting drug use and from unprotected sex with non-paying partners. At present these two factors have not led to high levels of HIV infection. However, these women are at risk of other sexually transmitted infections, including gonorrhoea and chlamydia which are themselves associated with considerable morbidity. In London, 44 per cent of women interviewed in 1989-91 reported a past history of gonorrhoea. In Sheffield 28 per cent of sixty-eight women had at least one episode of gonorrhoea during 1986-7; 24 per cent had chlamydia.

Concern about the risk of infection in women who work as prostitutes is not new. Attempts to control sexually transmitted diseases have often focused on prostitutes who are seen as a 'reservoir' of infection. Traditional epidemiology of sexually transmitted infections suggests the existence of a 'core group' of people, including prostitutes, who have a high prevalence of infection. The group then sustains sexually transmitted infection in the rest of the population.

This epidemlological model is relatively crude, and does not explain the high variability in risks of infection in different populations, but it has nevertheless underpinned a lot of interventions. Infection control strategies frequently focus on this notional core group.

This approach has often led to legal and social efforts to control prostitutes themselves rather than to control sexually transmitted disease. In the nineteenth century, for example, much of the legislation on venereal disease control was directed at inspecting prostitutes, denying them liberty if they were thought to be infected. In the UK, laws explicitly targeting prostitutes for compulsory examination were repealed, but the regulation of prostitutes still forms the basis of control programmes for sexually transmitted diseases in many countries. In Greece prostitutes are supposed to be registered with the police, and are required to attend a clinic twice a week for a stamp in their card to prove they are free from infection. Similar controls are found in parts of Austria and Germany.

In the 1980s, the debate about approaches to the control of HIV infection brought the issue of prostitution to the fore in many countries. By the mid-1980s there was fear that HIV would infect everyone who had multiple sexual partners, including prostitutes. This was reinforced by reports from different parts of the world where a high prevalence of HIV had been found in prostitute women. In 1985, researchers in Rwanda reported that over 80 per cent of prostitutes were infected with HIV. In Nairobi, the prevalence of HIV-I in prostitutes rose from 4 per cent in 1981 to 61 per cent in 1985. In the USA, the prevalence of HIV ranged from zero in Nevada to 45.3 per cent in New Jersey (Centres for Disease Control 1987). In Amsterdam 35.4 per cent of 96 prostitutes were found to be infected. While these reports may have hit the headlines, contrasting reports of a low prevalence of HIV among prostitutes came from other parts of Europe, North America and Africa.

It was wrong to assume, as many people did, that prostitution would confer the same risks of HIV in all places, or even that prostitution itself was comparable in different settings in the same country, or even city. The varied reports indicated that risks of HIV infection would vary widely between different groups of prostitutes, and this would reflect wider aspects of the epidemic, such as the degree of heterosexual transmission, along with the local conditions for prostitutes, including the degree of control over their working conditions, access to health care and the availability of condoms. The degree to which prostitution is associated with drug use and trade, which will itself depend on the history of prostitution locally, will influence HIV risk. Associations between prostitution and organized crime, notably the marketing of illicit drugs, have been documented from the early twentieth century to today.

It is clear that the risk of HIV infection, as with other sexually transmitted infections, varies widely. Strategies for reducing this risk must also be flexible. The work described in the rest of this was our response to this challenge, through an attempt to understand health risks encountered by prostitutes and to identify strategies for minimising these risks. At the end, we discuss whether this has provided a more effective and acceptable approach than the standard public health interventions which see prostitutes as a reservoir of infection that needs to be controlled and cleansed.

The PRAED Street Project

In the mid-1980s the likely impact of AIDS on different sections of the population was unclear, and initiatives emerged all over the country to try and reduce the spread of HIV. At St Mary's Hospital in London the genito-urinary medicine clinic already provided services for a number of prostitutes who were expressing concern about their risks of AIDS. We developed research to explore risks of HIV among prostitutes and, where relevant, methods to reduce this risk.

In 1986, Sophie Day began work as an anthropologist, supported by AVERT (the AIDS Virus Education and Research Trust). Helen Ward was working as a research doctor and already saw some prostitutes who used the clinic. After a few months, we developed a single research and service project, as described below, and in 1988 Helen Ward obtained support from the Medical Research Council to develop her research in an epidemiological direction.

We established specific clinic sessions for prostitutes, which later became known as the Praed Street Project clinic. It was a specialized service within the main genito-urinary medicine clinic. Women were able to make appointments to see the same staff, in contrast to the routine genito-urinary medicine clinic which operated on a walk-in basis with more than a dozen doctors. After attending the Praed Street Project clinic, women no longer had to explain or conceal their concerns.

The clinical service provided diagnosis and treatment of sexually transmitted infections, screening for HIV and cervical cancer, hepatitis B vaccination, advice on risk reduction and a range of referrals. From its inception, this clinic was linked to our research. A clinic that was useful to participants seemed an effective way of maintaining contact with women over time and, thus, establishing a cohort study. We conducted repeated interviews on a number of topics with women who returned monthly, or as frequently as they wanted, for a check-up. In this way, we were able to collect longitudinal data on HIV and STD risks in relationship to their social context. These included data on individuals and their partnerships, including condom use, drug use and numbers of sexual partners, as well as material on institutions, such as sectors of the sex industry and the apparatus for policing prostitution.

During the first few months, we became familiar with women and their accounts of work, and attempted to understand 'sexual health' from their points of view. We learned (on both sides) what language to use and how to ask questions in an appropriate way as well as what answers to expect. With time, the cohort design allowed us to develop some rapport and to explore issues which we could not broach during a single interview, such as family, sexuality and money. We were able to trace careers in prostitution as women were followed up for a period of several months or years. The longitudinal data also allowed us to check the reliability of our questionnaires through repeat interviewing.

The research interviews were conducted in a way that placed emphasis on discussion of issues raised by the women themselves, rather than being confined to pre-set research questions. Interviews allowed for detailed discussion of risk reduction in response to specific situations described by the women, and frequently encompassed issues such as family, relationships, fertility, the law and money, which had important effects on the ability of women to practice prostitution safely.

We were there to learn from the women about risk, and about what would be of use to them in terms of support and specific services. The Praed Street Project was then expanded and developed, as far as possible, in the direction indicated by participants.

The cohort provided a unique but by no means perfect framework for epidemiological and anthropological research. The cohort was not a random sample of all eligible women, there was a high rate of loss to follow-up and there was little information with which to investigate the consequent biases. However, we have incidence data on sexually transmitted diseases in those who did remain in follow-up, and can relate these to risk factors such as numbers of partners, types of sex and condom use.

As with the epidemiology, the study has both advantages and disadvantages from an anthropological perspective. We relied largely on interviews and conversations, many of which took place in the clinic.

Nonetheless, we collected such data over a period of years with participants whom we knew well, sometimes for as long as eight years. And, with time, we came to know women not just as 'patients' but at their workplace and, indeed, at court; among groups of friends and colleagues.

This basic clinical service and combined research continued until 1988, when we began to expand the project. The Medical Research Council awarded a grant for a larger epidemiological study in which prostitutes would continue to be interviewed in the clinic but also in the community, through field-work linked to outreach.

This grant allowed us to employ a research nurse, an interviewer and later a second doctor to assist in the provision of clinical services. The research nurse made the service more accessible for a number of women through greater flexibility and more time for formal and informal discussions. She was able to maintain personal contact with women, providing telephone help with booking appointments and reporting results (with the exception of HIV testing).

We also approached the Regional Health Authority (North West Thames) to fund an outreach worker to help us reach women who were not coming to the clinic. By 1988, in addition to those who presented to the genito-urinary medicine routine clinic, many new women were referred to us by friends and colleagues. This networking enabled us to meet women who might not have come to the general clinic, but it did not necessarily improve access to services for other women. The Regional Health Authority provided the funds for us to employ a worker for six months, initially to carry out an assessment of the need for outreach services, and second for premises (a Portakabin) where we could set up a drop-in centre.

With these additional resources we were able to expand the project considerably, both in research and services. The expanded research was not easy. We planned to enrol 200 women each year in a cross-sectional study to monitor trends in the prevalence of HIV infection, and to look more closely at the relationship between HIV and other sexually transmitted infections. We wanted to include women recruited through field work on the streets, in agencies, saunas, flats and other clinics in London. It took two years of hard work to recruit fewer than 300 women, and the majority of these were seen in the Praed Street Project clinic. Working outside of the clinic presented difficulties we had not fully anticipated, including the effect of heavy policing on the visibility of women working on the streets, fear of prosecution that made agencies and saunas reluctant to allow us onto their premises and the suspicions of women contacted by telephone about the nature of our work.

The same problems were found in relation to expanding the coverage of the services of the Project. We were concerned that the relatively low risk of HIV infection in women attending the Project clinic may have reflected the fact that these were the women who already had the best access to health care. Women with greater risks and less opportunity to make use of existing health services may have been missed by our services and research. We addressed these concerns through linking the research to the further development of services. If the services became more appropriate and accessible, the research would better reflect the situation of prostitutes in London; as the research improved, we would have a greater understanding of the women's s concerns in relation to health and health care.

The development of the Praed Street Project from 1988 to 1991 related to three main areas: an expansion of the range of clinical services provided; the opening of a drop-in centre and the related provisions of non-medical advice and support services; and out-reach work to make contact with women outside of the clinic.

Clinical Services

The Praed Street Project was based within a genito-urinary medicine clinic, but the diagnosis and treatment of sexually transmitted infections formed only a small part of our work. During the first seven years of the project, detailed records were kept of nearly 2,842 clinic visits made by 462 women. Women complained of symptoms on about half of the visits, at other times they requested screening for sexually transmitted diseases, cervical cancer, hepatitis B and HIV infection. In addition, advice was sought on contraception and fertility, general-health issues, and for psychological and social problems. Women frequently attended for reassurance following condom failures, reported on almost one-third of the visits, or in relation to other situations where they were concerned about having exposed themselves to risks of infection.

Most genito-urinary medicine clinics are relatively limited in the range of medical services they offer, but these are constantly under pressure from patients to expand, providing wider services for people who prefer the confidentiality which they feel is lacking in general practice. This has motivated many gay men to try and use genito-urinary medicine clinics as their source of primary care, particularly in relation to HIV disease. A similar pattern occurred with some of the women we saw. We therefore expanded the clinical service to provide more general health care-women would present with complaints such as sore throats, chest infections, minor injuries and skin problems. Sometimes this reflected poor access to local health services-one-third reported that they were not registered with a GP, and 11 per cent worked but did not live in London. On other occasions it related to problems of identity. It is difficult for a woman to disclose her work to a GP, who may be her family and children's doctor, but the health problem may be related to work. A sore throat may be associated with oral sex. An injury may be work-related. A skin problem may create problems for work in the future. Reluctance to consult other health care professionals also reflected stigmatization and actual, or anticipated, rejection.

One woman came to the clinic requesting a referral for infertility treatment. She did not want to go to the local hospital as she had been there before. On a ward round a doctor had introduced her to his students as a prostitute, whose infertility problems were assumed to be obvious from this label. This woman, like several others, had been refused infertility treatment because she was considered 'unsuitable'. In response we attempted to set up referral networks to agencies and professionals whom we were confident would not react in this way.

Where appropriate we provided basic primary care for women in the clinic, or referred them to appropriate specialists. It was not always easy to respond. One of the most obvious and frequent needs was for contraceptive services. Prostitutes are not alone in finding the existing provision of sexual health services in the UK sometimes difficult to fathom. Genitourinary medicine clinics provide screening for sexually transmitted diseases, HIV testing and counselling, cervical screening and diagnosis through colposcopy. Some also provide services for people with sexual problems. They do not in general provide contraceptive services such as prescribing the pill, fitting caps and coils. They may provide condoms, but for prevention of infection rather than prevention of pregnancy.

Family planning clinics on the other hand provide the full range of contraceptive services, also offer cervical screening, but are rarely able to carry out screening for and treatment of sexually transmitted infections. Both clinics may, or may not, offer referrals for termination of pregnancy. General practitioners provide a variable combination of the above services.

Between 1986 and 1989, we were unable to offer contraceptive services to women using the clinic, other than basic advice, referral to the local family planning clinic, and condoms. Initially even the condoms had to be obtained specifically for the project, through a combination of donations (from condom manufacturers) and research funding. Obstacles to developing the contraceptive services included territorial disputes between the disciplines of genito-urinary medicine and family planning, and, centrally, funding. Contraceptive services were funded separately from genito-urinary medicine. We eventually convinced the local district health authority and clinic management that this was a short-sighted policy, and basic contraceptive services were made available-but only to prostitutes using the Praed Street Project clinic, and to women with HIV infection. Other women using the routine genito-urinary medicine clinic still have to be referred elsewhere for anything other than emergency contraception. Once the contraceptive services were made available they became very popular with prostitutes and made up a steadily increasing part of the workload, accounting for approximately 10 per cent of Praed Street Project clinic visits in 1991.

Many women requested help and professional counselling, with work and other problems including relationships, drug use, depression and abuse. But there is a widespread lack of trust by women in prostitution of other professions. Social workers are feared most of all, but others, including doctors, health advisers and psychologists, are also threatening. Women expect, and their fears are all too often confirmed, a prejudiced and unhelpful response. Even the best professionals are likely to be insensitive to many specific issues facing prostitutes. To overcome this we initially offered some counselling within the Project, and set up ad hoc referral mechanisms to psychologists and counsellors we trusted. Later, we were able to offer more counselling within the Project, using outreach workers who were undergoing formal training and supervision.

From 1986 to 1992 the Praed Street Project clinic was open for around five half days a week. Women made regular appointments for a check up, or contacted us with specific queries relating to, for example, burst condoms, symptoms, pregnancy or requests for emergency contraception. Women taking part in the research would also be interviewed at each clinic visit, if there was time and it was appropriate. Interviews and conversations during the clinic interviews provided important data for the research, helping us to understand how risks of HIV and sexually transmitted infections were located, and dealt with, in relation to other concerns. Women talked of their work, the methods they used to reduce risks of infection, the impact of the law on their ability to work safely, personal relationships and family.

Health problems were often inseparable from other concerns. Pauline was worried about infertility. She described a miscarriage the previous year at the age of 17, and had not used contraception with her boyfriend since then but was still not pregnant. The pregnancy had been the result of a rape, the miscarriage blamed on an assault by her boyfriend. She began working on the streets after the miscarriage, but felt that the threat of being infertile meant it was not worth it.

She was concerned to find out if she could still get pregnant, worried that an episode of gonorrhoea may have blocked her tubes. A year later, she came in and was found to be pregnant by her boyfriend. Three months later we saw her after a termination, which her parents had pressured her into having. A year later she was pregnant again, and considering another abortion. Pauline related her concerns about infertility to her work as a prostitute-as long as she continued to work she was unable to construct a 'straight' life where she might have a baby. A few years later she had stopped work and was planning to get married-she had met an older man who had 'rescued' her from prostitution and with whom she planned to start a family. The last time we met she was retreating from the idea of marriage and of having a baby with him, fearing that she would be trapped as a house-wife. It appeared that once she had stopped working, fertility and having a child had become less dominant concerns.

Many women expressed similar concerns about infertility, frequently in relation to future pregnancies rather than wanting a baby at the time, while others wanted a child immediately.

Sandra was in her mid-20s and had been working for 18 months. She definitely wanted children, and described 'being at the stage of total paranoia at not being able to conceive'. Her fears about infertility related to past infections; 'funnily enough I've been cleaner in my working life than before. I had gonorrhoea, chlamydia and trichomonas when I had lots of boyfriends'. She used condoms, a natural sponge and spermicidal pessaries with all clients.

Three years later we saw her with her 18-month-old son and she was delighted to be pregnant again. She was still working and requested a check up, concerned about getting an infection that might 'rot the baby'. Throughout this time Sandra had problems with a violent boyfriend, the father of her children. She went into deep depressions, and was referred for counselling, which she found helpful. She stopped regular visits to the Project after her first baby was born, and used other services, although she was still seeing some clients. She has since completed a training programme and has a job.

Through developing the range of services on offer, the Project clinic met different needs for women working in prostitution. For some women it provided their only contact with medical care, for others it was one of a selection of providers of health care. Some attended private doctors for check ups and specialist care, some used drug treatment agencies, some consulted private doctors to obtain slimming tablets. Many women described other activities related to improving their general health and fitness, including running, swimming, aerobics and weight training. Women used complementary health care such as osteopathy, reflexology and aromatherapy, and some had cosmetic surgery.

Through the clinic we learned how prostitutes avoided infections at work, advice which we could in turn pass onto other women. The basic advice we offered was to use condoms for vaginal, oral and anal intercourse, and to ensure that there was no contact prior to putting on the condom. Women made us aware of problems of condom use in oral sex, including pointing out that lipstick, oil based, could weaken the condom. We heard advice about how to encourage men to use condoms, through developing negotiating skills and practical skills in applying the condom.

Several other methods of trying to reduce risks were described. Jenny told us how she used a contraceptive sponge, one or more spermicidal pessaries and was considering using two condoms with each client for vaginal sex. We saw Susan twice in 1986, and at one visit we discussed whether or not she needed a throat swab to check for gonorrhoea. She explained that if a client did come in her mouth, she would gulp down Listerine and spit out the semen. She preferred to do oral as she felt she could make them come quicker. If she had vaginal sex during a period she would douche, and then use a diaphragm and spermicidal cream.

The women we saw described using spermicidal preparations as additional protection from infection long before it was being advocated by 'experts' as a possible way of reducing HIV transmission. Prostitutes were also the first to express fears about the safety of using the chemicals contained in spermicides and condom lubricants-concerns that are now the subject of extensive research and debate.

Drop-In Centre

In 1988 we established Project offices separate from the main genito-urinary medicine clinic and opened a drop-in centre. The Praed Street Project clinic was still within the main clinic building. We first had a Portakabin in the car park below the clinic, next door to the Wharfside clinic, also a Portakabin, where HIV and AIDS out-patient clinics were based. This physical location added to our identity as 'outsiders', not fully part of the clinic and its more traditional services. But there were many advantages in this slight separation.

Women did not have to enter the main building to visit us and check out what we were offering them. Women could come in for informal discussions, collect condoms, be interviewed, make appointments for the clinic or simply meet other women over tea and coffee. This took some months to attract women but subsequently became very popular.

After several months the main clinic moved into new premises and we moved the offices and drop-in to another part of the hospital. It was not easy to identify such premises and obtain permission to use them-we were funded through research money and employed through the medical school, not the hospital. It was the District Public Health Department that finally agreed to provide us with the premises within the hospital grounds. The new premises were a great improvement. We had three floors of a narrow old building; one became the meeting room and drop-in, the other two were offices.The drop-in was open for particular sessions, but many women dropped in at other times for a chat, advice or to pick up condoms. Recurrent themes emerged and led to the development of specific forms of advice and support.

Legal problems were commonly discussed by individuals and groups of women. These related to problems with the police and courts over repeated fines, and specifically in relation to arrests when not working. Women find it difficult to contest a prostitutionrelated charge when they have a record because the evidence required to obtain a conviction is so minimal. Prostitutes have many other legal problems related to the criminalization of their work-the difficulties in establishing legitimate businesses and incomes lead to problems with tax, mortgages and other loans. Property may be held by others to avoid some legal problems, but this produces other difficulties when that other person, frequently a boyfriend, reneges on the agreement. We contacted a legal organization, Release, to provide advice sessions in the drop-in centre.

Women turned to us for help when they faced various crises and found it difficult to gain access to other sources of support, such as social services. We responded through providing advice on welfare and housing issues (informally at first, but later using trained staff), and establishing formal links with other agencies who could provide practical help.

Through opening a drop-in centre the Project established a distinct identity beyond that of the individual staff who provided particular services. Prostitutes became users of the Praed Street Project rather than 'patients' or 'interviewees'. A drop-in centre can transform relations between staff and users.The relationship between health worker and prostitute in clinic consultations, interviews and one-to-one counselling is unequal.However good the training and motivation of the staff, prostitutes are often, like other patients and clients of services, placed at a disadvantage. In a drop-in, where there may be several prostitutes and one or two members of staff, that relationship begins to change. The drop-in can create the conditions for Project users to collectively assert their positions and define their needs.

Some women clearly found it easier to discuss safer sex, problem clients and health concerns in the drop-in than in the clinic. Where possible the clinic doctor and nurse participated in the drop-in sessions in order to reduce the barrier between the two, but there remained some women who would attend the drop-in but would not use the clinic.

At the same time, the drop-in is not an appropriate place for other women. Some clinic attendees expressed horror at the idea of visiting the Project and drop-in, for fear of being seen there, meeting other women. Although they would likely meet other prostitutes in the waiting room of the Praed Street Project clinic, this was seen as less threatening to some women than being in a situation where they were together as prostitutes. For a project to meet the needs of all prostitutes, these differences between women need to be recognized and addressed.

The drop-in also served important functions for the staff working in the Praed Street Project. While it was often irritating to be interrupted in the middle of some work in order to answer the door to someone dropping in when the drop-in was 'closed', the informal contact with women in this situation was invaluable in terms of understanding their lives. In addition, the group drop-in sessions provided very positive feedback about the Project, and made us feel that the work was highly valued by users. This was a great strength at times when we felt rather less valued by other sections of the health service.

Outreach Work

We began outreach work in 1988. As in the clinic, research work and service provision were integrated, and 'field-work' was carried out at the same time as taking services out into the community. An outreach worker was employed to develop this work, specifically looking at health needs of women met in settings other than the clinic.

From 1989 to 1992 fieldwork and outreach took place on the streets of west, north and east London, in the magistrate's courts and in saunas, escort agencies and flats in west London. The aim was to find women working as prostitutes, to offer them condoms and health information, advertise the services available at the Praed Street Project, and to ask them about their work and health. Through this work we hoped to improve their access to services (at St Mary's and elsewhere), and to find out whether our research findings from the clinic were more widely applicable. Street outreach was made difficult by persistent heavy policing in west London. The main effect of the heavy policing-designed to reduce the visibility of prostitution in the area-was to make women difficult to find, and to make them reluctant to talk to us for fear of becoming more 'visible'. We contacted the local police to inform them of our work and to seek some assurance that they would not use talking to us as evidence that women were working. We received a verbal guarantee to this effect, but it was not always respected in practice by the police on the street.

Information collected during outreach was not standardized. Some women would talk to us for some time, and we would meet them repeatedly, others would be seen only transiently. Information was recorded from talking to sixty-two different women during the first few months of street outreach. Twelve (19 per cent) were already using the St Mary's genito-urinary medicine clinic-five of whom used the Project clinic, while seven used the general clinic without disclosing their work. Five more used other clinics, and six used local drugs services. Shortly after the outreach, a further ten women (16 per cent) made use of the Praed Street Project services.

This street work showed that while some women were already in contact with genito-urinary medical services, only a minority used them regularly, and many did not disclose their work. But discussions revealed that access to genito-urinary medical services was not necessarily the primary issue. A quarter of the women described problems with drug use, some of whom wanted needle exchange and other drug services which we were not able to provide. The other major request for advice related to reproduction: four women were pregnant and receiving no antenatal care; two described recent miscarriages, both related to violence; four other women described problems of conceiving and wanted fertility investigations. A range of other untreated health needs were described: two were worried about CIN, and two had never had smears; one wanted to come for an 'AIDS test', reporting that she had been refused one at another London hospital.

Several women reported pelvic problems. One said she had 'stomach pains' and subsequently attended for a check-up. A second woman suspected a pelvic infection while a third reported an untreated infection which had been diagnosed in prison. A fourth knew she had chronic pelvic inflammatory disease but had no GP or other health care. One woman thought she had a 'dose' (gonorrhoea). One said she was bleeding badly. One reported a vaginal discharge. Two wanted check-ups, as they had not attended clinics recently, in one case for sixteen years. A few women reported current treatment for their health; one woman was being treated for a cyst and another was receiving antenatal care.

Health needs were not easily distinguished from other aspects of street prostitution. Two women were worried about their children and the law. One, for example, wanted access to her child in the care of her mother. Two wondered about their rights on arrest as they were under-age; they were particularly worried that they might be sent home. Four women were currently suffering the effects of work-related violence (stitches, bruises, breakages, rape).

The above do not fully illustrate the range of health needs reported by prostitutes, nor the importance of field-work as a service in its own right as well as a means of accessing women to other health services. Many women took advantage of our visits to discuss health issues. In general, these issues were contextualized by reference to policing and the law on the one hand, and problems of safety with clients on the other. At times, health issues were also related to the difficulties of making a living. Much of our data on health were acquired gradually, after several meetings, as shown by a single illustration, concerning a woman, 'Christine', whom we met eight times.

The second time I met Christine, she described how she had been raped and beaten the previous month on the 'beat' (the street area where she worked). She attended St Mary's STD clinic, under her real (that is, legal) name, and she told neither the doctor nor the health adviser the circumstances of this rape. She did not describe her work. Because she had used her 'real' name, she did not report the rape to the police: she did not want her name revealed in court.

Two weeks later, Christine had been attacked by a man with a knife. She was not hurt. The police had arrived, but they 'just let the guy walk off'. At this meeting, Christine also described three past pregnancies, the first was a stillbirth, the second lived for 10 minutes and the third miscarried at 7 months. She had been told that she would not be able to have children and requested further investigations into her reproductive health.

At our third meeting, three weeks later, Christine was preoccupied. She had been sent a routine letter from St Mary's STD clinic. This had been opened by another woman and everyone was gossiping about what infection Christine might have. Christine was still suffering from the rape. Her GP 'simply prescribed sleeping pills'.

A doctor at St Mary's STD clinic offered 'only an HIV test'. Subsequently, Christine made use of the PSP doctor and drop-in.

At our eighth meeting, Christine was particularly concerned about policing in relation to her health. She had been arrested on the way to a video shop and kept in a cell all night, where she had suffered an asthma attack.

In summary, the street work identified a significant number of women who were not using our, or any other, service and yet revealed that they had considerable health care needs. The out-reach succeeded in establishing contact, and some of these women later used the Praed Street Project drop-in and clinic. In addition to the ten mentioned above, more subsequently attended, but in some cases it was many months or years later. On outreach we could deal directly with some of the problems raised-providing information on infections and explaining how to register for antenatal care, for example.

We were unable to follow most of these women up to see whether or not they did contact appropriate services because of the changing conditions on the street. Sustained heavy policing made it difficult for us as well as the women, and contacts were lost.

Magistrates' Courts are another useful place to meet women working as prostitutes-they usually appear before the court in the morning after being charged with prostitution-related offences the previous night. During 1990 and 1991 project workers made 115 visits to four London courts, and made 216 contacts with 119 different women. As on the street outreach, women were given condoms and information about the clinic; unlike the night-time outreach it was sometimes possible for project workers to bring women met in court directly to PSP if they needed medical or other services urgently. Thirty-five women met through the courts agreed to an interview for our research project. This work also brought us into contact with a number of male prostitutes. While PSP services were specifically for women, we could refer these men to other services (such as the Working Men's Project and Streetwise).

Women working from their own premises were contacted on the phone by research workers and by a PSP participant who had contacts with women working in flats who volunteered to do sessional work for the Project. The phone numbers are widely advertised in local telephone kiosks, contact magazines and local papers. This method was very labour intensive and rather frustrating, as many of the lines were disconnected, some women had several lines, and a few women did not want to talk to us.

We had more problems trying to contact women working in saunas, massage parlours and agencies. Unsolicited visits and phone calls generally met with hostility from the receptionists and management. This is not surprising, as these businesses are frequently approached by the police in different guises with the aim of bringing charges against them. Later on these attempts were more successful as we were able to use existing contacts met through the clinic or the drop in to introduce us into the saunas or agencies. Since 1992 this work has become much more systematic and is proving a successful way of making contact with women, particularly those who are new to the area.

Perspectives on the PRAED Street Project

In 1992 the various research projects came to an end. Attempts to secure continued funding from the Medical Research Council were unsuccessful because prostitutes were considered to be at insufficient risk of HIV to make continued follow-up valuable. By this time we had also completed a research project describing HIV risks in the clients and other male sexual partners of prostitutes, and were in the process of writing up the results of various aspects of the work.

There was a danger that the Project would end with the research, something we were determined to avoid. We felt that a clear need had been established for this type of project, and that the Praed Street Project team were uniquely placed to do this in west London.

We took proposals to the hospital, and the district and regional health authorities. The District Health Authority agreed to fund the drop-in and outreach project as part of HIV services. The initial team was a project coordinator, two outreach workers and a part-time administrative worker (who was never appointed). All three had worked on the research project and were skilled in working in this field. The medical side of the project was funded half through research (for a study of the acceptability of spermicides in condom lubricants) and half through routine clinic services.

The services have developed further since the main research ended, including initiatives such as the provision of self-defence classes for women, building closer links with drug agencies, and a new research project has been set up to look at the particular needs of prostitutes who use crack.

The range of services provided and the explicit commitment to an holistic approach to health does not sit easily within the clinically-led hospital structure. The work of the Project is labour intensive-it may take several contacts with a woman on the streets or in the courts before she attends even the drop-in centre, and more work before she feels it appropriate to have a check-up, contraceptive advice and hepatitis B vaccination. Some women will attend the drop-in more or less weekly for months at a time, with no specific problem that requires intervention. To Project workers and users the need for this intensive and sustained work is clear. Over the years Project workers have seen women move from abusive situations where they were extremely vulnerable, to a position of greater stability and independence.

We first met one Project user, Suzanne, in 1988. She found it difficult to use the clinic due to a lack of confidence and mistrust. Through regular visits to the drop-in, interviews and counselling she began to open up about her problems. She was in an abusive relationship which led to visits when she was injured, frightened, angry; she also needed treatment for a number of sexually transmitted infections. At other times she was happy and optimistic, which we found difficult as we knew it was unlikely to be sustained. But after many years of contact with the Project, she has found a way of taking control. She is completing a university degree and looking for a new job, has left her abusive partner behind. It is impossible to say how much the Project contributes to such a process, but from her perspective at least, it provided a setting where she could find support through all kinds of crises, knowing that she would not be rejected, and indeed that she, and her views, were valued.

From the perspective of other people working in the health service, the level of individual and group support provided to women using the Project appears as a luxury, as it does not conform to standard clinical practice. But the justification for the service lies outside the realm of standard clinical care, where efficiency is measured in throughput of patients. The Praed Street Project has a broader aim than identifying and treating infections.

From the public health perspective, prostitutes are seen as having poor access to standard health care as a result of stigma and marginalization, and the Project aims to improve access, removing barriers to the use of clinics. This in turn is important as prostitutes are likely to be in greater need of input from the health services because they are potentially at high risk of acquiring, and transmitting, infections. Additional resources directed at prostitutes may therefore be justified from a public health (*i.e.* population) perspective. However, the more successful the Project is in reducing the risks of HIV and other infections, the less such a view appears to be valid. If prostitutes are not at a high risk, why fund special prevention projects?

The Praed Street Project is one of many that have been established over the last ten years, the majority with a specific focus on sexual health and HIV risk. As part of a European collaborative survey, we identified over eighty projects in the UK that work in whole or part with prostitutes on the issue of health. Most operate with a similar holistic approach to health and explicitly reject abolitionist or regulationist approaches to prostitution. Advice and services are provided in the framework of 'harm minimization' that became the dominant approach to health promotion in relation to HIV-the health workers' role is not to comment on behaviour itself (such as drug use, sexual orientation or prostitution) but to help reduce the health risks associated with such behaviours.

There is a dilemma facing all projects working in HIV and sexual health in the second half of the 1990s. AIDS money is no longer 'ring fenced', it is part of the general budgets. Many innovative projects, like the Praed Street Project, were initially established in response to AIDS, and funded with ear-marked money. Now this is going, projects are forced to justify their role in relation to NHS managers' and purchasers' perspectives-usually shrouded in terms like 'health gain'. Projects are asked to provide rapid evaluations of their work, to define outcome measures which can be related to input resources.

It should be clear from the description of the Project and the case studies outlined that such assessments are not easy. Outcomes, such as the ability to leave a violent partner, may take many years to achieve. Health gain is easy to measure in terms of numbers of infections treated, but it is very hard to estimate numbers of infections prevented in a group using such a project. Finding outcome measures for broad health and support projects is going to be difficult, but is a challenge we need to take up if much of this kind of work is to survive.

In 1992, we (HW and SD) left the Project and had to move on to other jobs and research projects. Initially we retained an official role as part of a management committee of the Project, but that was later disbanded. Since then we have continued to have informal links, and to be involved in specific research projects, including the study of condoms and spermicides, and recently on crack-cocaine use.

Leaving the Project was difficult, but the distance and time does enable us to reflect on the work. What is missing from the perspectives outlined above is that of the women working in prostitution. Project workers work hard, are stressed and insecure, but are convinced of the need for the work to continue. Planners and managers are not so convinced, and want hard data to convince them of the need to provide such supportive services for prostitutes. Public health workers may see the value in the preventive and holistic approach.

Prostitutes will not all have a similar view. Many, and certainly those who regularly use the services, think that they are very valuable and react angrily to any suggestion of cutting back on services. But other women may be suspicious of the projects, seeing them as reinforcing the idea that prostitutes need to be helped and are in some way passive or victims.

Cheryl Overs, from the International Committee on Prostitutes' Rights, questions the hundreds of projects in the world designed to 'educate prostitutes'. She warns:

The funds are not directed at sex workers for their own sake, but because they are viewed as people particularly likely to infect others.. It is important not to misunderstand the nature of this benevolence-it has nothing to do with women's health, or the rights of prostitutes. There has been no change in policies or motivation, but rather these are pragmatic moves to protect the client.

If prostitutes' rights were the priority, the focus of prevention efforts would be to improve working conditions to enable women to insist on condom use and to work in safety without fear of male violence, or to prevent them from being unwillingly dependent on the protection of other people or the police. Human rights would be the central issue, as this would lead to greater control over working conditions and greater self-esteem.

It would be wrong to view all projects as the same, and many of the workers in them are concerned as much with self-esteem as they are with sexually transmitted diseases. Overs is right to remind us of the motives of many of those who fund these initiatives. But that should not blind us to the fact that many projects that have developed in response to AIDS have had beneficial effects for prostitutes. The distribution of free condoms, appropriate advice on safety at work, improved clinical services, access to sympathetic legal advice-all are valuable in their own right.

There is one further concern. Health promotion is often very worthy, but it can also be viewed as a form of social control. In relation to prostitution, health projects are concerned with promoting safer sex, to protect the woman and her client. At best, health promotion provides people with the ability to make informed choices.

At worst it imposes a conformity whereby anyone who chooses not to be healthy is seen as deviant. Within prostitute projects this may have the effect of excluding some women from contact because they do not conform, because they take drugs or do not want to have regular check-ups, for example.

On the other side there is a danger of 'medicalising' prostitutes. Recommending medical checks is crucial to diagnose asymptomatic infection, but there are dangers that this makes some women feel a great dependency, whereby they cannot be 'healthy' without the approval of a doctor. This form of medicalization may reduce rather than increase the control women have over their health.

A second, related, problem is that health issues have once again come to dominate much of the debate on prostitution. Those of us with an interest in the problems that prostitutes face have turned away from broader social aspects of prostitution towards the narrow concerns of a health promotion team. We have consequently tended to neglect the broader debates on prostitution, exploitation and stigma, except insofar as they have an impact on health issues.

The law, for example, is seen primarily as an obstacle to the effective delivery of health promotion messages and the ability of prostitutes to carry condoms, not as a systematic form of oppressing those who work in prostitution.

The last decade has seen a growth in 'experts' on prostitution. We are part of that phenomenon, and it is often tempting to speak out as advocates for the women we have worked with. To ensure that the interests and demands of prostitutes are not drowned by the focus on health, our 'expertise' needs to be balanced with, and challenged by, the voice of prostitutes themselves.

RESEARCH DESIGNS IN MEDICAL ANTHROPOLOGY BY TOURISM

Medical anthropology is primarily an applied subdiscipline, as should be apparent from the materials covered in this book. The roots of the subdiscipline reach back to an intellectual, academic interest in describing and understanding the ways in which various non-Western peoples have explained illness and given treatment to the sick; but the preponderance of research in the 1980s and 1990s has centered on pragmatic issues of improving the health and health care situations of contemporary people, both "Western" or "non-Western."

Health problems throughout the world constitute a sector of applied research that is by nature interdisciplinary; most health issues require data from the biological sciences, clinical medical practice and the social-behavioural sciences.

Research in health problems often involves other types of expertise as well; for example, the role of entomology is very important to understanding various vector-borne diseases such as malaria, typhoid and dengue fevers and the growing interest in research on health care systems requires information from economics and political science. Although there are many instances of research in which individual anthropologists, medical doctors, or biologists "did it on their own," such solo performances are increasingly suspect, given the complex data involved in health issues.

The interdisciplinary nature of the illness and health care sector is partly responsible for the fact that methodological issues are strongly affected by national and international agencies and other organizations that sponsor research. In the United States a very large share of health-related research is funded by the National Institute for Mental Health, National Institute for Drug and Alcohol, National Cancer Institute, National Institute on Aging and other federal agencies. On the international health scene, the World Health Organization (WHO), the U.N. International Children's Emergency Fund (UNICEF), the U.S. Agency for International Development (USAID) and a variety of other organizations sponsor health-related research.

Proposals for research in any of these national and international agencies are judged by interdisciplinary review panels, often (but not always) dominated by biomedical scientists. These factors have had considerable influence in shaping the directions of research methodology in medical anthropology. Also, increasing numbers of medical anthropologists are based in medical schools, schools of public health and other health agencies, in which collegial relations are strongly interdisciplinary.

On the other hand, a substantial portion of research in medical anthropology continues to be funded by the anthropology division in the National Science Foundation, the Wenner-Gren Foundation and other sources in which the review panels are primarily anthropologists. These anthropology-oriented sources are especially likely to be tapped for funding by medical anthropologists whose primary affiliations are in anthropology departments. In such cases the research designs and other methodological features are somewhat less affected by the interdisciplinary (particularly the biomedical) realm of discourse. It is probably fair to suggest that such "anthropology-oriented" medical anthropology is less often applied in nature. However, one can find many exceptions to these patterns.

The growth of medical anthropology over the past two decades has been especially evident in the applied, interdisciplinary realm. In applied research, the solutions to specific practical questions about health and illness are the central concern and development of theory plays a secondary role. Theoretical concerns are not totally ignored, but the areas of theoretical interest are often in "theories of the middle range," where conceptual issues are strongly intermingled with methodological strategies. Medical anthropologists often pay lipservice to aspects of grand theory, but the research is usually at a considerable remove from broader theoretical abstractions.

In any case it is possible to examine a great many issues in the methodology of medical anthropology without direct commitment to a particular theoretical position. In fact, much of anthropological method is essentially theory-less, in the sense that the basic methods of data gathering are the same regardless of the theoretical system adopted by the investigator. In field research it appears that practically all anthropologists use a mixture of interviewing (both structured and unstructured) plus direct observation (again, both structured and unstructured). Specific questions asked and specific targets for observation differ, depending on theoretical interests, but the processes of data gathering are broadly similar regardless of theoretical orientation. It is in the language of theoretical discourse that anthropologists differ markedly, even when discussing basically similar data. This is not to say that two different theoretical discourses necessarily disagree with one another; quite often the different theoretical vocabularies are in some sort of complementary, noncontrastive relationship.

Our examination of field methodologies in medical anthropology will be presented in a generally nontheoretical, or theory-neutral, manner. However, certain methodological tools and techniques will be presented with reference to particular research examples, which may include some of the theoretical language of the authors of the research. Research design becomes specific when we address specific questions. In much of the research in health care, as carried out by medical anthropologists and others, the basic questions very often consist of variations on three main (applied) thematic areas:

- Descriptive questions. What do people believe about illnesses—their causes and treatments? What do they do (*e.g.*, behaviours that increase or decrease risks of illness; specific treatment-seeking behaviours)? What are the characteristics of the health services and systems in which these actions occur?
- Analytic questions. What factors and systems explain variations in beliefs, actions and outcomes?
- Intervention-oriented questions. What are the ways to change and improve the health of particular populations, in terms of system changes, changes in knowledge and actions and prevention of illness-causing conditions?

These are not the only types of basic questions in medical anthropology, but a very large share of research is focused on specific issues related to these fundamental concerns. In a great many instances of research, then, the dependent variable of interest centers on a particular illness or condition--often the actual frequency of the illness. A great deal of medical and health care research, after all, is directed to lessening the frequency (incidence or prevalence) of specific illnesses. Just as frequently, however, the dependent variables center on people's choices of forms of treatment. Who uses "indigenous" treatments versus "cosmopolitan" resources to "do something" about a particular health problem?The independent variables are much more varied and they are by nature more directly reflective of basic theoretical approaches. The following hypotheses concerning "causes" or "factors" affecting treatment choices are all in the same grammatical form and can be examined with basically similar methodology, but they reflect different theoretical assumptions and language:

- People [in community x] avoid cosmopolitan health care because of their traditional health beliefs.
- People [in community x] choose indigenous versus cosmopolitan health care depending on their assessment of the severity of the illness and their ability to meet the costs of the specific health care.
- People [in community x] will go to cosmopolitan health providers and will follow the medical advice to the extent that the information fits with their explanatory models of a specific illness.
- People [in community x] see health care as a political expression and they choose or reject cosmopolitan health cam on political and ideological grounds.
- People [in community x] are likely to be more accepting of the newly introduced primary health care (cosmopolitan) if they have the opportunity to participate actively in the planning of the health service system.

Although these are only a small fragment from all possible research statements, generalizations, or hypotheses, they are useful in illustrating ways in which different researchers, with different theoretical approaches, often have the same implicit or explicit dependent variable (a behavioural outcome) in mind and they will use basically similar methodological approaches to gather the relevant data. In the five hypothetical cases, each researcher would presumably collect data on people's choices of health care alternatives, through direct observation or interviewing and would also collect information about the network of independent variables specified in their particular theoretical model. Some researchers may adopt a strategy of direct observation plus unstructured interviews; others might rely mainly on quite structured interviews; still others will opt for various mixtures of quantified and qualitative data gathering.

CONCEPTS AND DEFINITIONS

Before exploring the wide-ranging inventory of research designs in medical anthropology it will be useful to present some basic definitions of terms that are central to methodological discussions. These terms play a central role in the structure of research proposals, so they constitute a key element in the vocabulary of "grantsmanship," as well as in the analysis of different approaches to theory building and problem solving in medical anthropology.

Data

Data are the recorded results of empirical observations in fieldwork, both quantitative and qualitative. All field notes are data; the recorded responses on structured interviews and their transformations into computerized data sets, are data. Photographs, documents and other physical materials also constitute data. Note that we use the term data to refer to both the physical materials (including tape recordings) and the variables or "themes" or other attributes extracted from the primary materials. Sometimes we use the term raw data to refer to the actual physical materials, including unprocessed field notes.

Variables

A dependent variable is an outcome or condition or phenomenon that is to be explained or accounted for or predicted, by, reference to presumed "causal factors," "prior conditions," "determinants," "disposing features," or other conceptualizable antecedents.

An independent variable is any presumed "causal factor," "prior condition," "determinant," "disposing feature," or other conceptualizable antecedent that is thought to account for, predict, explain, or contribute to the existence or specific form of an outcome or condition or phenomenon.

In experimental and quasi-experimental research designs, it is almost always the independent variable that is manipulated. If a research project has an experimental and a control group, the nature of those two groups constitutes, or embodies, the major independent variable.

(Although many researchers have come to associate the notion of variables with statistical analysis, all empirical research can be usefully conceptualized in terms of variables, however implicit they may be in the actual research reports. Thus, data concerning particular variables may be "highly quantitative" or quite qualitative in presentation.

Hypotheses

A hypothesis is a more or less explicit statement of a hunch, expectation, or prediction of relationships or patterns that one seeks to test or examine in the course of a specific research project. Hypotheses, like operationalized definitions, are best seen as aspects of specific research projects.

Methodology

This concept refers to the logic-in-use in any research project whereby "raw" empirical observations are assembled and transformed into successively more abstract descriptive and analytic statements.

Methodology may be thought of as a series of transformational rules and processes (including definitions of key concepts) that guide data gathering and relate the resulting data systematically to the hypotheses and other conceptual models in terms of which research results are expressed.

Statistical procedures are one type of transformational system for arranging complex arrays of numerical data into patterns that can be expressed as theoretical models.

Models

A model is any representation of the interrelationships among a series of variables or constructs in a research domain. A model is thus an analogical, simplified, physical representation of the phenomenon in a particular instance of research. Commonly encountered models include maps, diagrams, scale models of physical things, as well as verbal descriptions that aptly portray essential elements of a complex domain. A famous model is the physical representation of the double helix used by the biologists Watson and Crick in arriving at the description of the DNA molecule. In anthropology, particularly in earlier decades, the most commonly encountered models were representations of kinship terminologies. For our purposes, the term model is the meeting ground between the theoretical and methodological realms of discourse.

A model embodies the elements derived from a particular theoretical perspective. Thus, the terms or features of a model are simplified portions of a general theory. At the same time, the model includes the elements or details about which specific data are to be gathered in a research project. Each element or concept in a model requires some sort of "operationalized" representation in the research activity.

Operational Definition

An operational definition (of a variable) is a statement of specific datagathering procedures that produce indicators for a given independent or dependent variable. The procedures often include statements of cut-off points, such as, "High blood pressure will be defined as a measured systolic pressure above 140 and/or diastolic pressure above 90." Here is another example: "Socioeconomic status in this research was dichotomized into two groups, landowners (having more than I acre of arable lands) and the landless."

Some researchers appear to consider the idea of operational definitions as referring only to quantitative research. However, the logic of this concept is the same, whether quantified or not. All concepts reported by researchers arise from data of some sort. The reader of any research can always ask, "What data serve as evidence for this particular statement?" Much of the writing in anthropology, including medical anthropology, presents information without specifying details of research methodology. Often we are left to guess at the operational definitions. But they are still part of the research structure, even if they remain unreported.

Triangulation

In this strategy in ethnographic research, data concerning a particular topic are gathered from more than one source, or using more than one technique, so that systematic comparisons (and possible corrections) can be made. Examples of triangulation include the systematic comparisons of the statements made by different key informants and the comparison of key informant statements with the results of structured quantitative surveys. Another common form of triangulation that has come into vogue is to compare focus group discussions with key informant interviews and/or quantitative survey results.

THE HOUSEHOLD AS A BASIC UNIT OF ANALYSIS

In most situations, the people of interest to medical anthropologists experience their health and illness and make decisions about health care in the context of the household or coresidential group. The specific operational definition of household may vary for different populations, but the general term refers to a group of people living together in a single domicile, sharing food and other resources, whether or not consanguineally related. Often researchers seek to delineate households as the people who eat from the same pot, even in cases in which more than one such cooking-eating group may be found within a compound or other complex domicile.In most community-based studies, the common practice is to carry out some sort of census or enumeration of all the households, in order to define the universe (the population) from which samples may be selected. Even when research is mainly participant observation and unstructured interviewing, it is good practice to establish a baseline census. When large numbers of households are involved, the basic census is limited to a small list of key questions:

- Name, age and sex of each person (and their relationship to household heads).
- Ethnic identifications of household heads.
- Occupations of adult members (including cash crops).
- Education of adult members.
- Religious affiliation of adult members.
- Physical indicators of house quality (usually number of rooms, floor material, roof and walls, number of windows).

The physical indicators of house quality are useful as an approximate measure of socioeconomic status.

In addition to these items, each household (and usually each individual) should be designated with a unique identification number, to relate all subsequently collected information and the selection of research samples, to the correct units. Commonly the identification number is composed of community, household, individual, as follows: 01(community)/ 001(household)/ 01(individual) = 0100101 (the first person in the first household in the first community).

In many countries the health ministry or one of the government health research institutes may have a standard census form that it wants all researchers to use. Such "nationwide" formats have the advantage that they permit some comparisons of the specific research population with other areas of the country. On the other hand, the standard forms often include portions that are obsolete or inappropriate for given regions. If possible, researchers will use the official protocol, with additions and modifications to fit local conditions.

If resources are available for gathering more information in each household, the additional items will reflect the specific research concerns, as well as special ecological and other local features important to specific health-illness issues-for example:

- Sources of water supplies.
- Sources and types of fuel and cooking facilities.
- Latrine, toilet facilities.
- Immunization status of children and women.
- Physiological status of women (pregnant, etc.).
- Usual source(s) of health services.
- Labour migration status of family members.
- Recency of arrival to this area and community.
- Community of origin of adult members.
- Foods produced by household.
- Animals owned or maintained by household members.
- Ownership of selected consumer items (radio, television, vehicles, etc.).

Many other items can be added to the list of basic questions concerning the universe of households. However, very few researchers can afford to collect even this much information from all households in their study communities. Quite often a researcher (or research team) will direct the extra questions to a subsample—perhaps every tenth household of the overall census. In this way at least approximate frequencies can be obtained for a variety of features that can then be studied in greater depth as research progresses.

The census, or enumeration, of all households in a study population has other functions besides the collection of specific data. Regardless of whether the process occurs at the outset of research or later, the census is an important opportunity to introduce the research group and purposes of the research, to all households in the area. In addition to the information about the project, each household can also be given information about any expected health interventions connected with the study. The census enumerators can distribute health education leaflets and information about clinic times and places and can recruit volunteers for local health committees. Census contacts can often help in identifying potential key informants, such as local healers.

THE ANTHROPOLOGICAL APPROACH

Compared to most other disciplines, the hallmark of anthropology, medical anthropology included, is the so-called holistic approach. This takes many forms, but in most research there is the assumption that for any particular outcome or phenomenon to be explained, there are a great many interrelated factors at work. In practice, this means that medical anthropologists are likely to collect a great deal of data about economic features, social relationships, cultural belief systems, political processes and other aspects of a community, even if the research intention is focused on a specific health question. Ibis holistic perspective often leads anthropologists to be highly critical of other disciplines when they appear to adopt single-factor explanations or seemingly simple explanations for illness conditions, health care responses and other issues.

The holistic perspective has important effects on research design. Whenever numerical analysis is involved, medical anthropologists are likely to be concerned with a large number of variables, requiring fairly complex statistical procedures. Also, attention to large numbers of factors, or variables, requires a considerable investment of time for each case, patient, illness episode, or other unit of analysis.

The time limitations (and limitations of personnel) in turn constrain the anthropologist to limit sample sizes severely. The typical project in medical anthropology is likely to have much smaller samples than, for example, corresponding research projects by epidemiologists, sociologists and demographers.

Another hallmark of medical anthropology is the central role played by the concept of culture. In recent years many other types of researchers have come to recognize the importance of cultural differences and cultural effects in relation to health issues, but for anthropologists, the concept has much greater importance in shaping the directions of research.

Earlier, before the subdiscipline of medical anthropology came into being, many anthropologists who studied matters of health and illness among non-Western peoples regarded the detailed description of traditional healers and cultural beliefs about illness to be the primary ethnographic objective. They often paid little or no attention to instances in which people used cosmopolitan medicines and practitioners. That is, the primary emphasis of earlier work was on the traditional belief system rather than on actual behaviour. In such studies, then, "the culture" was seen as the sole topic of data gathering.

The concept of culture has now assumed a more modest place in the theoretical and methodological works of many medical anthropologists. "Culture," and cultural differences, have come to be seen as one major cluster of variables, along with complex networks of other factors that account for, or explain, actual behaviours.

Ibis shift in the use of the culture concept constitutes a major achievement in anthropological methodology and metatheory. The development of the idea of culture as distinct from behaviour has made it methodologically possible to speak of (and carry out research on) the variable effects of culture on behaviours.

Not all anthropologists share this definition of culture, but there is a widespread tendency to consider culture as idea systems, systems of symbolic meaning, or other variations in language that all focus on people's mental processes. For example, a widely cited book by Arthur Kleinman states that "we can view medicine as a cultural system, a system of symbolic meanings anchored in particular arrangements of social institutions and patterns of interpersonal interactions". Similarly, Horacio Fabrega, in his book Diseaseand Social Behaviour and Social Behaviour, commented that "illness, for example, offers an additional opportunity to study how behaviour is structured and organized by underlying cultural rules". He then noted that "culture by definition represents a 'man-made,' socially relevant, experientially derived set of rules for living."

Regardless of researchers' specific definitions of culture, one of the central contributions of anthropology to applied studies of health issues is the delineation of the complex ways in which cultural belief systems interact with other factors in affecting rates of disease, definitions of illness, differential responses of illness and other outcomes of interest. Although other disciplines pay some lip-service to the idea of culture in relation to health and illness, medical anthropologists are thought to be the methodological experts in the study of cultural factors. To a considerable extent, the continued increases in acceptance of medical anthropologists in the interdisciplinary community of health research are due to increased recognition of the cultural factor as crucial to understanding all aspects of illness and health care.

The concept of culture has led to a generally accepted distinction between disease and illness. Illness refers to the culturally defined feelings and perceptions of physical and mental ailments and disability in the minds of people in specific communities. Disease is the formally taught definition of physical and mental pathology from the point of view of the medical profession. Both terms are, of course, "culture."

The terms refer methodologically to the contrasts between two distinct cultures that meet when patients interact with physicians, whether in modern urban settings or Third World health systems.

A large share of the research in medical anthropology of the 1980s and the 1990s has focused on situations of cultural pluralism, in which populations with various indigenous health cultures are in more or less extensive contact with the trappings of cosmopolitan health culture. Accordingly, their cultural systems (or "rules for living") include beliefs and rules about the introduced cosmopolitan medications and practitioners, intermingled with the cultural ideas concerning the indigenous healers and treatments. Studies of health care and health issues in urban communities in North America are set in a context of cultural pluralism—as most "mainline" and middle-class people are aware of various alternative health care choices.

CULTURAL VIEWS OF ILLNESS

Arthur Kleinman's formulation of explanatory models (EM) of illness has taken a central place in research on specific sicknesses, as medical anthropologists and others have sought to present a coherent picture of the specific cultural features that affect peoples' health behaviours. The explanatory model for a particular illness consists of:

- Signs and symptoms by which the illness is recognized;
- Presumed causes of the illness;
- Recommended therapies;
- The pathophysiology of the illness;
- Prognosis

As Kleinman points out, individuals are likely to have quite vague and indefinite models of explanation for their illnesses, depending on past experiences of the patient and her or his circle of kin and friends. On the other hand, some individuals in any given community have quite coherent explanations and expectations concerning a specific illness; and the "experts," the healers in the community, would probably on average have more coherent definitions than laypeople, with regard to illnesses and the relevant therapies. In any case, recent research by medical anthropologists has frequently made use of the EM construct as a focus around which a variety of questions can be raised concerning treatment behaviours and other features. Some of the examples of research designs described below focus on methods for systematic relating of explanatory models and treatment-seeking behaviours.

In the past two decades researchers have increasingly recognized the methodological importance of intracultural and intracommunity diversity in people's beliefs and practices.

Ibis tendency in research arose in part in relation to the growth of cultural pluralism, especially in matters of health and illness. Medical anthropologists have come to realize that even in seemingly "isolated" communities, individuals and families differ in their degree of adherence to traditional, indigenous health practices, as well as in their attitudes about medical-health ideas and materials newly introduced into their regions.

As a direct consequence, researchers have recognized the need for representative samples of individuals and households, from whom cultural data are collected. The older ethnographic methodology, based on a few selected key informants plus participant observation, is not entirely abandoned, however. Indepth interviewing of key informants, along with participant observation, are still essential aspects of anthropological research, particularly in early, exploratory phases of study.

The qualitative, descriptive materials from this ethnographic work are essential for making sense of the more quantified materials gathered from samples of observations or structured interviews.

RESEARCH DESIGN: CLINICAL AND COMMUNITY APPROACHES

At the outset of research on health issues a major decision must be made: to focus the study on cases and events in clinical (health service) settings or to define the research population as community based. That decision has major implications for both qualitative and quantitative aspects of research design. Some researchers have found it useful to combine clinical and community-based samples. One very useful model is to start with a community in which cases of illness are identified. Differences between the users of health services and the nonusers can be explored in detail. In addition, the interactions in health care settings can be studied in the user subpopulation.

A clinical population can be defined as any group of patients, clients, or cases selected from the persons found at a particular health center, hospital, or individual healer's location. Clinical populations are selected for research whenever a portion of the research issues focus directly on the activities of the clinic or when it appears that a substantial part of the "cases" of a particular illness are to be found at the clinical setting.

Medical anthropologists have focused increasing attention on the cultural systems, technical workings and other aspects of health care in hospitals and other health care settings. Direct observation of practitioner-patient interactions has become an especially important methodological focus, as researchers seek to define more precisely what really happens in therapeutic encounters. K. Finkler spent two years observing physician-patient interactions in a large hospital in Mexico City.

She was present at 800 consultations and she collected detailed narratives from patients about their illness and systematic data concerning their family backgrounds. Follow-up visits were made to the homes of 205 of the patients to get fuller documentation of their illness experiences and perceptions of their interactions with the physicians. Her massive data collection also included in-depth interviews of seventeen physicians concerning their treatment philosophies and practices. Hospital records provided further depth of information.

Earlier, Finkler had carried out systematic observations among healers at a spiritualist temple in a rural region in Mexico. Her data in that study included 1,212 healer-patient interactions. Because of the similarities of data collection methods in the two studies, she was able to make systematic comparisons between the systems of treatment, identifying broad similarities and significant differences. She noted that "both Spiritualist healers and physicians impose a mind-body dualism on their patients." Also, "In both regimens, the patient takes the role of a passive recipient of the practitioner's ministrations and in both regimens, the practitioners require their patients' compliance reprimanding patients for not having followed prescribed treatments".

On the other hand, Finkler found major differences between the two healing systems: the explanations of illness causation (and diagnoses) are very different; recruitment to the healing role differed greatly; treatment repertoires of spiritualist healers were usually more complex than those of the physicians, who relied mainly on medications. Contrary to widespread belief among anthropologists and the general public, the physicians she observed spent almost twice as much time with first-time patients than did the healers. On the other hand, "Perhaps the most crucial difference... is this: [spiritualist] healers resolve conflicts for patients that physicians cannot because the biomedical script requires physicians to focus on discrete physical pains".

Studies of provider-client interactions have been directed to the work of other practitioners besides doctors and healers. Rayna Rapp conducted an extensive study of genetic counselors, during which she "observed five genetic counselors working for New York City's Department of Health during their counseling sessions... sitting in on more than 200 intake interviews".

Where specific aspects of the client-provider interaction are studied, the sample unit is often the specific encounter rather than the population of individuals. Accordingly, in some cases the sampling frame is specified as "all clientprovider interactions occurring during period," and a system of randomising can be applied to the time periods themselves.

A study by Trevathan of childbirth events in a bicultural community provides another illustration of research where the data can be gathered only in a clinic setting. In the case of childbirth, the significant questions often center on the expectations of mothers in relation to a particular clinic regimen. Accordingly, Trevathan selected a birth center with a large flow of clients. She enrolled in the one-year midwifery training programme of the birth center, after which a study of mother-infant interaction was initiated. "Every woman who registered for prenatal care at the Birth Center and whose delivery was expected between October 1978 and May 1979 was informed of the 'bonding study.' Volunteers were also recruited during childbirth education classes. In the eight-month period, 152 women agreed to be in the study, approximately 50 percent of all those who delivered during that time period". In this example, focus on cases in a particular clinical setting, where the researcher was a participant, permitted her to maintain close control of the research environment. On the other hand, the generalizations (*e.g.*, concerning differences between Spanish-speaking and Anglo mother-infant pairs) cannot be extrapolated to the general population.

Studies based on clinical samples are often limited by the number of patients in a particular facility. For example, Cohen and colleagues compared and contrasted the explanatory models of diabetes patients with those of clinical staff in a diabetes clinic of a large midwestern university hospital. Their samples consisted of thirty-nine diabetes patients and fifteen professional staff. Despite the small sample sizes, the study shows interesting areas of discrepancy between the diabetes patients and the clinical staff, particularly in their interpretations of etiology, severity and pathophysiology of the illness. Patients and clinical staff were in close agreement concerning the appropriate treatment for diabetes. Studies focused on cultural patterns such as explanatory models of particular illnesses can often accomplish their objectives using rather small samples.

In the cases mentioned, the clinic populations were appropriately selected because of the nature of the research topic. However, clinic populations should never be considered as representative of the general (community-based) population. In almost every case, a particular hospital or other health setting receives only a selected, nonrandom portion of the population that exhibits a given illness or condition. Other cases may remain home, untreated; still others are found at the various alternative treatment facilities. Even an exhaustive tally of all cases in all facilities does not produce a representative picture of a given health problem, except perhaps with illnesses so severe and so clearly identified, that nearly all of them can be found.

Clinic-based samples, if used as the sole data collection strategy, also have another potential weakness. Patients at health facilities appear as individuals, separated from the family networks in which they normally reside. Full, holistic understanding of people's expectations and reactions concerning illness and health care requires consideration of the household setting as it affects cultural responses. Thus, researchers such as Finkler have often carried out follow-up interviewing of patients in their homes, after observing their interactions in the clinic setting.

Generalizations about the frequencies of health care problems and choices of treatment require sampling from the relevant community population. Epidemiologists often refer to that community-based population as the "denominator," which is essential to study if one is interested in precise estimation of rates (or changes of rates) of particular illnesses or health care practices.

CLINICAL SAMPLES WITH MATCHED CONTROLS

Generalizations from clinic-based samples can often be greatly strengthened by selecting a control group from the same population that the clinic patients represent. K. Finkler, in the study of spiritualist healing mentioned above, introduced this method in her study of the patients. The data from the clinic (temple) sample were systematically compared with a control group (N = 372) "geographically matched with subjects interviewed in the temple corresponding to the villages [from which the patients originated]". Use of the control group permitted Finkler to state that the regular clientele of the temples did not differ significantly from the general population in perceived illness.

STRATEGIES FOR COMMUNITY-BASED SAMPLES

Most research in medical anthropology has been structured in terms of communities or (sometimes) communities within communities. One or more communities in a particular region are chosen as primary sites for research, usually (not always) because of the prevalence of a particular health issue or problem in the selected region. Once the community or communities have been selected, sampling and other aspects of research design depend a great deal on two main factors:

- The nature of the specific health problem addressed
- The geographic characteristics of the communities.

Community-based research is particularly congenial to medical anthropologists because the holistic methodological perspective requires a research context in which the field researcher enters into fairly long-term contacts with the people and is able to combine a great deal of firsthand participant observation with equally extensive interviews and conversations with people.

Regardless of the specific topical focus, fieldworkers usually involve themselves in the daily lives of the people they study, even if only for short periods of time.

Often the researcher focuses on a single, well-chosen community of intermediate size. Where local villages and hamlets contain small numbers of households, it becomes necessary to include several such communities. Research that is concerned with a particular illness of specific population segment (*e.g.*, asthma among small children) requires that the population be large enough to contain an adequate sampling of households with small children experiencing the illness.

Sizes of study samples vary greatly, depending on overall community size, prevalence of specific illnesses studied, the types of data gathered and the resources (including time) available.

Nichter and Nichter described a survey carried out in South India, in which a small number of questions concerning food intake during pregnancy, preferred size of baby and relations of food intake to baby size constituted the very simple interview protocol. The simplicity of the interview schedule made it feasible to manage a sample size of 282 participants.

Approximately 100 households appears to be a common ballpark figure in much medical anthropology research.

In many cases medical anthropologists find it necessary to collect data from. multiple samples of informants or respondents, in part because of the difficulties in getting adequate representation of the various subgroups in a population.

Also, different samples are sometimes selected in order to focus on particular topical areas. In a study of childbirth and obstetrics among the Bariba ethnic group in Benin, Sargent gathered data from several samples:

- 26 postmenopausal women in a rural Bariba village;
- 123 pregnant urban women of the same ethnic group (a clinic-based sample);
- 35 pregnant Bariba women contacted in their homes;
- 50 urban Bariba women currently employed in a cashew factory;
- 77 Bariba women who delivered at the Parakou hospital, whom she interviewed "concerning pregnancy and delivery expenses and hospital experiences".

Thus, Sargent found it important to combine community-based and clinic-based samples in order to get a holistic perspective on childbirth and maternity in the population. When researchers have sufficient co-investigators and research assistants, samples can be larger. Browner and associates carried out research on reproduction and health in a township of 1,800 inhabitants in highland Oaxaca, Mexico. "In addition to participant observation and intensive interviewing of selected key informants, single interviews were conducted with a 54 percent sample of the municipio's adult women and their husbands. One-hundred eighty women and 126 men were interviewed, with the sample constructed to represent the age, residential and linguistic backgrounds of adult population".

Many anthropological studies utilize multiple community samples. In some cases several communities or hamlets must be included for representativeness in a complex population. Gittlesohn, in a study of intrahousehold food distribution patterns, defined his research population in rural Nepal in terms of a network of six villages, in order to include all relevant caste groups.

Quite often the selection of multiple communities is used to operationalize a significant, usually independent, variable. Bentley chose three villages in north India as the population for study of household management of childhood diarrhea, in order to have an experimental and control group. One village was the site of an oral rehydration therapy (ORT) intervention programme and two villages nearby were selected as controls in order to test the efficacy of the ORT programme.

In a study of "ethnicity, ecology and mortality in Northwestern Thailand," Kunstadter gathered data from a number of different communities, both highland and lowland. "Community type is the basic unit of comparison. Disaggregation of the population according to type of community shows that fertility and mortality patterns are systematically associated with ethnicity and ecology (location and basic economy). Populations in the study area allow control of ecological and ethnic variablility by comparing, for example, the same ethnic group in different ecological settings (Northern Thai in Town, Suburb and Lowland Rural communities) and different ethnic groups in the same ecological setting (*e.g.*, Highland Skaw Karen, Po Karen and Lua' with similar swidden economies)".

In a similar vein, Hackenberg and associates selected four communities in the Philippines—two sedentary and two migrant groups—for testing specific hypotheses about the effects of migration and modernization on hypertension levels. Gebrian used a multicommunity design in a study of nutrition, rates of immunization and other characteristics in a thirty four-community region in southwestern Haiti. She compared communities in terms of "distance from health center," "level of community participation," size of population," and other independent variables in testing hypotheses about the effectiveness of primary health care operations.

SAMPLING IN URBAN COMMUNITIES

Medical anthropology in urban sites, particularly in North American settings, very often focuses on one or more ethnic groups within the general population. The selection of such ethnic (or other) subcommunities poses special problems, particularly in identifying the total population of ethnic households from which sampling will occur. A typical strategy is to identify one or more urban "neighbourhoods" thought to be concentrations of the particular ethnic group. In Hartford, Connecticut, Schensul and associates selected two neighbourhoods; a public housing project and an area of privately owned houses. After arbitrarily delimiting the two neighbourhoods, a system of random sampling was adopted by which 143 households were selected for interviews.

Janes described the difficulties in selecting a sample of Samoan migrants in northern California for his study of hypertension. "The sample selection process involved the following steps: a list of the church membership of two large church congregations was obtained, numbering about 130 households. From this pool, 60 households were chosen at random. This resulted in 89 interviews with men and women in these households.

In addition, with the aid of a Samoan research assistant, who was also a well-known and respected member of the community, I selected a sample of 25 individuals from other religious denominations". The contrast in style between intensive, small-sample research and the collection of survey data in an urban setting is particularly striking in the work of Scrimshaw in the Ecuadorean city of Guayaquil. In the ethnographic phase of research, "sixty-five families in one small area of the squatter settlement were studied for six months using participant observation, conversation, informal interviewing and observation".

An interview schedule was then designed for gathering quantitative data on migration, fertility and induced abortions and was administered to approximately 2,000 households in a squatter settlement and the "central city slum" area, using probability cluster sampling.

Scrimshaw demonstrated that her ethnographic sample of fewer than 100 households was in many ways quite similar to the large-scale sample in terms of frequencies of fertility attitudes and behaviours.

BASIC DATA-GATHERING TOOLS

Key Informant Interviewing

Open-ended qualitative interviewing of key informants has long been the foundation stone of anthropological data gathering. Even in projects with a major focus on quantitative survey methods, there is almost always an initial phase of ethnographic exploration—in the form of informal interviewing.Some unstructured conversations and interviews should always be carried out with a variety of informants before more structured quantitative data gathering is initiated. One major aim of the qualitative research is to develop a good sense of local vocabulary in relation to health problems. The forms of even the most routine questions and observations should be shaped by knowledge of the local language and ecological conditions.Traditionally anthropologists have relied heavily on serendipity in locating key informants.

Loitering about in public places usually leads to contacts with some local persons who happen to feel like talking with the outsider. A somewhat more structured approach is to go from household to household, to visit and to explain the intended research project to individual families.In health care research, whether clinic based or community based, medical anthropologists often follow a sequence of contacts, beginning with local administrators, health authorities and other leaders in the political and administrative hierarchy. Following that sequence of contacts with informants, it has become useful to distinguish three main types of key informants:

- Type 1 key informants: Administrators and officials. The first key informants one contacts are likely to be personnel in government services, police and administrators in nongovernmental organizations, who am broadly familiar with local situations and activities because of their official dudes. These first-line key informants can help data gatherers to get started in the target community, as they am often gatekeepers who can grant (or refuse to grant) access to clinics, hospitals and community health workers.
- Type 2 key informants: Health workers and community outreach workers. In most areas, both urban and rural, them am outreach workers of health services and other social programmes, in government services as well as nongovernment organizations. These informants are particularly important because they can provide direct contacts with people in the target populations. Also, the community outreach workers are often in situations of mediating between service programmes and the people's household-based health beliefs and practices.
- Type 3 key informants: Members of the target population. Ethnographic research is rather incomplete until extensive informant

interviews have been carried out with members of the target population. In the case of women's and children's illnesses it is commonly expected that the anthropologist visits a number of households, seeking out women who have had a lot of experience with illness management and who am willing to spend considerable time in discussing "cases" and "episodes" of illness. Cam should be taken that these key informants are drawn from several different parts of the community in order to ensure representativeness of the sample, even though key informants are never selected on a random sampling basis.

The numbers of conversations and other contacts with key informants will vary greatly, depending on their availability, their breadth of information and willingness to spend many hours with the interviewer. Typically medical anthropologists, like other ethnographic fieldworkers, rely on a small number of key informants (usually fewer than ten) for a large part of their detailed information, with smaller amounts of contact with their secondary key informants, who are nonetheless very important for cross-checking and triangulation of data.

In some cases anthropologists select samples of informants from different sectors of the local population after carrying out a household census to identify types of households and other variations. Small numbers of representative families (*e.g.*, families with children under five, households with pregnant women, nuclear versus extended households) can then be visited for in-depth ethnographic interviewing.

Ethnographic interviewing and unstructured observations in homes is the crucial stage in many projects, during which the complexities of health care decision making, types of home treatments, attitudes and relationships to health facilities, economic and political issues and many other details of local life are studied extensively, in preparation for carefully designed, structured observations and interviews. The informal contacts with selected households can also include some pretesting of portions of data-gathering formats intended for the more structured portions of the study.

Structured Data Gathering in Samples of Households

Many health-related research projects include several different structured datagathering operations, sometimes using somewhat different samples for the various observations. For example, Bentley, in her research on diarrhea management in north India, interviewed in a random sample of 199 households to collect data on beliefs and knowledge about the causes and prevention of diarrhea and other aspects of explanatory models. In a later phase of research, mothers of children with diarrhea episodes were interviewed as well as observed in 50 households, to get actual behavioural data. In his research on intrahousehold food distribution in Nepal, Gittelsohn selected six villages within a panchayat, from which he identified a random sample of 115 households. A number of different interviews and observations were carried out, including a socioeconomic interview, several twenty-four-hour dietary recalls, anthropometric measurements of both children and adults, repeated direct observations of meals (total of 354 meals recorded), collection of morbidity data, in addition to key informant interviews and informal chats with many of the people in the sample. The resulting data set contained twenty-one separate subfiles, totaling 70,000 lines.

COMBINING QUALITATIVE AND QUANTITATIVE DATA: SOME EXAMPLES

Case 1: Explanatory Models of Illness and Decision Making.

One of the more thorough and impressive studies of people's modes of choosing among health care alternatives is that of James Young, in the town of Pichataro in western Mexico. The study is important because it illustrates structured interviewing with small numbers of key informants, after which the methodology shifted to collection of actual illness episodes.

In the first phase of research Young and his wife, Linda Garro, carried out a census of the 509 households in the community and began key informant interviews concerning common illnesses and their characteristics. General ethnographic interviewing was necessary to identify specific types of health care resources utilized by the people, as well as to develop the basic list of locally recognized illnesses concerning which cultural models of explanation and choice making could be derived.

With a provisional set of forty-two physical and behavioural symptoms of illness (each written on a separate card), the researchers asked five literate informants to sort these into piles in terms of severity. The same informants were also asked to sort the illnesses (diagnostic labels) into piles in terms of severity.

In order to get in-depth information concerning the culturally defined characteristics of each of the illnesses, a set of forty-three different illness attributes (questions) were asked of each of the thirty-four illness terms identified in early stages of the research. Ibis time-consuming interview required a number of sessions with each of the ten informants—six women and four men.

The most time-consuming process was the collection of a corpus of actual illnesses, for the testing of the decision model derived from analysis of the data on illness definitions and characteristics. From the original census data, a representative sample was drawn. "Over a six-month period, sixty-two households were visited on an approximate biweekly basis and records were made of each illness occurring among its members". A total of 323 cases were collected.

This research project is very revealing, as it includes a thorough mixing of qualitative and quantified procedures, progressing from pattern identification of illnesses, to the testing of models concerning the ways in the patterns influenced actual behaviours (in the 323 episodes).

Case 2: Modernization and Arterial Blood Pressure

"Hypertension," or more accurately, differential blood pressures, is particularly interesting as a focus of research because the disease is relatively symptom free. As a result, in most indigenous communities there has been no traditional concept. Nonetheless, a great many cultural groups, including many Native American communities, now have cultural models of "hypertension," learned (and modified) from the doctors, nurses and others in cosmopolitan medical services. Studies of factors affecting differences in blood pressure levels (and outright hypertension) involve use of an overt biomedical measurement (using a sphygmomanometer), plus the observation of cultural, psychological, social and other factors thought to affect arterial blood pressure levels. The following case is important because it exemplifies an increasingly frequent type of study, in which medical anthropologists collaborate with epidemiologists and other biomedical researchers in projects sponsored by international agencies.

Dressler and associates chose an urban area in of Ribeirão Prêto, a city of 400,000 in Southeast Brazil, for the research. "A variant of cluster sampling was used to draw a sample of 139 individuals. Four broad clusters based on residential and economic sector were chosen and then random samples of 20 households were chosen from each cluster".

The clusters that the researchers selected represented agricultural day laborers, continuously employed plantation workers, factory workers and a fourth cluster of bank employees.

For the dependent variable, the research group used the mean values derived from five separate measurements of blood pressure using a DINAMAP Vital Signs Monitor Model 845XT. The automated equipment for measuring blood pressure is much more reliable than ordinary sphymomanometers, as it "virtually eliminates inter-observer variability". Ibis is an example of use of state-of-the-art equipment and methods to manage the biomedical variables in an interdisciplinary project.

Other variables were "index of style of life," composed of ownership of items of material culture and "economic resources," representing occupations of all adult members of the households. From these two measures, an index of "life-style stress" was computed, based on the discrepancies between the two indexes. Dietary data were collected using a series of four twenty-four-hour recalls. Other variables included individual perception of "relative deprivation," "life changes," and the usual age, sex, education and race, as well as height and weight.

The lifestyle index in this study is particularly interesting because it includes ownership of consumer goods (colour television, vehicle, food blender, camera, telephone, etc.) and also items such as yearly trips to Sio Paulo, vacation trips, magazines read per month, newspapers read per week and number of books read per year.

The statistical analysis (multiple regressions) replicated Dressler's previous study of hypertension in St. Lucia, again demonstrating the importance of lifestyle stresses as predictors of differences in blood pressures. In his earlier research, Dressler had carried out extensive qualitative ethnographic research in addition to the quantified data gathering.

The Brazilian study, on the other hand, included very little qualitative data gathering.

Case 3: Diarrhea Research of the 1980s

This case departs from the focus on individual projects in order to examine some features of a concerted programme of research on diarrhea that has played a central role in the child survival programmes of the 1980s and 1990s, particularly involving Oral rehydration therapy (ORT). Infant and childhood diarrheas have been a leading cause of mortality in most parts of the developing world. Beginning in the 1980s, it became apparent that a major reduction in infant and small child mortality could take place if ORT were regularly used to offset the dehydrating effects of diarrheas, even though ORT is not itself a cure for the illness.

Practically every developing country now has a programme for promotion and dissemination of ORT. In most cases the emphasis is on teaching people to use ORT packets disseminated throughout the primary health care systems; however, some programmes have sought to train people to mix home-made oral rehydration solutions, following simple recipes. There has also been promotion of rice-based and other cereal-based ORT.

Despite the apparent success in some of these campaigns, most national programmes have encountered difficulties in convincing the majority of people to use ORT. And in many instances even the acceptors of the therapeutic regimen do not use ORT in an appropriate manner.

Problems with people's acceptance and proper use of ORT in most developing countries have led to widespread realization of the need for research, including anthropological data gathering, to identify the points of difficulty and to develop ways for improving programmes.

The study by Bentley in north India is one of a large number of studies by anthropologists during the 1980s. Several of these studies were published in a special edition of Social Science and Medicine.

Biomedical, thinking and directions of research with regard to childhood diarrhea have progressed from a simple focus on ORT, to the examination of complex issues around breast feeding and other dietary behaviours, patterns of use (and misuse) of pharmaceutical remedies and many other culturally mediated beliefs and behaviours. With the realization of complexity has come a greatly increased interest in the possibility that specifically anthropological methods may hold the keys to better management of the diarrhea issue.

A major first step to disentangling the "diarrhea problem" was the shift of focus from the biomedical construct, "diarrhea disease," to the variety of cultural constructions—the emically defined patterns related to diarrhea as illness. One of the more influential studies earlier in the decade was Nations's study of an economically impoverished area of northeast Brazil. She noted the points of incongruity between the prevailing allopathic approaches to diarrhea and the perspectives of the mothers and local healers among the people. She called for new approaches to diarrhea control:

In short, the foremost concern of this alternative approach to diarrheal disease control is to support rather than suppress popular village healing. Doctors must adapt medical terminology to popular usage. They must learn the popular folk explanations for childhood illnesses and explore their relation to biomedical etiologies. Health professionals must also give villagers dietary advice in a way that does not violate harmless food beliefs and that assures the traditional healers power in village medicine. Still, peasant families must also have easy access to effective modern means to save children dying from severe dehydration.

Key informant interviewing to elicit varied terminology for diarrhea, emic types of diarrhea and the exploration of the explanatory models (EM) for diarrhea in given cultures have become core elements of most community-based diarrhea research, even by nonanthropologists. In north India Bentley found that mothers identified five types of diarrhea: "bloody,": "watery," "bits-and-pieces," "green," and "yellow". Scrimshaw and Hurtado found that explanatory models of diarrhea in Guatenuda included those caused by the mother (due to emotion, physiological condition, etc.). foodrelated diarrhea (hot, cold, "bad," excess), as well as those due to tooth eruption, "fallen fontanel," evil eye, worms and "cold enters the stomach." This complex array of different causes is associated with different choices of therapies.

In a rural area of central Mexico, Martinez asked mothers to sort into groups the various foods that had previously been identified as "foods given to children during diarrhea." The pile-sort task results were then submitted to multidimensional scaling.

Martinez asked his community health workers to examine the scaling results and to interpret the dimensions. The general result included the finding that women were differentiating between foods that were appropriate during acute phases of diarrhea and those that are usually fed during the recovery phase.

Most of these ethnographic researchers have used some sort of sampling procedures, but the exploration of folk taxonomies, explanatory models and other aspects of emic views of diarrhea do not generally depend on statistical analysis, other than, at most, frequencies of recognition of taxonomic categories. While some variations are always found in the numbers and types of categories identified by different informants, the range of variation is not usually extensive.

Quantitative survey techniques, on the other hand, are generally used to assess the strength and prevalence of beliefs about causes of diarrhea and especially for assessing frequencies of crucial elements such as cessation of breast feeding, curtailment of solid foods and other potentially harmful behaviours arising from cultural belief systems. Survey techniques have also been used to find out the percentage of people who have heard of ORT, as well as the rates of recent use of this therapy. Coreil and Genece report a survey concerning adoption of ORT among Haitian mothers, carried out in the coastal town of Montrouis and the surrounding villages. As is usual in this kind of study, several weeks of ethnographic investigation were carried out before the survey was initiated. "A random sample of 300 mothers or caretakers of children 0-5 years were interviewed. Census records allowed us to identify all the 1714 families in the health programme with preschool children"). The researchers made use of two survey teams, "each consisting of 3 interviewers and a supervisor. The project director (author) trained and closely monitored the teams. The 65-item questionnaire was pretested on 15 mothers from an adjacent community". The statistical analysis consisted of a multiple regression to examine the relative strengths of several hypothesized predictors of ORT knowledge and use.

The third major sector of anthropological research on diarrhea has been directed to prospective study of behaviours in the case of actual diarrheal episodes. This methodology requires three main ingredients:

- A representative sample of households containing small children of the requisite age;
- A method for monitoring households so that episodes of diarrhea are quickly identified as they occur;
- A well-designed protocol for direct observations and interviewing concerning the identified cases.

Monitoring and follow-up of diarrheal episodes is time-consuming, as each visit should include direct observation if possible, as well as interviews of caretakers concerning modes of treatment, visits to health care facilities, feeding behaviours, condition of the child and many other details. As studies of diarrhea have shifted towards possible prevention strategies, interest is developing concerning direct observation of hygiene and sanitation in households, including hand washing, modes of cleaning up after children's diarrhea, maintenance of drinking water and other behaviours. All of the recent studies of actual behaviours have demonstrated that them are wide discrepancies between people's answers to surveys as opposed to actual behaviour as observed directly by the researchers.

At the same time, direct observation of complex health-related behaviours is a relatively underdeveloped aspect of anthropological research and more experimentation is needed to refine the methodology.Collaboration of medical anthropologists with epidemiologists, biomedical researchers and others has been particularly fruitful in the sector of diarrhea control.

This is partly because of the widespread realization that qualitative ethnographic work and other anthropological research tools play a vital role in furthering practical understanding of key issues, particularly about the ways in which complex health beliefs, or explanatory models, affect health care decision making.

Case 4: Focused Ethnographic Study of Acute Respiratory Infections in the 1990s

G. Pelto and associates at the World Health Organization (WHO) have recently developed a systematic ethnographic approach to the examination of people's cultural explanatory models of acute respiratory infections (ARI) in very young children. Serious respiratory infection (usually pneumonia) is a major killer of children under five years of age, currently accounting for more than 4 million deaths annually. In order to promote effective responses to serious ARI among mothers and other caretakers, the WHO planning team developed a set of interrelated data-gathering techniques that produce a relatively clear picture of the explanatory models, as well as behaviours and evaluations associated with the culturally defined ARI illness domain. Here are the main elements in their focused ethnographic study (FES) strategy:

- Data gathering begins with key informant interviewing about respiratory illnesses and their treatments in the local area. The interviews also include a "free-listing exercise" to obtain the vocabulary of signs and symptoms, as well as local, culturally specific names for children's respiratory illnesses.
- Illness episodes of ARI are collected from small samples of mothers in order to assemble more information about behaviours connected with the different categories of signs, symptoms and illnesses.
- Mothers are shown short video clips of sick children (including some with pneumonia) and are asked to identify symptoms and explain "what is wrong" with the child (what illness does the child have?). The mothers are also asked whether they have perceive the child to exhibit "rapid breathing" (an important symptom of pneumonia).

- The sample of mothers is asked to respond to hypothetical vignettes of children with
ARI symptoms. The descriptions are varied systematically to highlight differences in response (recommended actions) for more severe and less severe symptoms.
- The respondents are asked to do simple sorting tasks with sets of index cards, to indicate which specific symptoms are associated with local illness terms. The card sorting is also used to get systematic ratings of severity of the various signs, symptoms and illnesses. Weller (1980) and others have used similar sorting tasks for cognitive mapping of various cultural domains.
- Structured interviewing in the form of paired comparisons (Weller and Romney 1988: 45-46) is used to elicit the mothers' choices of health care providers. The list of alternatives (doctors, healers, clinics, etc.) is obtained from the key informant interviews.
- Interviews with mothers (and other caretakers) bringing small children to clinics provide more direct information on actual health-seeking behaviours in relation to particular symptoms. A key question in that context is, "Which of the symptoms [that you saw in your child) were the ones that led to your decision to come for health care?"
- Interviews with pharmacists and vendors concerning their prescribing patterns for ARI symptoms and interviews with various indigenous and cosmopolitan practitioners are included for rounding out the picture of the local people's management of ARI episodes. Also, home inventories of herbal remedies, pharmaceutical products and other medicines are obtained from the sample households.

The FES strategy adopted in the WHO ARI programme is a mixture of qualitative and small sample quantitative techniques, many of which are clearly described in Systematic Data Collection, by Weller and Romney. The tools and techniques for cognitive mapping of cultural domains, as well as other basic ethnographic methods for this type of study, are also described in Research Methods in Anthropology.

This example of the use of explicitly ethnographic research methodology at the WHO is part of a rapidly developing trend in international health organizations. There is now widespread interest in adoption of the research approaches of medical anthropology, partly connected with a growing recognition among biomedical personnel and health care planners, of the importance of cultural and social factors in affecting the success of health care programmes.

The FES battery of data-gathering techniques is a useful example of the strategy of triangulation in ethnographic research. Data concerning people's recognition and definitions of symptoms and illnesses are collected in illness episodes, free-listing exercises, viewing of the videos and structured sorting tasks. Thus, the data provide systematic cross-checking of both illness definitions and the behaviours associated with them. Also, the authors noted that in their methodology, "Data on antibiotic use patterns are obtained from several FES procedures, including the narratives of past ARI episodes, scenarios, home inventories [of medicines] and interviews in clinics, with pharmacists and with practitioners". Based on those multiple data sources across a number of different research sites, they found that there are widespread problems in misuse of antibiotics: "

- Antibiotics used for mild upper respiratory infections;
- Failure to continue with a full course of antibiotic treatment;
- Saving medication from a partially completed course to use for another episode".

DISCUSSION OF THE CASES

The four cases illustrate a few of the many trends in contemporary medical anthropology, particularly in fieldwork in primary health care in developing countries. To an increasing extent, medical anthropological research is directed to intensive study of specific sicknesses—either in emic, culturally delimited terms of illness or through study of a biomedically derived disease, for which the relevant cultural explanations, behaviours and other features are explored. Research directed to specific pathological states has the large advantage of delimiting and controlling the range of relevant health behaviours to be studied.

Also it permits the anthropologist to become at least moderately knowledgeable about the relevant biomedical aspects without having to spend months in studying medical textbooks.Most field research in medical anthropology—in these cases and other studies like them—includes varying mixtures of the following ingredients:

- Initial selection of field site where the sickness condition(s) of interest are prevalent enough to be studied. Quite often the field site is selected because of an ongoing health care programme.
- General, descriptive field research, particularly key informant interviewing, in the area, much like other anthropologists in the first phases of getting acquainted with the local environment and its people.
- Census or enumeration of the local population in order to gather general descriptive information and to acquire the framework for later representative sampling.
- Key informant interviewing and participant observation focused on the particular pathology, to explore "explanatory models," taxonomies, as well as a variety of other areas of cultural knowledge concerning the topical focus.

- Use of pile sorts, triad sorts, sentence frames, or other structured methods with small numbers of informants, in order to refine various aspects of the explanatory models and other aspects of the cultural belief systems.
- Structured direct observations of management of illness, hygienic-sanitation behaviour and conditions, provider-patient interactions and other behaviours central to the research.
- Structured interviews for eliciting data on main independent and dependent variables from representative samples, in order to test specific hypotheses and to verify major patterns and processes tentatively identified in earlier steps of research.
- Extraction of data from patient records in hospital, clinic, or other health care facility where available. In the usual case, extraction of such data requires permission not only from the administrative personnel who control the records but also from the individual patients or their families. Such records may also include data from special bioclinical observations, including blood pressures, blood samples, urinalysis, x-rays, clinical assessments by doctors and other procedures.
- Analysis of both qualitative and quantitative data, using either micro- or mainframe computers and often both.
- Presentation of results of research and policy recomniendations to persons in the research community and other groups involved in health programme operations.

In addition, medical anthropologists generally collect large amounts of descriptive, contextual information about the community, environmental features, political and economic structures and other relevant material. Most research projects do not, of course, include all of the qualitative and quantified procedures just mentioned. Depending on the time frames of research, the specific questions studied and personnel and funding available, individual projects can range from small-scale studies using one or two of these basic tools, all the way to comprehensive, multiyear programmes of data gathering that expand beyond this core list.

RAPID ETHNOGRAPHIC ASSESSMENT PROCEDURES

Applied ethnographic research is frequently seen as a desirable first step before health care programmes are put into operation. Also, increasing numbers of epidemiologists and other quantitative researchers are realising the importance of ethnographic research for fine-tuning their approaches to planning of structured interviewing and other research operations. Ilree main reasons for initial ethnographic research are:

- To provide locally relevant cultural information to be used to improve health care programmes.
- To provide a baseline of data from which to measure change and effectiveness in such programmes.
- To identify locally relevant cultural taxonomies and explanatory models, in order to frame meaningful questions in structured interviewing and observations.

Very often such initial ethnographic research must be completed in a few weeks, so as not to delay the introduction of the health care programme itself However, anthropologists have traditionally resisted what some people have referred to as "quick-and-dirty" applied research. Based on the general holistic principle common to most sociocultural anthropology, some ethnographers have argued that many months are required just to become familiar with all the relevant cultural features and to become known in a given community setting. Also, learning the local language(s), often thought essential to good ethnographic work, requires a great deal of time.

Despite some trepidations concerning rapid ethnographic research, there was a substantial increase in sophistication in systematising this type of data gathering. In several instances the guidelines for specific data gathering have been set forth in field manuals, particularly when similar data were to be gathered in several sites by different research groups. One of the early examples of such a field manual was prepared by Marchione for the Infant Feeding Practices Study, undertaken by a consortium of researchers from the Population Council, Cornell University and Columbia University School of Public Health. 'Me plan of research called for approximately ten weeks of ethnographic reconnaissance, with a suggested sample of thirty to fifty informants. The informants were to be selected from the same communities in which a later, structured interview survey was to be carried out.

A more comprehensive manual for rapid anthropological assessment was designed by Scrimshaw and Hurtado for use in an ambitious programme of research sponsored by the United Nations University, initiated in 1983-1984. Social science researchers in fifteen countries carried out projects that ranged from two or three months to six or eight months, using the draft set of guidelines. The researchers and their methodological consultants convened in Bellagio, Italy, in 1985 to review the resulting data and to modify aspects of the methodology. The revised set of research guidelines, the RAP Manual was then published for general use in health and nutrition programmes. The manual includes an appendix with data collection guides including morbidity history of adult household members, inventory of household remedies, use of health resources, interview with health staff, provider-patient interaction and others.

Scrimshaw and Hurtado commented, "A great deal of practical, diagnostic and applied work can be accomplished in a shorter time and by using a simpler approach". The authors of the manual point out that a great many health care programmes have been initiated without any sort of culture-specific map to guide health personnel in adjusting to local belief structures, ecological conditions, economic restraints and other factors affecting peoples' health-seeking behaviours.Among these several different examples of rapid research techniques, there are several common methodological themes:

- It is commonly assumed that some descriptive materials on the local cultural system(s) are available, so that the researcher does not need to spend time finding out about the economic system, kinship and social organization and other general features.
- Familiarity with the local language on the part of the researchers, or else use of local research workers as interviewers, is generally assumed.
- The extensive version of the holistic assumption is rejected in favour of a more limited style of multifactor research. For example, in research on diarrhea or acute respiratory infection, it is assumed that data gathering can focus very specifically on the illness itself, plus a clearly specified list of contextual factors. Very little general ethnography is needed.
- The specific ethnographic data to be collected are thought to require small numbers of informants. Samples of thirty to forty respondents are usually sufficient to establish the local vocabulary, explanatory models and other patterns.
- When research is limited to small numbers of informants, contacted during a fairly short time period, considerable care is usually exerted to ensure representativeness of the sample, in terms of local subgroups, age and sex distribution, socioeconomic status and other dimensions of variation.
- The use of focus group interviews or group discussion sessions is commonly used in the exploratory phases of the research.
- Inferential statistical analysis is seldom appropriate in the rapid ethnography methodology, but descriptions can include presentation of frequencies of responses in various categories.
- The rapid methodologies sometimes include limited use of survey methods near the end of the data-gathering process.

The rapid methodologies have developed primarily in response to the requirements of applied primary health care programmes. In many cases the rapid ethnographic assessment is needed to produce basic data for designing health care intervention programmes.

However, the Rapid Assessment Procedures manual by Scrimshaw and Hurtado was developed in relation to evaluation of ongoing nutrition and health care programmes.

USE OF MICROCOMPUTERS

A second major methodological development of the 1980s and 1990s is the ongoing evolution of computer utilization in research. To an increasing extent, medical anthropologists (and many other types of researchers) are carrying microcomputers into fieldwork for both qualitative and quantitative data management. The most common use of microcomputers is for writing field notes. The legendary tediousness of writing field notes and analysing them is somewhat lessened through use of versatile word processing software. Failures with microcomputers were numerous in mid-1980s fieldwork, but laptop and notebook computers are now quite sturdy and reliable. Fieldworkers are nonetheless urged to print out hard-copy field notes frequently and to make backup copies onto floppy diskettes.

In larger, multidisciplinary projects involving collection of various epidemiological, social and cultural data, the maintenance of computerized data systems becomes a major task. With proper team organization, data entry at the research site makes it possible to check computer printouts against the original raw data and to send researchers back to households to retrieve missing information. For community-based data capture, it is advisable that database programmes be tailormade so that the blanks for entering numbers and words mimic the basic interview forms.

In Gebrian's primary health care project in Haiti, the field-based computer allows the programme coordinator to send printouts of household data summaries back to individual communities, so that health committee's receive feedback concerning local health status (*e.g.*, percentage of malnourished children) for planning purposes.

A major advantage of the microcomputer in fieldwork is the ability to carry out data analysis, both qualitative and quantitative, with at least some automated help. For extensive text data (field notes) most word processing programmes include at least minimal search or find routines.

Full-scale indexing of field notes, for more complex searches of key words, can be done with programmes such as FOLIOVIEWS, GOFER, or ZYINDEX.

High-powered statistical analysis for microcomputers is available in SAS, SPSS, SYSTAT (Windows-based) and other statistical software. Practically all of the complex statistical analysis that required mainframe computers fifteen years ago can now be carried out in the field using easily portable computers. The use of microcomputers in field research is now quite common among many research groups in developing countries as well.

Until recently anthropologists have not had simple microcomputer programmes available for construction and analysis of triad sorts and pile sorts and for developing and testing Guttman and Likert-type scales. However, a new programme developed by Borgatti, called ANTHROPAC, is now available for these fieldwork operations.

The programme is menu driven and quite easy to use. Borgatti has also incorporated procedures for network analysis, another important tool for ongoing analysis in the field.

Communications from field sites to home base often depend on slow-moving mails, but large amounts of data and voluminous reports can be conveniently shipped on floppy diskettes. Where telephone services are reliable, a great deal of communication, including transmission of data files, can be accomplished through e-mail, directly from computer to computer. E-mail simply requires that each end of the system have a modem for connecting computer to telephone, plus appropriate software to facilitate sending and receiving. Many researchers use a variety of different electronic communications systems for messages and data file transmissions, both domestic and international.

1980s and 1990s have seen impressive advances in research design and data-gathering techniques in medical anthropology. These developments are due in part to influences outside anthropology, through interdisciplinary communication. Widespread acceptance and recognition of medical anthropology as an essential ingredient in research on illness and health care has brought about increased sharing of methodological techniques among the biological, clinical, epidemiological and social sciences. The mutual interactions of anthropology and epidemiology have been particularly important, as documented in Anthropology and Epidemiology, edited by Janes, Stall and Gifford. Cooperation between epidemiologists and anthropologists has led to methodological shifts on both sides. Medical anthropologists have come to pay more attention to matters of sampling and representativeness, along with new techniques of statistical analysis. The Applied Diarrheal Disease Research Programme, PAHO, WHO, NIH and other organizations have insisted that ethnographic fieldwork should be described in concrete, easily understood terms and these influences have led anthropologists to be more specific about techniques, leading in turn to increased standardization of procedures.

In the area of structured direct observations, anthropologists, epidemiologists, nutritionists and psychologists seem to have all learned from each other. Earlier anthropological observations tended to be unstructured and ad hoc, without much concern for representativeness. Some of the other disciplines, on the other hand, had developed methods that were highly structured but badly suited to specific field conditions. Medical anthropologists have played an important role in helping to develop culturally appropriate modes of observation that can be structured sufficiently to permit statistical analysis.

The advent of microcomputers has certainly had a direct technological impact on medical anthropology. The availability of easy-to-use statistical software has encouraged researchers to develop more systematic numerical as well as qualitative data gathering. Some of the impetus for improvements in computerized data gathering and analysis has come directly from anthropologists with long experience at mainframe operations. Researchers in other disciplines also contributed techniques and tools that anthropologists have found useful.

The continued spread of the HIV-AIDS epidemic and growth of needs for research to develop intervention programmes have also contributed to developments in medical anthropology. The Global Programme on AIDS at WHO has included increasing numbers of anthropologists, particularly reflecting the need for systematic ethnographic fieldwork in relation to high-risk behaviours that contribute to spread of HIV infection. Everywhere in HIV-AIDS intervention programmes one hears frequent reference to needs for qualitative, ethnographic research. The needs for careful, systematic ethnographic work are particularly evident in relation to hard-to-reach populations such as injection drug users, men who have sex with men and commercial sex workers.

One of the major motivations for improved research methodologies, both qualitative and quantitative, arises from the requirements of applied communitybased health programmes. Health programmes, particularly in developing countries, measure effectiveness in terms of reduced levels of infant mortality, morbidity and other indicators.

Whenever data gathering is intended to have direct programmatic consequences, within organizations whose personnel are largely nonanthropologists, there is a considerable pressure to improve the credibility of data gathering and data analysis. The conventions of report writing and oral presentations of research result in international health circles also foster consciousness of methodology. Our impressions, based on many recent experiences and informal communications among medical anthropologists, are that the transmission of effective research methodology is not strongly developed in our graduate training programmes. Most medical anthropologists have improved their methodological skills in the school of trial and error, in the course of work in interdisciplinary projects. As a result, colleagues who happen not to be involved in interdisciplinary team research can find themselves with fewer resources for keeping abreast of methodological developments.

Methodological skills are scarce resources and have direct economic value-in employment, promotion and the like—in addition to their contribution to excellence of research output. To an increasing extent, researchers who are marginalized in relation to the main international communications networks may be falling behind in methodological terms, leading to relatively weaker, less useful research. The problem of effective dissemination of research methodologies is especially important for anthropologists in Third World countries. Fortunately, the research promotion efforts of international health organizations and foundations have been effective in promoting more sophistication in research methodology, including use of microcomputers, in the developing countries.

During the past several decades, the research methods of anthropology have served as the primary source of development for research approaches in medical anthropology. At the same time, the field has also drawn on other socialbehavioural sciences for both methods and theory.

The expanding focus on application of research findings and the use of community-based information in intervention programmes is leading medical anthropologists into closer collaboration with other types of professionals and introducing other approaches to the collection, analysis and interpretation of data.

These encounters are giving rise to new approaches that develop as the result of the interaction between wellestablished anthropological approaches with those of public health, health services and social action. The materials we have reviewed provide examples of some of these new directions and we can expect to see others as the field matures.

HEALTH CARE AND REGULATION

Health Tourism is a concept where a patient travels to another country for medical treatment in order to save costs, or get treatment faster or even to avail of better medical facilities. Most patients from countries like USA and UK travel to developing countries such as India for treatment because India offers some of the cheapest pricing options of treatment, offers a good holiday, there are no waiting lists or queues to stand in, the doctors are comparable to anyone in the world and finally, language does not pose a problem as most people speak English. Although the cost difference between treatment in India and Thailand is not much, India offers what you call a language advantage — a patient would surely prefer a country where English is widely spoken. Also, it is believed that the facilities in India are more suited for International patients.

India is also working hard to increase it's infrastructure to better suit the needs of patients coming to India for treatments such as heart surgery, knee replacement, other orthopaedic treatments, cosmetic surgery, eye care, dental treatment or any other treatment for that matter. This is one of the primary fields which India intends to explore during the coming years. Well, many highly qualified doctors have had some form of training from abroad, specially USA and UK. Indian surgeons and doctors are known for their skill and research throughout the world. India has over 150000 medical tourists each year and this figure is rising at a high pace. Some recent programmes recently on BBC and CNBC have reinstated the fact that medical tourism is a good idea if — you want to save costs, you need the treatment to be done at your time and convenience, you need a high quality budget incorporated.

Alison was 16 when we first met. She was referred to us by a social worker because she was already known to be HIV positive. She had been working as a prostitute for at least three years, and thought she had got HIV from a boyfriend who was also positive. Over the next six years we saw a lot of her. She began to inject drugs regularly, continued to work as a prostitute and spent time in prison for petty crimes. After a few years she became depressed and worried about her illness, and then developed AIDS.

Danielle was in her mid-30s when she began using the project clinic. She made a relatively good living from her work as a prostitute. She had drifted into prostitution and continued to work to support her daughter after she left her husband.

We got to know her very well, seeing each other regularly over a period of seven years. Generally we met in the clinic, where she came for monthly check-ups even though she rarely had any problems. She was an 'ideal' consumer of health services and advice as she was extremely concerned about HIV. During our last meeting she explained how she was still looking for alternative 'straight' jobs, but the money was not good enough. She was killed by her boyfriend.

We set up the Praed Street Project in 1986 to look at risks of HIV and other sexually transmitted disease in women working as prostitutes. We combined epidemiological and anthropological research with the development of a clinic and other services for prostitutes. When we completed our research in 1992, the prevalence of HIV infection had not changed, remaining around 1 per cent.

Our research was based on a cohort of women who were followed for up to seven years. During that time our perspectives on research and the development of services became much broader.

Four women died during the last two years. Two had AIDS; both were infected when they joined our study, one through injecting drug use and the other probably through heterosexual contact with an infected non-paying partner.

The other two women did not have HIV; they were both murdered. These deaths are reported as a reminder that AIDS is only one of many issues facing the women. They presented with other health problems: sexually transmitted infections, recurrent problems such as thrush or cystitis, concerns about fertility and infertility, psychological problems and physical injuries.

Health issues were themselves raised in relation to wider concerns about money, housing, conditions at work, police, family, relationships, violence at work and at home. Through developing the Praed Street Project we attempted to address some of these broader concerns, providing a range of services that go far beyond those normally associated with genitourinary medicine and sexual health. Many other projects across the country have faced the same issues and, like the Praed Street Project, are now under threat as specific AIDS budgets are withdrawn and health authorities and clinics are likely to focus narrowly on HIV prevention for those at highest risk-which at the moment does not include prostitute women. This is primarily a history of the Praed Street Project, of the people who worked in it and of those who used it, with the aim of elucidating different perspectives on our work. We start with a brief discussion of prostitution and the risks of HIV and other sexually transmitted diseases as a background to our work.

3

Health Tourism and Economic Development

Health and sex tourism occupies marginal spaces that are in themselves a component of the inherent marginality of tourism in contemporary Western society. The previous discussed how sex tourism may well be illicit, but, as earlier noted, the inter-relationship between sex tourist and sex worker may also move from the symbolic to the pragmatic and thence progress to the functional. The marginal spaces of sex tourism are therefore consistently shifting according to different social, cultural, economic and political factors. Indeed, the contested, multi-layered, nature of sex tourism implicitly suggests that this, at times, transitory space of inversion, provides the capacity for new understandings, perceptions, relationships and representations of sexuality, travel and the sex industry.

Due to its increasing visibility, health and sex tourism therefore possesses the potential to act as a catalyst for encapsulating or creating social change, and in Australia and New Zealand, the countries with which the authors are most familiar, this has certainly become evident with respect to changing attitudes towards the sex industry. Such changes become codified through the regulatory actions of the state which has historically served to implement a moral code with respect to sexual behaviours through legal sanctions. Indeed, the role of the state with respect to sex tourism may not necessarily be one of prohibition or prevention. In some jurisdictions sex tourism has been implicitly or even overtly encouraged in order to attract foreign exchange and encourage economic development. This, to some, perhaps paradoxical relationship between sex tourism and the state, reflects the complex multilayered nature of understanding sex tourism to which we have often referred within this book.

However, in examining this relationship we will also note the various intersections that exist with other considerations in the development of an understanding as well as the position of sex tourism within contemporary capitalism. The first discusses various aspects of the interrelationship between sex tourism and economic development in South-east Asia, a region often featured in discussion of the development and control of sex tourism. Then discusses was some of the issues that surround decriminalisation, legalisation and control, including problems with respect to controlling sex tourism in the communications age. Then goes on to examine the way in which the state and contemporary capitalism effectively commodify the body in a manner which not only creates the spaces of marginality in which sex tourism exists but which also commodifies that space itself as a place to be consumed.

Sex tourism has been recognised as an overt component of the touristic attractiveness of several countries of South-east Asia since the late 1960s. In South-east Asia the institutionalisation of sex tourism occurred when the prostitution associated with American military bases and Japanese colonialism was transformed into a component of the international tourism industry and an integral component of national and regional economic development. Prostitution is technically illegal in many South-east Asian countries, but the law is poorly enforced. The prevailing sentiment appears to be 'that what a tourist does in the hotel room, is none of the authorities business', particularly when it results in economic returns to a region and members, usually male, of the local authorities and business classes. Given the illegal and often casual nature of much sex tourism it is extremely difficult to determine the exact number of s e x tourists to the region. According to one estimate from the mid-1980s, 'between 70 and 80 per cent of male tourists who travel from Japan, the United States, Australia, and Western Europe to Asia do so solely for the purpose of sexual entertainment'. The present-day figure is unknown especially as there has been a massive growth in interregional travel and trade. The changing nature of tourism in the region which now has greater emphasis on family-oriented resort tourism, marine and ecotourism has possibly meant that the relative number of sex tourists to other markets has declined but the number still remains significant.

From a feminist perspective, the study of the sex tourism industry encapsulates many of the problems which are fundamental to women and development: 'Prostitution is both an indiction of an unjust social order and an institution that economically exploits women. But when economic power is defined as the causal variable, the sex dimensions of power usually remain unidentified and unchallenged'.

As Claire and Cottingham report, often women who have fled rural poverty only to be forced into prostitution by urban unemployment, are 'victims of the double standard. Women who have been raped, jilted, or taken advantage of no longer fit the chaste wife-mother-sister ideal and are ostracized by nearly all sectors of society'. Historically, the economic and social problems of Asian women tend to be viewed by Western feminists as stemming from the patriachial nature of local cultures.

For example, Truong (1983) reported that 'in eastern societies, concubinage and brothels have existed for centuries and carried a distinct class connotation'. The influence of the patriarchial nature of society on the manner in which sex tourism comes to be defined as a 'problem' does not negate the substantial insights made into sex tourism by feminist researchers. However, researchers such as Ong argued that 'the new commerce in the labour-power and bodies of Asian women, is more rooted in corporate strategies of profit maximisation than in the persistence of indigenous values'.

From the perspective of political economy, sex tourism may be regarded as a result of shifts in the international division of labour within a globalised economy and the development of consumerism in Asian countries of which tourism is a major constituent.

Such shifts may only serve to reinforce the gendered nature of local power relations in which some bodies assume the function of commodities to be consumed by tourists or locals.

The role of tourism in the relationship between consumerism and globalisation is observed by Bishop and Robinson (1998:108): 'Not only is shopping increasingly understood as the moral equivalent of sightseeing for the tourist, but the tourist locale - even the land itself - is represented as consumable goods.' Furthermore, to Bishop and Robinson 'With all tourist sites, commerce depends on the construction of a desirable other - often one that titillates as well as appeals - capable of attracting outsiders'. They then went on to argue:

This construction can create inequitable interactions between local and traveller that actually serve to reinforce disparity while being represented as mutually beneficial. In these international interactions, including the sexual ones, the flow from centre to periphery, from here to there, is virtually unidirectional; the trickle in the opposite direction largely provides education for an academic elite and political class. The disparity of interactions can be charted in this flow: when 'they' come 'here', we educate them; when 'we' go 'there', they service us.

Despite their criticism of the tourism studies literature, the well-articulated critique of sex tourism by Bishop and Robinson which had integrated political economy and cultural studies traditions had been anticipated within the tourism field. For example, Graburn argued:

The phenonemon of prostitution in the third world is particularly crucial because of the economic power differential between the buyer and the seller. Furthermore there is a direct analogy between prostitution in the Third World and that in the metropolitan resort centres where the prostitutes are disproportionately drawn from disadvantaged sections of the population who may have similar economic problems illuminating forms of 'internal colonialism' commonly found in stratified, industrial societies.

The flow of international capital and visitors to the less developed countries has led several commentators to conclude that tourism is prostitution and an inevitable consequence of mass tourism. For example, Rogers stated:

The nature and character of modern tourism which is strongly centreed around [an] unquenchable [thirst for] profit and the sexual gratification of men from the First World cannot but breed and perpetuate the prostitution of deprived and dispossessed women and children of the Third World.

More recently, Seabrook (1996:167) argued that 'resistance to sex tourism should be part of a wider campaign against tourism in general The ideology of cheap holidays is part of the ideology of cheap goods, cheap labour and cheap sex.' Such sentiments would be anathema not only to many in the tourism industry, but such a perspective also indicates a sharp departure from much of tourism research which generally ignores questions of ideology, gender and the capitalist system within which tourism is situated and the often marginal nature of the tourist experience itself.

However, as argued throughout the book, failure to recognise the marginal and multilayed spaces of tourism only serves to further marginalise many of the workers who occupy those spaces. If solutions are to be found to the vexed issues of sex tourism, it therefore becomes essential that debate and ideas be allowed to come into a wider public sphere in which they can be adequately interrogated rather than continue to be blindly ignored.

Tourism is a major industry in South-east Asia. For most of the countries in the region tourism is one of the most important sources of foreign exchange and employment generation. International tourism visitation has demonstrated almost continued growth since the late 1970s at a rate well above the world average. According to Bacani (1998) tourism accounts for around 10.3 per cent of Asia's GDP. Perhaps somewhat paradoxically, the 1997-98 Asian financial crisis has served to make tourism even more important for the region as countries seek to gain urgently needed foreign exchange and attempt to encourage renewed growth at a time of economic recovery. Tourism has therefore been integral to the region's economic development. However, the commodification of the human body by the sex tourism industry cannot be explained simply by reference to state economic strategies. Instead, as the above discussion suggests, there are multifaceted and interrelated reasons for the development of sex tourism in the region.

One of the authors identified four stages in the development of sex tourism in an earlier account of sex tourism in the region: indigenous prostitution, economic colonialism and militarisation, substitution of international tourists for occupation forces and rapid economic development. The discussion below presents a revised account of sex tourism development with provision being made for the internationalisation of legal and political responses to sex tourism in the mid-1990s and the impacts of the Asian financial crisis in the late 1990s.

INDIGENOUS PROSTITUTION

Prostitution in South-east Asia clearly existed before the arrival of tourists with 'domestic' prostitution continuing to constitute a major component of most countries' sex industries. Writers such as Truong (1990) and Hill (1993) have argued that Buddhism plays a major role in perpetuating the patriachial nature of Thai culture. This point is also reflected in the comments of Skrobanek (1996: vii) who commented that 'certainly there are elements in Thai society which contribute to the growth of commercialisation of human relationships, both in the family and community, and to the commodification of women's body and soul'. An issue raised by a number of other commentators. For example, Richter, in her seminal work on the politics of tourism in Asia argued, 'Perhaps because Thailand was never colonized, and also because the nation has a history of concubinage and prostitutes in its traditional culture, opposition was slow to recognize the difference in scale, violence, and social decay implied by sex tourism' (1989:84).

More recently, Seabrook (1996:79-80) observed that 'the monastery, military and monarchy had degraded the social and cultural position of women to such a degree that it was easy for the market to do the rest'. Indeed, the importation of elements of Brahminical culture into Thai society has allowed concubinage and polygamy to be legitimised and has cast a ready-made framework within which sex tourism can be culturally acceptable. As O'Malley (1988:107) argued, 'The result was an erotic industry promoted by a government hungry for foreign exchange and built upon the solid base of a hundred years of institutionalized prostitution.'

While social and religious institutions have had a significant role in commodifying women, Buddhism cannot itself be held solely responsible. As Bishop and Robinson (1998:160) noted 'virtually all the world's major religions include patriarchal power structures that do not necessarily lead to the establishment of prostitution as a major industry despite rumours to the contrary, Buddhism explicitly prohibits the practice of prostitution.' Indeed, it is with respect to patriarchal power structures that common elements emerge between the various countries of the region that have engaged in sex tourism.

For example, one of the ironies of the current Japanese involvement in sex tourism is that the Japanese used to export their own prostitutes Kara-Yuki San to their colonies. Kara-Yuki San were bonded Japanese women who were sent abroad to serve as prostitutes in ports frequented by Japanese merchants and soldiers. However, since the 1920s when the Japanese government issued the Overseas Prostitution Prohibition Order and with the prohibition of legal prostitution in Japan in 1958, women from the former colonies 'are now imported into Japan as prostitutes'.

As previously noted, such was the significance of prostitution in Japan's male-dominated culture that following both the 1911 and 1923 earthquakes the reconstruction of licensed prostitution quarters took priority over the rebuilding of schools. Moreover, domestic prostitution may not only be based on gendered power structures but also on race and culture. For example, in Taiwan the majority of prostitutes are not Han Chinese but instead come from the island's aboriginal population which is PolynesianMalayan in origin and which lives in the marginal rural areas. Similarly, many of the minority ethnic groups in Myanmar and Thailand are often disproportionately represented in prostitution in relation to the percentage of the general population they represent. Therefore, the factors which lead women and men into domestic prostitution may be regarded as an inter-related series of marginalities relating to gender, race and economics, and it was upon this set of unequal power relations that the second stage of sex tourism development in the region was built.

Economic Colonialism and Militarisation

The second stage is that of economic colonialism and militarisation in which prostitution is a formalised mechanism of dominance and a means of meeting the sexual needs of occupying military forces. In this stage the occupied culture's general acceptance of various forms of prostitution has been used as a justification for economic or military enforced prostitution or, as in the case of Japanese militarism in the 1930s and 1940s, was used as a means of exercising power on host populations. In addition, this stage commences the economic dependency of certain sections of host societies on the selling of sexual services as a means of economic growth and development. For example, in the case of Taiwan, hot spring resorts which provided for the spatial concentration of tourist-related prostitution activity were first developed under the Japanese colonial era between 1895 and 1945. According to Robins-Mowry:

The Japanese Government organised a system to service the Occupation troops, systematically recruiting women - patriotically - to serve as prostitutes. From their own experience on mainland China, the authorities considered this essential for any military occupation. The women were recruited, according to Morosawa Yoko, as the 'breakwater to protect Japanese women's chastity' - meaning, of course, the chastity of less needy daughters and wives.

However, military-related prostitution continued after the end of Japanese military occupation with the resort of Peitou achieving rapid development in the post-war era with legalised prostitution until 1979 as a favoured rest and recreation area for American forces.

Militarisation also played a major role in the development of the Filipino sex tourism industry. While the United States retained a military presence in the Philippines, the 12,000 registered and 8,000 unregistered hostesses in Olongapo City provided the major source of sexual entertainment for the US military personnel based at Subic Naval Base and Clark Air Force Base. The City was economically dependent on the military presence and a number of city ordinances were written which allowed prostitution to be legitimised, regulated and protected by the local state. For example, the city enforced an anti-streetwalking ordinance which ensured that the soliciting of customers could only occur inside clubs thereby assuring club owners of fees derived from the provision of sexual services. The American military presence was also formalised in Thailand when in 1967 the Thai government signed an agreement with the US government to provide Rest and Recreation facilities in Thailand for American troops in Vietnam.

The American military presence in South-east Asia, and in Thailand in particular, created the foundation for sex tourism in several ways. First, it maintained and reinforced indigenous power relationships which were exploited through prostitution. Second, it served to commodify local bodies for the pleasures of foreigners and thereby increase the market value of female sexual capacity. Third, it created a series of economic structures and dependencies which would be filled by the international tourist once the military forces departed.

International Tourism

The third stage was marked by the substitution of international tourists for occupation forces. Following periods of occupation and the restructuring of traditional economies within the post-war international economic order, sex tourism became a formal mechanism for obtaining foreign exchange and of national development. A common element in this third stage is the authoritarian nature of governments during periods in which sex tourism was being promoted by government and the tourism industry. For example, the authoritarian nature of successive South Korean governments through the 1970s to the late 1980s played a major role in the commoditisation of women through kisaeng tourism. Prospective kisaeng endured lectures by male university professors on the crucial role of tourism in the South Korean economy before obtaining their prostitution licences.

At the government 'orientation programme' for sex workers, women were told 'Your carnal conversations with foreign tourists do not prostitute either yourself or the nation, but express your heroic patriotism'. Perhaps more telling is the report of the South Korean Minister for Education who stated that 'the sincerity of girls who have contributed with their cunts to their fatherland's economic development is indeed praiseworthy'.

It is possible that the denial of individual rights by authoritarian regimes may have encouraged the perspective that individuals are sexual commodities to be utilised for furthering the national economic good. Similarly, the Thai government placed great emphasis on the promotion of RandR and tourism in the economic development of Thailand. For instance, in 1980 Booncha Rajanasthian, Thailand's Vice Premier, asked all provincial governments 'to consider forms of entertainment that some of you might consider disgusting and shameful, because we have to consider the jobs that will be created'.

As part of the development of international tourism not only were bodies incorporated into the international tourist economy but also the culture. For example, 'The stereotype of Thailand as the playground of the Western world dominates the public imagination outside the country and is continually reiterated in the popular media'. Indeed, advertising for many of the South-east Asian nations openly plays on the notion of the 'exotic orient', South Sea romanticism and the image of a 'lost paradise' which has existed since the seventeenth and eighteenth centuries. For instance, Davidson (1985:18) reported a Frankfurt advertisement which stated, 'Asian women are without desire for emancipation, but full of warm sensuality and the softness of velvet', characteristics which are related too in more contemporary tourism advertising. For instance, Singapore Airlines proclaims 'Singapore Girl you're a great way to fly' along with soft images of airline hostesses waiting to provide service for customers.

Rapid Economic Development and International Controls

The fourth stage of sex tourism for most of the nations of the region was that of rapid economic development. As the author commented in 1992. 'It is as yet unknown whether increased standards of living will reduce dependency on sex tourism or whether the growth of consumerism will become a new factor in the maintenance of the sex tourism industry.' Indeed, in 1976 the head of the Tourist Authority of Thailand commented that 'prostitution exists mainly because of the state of our economy. If we can create jobs, we can provide per capita income and do away with prostitution'. However, while economic growth was undoubtedly rapid from the 1970s through to the mid-1990s it was also uneven. For example, the regions of the northeast and northern provinces of Thailand along with displaced minorities from Burma on the Thai-Burmese border have continued to provide a major source for child and female prostitutes. The economic marginality of the regions forces many rural households to depend on the remittances provided by migrant girls. The northern Thai provinces have continued to remain structurally disadvantaged within the Thai economy with much of the export and large-scale tourist growth concentrated in the southern and central provinces and 'if no new income sources are created by the typical prostitutes' earnings; a vested interest and dependency upon the continuation of the sex industry is created in the rural hinterland'. Therefore, given the lack of economic development in the north, there would appear to be an assured supply of workers for the sex industry based in the nation's urban and industrial centres. As Bishop and Robinson argued:

It is hard to see how economic growth arising from prostitution-based tourism could do away with prostitution. On the contrary, since the market sets up a permanent demand for a sex and age-specific labour force which, as it happens, ages very rapidly, the way to assure the constant availability of fresh supplies from the rural areas is precisely to pursue national planning policies that systematically de-emphasize agriculture and displace fishing and to withhold resources where they historically constituted the economic base.

Nevertheless, some controls and limiting factors on prostitution have been put in place. Most significantly, AIDS has become a major source of concern to governments in the region. For example, in 1989 the Thai Public Health Ministry actively started campaigning against prostitution and the promotion of Thailand as a sex tour destination. The primary reason for the campaign was the recognition that sexually transmitted diseases such as AIDS could pose major problems for Thailand's rapidly growing tourism industry and for the Thai economy in general.

The Asian Development Bank calculated that 'through the death and disablement of AIDS sufferers - usually from the economically productive 20-40 age group - Thailand had lost almost $3 billion so far and by 2000 this would rise to $3.5 billion a year if the disease went unchecked'. The concern for the manner in which the AIDS dimension of sex tourism was seen to be harming the country's tourism industry is well indicated in the comments of the Thai Deputy Public Health Minister, Suthas Ngernmuen:

Thailand's profitable tourist industry has been an inhibiting factor in promoting AIDS awareness. More than two-thirds of the overseas visitors entering Thailand are single men, and medical officials avoided publicising the appalling AID statistics for fear of damaging the country's healthy tourist business. But it is long past time for the government to change Thailand's image as a sexual paradise.

We should promote tourism in more appropriate ways, and campaign more against AIDS.

Sex tourism therefore represents a major dilemma for the Thai authorities. Sex tourism continues to be a major tourist attraction and hence a source of foreign currency but authorities are increasingly worried by Thailand's reputation as the sex capital of Asia which may repel other potential markets. For these reasons the Thai government created the 'Visit Thailand year ' in 1987 in order to refurbish its image and to de-emphasise sex as an attraction. Nevertheless, as economic growth continues to be uneven, peripheral rural areas will continue to furnish Thailand's sex industry with its raw material.

As well as attempting to change image and marketing campaigns, countries in the region have also begun to work together in order to stop child prostitution. Led primarily by ECPAT (End Child Prostitution in Asian Tourism), an international campaign has successfully managed to get child sex tourism legislation enacted in a number of countries in the region and in Europe. For example, Australia enacted the Crimes (Child Sex Tourism) Amendment Act

1994 to deal with the activities of Australians who travel overseas for the sexual exploitation of child prostitutes; those responsible for organising overseas tours for the purpose of engaging in sexual relations or activities with minors; and those who otherwise profit from child sexual exploitation. As Hall (1998) argued, ECPAT has been able to create an awareness among both politicians and the public about child sex tourism in South-east Asia. Such was the success of the ECPAT campaign in creating moral indignation and therefore political action that it almost passed by without notice that the term 'sex tourism' is not even defined in the Act.

Undoubtedly, ethical concerns over undesirable social impacts of international travel were at the forefront of debates over the Act. Unfortunately, such 'awareness' of the negative impacts of tourism has been restricted to a narrow range of Asian concerns.

Little concern was expressed in discussion of the legislation about the sexual activities of international visitors to Australia and the various campaigns of the Australian Tourist Commission which sought to display bikini-clad women in order to create a favourable and attractive image to certain market segments. In this situation, it may therefore be argued that while something has been seen to be done in the solution of 'sex tourism' issues, in reality, very little fundamental change has occurred.

The Impact of the Asian Financial Crisis

The contemporary stage of sex tourism development in South-east Asia is one marked by the impacts of the financial crisis which began in mid-1997. As noted above, tourism has become even more important to the various countries in the region as a source of foreign exchange. As previously noted, in this climate the commodified body, usually a woman's, remains an important source of income generation through sex tourism and trafficking. Governments therefore implicitly, and occassionally explicitly, exploit bodies as a natural resource in much the same way as the rainforests of the region are sold and raped. Indeed, the opening up of Vietnam, Laos, Cambodia, southern China and Myanmar to tourism and the effects of the financial crisis has only sought to expand the range of low-cost sex tourism opportunities for visitors to the region. In this setting sex tourism to the region remains as problematic as when it first began to be discussed in the media in the late 1970s.

The Political Economy of Sex Tourism

Sex tourism is integral to the economic base of several regions of South-east Asia. The Philippine Women's Research Collective (1985:36) argue that the 'insidious tourist first attitude' of many governments and their advisers has transformed the processes of development to place the economic 'needs' of a modernising economy well ahead of wider socio-economic concerns which feed into the growth of tourism-related prostitution such as rural migration. More critically, Enloe succinctly observed:

Sex tourism requires Third World women to be economically desperate enough to enter prostitution; having done so it is made difficult to leave. The other side of the equation requires men from affluent societies to imagine certain women, usually women of colour, to be more available and submissive than the women in their own countries. Finally, the industry depends on an alliance between local governments in search of foreign currency and local and foreign businessmen willing to invest in sexualized travel.

If Enloe's analysis is correct, and much of the argument in this would agree that it is, then how do we control sex tourism? Fish (1984a, b) has argued that an effective means of controlling sex tourism would focus on placing a heavier proportion of the costs of law enforcement and sanctions on the hotels, agencies and their customers. However, such an approach built on the assumptions of schedules of the elasticity of demand fails to recognise the broader economic, political and socio-cultural context within which sex tourism occurs. Short-term measures such as counselling may be useful, but sex tourism demands long-term solutions. 'Banning prostitution may be counterproductive and only create even greater hardship for the already impoverished women who engage in it'. Similarly, Truong (1983:534) argued that 'legislation to protect prostitutes, and to improve their working conditions and occupational health, is preferable to legislation that would deprive them of their livelihood'.

The issue of the right to be a prostitute remains extremely controversial and is an example of the problem of competing rights which has exercised critics of the efficacy of rights approaches. For example, Klerk argues, 'It would be a violation of the principle of self-determination of individuals to forbid to prostitute. Moreover, a prostitute has the right to let another person exploit her, and she might have good reasons for that.' Therefore, from Klerk's perspective, it is 'not logical to restrict the concept of traffic to prostitution', when it accepts prostitution as a 'normal job'. Indeed, a very strong case exists for prostitution to be professionalised. Lap-Chew states:

The more 'professional' the sex worker, the more care she takes of herself. The more 'legal' or 'legitimate' she feels, the less she will be afraid to report abuse and exploitation, the more she will seek health and other kinds of care for herself and be able to develop a degree of professionalism in her work. Is this not an argument in favour of recognition of prostitution as a form of legitimate work?

In contrast, Barry, in writing up the final report of the International Meetings of Experts on Sexual Exploitation, Violence and Prostitution argues, 'Clearly prostitution cannot exist as a right because it negates already established human rights of the prostitute woman to human dignity, bodily integrity, physical and mental well-being'. Similarly, Jeffreys observes that the establishment of the right to prostitute, 'transforms the right of some men to abuse women in prostitution and of others to make a profit from that use - interests which arguably provide the real fuel for the pro-prostitution position - into a woman's rights to have her human rights violated'. In seeking to argue that there is little sense in separating trafficking from prostitution, she then goes on to cite Raymond (1995:2) who states, 'Prostitution, of course, is the goal of sex trafficking and builds the base for the trafficking in women and children. When prostitution is accepted by a society, sex trafficking and sex tourism inevitably follow.'

The authors do not accept the position of Jeffreys in quoting Santos, that: those who accept that prostitution is 'an inevitable social institution' accept that, sex, however it is obtained, either by coercion, commercialization or even seduction, is a male right, and that bodies of women and children, and men too, can be and should be packaged and sold as a commodity because there is a buyer and there is a seller.

As Fraser and Nicolson observed:

To construct a universalistic social theory is to risk projecting the socially dominant conjunctions and dispersions of her own society onto others, thereby distorting important features of both. Social theorists would do better first to construct genealogies of the categories of sexuality, reproduction and mothering before assuming their universal significance.

Instead, the authors follow the approach of Anti-Slavery International (ASI) (1995) which: believes that the definition of prostitution as commercial sex work has more scope than an exclusively abolitionist approach for enhancing the welfare of women and men whose sexual services are sold. By looking at commercial sex as work, in labour conditions, those involved can be included and protected under the existing instruments which aim to protect all workers and, where appropriate, forced labour and migrant workers; all persons from violence; and women from discrimination.

The approach of ASI focuses substantial attention on issues of child and forced prostitution but recognises the right of individuals to engage in sex work if they so wish. It is the argument of the authors that prostitution needs to be legalised so that the conditions under which the sex worker operates and the sex industry is run are as transparent as possible to external evaluation. The illicit marginal spaces need to be brought out of the shadows if they are to be effectively controlled. To deny the concept of sex work as being a professional service, as having like other jobs its good or bad days, is to continue to marginalise and stigmatise. This short-term measure would hopefully improve the health and economic conditions of prostitutes at a minimum. However, in the long term it may also lead to greater transparency of the web of institutionalised exploitation within which trafficking does, and tourism may, operate and reinforce in some circumstances, such as those that exist in parts of South-east Asia. Campaigns, demonstrations and rallies against sex tourism are likely only to lead to superficial changes to the sex industry. For example, ECPAT's campaign against child sex tourism in Australia, noted above, has had only a marginal impact on creating a broader understanding of sex tourism issues in Australia.

One cannot condone sex tourism, especially child sex tourism, if it is coercive in nature. However, it is also important that decisions and policies that are formulated with respect to sex tourism are given serious and considered debate. In the case of sex tourism in Australia this did not happen. The Australian Child Sex Tourism Bill was able to pass because it focused on a small area of sex tourism policy on which moral, and to a lesser extent, ideological consensus could be reached. Such was the success of the ECPAT campaign in creating moral indignation and therefore political action that, as previously noted, it almost passed by without notice that the term 'sex tourism' is not even defined in the Act. As Mr Slipper, member for Fisher, noted 'that the bill should more properly be entitled the Crime (Overseas Exploitation of Children) Bill.

I think that name is a more appropriate name for the bill. The bill's title at the moment tends to be emotive, but I suppose that is a matter not of substance'. Child sex tourism is an important issue, but the numbers of children engaged in prostitution because of tourism is nothing like that of those sex workers who are above the age of consent in the countries in which they work. As the PJCNCA observed:

Most sexual offences against children are committed by their relatives and neighbours who are not paedophiles in the strict sense of the term and who do not operate in any organised or networked way. There is no evidence to suggest that organised paedophile groups have ever resembled what are traditionally thought of as 'organised crime' groups in size, aims, structures, methods, longevity and so forth. There is no evidence of any current organised promotion or arrangement of tours by Australian paedophiles to overseas destinations known to be attractive to them. However, informal networking among paedophiles may assist some tourists going overseas to commit paedophile offences.

Tourism is clearly an element in the reason for prostitution occurring in certain locations in South-east Asia and Australasia, but so also are gender, culture, the pattern of economic development, racism, poverty and wealth distribution, highly patriarchal societies and material interests. In examining media reports and, more particularly, government reports and parliamentary debates on the child sex tourism debate in Australia there is often an impression given that 'something has been done'. Perhaps it has. Nevertheless, because of the failure to closely examine the marginal space which sex tourism occupies, broader questions are being left unasked and extremely significant issues, such as gender, economic and power relations, are typically relegated to academic rather than policy discussions. As Hall (1998) argued:

Governments of countries, such as Australia, while taking action on child sex tourism, fail to recognize that in their own tourism advertising, they also promote the commodification and objectification of the sexual body. But, of course, the portrayal of available female bodies on Bondi or Bali has absolutely nothing to do with child sex tourism. does it?

This failure to acknowledge the embodied nature of tourism is highly significant. The tourism industry 'rests on the physical display of bodies perceived as fundamentally, radically, different from those of the majority of the audience who pays to see them. The live presence of the performers is crucial to this economy of pleasure, for it provides the guarantee of the authenticity on which such commodification exists'. Sex tourism is an integral part of the commodification of body, culture and place on which the tourism industry is based. However, the commodification of sexuality is wider than just individuals. It also has to be seen in relation to places. Sites of seduction are created where the tourist and the investor are to be seduced.

There may be 'red light' districts or they may be the alluring promises of place promotion. Either way tourism becomes not simply a provider and creator of demand for prostitution, but in the very processes of creating places attracts an attention whereby tourism becomes a catalyst for subsequent change. As noted earlier in the book, if Butler's (1980) destination life cycle can apply to resorts in general, so too it might apply to specific red light districts. Moreover, in the communications age, the commodification of the body through cyber-sex tourism means that the potential for the state to effectively control sex is becoming even more doubtful. Ironically, the various measures proposed by governments to control sex sites serves to commodify bodies even more.

For example, despite the existence of software content such as Net Nanny which can restrict access by children and the detailed agreements regarding age and intention on many Internet pornography sites, governments seek to restrict access further through utilising age checks such as cyber identification procedures or credit cards - both of which increase the cost of access and the commercialisation of sexuality on the web. Arguably, such commoditisation of sex on the Internet may only further reinforce the creation of a global economy of pleasure of which sex tourism is a part.

Alternative ways of seeing non-commoditised inter-personal relationships are possible but they lie outside of the domains of the dominant culture of contemporary global capitalism. Establishing sites of opposition to the commodifying culture of capitalism is important. The dialectical relationships which provide the means to influence directions, create tensions, and therefore generate new spaces within which relationships can be founded. The liminoid nature of sex tourism, which is by its nature a conceptualisation of shifting boundaries, unclear definitions, differing constructions and disjunctions in society, also provides the possibility for developing new relationships and understandings. Within the global tourism economy of pleasure sex workers need to be recognised as professional providers of sex services in order to ensure that they are not exploited. Such a recognition implies that global measures such as trading and labour agreements therefore provide a significant base with which to improve the conditions of sex workers. However, it also implies that prostitution must be recognised as work.

Discussion and investigation of sex tourism and the wider links between sexuality and tourism in the commodification of the body may also become a catalyst for subsequent change:

In a period of academic discourse that celebrates 'posts' (postmodernism, postcolonialism, postnationalism) and a new sense of hybrid positionalities and fluidity of categories, it is imperative that we give adequate weight to the intransigence of physical evidence in systems of social differentiation and track these operations in public discourse. Tracking that trace is the only way potentially to disrupt it and to reconfigure the possible meanings of bodily presence.

'Recognising sexual alienation as part of a totalising system makes it hard to accept easy answers about what is to be done about sex tourism, because all are, at best, partial solutions'. Profound change can only occur within a wholesale transformation of economic, social, gender, and political relations. The issues of sex tourism need to be seen as part of wider questions of sexuality, commoditisation, and tourism and the politics of moral and sexual control. However, such transformations require a starting point which, at the very least, requires recognition that sex tourism is part of a series of relationships between supply and demand, worker and client, the individual and society, and that the rights of workers can no longer be ignored.

From the perspective of a non-positivistic research tradition, any reporting of research is eloquent when the text is re-construed from a stance of examining both that which is said, and that which remains silent. In that sense the writing of a book about matters as controversial as sex tourism is in itself a difficult task. As Manderson (1992) noted, it leaves the authors exposed, even while judgements on the authors' work convey meaning about those who make comment. Further, to include in a book research undertaken at a primary level that was based on, in some cases, comparatively long relationships with informants, makes the task all the more difficult.

As has been discussed, the authors have sought to examine on the one hand, issues of motive and, on the other, their relationship with informants. In the previous, one value judgement that is a result of this work has been made explicit, and that is that women possess a right to work as sex workers if they so wish, albeit it is recognised that the conditions that give rise to 'choice' may be constrained by economic necessities among other factors. In short, the authors deny that all sex workers are, by definition, victims. Yet, as hopefully is made clear on sex trafficking, it is equally recognised that power structures exist whereby there is undoubtedly exploitation.

Legalisation and/or decriminalisation (as may be deemed appropriate by those involved) of the industry is not seen as an answer to all the problems, but it is seen as a means of securing better support mechanisms in terms of health, protection and self-assessment by those men and women who work as sex workers.

Such a course of action runs the danger of perpetuating those systems that create the conditions for sex tourism, but from a purely pragmatic perspective the authors would ask, how many women (and men) need to continue in danger from middle men who withhold monies, health protection and can continue to threaten sex workers, while the wider social problems of inequitable distribution of economic power are 'put right'? In the act of writing though, what has thus far been left unsaid is the relationship between writer and reader.

If the authors have had to deal with considerations of voyeurism, where does that leave the reader? Sex is about intimate matters of self-identity, and therefore can any reader come to an issue such as sex tourism with a mind stripped clean of perceptions, judgements and a sense of their own relationship to the topic, whether it be curiosity, fascination or seeking to clarify their own views? Through adopting a conceptualisation of margins, the authors have sought to develop a series of tensions that portray sex work and sex tourism as paradoxically simultaneously embedded in and yet marginalised by wider society.

Margins, it was argued, illustrate by drawing boundaries and illuminating alternatives. They are additionally multi-layered in meaning, and it is hoped that this book has shown that sex tourism as it is known today has historical antecedents in the nineteenth century that have cast long shadows. It was not the intention of the authors when they commenced this project, to engage in a polemic.

Hopefully the reader feels that this has not been the case. But just as the authors have felt compelled to eventually establish a judgement, so too, it is hoped, the reader will be better able to make their own judgements, be that what they will.

4

Health Tourism and Prostitution: A Symbiotic Relationship

The health and sex tourism is an interaction between two liminal peoples, peoples separated from the mainstream of society through a process of fragmentation derived from the Industrial Revolution. It was also argued that, within the semantic component of comparative symbology, they represented a signal relationship to mainstream society by postulating alternatives which meet needs denied by that society. This analysis supports the thesis proposed by Downes and Rock (1988:203) that 'Those who deny or defy important separations and definitions within society do more than merely break a rule. They may be thought to challenge the very legitimacy and structure of order, becoming agents or instances of chaos.'

But there exists too a pragmatic relationship - the relationship of client, customer and market transaction, and the market transaction possesses the role of bringing the alternative lifestyles of tourist and sex worker within the capitalist structures that dominate western society. The question has to be asked, is there an even closer relationship between tourism and prostitution than simply having historical antecedents in social forces that gave rise to the current situation? This present situation can only continue because either a mutually advantageous social exchange takes place if we are to follow Ap (1992) and his conceptualisation of social exchange theory, or, to follow Bishop and Robinson (1998), an unequal and exploitative condition has been created.

There is little doubt that such an exploitative condition exists. Even the most superficial review of sex tourism must recognise the brutality that occurs within prostitution. For example, with the growth of prosperity in China there has come a growth in pornography, prostitution and trafficking of women. The South China Morning Post reported the police rescuing 10,000 women from slavery in Hunan Province. The Herald International Tribune of 7 September 1991 reported that Vietnamese women were being lured into prostitution in China. With the growth of prosperity in China there has come a growth in pornography, prostitution and trafficking of women. The campaign group, End

Child Prostitution, Pornography and Trafficking (ECPAT), based in Bangkok, notes that 'The commercial sexual exploitation of children has paralleled the growth of tourism in many parts of the world'.

ECPAT estimate there are 60,000-100,000 children involved in the sex industry in the Philippines, that 20 per cent of Vietnam's growing commercial sex industry is comprised of children under 18 years of age, and in Phnom Penh in Cambodia 31 per cent of sex workers were between the ages of 13 to 17. Trafficking in young women is reported in Bangladesh, Burma and India. Sexual exploitation of children is part of a wider exploitation as young children are forced to work in factories, building sites and sweat shops. Muntarbhorn (1996) notes: 'There can be no more delusions - no-one can deny that the problem of children being sold for sex exists, here and now, in almost every country in the world.'

There is also emerging a literature which argues that the bars of Patpong that cater for the farang are not entirely exploitative, but permit economic support for rural families and generate opportunities for women that might not otherwise exist. Phillips and Dann (1998) emphasise the 'white knight' syndrome of guilt assuagement by 'white' men. Thus the 'client thinks of her as a girlfriend, and she calls him her boyfriend (feng). The legitimacy of the relationship has been established' (1998:68). The bar girl becomes an entrepreneur: she schedules the return trips of her boyfriends so that they do not coincide with each other, and she herself has become quite the cosmopolitan traveller with a passport showing trips ranging from the United States to Switzerland. It is quite a skill to be able to play such a large part in the life of a man whom she has only known for a week.

Yet the reality of this relationship is that it is based upon a hierarchy where the benefits are assumed by only a few, and where each new, young arrival from the fields is a rival for the monies of the farang. Odzer (1994), who in her own research role displays the ambiguities and paradoxes of Patpong life and the exotic spell of the 'other', and who is not unsympathetic towards those who people the soi of Patpong, nonetheless clearly recognises a potentially cruel hierarchy when she writes:

A hierarchy of jobs existed on Patpong. Working in a blow job bar. or performing in Fucking Shows was at the bottom. Next came dancing nude and performing trick shows in rip-off bars then dancing nude and trick shows in non-rip-off bars. Bikini dancing in ground-floor establishments was high status, but working in evening clothes without having to dance was higher. A distinction existed, however, between pretty women in dresses, who were brought out often, and less ravishing, perhaps fat, older women who served as hostesses only. Hostess-only types were pitied. Attractiveness and sex appeal were major elements of Patpong prestige. At the top of the status hierarchy were the beauties who didn't work for a bar at all but came and went on their own time.

The hierarchy is based not on personal worth but on the dexterity of the vagina and the possession of 'good' looks. Additionally, Bishop and Robinson (1998) argue that the economic value of the bars of Patpong only continues to perpetuate an economic system based on economic and social inequalities rather than seeking to remove those inequalities. Ryan (1999), while recognising the economic and possible enhancement of self-identity of the women who work within these Thai bars, still nonetheless asks whether this is a desirable means of achieving these ends.

Such hierarchies as described by Odzer (1994), such conditions of slavery are based on exploitation, and this must be recognised and stated. This is done later in this book when examining the conditions of sexual slavery and the trafficking in sex. The research of the present author has not, on the whole, been of such conditions. Most of the author's research has been undertaken in the societies of New Zealand and Australia where licensed massage parlours exist and where generally street work is but a small segment of total prostitution. Hence the extreme conditions of exploitation as found in Eastern Europe or Asia are not found. This is not to say that exploitation does not exist within these Tasman societies. As will be discussed, at one level exploitation of women, transsexuals and gays exists where some, due to low income, feel that no other choice exists but prostitution. At another level, massage parlour management can be exploitative. In one instance known to the author a female proprietor sought to impose on the sex workers a contract which required the women to pay $200 to work at a particular parlour in New Zealand. The contract also stated that non-appearance for a shift was automatic grounds for dismissal, while, in an attempt to bamboozle and frighten, the contract also included clauses such as the women being responsible for any contravention of the Resource Management Act, an Act which in New Zealand is primarily concerned with environmental protection and had no relevancy to the situation within which the women found themselves.

Within Australia there is no common legislation, with each State or Territory being responsible for its own law in this matter. The condition in Queensland has been particularly open initially to corruption and, second, one of risk for women. The 1987 Fitzgerald Enquiry in particular found evidence of large-scale corruption by the police. Inspector Allen Bulger of the Licensing Squad was found to have received AUS$274,000 from various criminal sources, while the Licensing Squad itself earned AUS$1,787,750 of 'black money' - including payments from well-known massage parlour owners, Hector Hapeta and Vittorio Conte. Sullivan says of the Enquiry that 'evidence presented to the Fitzgerald Enquiry during 1987-88 suggests that the heavy criminal penalties for all prostitution-related activities established in Queensland facilitated the establishment of an extensive system of police graft and corruption during the 1970s' (1997:154). This corruption extended into the heart of the political system with a leading Queensland politician, Don Lane, also being jailed for his part in the protection of corrupt officers. However, subsequent legislation which has made it illegal to work in a brothel and does not permit support services for women working for escort agencies has exposed women to risk.

For example, there have been cases of women brutalised and murdered, partly, it is argued, because it is illegal for them to have drivers handy who can act on their behalf, or for them to have help at hand by having others in the same house. Thus, the condition of women being abused within western societies must also be recognised. The main purpose of this is to further explore the relationship between tourism and primarily heterosexual prostitution, but at a functional as well as symbolic level. This will be done by first briefly reviewing some of the literature that describes the use of sexual imagery in tourism advertising. Second, an argument will be made that many of the things that actually motivate holiday taking can be applied to visiting a prostitute. Given the opportunity provided by travel, it is thus not surprising that many men are able to fulfill holiday motives of relaxation and pleasure by spending time with female company.

Third, by adopting a stance that the commercial transaction between two consenting adults characterises the client-prostitute relationship, the claims that commercial sex enhances personal identity will be examined. However, even within this context the conceptualisation of the liminal is not without relevance.

It has been argued that the tourist is a socially sanctioned marginal person, but the sex tourist goes one step further into liminality by entering what has been constructed as the world of the profane. It is, in Sutton-Smith's (1972) terminology, a move into anti-structure.

Hence far, in the concept of liminality, of people on the margins of society, has been used as a device to analyse both tourism and prostitution. However, as used by Turner, especially in his work The Ritual Process: Structure and Anti-structure (1969), the concept applies to moments within tribal societies. He draws our attention to initiation ceremonies whereby an individual is ritually made marginal until taken in by the community.

By 1982, however, Turner, adopting SuttonSmith's views, referred to liminoid phenomena. These he saw as being characteristic of democratic-liberal societies. He writes:

In the so-called 'high culture' of complex societies, liminoid is not only removed from a rite de passage context, it is also 'individualised.' The solitary artist creates the liminoid phenomena, the collectivity experiences collective liminal symbols.

This does not mean that the maker of liminoid symbols, ideas, images, etc., does so ex nihilo; it only means that he is privileged to make free with his social heritage in a way impossible to members of cultures in which the liminal is to a large extent the sacrosanct. Thus sex tourism can be called a liminoid phenomenon because:

- It is individualised and contractual.
- It occurs at 'natural disjunctions with the flow of natural and social processes'.
- It is co-existent with, and dependent upon, a total social process and represents its subjectivity and negativity.
- It possesses the nature of being profane, being a reversal of roles, an antithesis of the collective, but possessing its own collective representation.
- It is idiosyncratic, quirky and ludic. 'Their symbols are closer to the personal-psychological than to the objective-social typological pole'.
- Ultimately they cease to be eufunctional, but become a social critique exposing injustices, inefficiencies and immoralities of mainstream economic and political structures.

The moment of intercourse between client and prostitute is obviously a contractual one between individuals. The language of the massage parlour betrays this in most instances. What occurs behind the door of the bedroom is 'between the lady and the gentleman' - it is not the concern of the parlour manager. Of course, this may in part be due to the legal situation. One massage parlour manager in Christchurch, New Zealand explained why his notice board did not list 'all-inclusive prices' on the grounds that to do so would mean that the police would interpret his parlour as being a 'brothel' and hence illegal. Rasmussen and Kuhn (1977:13) note that 'Another important technique used to protect the masseuse from legal constraint is the word game.'

The nature of the space and culture of the red light district or the massage parlour is one that normalises the process of commercial sexuality, and, as will be argued, creates its own 'collective representation' of symbols and pragmatism.

It is quirky, and it can be fun. In a paper co-written by this author the second author, a stripper, said of the paper, 'It's fine, but we have lost the fun, the laughs of the clubs' (Martin, personal communication). In meetings with Susie Kruhse-MountBurton, Susie also noted that you have to have 'a sense of fun and of the absurd for this business'. Finally, it is a central thesis of this book that as the inter-relationship between sex tourist and sex worker moves from the symbolic to the pragmatic, it thence progresses to the functional. It thereby possesses a potential as a catalyst for encapsulating or creating social change due to the way that people respond to its increasing visibility.

This is evident in changing attitudes towards the sex industry. Thus, for example, in New Zealand a Private Member's Bill has been drawn up which seeks to decriminalise prostitution. This compares with the perceived lack of visibility of the sex industry for farangs within respectable middle-class Thai society that is discerned by Hamilton and Bishop and Robinson (1998) as one reason for the sustained existence of the industry. They argue that it is this defensive lack of recognition that explains Thai resentment about Longmans and Microsoft making references to the Thai sex industry in directories and encyclopaedias and their unwillingness to host, in 1998, the filming of another version of The King and I. For Bishop and Robinson this 'deadening silence', this organised forgetfulness or asphasic gap, is deliberate.

It is described as a 'will-to ignorance'; a coping mechanism at best and a political manipulation at worst. Thus the functionality of sex worker-client relationship in the Thai case is demarcated as 'an other' within Thailand itself, and by such demarcation is 'en-bounded' as beyond discussion even while its economic benefits are accepted. However, before entirely accepting this thesis it does need to be noted that The Bangkok Post and The Nation, two significant Thai newspapers, have run articles on child prostitution and child enslavement on many occasions. In addition, anyone who accesses The Bangkok Post Internet pages, can easily find several stories reporting problems relating to sex tourism. Thus it is the degree of the 'killing pretense', 'this privilege of unknowing' that must be questioned.

Given the legislation approved by the Thai Parliament on 4 September 1996 with its penalties for those who procure prostitutes under the age of 18 years while creating four remand homes for under-age prostitutes for education, counselling and training, one wonders how 'forgetful' this debate is. Nonetheless, the report of the debate in the Bangkok Post of 21 December 1996 is not without interest as to where blame is being laid, for example, Police Major-General Surasak Sutharom is quoted as saying that 'Sex workers who returned home with their pockets full of money were one factor attracting the younger generation to jump into such illegal business.'

However, it might be objected that the coverage of sex tourism by The Bangkok Post does not invalidate the argument of asphoria advanced by Bishop and Robinson as this paper is written in English. However, it is felt their thesis can still be questioned. For example, Jackson writes:

In researching the history of prostitution and attitudes towards women in Thailand, Scot Barmé (personal communication) reports an almost complete absence of references to homoeroticism in Thai newspapers and popular magazines from the 1920s and 1930s. This contrasts with the voluminous press reporting of heterosexual prostitution and the changing roles of women at the time, and the existence of a thriving underground history in heterosexual pornography.

Certainly a considerable Thai-sourced literature exists on problems relating to prostitution and can be easily found, particularly after the initial incidence of AIDS and little of this literature is cited by Bishop and Robinson. They appear to reach their conclusion by an analysis of economic data which is silent on the contribution made by prostitution to the Thai economy, but given the problems associated with calculating the contributions of tourism per se to an economy, it is hence not surprising to find that the statistical database for assessing the role of sex tourism in Thailand's economy is far from complete.

Again, the thesis adopted by Bishop and Robinson can be criticised as to the politico-economic manipulation of Thailand by western interests. For example, Aramaberri (2000) estimates that the value of sex tourism to the Thai economy is approximately 1.3 to 2.5 per cent of GNP, and at most just under 6 per cent of exports. Aramaberri concludes that the use made of the economic data by Bishop and Robinson is incomplete and selective, and the 'authors use the globalization synecdoche only to pave the way for the real purpose of the book: a moral advocacy against prostitution'.

This is not to say that Bishop and Robinson may be wrong, but rather simply seeks to say that their thesis requires closer examination. What the debate does illustrate is one aspect of the nature of liminoid phenomenon - it is by its nature a conceptualisation of shifting boundaries, unclear definitions, differing constructions and disjunctions in society, even when as significant as sex tourism.

SEXUAL IMAGERY IN TOURISM ADVERTISING — COMMODITIES OR EXPLOITATION

It has been argued that the first link between tourism and prostitution occurs at a symbolic level through the sexual images used by the tourism industry. Oppermann et al. (1998) review sexual imagery in examples of tourism promotional literature in Oppermann's book on sex tourism. While examples of sexual innuendo are found, they conclude that in some countries' advertising it exists but to a very small extent. They also specifically identify tourism promotion emanating from the Tourism Authority of Thailand and conclude that 'The majority of images presented in these brochures and booklets presented visitors and locals in realistic and modest dress and their actual less-than-perfect appearance'.

Two immediate observations may be made about this work. First, it does not use the word 'gender' and thus the analysis is undermined by a failure to distinguish between gendered representations and those of a more sexual nature. Second, the research was limited to the official promotional material of tourism authorities, and thus excluded from consideration the more explicit advertising material that is aimed at sex tourists.

Marshment (1997) also reviews the use of sexual imagery in the advertising of mainstream tourism products, namely the products of British package holiday companies. She argues that while there are images of the woman in a swimsuit, such a figure 'signifies the pleasures of idleness and luxury that certain representations of the beach holiday offer. There are no comparable images of men ... she is not part of the package holiday, but a signifier of it' (1997:20). Marshment argues that at face value gender is not a factor in the selling of holidays, but in these cases of package holidays there are gender constructions of definitions of the marketplace.

The market is the nuclear family, they are heterosexual, with ideals of companiate marriage and are associated with a range of definitions of ordinariness. For Marshment, however, there is evidence of just how gendered are the representations of our culture. She argues that the embodiment of pleasure is the female body, not the male, and that is why it is the female body that is used to represent the pleasure of the beach holiday. Even more specifically, it is the young, slim female body, while the exoticism of the 'other' is tamed by the use as a signifier of the young, slim, and demure female figure.

Considering that these images are derived from mainstream holidays, arguably these results are not surprising. If one is looking at the holiday images of British package holidays which are aimed at the mass market, then the use of homosexual imagery is going to be primarily absent. However, if one resorts to the media aimed at the gay market, magazines such as Boyz, Cafe and Attitude, then one does find pleasure being signified by young, slim male figures. Equally the messages of sex tourism are generally far more explicit. How explicit these images will be are partly constrained by the media being used. Press advertising for Auckland's massage parlours offers a range of images. Some refer to gentlemen's clubs with nothing more than a picture of the premises, but many feature pictures of the women with short descriptions. These emphasis bubbly personalities, fun women to be with - thus 'Suzanne is Asian and aims to please and tease', while 'Terri is not shy and nor should you be'. Some indicate specialities or offer 'toys'. While the photographs are of women wearing little and being topless, these are not passive women.

Indeed, domination services are offered. The images contrast with those offered by the videos of Dexter-Horn productions. In the case of The Erotic Women of Thailand images are presented of seemingly embarrassed young women having showers with a voice-over which emphasises that these are not models but real women that you can meet. Towards the end of the video is an explicit appeal to men who are disillusioned with 'demanding, liberated North American women'. Thai women are 'real' women because they are submissive. O'Connell Davidson (1995) traces similar attitudes of British sex tourists in Thailand.

This implies that the market for these 'exotic-erotic' trips are men unable to cope with the self-confident women of the West, and there is evidence for such a thesis. Seabrook describes the situation thus: Westerners think that sex is the ultimate authentic human experience. The young women and men of Bangkok know better. Because the farangs are so lonely, because they are such isolated individuals, they imagine that it is through sex that human beings come closest to one another. They think they see the profoundest communication in what is the loneliest experience in the world. They think like this because they are so far away from each other, they have to reach across the empty spaces of their separateness before they touch another human being.

What strikes this author about a tape like that of The Erotic Women of Thailand is just how little fun the whole process is shown to be. The shots taken in the clubs have, judging from the voice-over, an illicit thrill not because of the scenes they show, but because filming is not permitted and thus it is an 'adventure' to take such shots. The result is one of grainy shots of poorly lit rooms showing bored women in their underwear. The images are not sexy or erotic and if pornographic are thus because of the allusions being made. That they are thought to be erotic says much about the state of mind of the viewer.

If we are to look at sex images in relation to sex tourism, then the search for imagery has to go beyond the sources of imagery analysed by Oppermann et al. (1998). However, as noted, the nature of the image presented is modified by the media in which it is presented. The imagery presented by small adverts in easily accessible newspapers differ from those in men's magazines, or in the magazines aimed at lesbian, transsexual and gay readerships, all of which are more explicitly sexual. In heterosexual imagery 'close-up action' is often promised. Some women advertise 'back entry' or an experience of 'showers'. The photographs are of topless women; some offer 'double action' or 'voyeur sessions'. Touts in the soi of Patpong offer leaflets describing fucking shows. Gay readers are offered just as great a range of services as their heterosexual counterparts.

Detailed guides exist, for example The Best Gay Guide to Amsterdam and Benelux (1992). If this is thought to be offensively explicit it is of interest to note that while writing this, left in a staff room the author found a copy of Cleo for August 1998. Articles in this women's magazine included 'Your vagina - what's normal'? and the latest in pubic hair designs. For the virtual sex tourist of cyberspace, as is described by Kohm and Selwood (1998), there exist a full range of sites which provide information, pictures and reader's reviews.

Explicit sexual imagery is easily found. What is of interest is the interpretation of such imagery. For many the images are simply pornographic. But if one uses the dictionary definition of pornography as being the explicit description or exhibition of sexual activity in literature, films, etc. intended to distinguish erotic from other, more aesthetic, representations, then several problems quickly emerge.

First, does such an intent exist, second, how does one judge the success of such intent, third, is there need to show the outcome of the intent to stimulate? Sullivan (1997) demonstrates the problems involved in attempts to legislate such imagery. She describes the anti-pornographic view by excerpts from Parliamentary debate: thus they came to believe that pornography is a violation of the rights of women. They found that the majority of all this material is based on treating women not as persons but as things, and on degrading and humiliating women.

Yet, as evidenced by the example of Cleo for August 1998, it is possible to publish an article for the general readership of women which ostensibly would have at least a purpose of titillation. Thus the article goes on to note that the school's objectives include providing 'an arena in which single people can meet each other. The school is always booked solid around Valentine's day'. Sexual freedom is being increasingly constructed around females being able to enjoy their own sexuality. With reference to Cosmopolitan magazine, Janet Lee has remarked:

Cosmo exhorts the female reader to construct herself through self-discipline, and the reward for this is physical pleasure - or, more specifically, sexual pleasure... The 'new woman' Cosmo version is the sexy woman. Sex equals not only fun, but independence and success. And Cosmo claims to have the knowledge that will tell you how to have it all - sex, success and liberation.

Hence, the images of sex available to females that were once comparatively difficult to access in the mass media are now very accessible to women. A further examination of the sexual imagery associated with sex tourism reflects a further complication to the thesis of marginalisation that has been advanced previously. That thesis has been based upon a conceptualisation of fragmentation, of differentiation. The language of sexual imagery in sex tourism as derived from the actual advertising of commercial sexual services both reinforces and counter-balances that thesis. It reinforces the thesis because at one level it represents a change in the nature of the tourist's liminality.

The images once constrained to pornographic magazines are now to be found in women's magazines, and the by-product of this is to drive the commercial sex industry to ever more explicit images until there is little more left to exploit. Dragu and Harrison (1989), writing from the perspective of the former being an ex-stripper and the latter a writer of pornographic stories, observe that in the nineteenth century, there was a time when even the mention of women's legs was considered to be shocking and indecent. They note:

We have always focussed our suppression of sex on its purely physical aspects, and so it is natural that we also pursue sexual revelation at the physical level. This is a perfectly valid process, and one that has served us well for a long time, but we seem to be reaching the end of the line. Today, even a good long look at a woman's inner labia is loosing its charge.

They argue that the belief of sexual thrill lies in the realm of what is forbidden, and as that boundary moves, so sexual entertainment may be moving into decadence. A by-product of this is that such entertainment increasingly fails to satisfy and the concentration on the purely physical denies the spiritual and emotional - they liken it to fast food, we keep consuming but it never satisfies. Furthermore, what is emerging is the growth of the female as the consumer - they too emulate their male companions as searchers for sexual entertainment. However much both males and females learn that masturbation can be satisfying, love-making is better with a partner. The past boundaries and roles between sex tourist, commerciality, gender of sex tourist and provider of sexual service, consumer and provider of sexual entertainment, are being eroded.

It has been argued that the tourist is a marginal person, but that the marginality is sanctioned by society. But by becoming a sex tourist, by responding to the imagery of sexual service, that tourist might be said to be transgressing from the licit to the illicit. The tourist now begins to share the possibility of condemnation. Ryan and Kinder (1996a) stress the importance of concealment of the client. In an analysis of Auckland's red light district they write:

From the viewpoint of the tourist seeking a passive or active sexual entertainment ... Fort Street represents a safe 'crimogenic' place. Indeed, in many senses the term [crimogenic] is perhaps inappropriate for Fort Street. It offers a high degree of physical safety.

They go on to comment, using the concepts of 'Routine Activities' and Felson's (1986) concept of 'Guardians', that the tourist seeks anonymity and in doing so will 'adhere to a set of rules, for to do otherwise is to risk the concealment necessary'. Thus, by transgression of the boundary between the sanctioned marginality and that not so sanctioned, the tourist now requires the sex industry to provide safety and confidentiality. The reality of this provision thus permits enjoyment of a leisure pursuit - the cocoon of confidentiality permits a legitimisation of the act of patronage by those within the demarcated zone, which is both spatial and social. Hart, in her description of a Spanish barrio or neighbourhood where prostitutes worked described it in this way.

Within the barrio, sex as leisure was not an unambiguously illicit or illegitimate pursuit. Many clients did voice misgivings about being there (on a periphery), and often went so far as to describe their presence in the barrio as a 'vice'. However, they were able to enjoy this 'vice' in an atmosphere in which this was accepted as a leisure pursuit, albeit one that was considered to be rather different to others.

In research one client touched on this when he said: 'The parlour is where I relax, no-one knows I'm there, it is my time, my hour out of the hassles, I'm not anyone but me having a nice time with nice company.' This pursuit of sex as a leisure activity, this placing of prostitute and tourists within the same domain of the space of prostitution has many implications that lead us to conceptualisations of de-differentiation.

Competing definitions of the commercial sexual space exist. Prior to advancing a thesis of the de-differentiation offered by the locus of client-sex worker interaction and the imagery and pragmatism associated with it, it is necessary to state the arguments and views of those who will have none of what they perceive as self-deluding semantics. Kathleen Barry has played a leading role in the Coalition Against Trafficking in Women (CATW). The Coalition wishes to further enforce the 1949 Convention of the United Nations of 2 December, entitled 'Suppression of the Traffic in Persons and of the Exploitation of the Prostitution of Others' by creating a freedom from all sexual exploitation. Barry herself in her book, Prostitution of Sexuality, makes her views quite clear. Thus, for example:

A lover, husband, or boyfriend who promotes the sexual exploitation and commodification of women is a pimp, and together, pimping and procuring are amongst the most ruthless practices of male power and sexual dominance. These practices go far beyond the merchandising of woman's bodies for the market that demands them; they crystallize misogyny in acts of male hatred of femaleness as rendered into a commodity for whom the marketer and the purchaser have contempt.

For an activist like Marcovich, a founder of the Movement for the Abolition of Prostitution and Pornography, prostitution is akin to slavery. She describes it as a market system based on a society which legimitises this market, on the actions of pimps, money and the clients, always men, who buy the sex act, pieces of body: vagina, anus, breast, mouth and hands of women ...

the prostitutes, women who are victims of this market, who, to support the violence of being denied as human, of being penetrated and tortured 1, 10, 100 times a day by men for whom they have no desire, split their spirit and their body in two, become addicts to drugs or alcohol, when becoming ill much later with anal or vaginal cancer.

From these perspectives the issue is simply one of male exploitation of power. The sexual imagery of the sex industry is not about questions of identity, but solely about the exploitation of the female body for pecuniary gain by men.

The almost diametrically opposite viewpoint is stated by Murray. She argues that feminist arguments of the type postulated above are based on a false premise for there is nothing inherently wrong in the commodification of sex. Further, she argues, academia has given credence to such arguments of commodification and thus legitimised them. But Murray also notes 'The academy has progressed from women's studies to gender to sexuality, getting closer to the cunt of the matter while continuing to marginalise class, race and alternative subject-voices' (1998a: 70). For Murray the voices and images of commercial sex are not yet diffuse enough. Nonetheless she discerns that at last:

Dyke whores are no longer double deviants, in some parts of the West at least. After being invisibilised by some feminisms, dyke whores have come out in a babble of trendy deviances, though the working-class junkie whores are still invisibilised. There are new games to play, where the referee is not the only one with a whistle.

The imagery of commercial sex and sex tourism is becoming more diverse and the flâneur and voyeur is no longer simply male or heterosexual. The differentiation of whore/madonna of the nineteenth century is becoming the subject of a post-modernist de-differentiation where madonna reads Cleo, can respond to the advertisements that feature the services of 'Tony' or 'Steve', admire the Chippendales and other male-based sex acts aimed at women, and where the whore is butch, or gay, or black and definitely proud.

From the position of those feminist groups who work with sex workers, the views of CATW seem extreme. Lisa Hofman, Director of the Dutch Foundation Against Trafficking in Women, is cited by Chapkis as saying:

We were shocked when we went to an anti-trafficking conference in New York in 1988 and discovered how out of touch with working women the U.S. Coalition ... seemed to be. I think it's very significant that that particular group only works with women who have already left prostitution.

Hence, in conclusion of this section, there exist many more explicit sexual images associated with sex tourism than those examined by Oppermann and his co-authors in his book. Essentially, the chapter by Oppermann et al. (1998), in the view of this author, is not about sex tourism at all and thus perhaps is misplaced. To find the images related to sex tourism it is necessary to examine the images of the sex tourism industry, and as might be expected, these images are diverse. First, they are often 'explicit' by the norms of 'normal' society - but as has been pointed out by reference to a popular women's magazine, these norms themselves cover a wide range of acceptabilities. Second, the images of the commercial sex industry are not solely related to heterosexual sex or straight sex. Third, as illustrated by the statements by Murray, those portrayed in the images do not feel necessarily degraded by the images.

As will be discussed below, they can feel empowered. Images imply recognition, and images are picked up, used and, yes sometimes abused, by the media operating in mainstream society. However, sex workers have known through discrimination that they have never entirely controlled the images of their industry. The paradox is that as images become adopted, distilled, disseminated, they assume their own lives which become divorced from that which was illustrated, but in doing so enter a public consciousness which permits the prostitute voice to emerge from behind the image. As Kempadoo (1999:27) writes of sex work 'being simultaneously a form of domination and exploitation as well as a place that enables assertions of freedom in the context of oppressive racialized economic orders'.

As will be argued, there exist links between the 'macro-context' of the social understanding of sex tourism, and the 'micro-level' of its meaning for individual actors. Foucault notes in The Carceral that 'the modelling of the body produces a knowledge of the individual, the apprenticeship of the techniques induces modes of behaviour and the acquisition of skills is inextricably linked with the establishment of power relations'. It is now to the 'apprenticeship' and the functional relationship that we turn.

MOTIVATIONS FOR HOLIDAYS AND/WITH COMMERCIAL SEX

Some of this section will draw upon past research published by the author, either alone or with co-authors and from previously unpublished notes relating to that research. It will also cite other work that generally confirms these findings, but it is again important to establish a caveat on the location of that research. It is primarily based in New Zealand and Australia with some insights from the UK and thus is not immediately applicable to situations outside of those countries. Some generalisation is possible, but care must be taken when seeking to apply the findings to other regions of the world. The position in South-east Asia and Eastern Europe may mean that some of these findings will not be applicable to those parts of the world, or to some aspects of sex tourism such as that relating to paedophilia.

Many researchers have examined the motivation for tourist behaviour. Crompton (1979) notes that travel consumers are not motivated by the specific qualities of the destination and its attractions, but rather by the broad suitability of the destination to fulfil their particular psychological needs. He proposes that 'instead of distance, culture and climate being used to classify destinations, one can envisage clusters of vacation centres which are predominantly self-exploration, or social interaction or indeed sexual arousal'. In this sense the term 'sexual arousal' is being used literally and not as a metaphor, and it may be argued that parts of Thailand, Amsterdam or any red light area meets this definition. Mathieson and Wall (1982) refer to the physical motivational category which includes motivations such as refreshment of body and mind and pleasure - fun, excitement, romance and entertainment.

It is not hard to extend these motivations to the client visiting a prostitute. Yiannakis and Gibson (1992) developed a typology of holidaymaker clusters based upon three different continuums. The first is the desire for a vacation that is either highly structured or has little structure. The second axis indicated whether the tourist preferred their tourist destination to be a stimulating or tranquil environment. The final axis was a continuum to determine whether the tourist aspired to visiting a strange or familiar environment. Hence the tourist seeking contact with prostitutes might choose a vacation with a structure that permits flexibility, seeking a stimulating environment, but also one with familiarity. They describe the 'action seeker' as 'Mostly interested in partying, going to night clubs and meeting the opposite sex for uncomplicated romantic experiences'. This type of tourist has been previously described with reference to the work of Wickens (1994). Wickens also returns to the same subject in her later work of 1997. Describing a category of tourist which she terms 'Raver' she reports one as saying:

Without the emotional baggage of love, I enjoyed the lust in the brief sexual liaison I had with Kosta. I met him in a bar ... He sent a drink across to me... and ended in bed. No, I didn't experience any emotional pain when we parted a few days later!

This example is telling as it offers evidence of the de-differentiation modern tourism offers to its clientele. Compare this statement with that of a former prostitute, Maryann, as recorded by Chapkis:

I think that the assumption that being a prostitute ruins a woman's experience of sex is part of that [*i.e.* the view that sex can only mean one thing to women]. Men need to think that women can't have sex without intimacy, and that if they do that it's bad for them. Like a woman only has sex with a man because he and he alone has something she can't live without. In fact, an important part of prostitution for me was realising that sex didn't have to be about intimacy. There is great power in the realization that you are, in fact, in control.

In much of the debate on sex tourism it seems as if the argument has been hijacked by a feminist rhetoric within which the client is the male and the prostitute female, and the relationship is heterosexual. It also implies that the prostitute is the victim. These scenarios are incomplete. For example, Albuquerque (1998:109) describes how Barbadian beach boys size up potential female clients and 'a relatively wealthy, attractive, thirty-something French Canadian tops most lists'. At another level the issue of degradation is sometimes perceived by the client. Thus Kruhse-MountBurton notes that: prostitution in the Australian context is often appraised by clients as deficient, in that prostitutes are criticised for being emotionally and sexually cold and for making little effort to please, or to disguise the commercial nature of the interaction.

Additionally, not only may the client be female, or gay, but the prostitute a lesbian while meeting the needs of heterosexual male clients. It seems as if in the nineteenth century the existing hegemony stated that for a women to have sex outside of marriage was itself bad for the woman and her soul. The nineteenth century is also full of examples of women for whom to have sex without love was also equally harmful (for example, Anna Karenina or Madame Bovary). Wickens's example is of a woman who wants and enjoys sex without a wish for long-term relationships. One of the modern myths is that it is harmful for a woman to have sex without desire; that, in short, it harms a woman who commodifies her sexuality.

However, from an increasing number of interviews with sex workers the evidence mounts that this is simply not the case. For example, in interviews with New Zealand prostitutes, Jo said, 'I did it because I wanted to, it was as simple as that. And when I didn't want to do it, I stopped.' Terri said, 'If I didn't want to do this, I wouldn't be here - it's a job of work.' Amber, an exotic dancer of ten years' experience said, 'It's really very simple at one level - it's just a job of work, it pays the bills.' This is not to say that the work cannot be fun or enjoyable. Sharon notes that on one occasion she had such fun with a 'real Italian Romeo type' that she let him off free of charge, but quickly adds that this is not a normal circumstance. The old question, do prostitutes enjoy it, can elicit many answers, but the stereotypical responses of 'no they don't' denies the concept that sex without love can be fun, and that as a job of work, there are good days and bad - and on a good day it may be possible to have a good time with a client. Jo Doezema, an Amsterdam-based prostitute says:

So there are parts of my life I don't want to share at work. So what? Do I have to give all of myself and not hold anything back in order to legitimately be able to say that I like my work?

She goes on to make the point that if prostitutes say they enjoy their work, their view is dismissed as one whereby the prostitute does not realise she is being destroyed. Burrell (1997) reports that at a conference in the UK, many prostitutes were angered and dismayed at what they felt were simplistic feminist arguments portraying them as victims. It is, quite simply, a role that is rejected time and time again by many working women.

The tourist may seek fun while on holiday as a source of relaxation. Is the person who waits at the table stigmatised for providing a fun ambience while serving them? Generally the answer is no. Can it be doubted that the waiter might not, on occasions, actually be having fun while serving a group of cheerful holidaymakers who make his or her task that much easier? Again, the answer is no. Why, then, the difficulty in believing that those sex workers able to work in an environment which generally respects them as a person and which provides her or him with control, might not also have some fun, or be professional in the service being provided?

To deny the concept of sex work as being a professional service, as having like other jobs its good or bad days, is to continue to marginalise and stigmatise. When this author asked a member of the New Zealand Prostitutes Collective why she persisted in her role, the response was to bring about a 'normalisation' of sex work. Yet perhaps marginalisation is 'safer' for many people, because, as already noted, not to stigmatise means a need to recognise that non-prostitute women may also wish to either have male sex workers, or to seek male patrons for purposes of their own. That, in short, the bourgeois repression of sex in Western society may not have advantages, but in fact may psychologically cripple. Wickens's 'Ravers' may not be paid in money, but they are paid in terms of having the good time they desire.

Around prostitution are created many fantasies. Some are sexual, some are cultural (how often has the whore with a heart of gold been portrayed in Hollywood films? Even Rhett Butler in Margaret Mitchell's novel Gone with the Wind had the support of his good whore). Tourism too is a time of fantasy. Disneyland peddles its fantasies and myths of American culture - what Hollinshead (1997) has termed its 'Distory'. Tourists arrive at Disney and other locations to be immersed in myth, to play out roles. Today photographers offer services whereby they will create photographs of us all as models or figures of fantasy. What previously had been a private fantasy becomes projected onto our film or in a set - how close to reality are the worlds portrayed by the film, West World? Certainly, Ryan and Kinder (1996a) found evidence of clients seeking fantasy. They cite the example of 'Tony', who notes that 'it is more exciting, more uninhibited and there is no holding back. I enjoy the whole experience, the sex, the fantasies, being able to "talk dirty" and the fact that there are no demands on me.' Winter (1976:10) comments: 'Some clients thrive on the ability to engage an anonymous prostitute for sexual relations: to them the whole experience is a novel sexual adventure filled with surprises and fantasies.' However, for the sex worker, there may be little such novelty or excitement.

Like holidays, a visit to a prostitute can meet relaxation, social and friendship needs. Evidence of this emerged from conversations with clients reported by Ryan and Kinder (1996a). 'Charlie' stated that he sees ladies to 'get a little bit of happiness'. 'Fred' commented: 'I just usually want a cuddle and some company. It gives me friendship and some social activity.' 'Nick', a business traveller who often visits prostitutes stated that he used 'high class' escorts who are usually well educated, that he had a need to interact with them on an intellectual level - that 'it is more important to be with the girl and have intelligent, cheerful conversation, than just to have sex'.

Additionally, tourists visit different places in order to see and do new things - they search for novelty. So too do those who visit prostitutes. 'Sam' met escorts 'because of a search for variety'. Michael 'feels the need to do something different'. Peter, who frequently uses prostitutes when on business trips, commented: 'yes, my sexual [activity] is different than with my normal partner ... [it] involves excitement at the unknown'. Again, 'Basil' stated: 'Trying to get more of a cover of what different people are like - mainly for the variety.'

Holidays have also been noted by Crompton (1979) as opportunities for regression into childhood.

The tourist visiting a prostitute may also be engaged in another form of regression. Sheehy (1971) has made the observation that, for a man, prostitution represents an opportunity of 'buying the nostalgic illusion that things are how they were when he was a boy'. Further, if holidays present opportunities for the many to enjoy, however limited the time, the lifestyle of the wealthy, so too sex tourism, particularly in Asia, permits an exhilaration usually open only to the wealthy, that is of having access to many women of youth and beauty. It can also be regarded as an acting out of the fantasy of being powerful. Lindi St

Clair is quoted by Thomson (1996) as saying, 'Let's look at half these politicians. Let's look at half the royals.

Who would give them a second glance if they weren't rich and famous? Power makes an ugly man attractive.' And every man, ugly or not, who walks into the massage parlour has the power of paying the fee. Within this act lies the repugnace felt by those feminist commentators like Barry who see prostitution as being the act of purchase of female body parts, but the parlour does offer its culture and its norms, and within this environment the sex worker does exercise considerable elements of power as will be discussed below.

The 'holiday romance' that can be found in literature and fact (although not often researched) has several features. One is that it is understood by both parties to be temporary - that its boundaries are those of the holiday place and period. There were examples of respondents in the Ryan and Kinder research, as with Wickens's example cited above, who simply wanted sex without emotional involvement. Indeed, parallels could be drawn between the actions of some younger respondents and the type of tourist featured in media portrayal of 18-30-year-old holidaymakers. 'Ted', aged 25, was one such example. He went to a prostitute the first time two years ago when 'out with the boys and we were drinking'. He had no time for emotional involvement with a girl; 'I don't want to have to go through all that bullshit.' However, this attitude was not found to be common, and was primarily shown by younger clients (Ryan and Kinder, 1996b). Both Seabrook and O'Connell Davidson describe the type. O'Connell Davidson (1995) divides the clientele into three, 'Macho Men', 'Mr Averages' and 'Cosmopolitan males'. 'Macho Man' looks to have sex with as many women as possible. Seabrook (1996:36) describes the short-term tourists to Patpong as 'extremely insensitive' and having 'little imaginative understanding of the people whose lives touch theirs' ... "A shower, a shag and a shit, the three biggest pleasures in life, " said one man with his mates.'

However, Seabrook goes on to write that behind the bluster, the attempts to assuage the guilt in drinking, even these men at an individual level 'become more thoughtful, and are interested in the lives of the women who service them; but they feel that by giving a generous tip, "treating them decently", they have acquitted themselves of any debt to the women'. There is a significant literature relating to sex tourists who want friendship with young women. Kruhse-MountBurton (1995:194) cites one interviewee as stating: 'It's true there is no chance of rejection. But now maybe I'm a bit idealistic in the sense that I think, wouldn't it be nice if during that day, and that encounter, that there developed a genuine friendliness.'

Cohen (1986) reproduces letters sent by former clients to the Thai women with whom they have shared time. In the Ryan and Kinder research similar motives were also stated by respondents. Thus one man said: 'It's like meeting a girl friend for the first time ... the affection may be purchased, but I am continually pleasantly surprised by just how nice the women are, and that I very much appreciate.' The difference in attitudes, between seeking or rejecting emotional support is possibly demonstrated by the language used by respondents in Ryan and Kinder's work (1996a). Those who share 'Ted's' views seemed to have a greater tendency to 'use a prostitute'; others would 'visit a prostitute'. Such language difference can be held to be significant, and Ryan and Kinder offer a simple content analysis by frequency counts of use of various expressions. However, such a simple analysis remains but that, simple, as it does not take into account the point made by Seabrook (1996) that within other contexts most males seem to incline to at least some reflexivity as to their role as clients.

Another reason advanced for holiday taking is that of ego and status enhancement. Such motivation can also be discerned, albeit perhaps indirectly, with sex tourism. O'Connell Davidson (1998) provides evidence from her interviews with sex tourists in Cuba and Thailand which provide support for this motivation being present. Thus she cites one white British sex tourist in Cuba as saying:

It's funny, but in England, the girls I fancy don't fancy me and the ones that do fancy me, I don't fancy. They tend to be sort of fatter and older, you know, thirty-five, but their faces, they look forty. But in Cuba, really beautiful girls fancy me. They're all over me. They treat me like a star. My girlfriend's jet black, she's beautiful.

For O'Connell Davidson a complex set of identities arise in such cases. The men value a certain form of female identity, they are able to possess that through economic power, they attribute value to the person 'possessed', and thereby re-value themselves. An implicit theme within this analysis is the psychological immaturity of men who are unable to see past the physical. Yet what is paradoxical in such situations is that within the situation men will often rationalise the relationship in terms of the senses of friendship, companionship and concern they will feel for the woman concerned.

It raises the question whether the re-evaluation of self on the part of males actually permits the better side of their character to emerge. Such a thesis would support the priestess function described by writers like Bell (1994), Jordan (1991), McLeod (1982), and Delacoste and Alexander (1987). Unfortunately, to sustain this thesis would require evidence of a behaviour change when men return home from locations like Thailand and Cuba, and what evidence that does exist seems to support Cohen's (1986) contention that, on the contrary, men simply seek to return to the land of their beautiful women. Cohen begins his paper on the correspondence between farangs and Thai girls with a quote from Grey, namely:

Excessive love for the exotic can destroy the white European in the Orient. Many men think they go away from here with their souls intact - but they find in their own countries they've been profoundly changed by their experiences without knowing it. They become outcasts among their own people because everything at home seems insipid in comparison with the East. Then they're lured back by the siren call of what has already ruined them.

However, it has to be observed that such behaviour is not unique to sex tourism. Ryan (1997) relates stories of how the cathartic experience of tourism lures people back to the holiday destination. As stated, and citing from his own experience as a windsurf instructor in a holiday destination, he identifies the nurse who returned as an instructor, the personnel manager for a large British retail chain who did the same, the man who sold his business in order to teach people to sail catamarans, the couple who started a cycling company in order to live in France. The liminal possesses the ability to create a permanent marginal status wherein the ritual of the liminal provides psychological support.

Another motivation that emerged from the New Zealand research (albeit associated with concealment needs) was role of prostitutes in family bonding - a need recognised in the tourism literature as one met by holidaying. For example, 'Roger' is happy in his marriage, but feels a need to visit prostitutes for a sexual relief. He would never want his wife to find out as it would ruin his marriage and trust between him and his wife. For almost all the men involved, concealment and discretion were of paramount importance, often because of a need to sustain a marriage.

In this listing of motivations, there are leitmotifs, namely, the desire for sex and concealment. The desire for sex is, as already noted, not unknown to observers of tourist behaviour. Nor, but from a different perspective, is the desire for concealment. Pizam and Mansfeld (1996) illustrate the link between crime and tourism, and the fact that tourist locations can offer concealment for criminal action. In the context of the tourist and the prostitute, the tourist location offers the concealment of anonymity which reduces ties of responsibility. However, what emerges from the discussions with clients and prostitutes is, for some, a need to conceal actions from cared for others. Clients wish to conceal their actions from their partners, and for many prostitutes, there is a wish to conceal their actions from parents and/or children. As already argued, such a need arises from a societal viewpoint that while recognising the existence of sex work, many still prefer to marginalise it to the 'safe' location of the massage parlour or red light district in order to avoid questions relating to sexual identities and relationships within mainstream society.

To summarise this, thus far, it may be said that all the motivations that exist for holiday taking - relaxation, fantastical escape, family bonding, adventure, doing something different - all of these motivations equally apply to visiting a sex worker. The other reason for visiting a sex worker is the search for sex, and it has been often argued that the atmosphere of holidaying is signified by female figures. While this has tended to agree with Marshment's contention that mass package holidays may be gendered in imagery other than overtly sexual in appeal, it needs to be recognised that within popular literature as well as the academic, the fourth 's' of the holiday after sun, sea and sand, is indeed 'sex'. Baillie notes that:

Tourism promotion in magazines and newspapers promises would-be vacationers more than sun, sea and sand; they are also offered the fourth 's' - sex. Resorts are advertised under the labels of 'hedonism', 'ecstacism', and 'edenism'. One of the most successful advertising campaigns actually failed to mention the location of the resort: the selling of the holiday experience itself and not the destination was the important factor.

However, it is not necessary to look for relationships between tourism and the sex industry solely in terms of the hedonistic advertising adopted by the industry. Simply put, both holidaying and visiting a prostitute or visiting a strip club may be regarded as forms of leisure activity. O'Connell Davidson (1998) reviews that form of sex work which she describes as ritual reinscriptions where young men are introduced to sexual knowledge. She writes that:

Although even the most reluctant client may go on to become sexually excited by the process of selecting and then exploiting a prostitute, it is important to note that participation in the form of prostitute use [of this type] ... is not generally motivated by any particular sexual desire or desire on the part of individual participants. Nor does it involve sexual abandon.

A further factor enforces the linkage between tourism and sex work. This is opportunity. Ryan and Kinder (1996a) seek to explain this by reference to two diagrams reproduced. The first is derived from Tonry and Morris (1985) whose work was based on studies of criminality and deviance, especially with reference to 'opportunistic' criminality. The argument is advanced that the readiness to undertake what was termed an 'unworthy act' arises from an interplay between background, needs, past learning and an evaluation of whether it is possible to both commit the act and escape undetected. It is worth highlighting that opportunity alone is not a sufficient variable. There exist a series of salient factors that shape a reaction to the 'chance event'. In the case of sex tourism it may be argued that the opportunity to visit a prostitute arises within a context of hedonism, relaxation and escape.

However, this context and opportunity are again not sufficient unless the need exists to an extent where a readiness to act is formed. That readiness may be in a context of anonymity, but as Seabrook (1996), O'Connell Davidson (1998) and Ryan (1999) make clear, in some cases that anonymity is set aside in the pursuance of male rites of mateship or togetherness. Ryan and Kinder (1996a) suggest an event model which does emphasise anonymity. An area (a red light district) is selected and then either rejected or seen as 'acceptable' and then subsequently a specific location (brothel, or in the case of street prostitution, road) is then selected as protecting the sought for anonymity. Thus, while motivation to act may exist, it can be frustrated by the nature of the place. Obviously being away from home reduces the likelihood of the constraining variables being operative. The definition of 'recourse to prostitutes' as 'unworthy' is now perceived as being problematical given the different layers of meaning associated with commercial sex. Tonry and Morris (1985) link commercial sex with excessive drink, drugs, theft, etc., but this link is far from automatic, especially given the conditions of touristic destinations. Utilisation of the term 'unworthy' is here simply a reproduction of the original paper, but is not a term the present authors would automatically subscribe to.

The pragmatic or functional test of Turner's (1974) comparative symbology thus includes the spatial layout of the place. The relationship between holiday motivation and that of visiting a sex worker is also symbiotic. As noted, both are leisure pursuits. The tourist trip provides opportunity. The tourist industry sustains the sex industry in part by enabling demand to be operationalised in locations away from home. The tourism industry also sustains a pattern of global economics whereby the dominance of the one party ensures the economic dependency of the second.

But a further pragmatic outcome is whether the interaction between the two parties has satisfied the needs of the sex worker and tourist, and this can be interpreted in terms of the result of the interaction upon the self-image of each. Such an analysis is consistent with the adoption of Turner's argument, previously noted that, tourist-sex worker interactions occur at a personal-psychological level. It thus appears that any analysis of sex tourism is operating at two levels of analysis. There is the micro-analysis of individuals who justify their actions, and the macro-level of analysis where the aggregation of individual acts is sustained by socio-political-economic matrices of interaction whereby some have monetary power to wield and others have no other way of accessing money other than to engage in prostitution. At the personal level there may be a choice to engage in sex work, limited choice or forced labour. The conditions under which the sex worker engages in sex work are important in shaping the personal-psychological level of interaction, and the consequent damage that might be done to people.

Hollinshead (1999) also identifies elements of tourism, which, for our purposes, can also be utilised to help explain the relationship between tourism and prostitution. He argues that tourists are drawn towards 'selectively celebrated sites', they delight in the 'exotic', and that they are self-indulgent. He also advances the notion that the 'tourist gaze' (Urry, 1990) is important because it helps render a more romantic and illusory world with the consequence that it transforms places and people, and creatively empowers 'the vision of people of and about the world'. From what has been described, these processes can be seen to be operating within sex tourism just as in other forms of tourism, as Hollinshead would no doubt contend would happen.

Locations like Amsterdam, Patpong, or other red light districts attract clients and the tourist as voyeur, but in doing so the 'Gaze' itself acquires a political power based on a questioning as to why, how and should such places exist in the way in which they do. As Hoy notes, in the Foucaldian view of the world:

Power in a game of chess is [not exercised] by one piece over another at the moment of capture. On Foucault's model, the capture is indeed a 'micropower', but it is also the effect of the overall arrangement of the pieces at the time as well as of the strategy leading up to and including the capture.

Thus tourism becomes not simply a provider and creator of demand for prostitution, but in the very processes of creating places attracts an attention whereby tourism becomes a catalyst for subsequent change. If Butler's (1980) destination life-cycle can apply to resorts in general, so too it might apply to specific red light districts.

THE CHANGING URBAN SCENE

Man's Environment attains a high degree of simplification in the modern metropolis. At first this may seem surprising: We normally associate metropolitan life with a diversity of individual types and with variety and subtlety in human relations. But diversity among men and complexity in human relations are social and cultural phenomena. From a biological point of view, the drab, severe metropolitan world of mortar, steel and machines constitutes a relatively simple environment and the sharp division of labour developed by the modern urban economy imposes extremely limited, monotonous occupational activities on many of the individuals who make their livelihood in a large city.

These have not always been the characteristics of urban life. The metropolitan milieu represents a sharp departure from the forms and styles of life that prevailed in communities of the pre-industrial era. Early towns produced highly varied and colourful environments. Students of the medieval commune and the Renaissance city never fail to single out the humanising artistic touch that the urban dweller gave to his home and to everyday articles. Craftsmen seldom permitted the function of an object to completely dominate its form. Decorativeness is to be found even in tools and weapons—objects which in our day are noteworthy for their purely functional design.

This high sense of individual artistry was nourished by a vocational tradition that directed the workman to nearly every phase of the making of a product. The craftsman often prepared his raw material with his own hands, smelting his metals or tanning his leather.

The great architects and engineers of the Renaissance not only designed a structure but also participated in its construction. The roundedness of the Renaissance man, which we look upon with so much envy today, was due in large part to a unity of mind and body, to a combination of thought and physical activity.

Early urban life was leisurely and relaxed. Craftsmen worked more or less in accordance with a pace established by physiological cycles, accelerating the tempo of their work during moments of energy and slowing down or halting entirely during periods of lethargy. The rate of physical activity was determined by the body's vitality rather than by external agencies, such as machines. Men did not try to "conserve" their energy and distribute it uniformly, as though it were an inorganic resource; human energy is seldom "conserved," in this simple, mechanical sense. Craftsman and artist worked by "fits and starts," giving themselves over to a task to the degree that their bodies were amenable to physical activity and artistic endeavor. Labour and art were seldom forced. The tempo of work varied, from hour to hour and day to day, with the changing vitality of the body.

The town developed in an agricultural matrix. Farms lay directly outside the city, not in a far-removed perimeter that the traveler could reach only after a long journey through suburbs and "exurbs." A short stroll carried the urban dweller from the market place, on which the principal cultural activities of the community were centered, into open fields and orchards. Farmer and city man intermingled freely. In many cases, the urban dweller combined the work of a craftsman with that of a food grower, often maintaining a small garden inside the city walls to supply some of his own food. "One must not look at the narrow streets between the houses without remembering the open green, or the neatly chequered gardens, that usually stretched behind," observes Lewis Mumford.

Food staples were grown nearby, on farms that produced a variety of crops. As soon as a crop was harvested, it found its way quickly to the market place and from there to the urban consumer. The city dweller was never completely urbanized, in the narrow sense, as he is today. Gardening within the city and easy access to the countryside helped to fuse all aspects of urban and country life.

Early city life, to be sure, was burdened with many problems that have largely been solved by modern science and technology. Diet was severely restricted, especially in medieval times and fresh foods were available only during the growing season. Sanitation remained primitive for centuries, although Mumford points out that the existence of open spaces in the medieval town "shows that sanitary arrangements were not necessarily as offensive as they have been pictured, nor vile smells as uniformly ubiquitous."

Agricultural techniques were crude and few advances were made in transportation until railroads came into existence, but the early towns put the tools and the knowledge at their disposal to the best possible use. Life was usually serene. "One awoke in the medieval town to the crowing of the cock, the chirping of birds nesting under the eaves, or to the tolling of the hours in the monastery on the outskirts, perhaps to the chime of bells in the new belltower.

Song rose easily on the lips, from the plain chant of the monks to the refrains of the ballad singer in the market place, or that of the apprentice and the house-maid at work. As late as the seventeenth century, the ability to hold a part in a domestic choral song was rated by Pepys as an indispensable quality in a new maid. There were work songs, distinct for each craft, often composed to the rhythmic tapping or hammering of the craftsman himself. FitzStephens reported in the twelfth century that the sound of the water mill was a pleasant one amid the green fields of London. At night there would be complete silence, but for the stirring of animals and the calling of the hours by the town watch. Deep sleep was possible in the medieval towns, untainted by either human or mechanical noises."

Modern science has eliminated nearly all the difficulties that earlier urban communities faced. Owing to advanced means of transportation, the city dweller now enjoys a highly varied diet and the metropolis receives abundant supplies of foods of all types the year round. Sanitation has reached a high technical level; the daily wastes of millions of people are removed without hazard to public health. And yet for every difficulty science has eliminated, the metropolis has created a new and greater problem in our manner of urban life.

The metropolis lacks nearly all the humanising features of early urban life. In the medieval and Renaissance towns, intellectual activity and art were combined with physical labour; in the metropolis, intellectual activity, art and physical labour are sharply separated. The civil engineer who designs a structure seldom participates in its construction; his counterpart in the field rarely engages in design. Architects like Frank Lloyd Wright, who concerned himself with nearly every phase of construction, are rarities. Most jobs in the metropolis are sedentary and monotonous. Some of the more rapidly growing occupations require very little mental or physical work; they are mindless as well as sedentary. Work of this kind is typified by the tasks of the billing-machine operator and the dictaphone pool typist, whose principal qualification is the ability to endure an excruciatingly vacuous routine.

The current occupational trend is towards an extreme simplification of the labour process. Work is fragmented, limited and overspecialized. Modern industry has broken down many highly skilled crafts into repetitive tasks that the worker can perform mechanically, by habit, without losing time either in thinking or in changing tools.

Work tends to become sedentary, not because the comfort of the worker is kept in mind, but because any unnecessary movement of the body tends to diminish output by interrupting the smooth, uniform flow of labour. The same trend is evident in intellectual and artistic work, where over-specialization tends to replace creative activity with mechanical operations. While many such jobs allow for considerable individual leeway, progressively fewer faculties are used or developed. In the worst cases, physical work is limited to a few dexterous operations of the fingers, mental work to a few dexterous operations of the mind.

Labour becomes highly intensive. The few faculties that are brought into play are employed at continually higher rates of speed. Work is viewed more as a function of habit than as the function of individual resources and talents whose use requires patience and tolerance. Thus, many jobs not only tend to restrict the use of certain parts of the body, but employ other parts excessively. Forms of work which once mobilized the human organism as a whole are supplanted by occupations that tax the eyes or the nerves. While the mind is dulled and the human musculature becomes flaccid, nerves become overly sensitive and raw. The anxieties and tensions created by intensive, sedentary work are reinforced by an exaggerated responsiveness of the nervous system as a whole.

The metropolis offers very little to counteract the oversimplification of the daily work routine. The urban dweller encounters few changes in colour to awaken his visual senses; he receives virtually no respite from the artificial world in which he is immersed during working hours. Areas in which he can walk freely on soil and amid vegetation are disappearing; new dwellings, most of them noteworthy for their lack of architectural inspiration, are encroaching on the last open spaces in American cities. Public parks are likely to be congested during the day and in the evening they often attract delinquent elements, whose presence discourages the respectable urban dweller from venturing into their precincts. American urban life has retreated indoors. This retreat is due partly to the erosion of human solidarity in large cities, partly to the seductive powers of the mass media. The average urban dweller is likely to pursue the same insensate, sedentary way of life during his leisure time that he follows during his working hours.

Many aspects of metropolitan life, while trivial in themselves, aggravate the effects of urban modes of work. The nervous strain that the city dweller feels at his job begins to gather within him even before he gets to work. He encounters inconveniences, rudeness and congestion on public conveyances; he is beleaguered by countless small anxieties, many of which seldom rise to the level of consciousness. An all-pervasive irritation collects within him on his way to work, at work, between working hours and on the way home. Mechanical noises are everywhere. They invade even the hours of sleep as a result of the growing web of highways that reaches into every part of the city. Advertising media assail the senses with garish images and sounds; their message is crude and elemental, designed to startle and perhaps to shock the viewer into a response. Recreation seldom furnishes the average urban dweller with the experiences denied to him in the daily bustle of life—moments of genuine serenity, silence and gentle changes of scene. More often than not, urban recreation merely removes him temporarily from the afflictions of his environment without replenishing his reserves. It provides him with surcease from anxiety and nervous strain rather than with restoration of vitality.

Unfortunately, these problems are no longer confined to the city. The metropolis establishes the social standards of the entire country. Owing to its commanding economic and cultural position, it sets the pace of national life and establishes nearly all the criteria of national taste. Many distinctively urban forms of work and play have invaded the most remote rural areas of the United States, where they generate the same stresses in the villager and farmer that they do in the city dweller. The nature of agricultural work, moreover, is changing. As farming becomes increasingly industrialized, diversified physical work is reduced to a minimum by machines and one-crop agriculture. Although the farmer still pursues a less hurried way of life than his urban cousin, he is often beleaguered by even greater economic problems. Both in the city and on the land, a new type of man seems to be emerging. He is a nervous, excitable and highly strained individual who is burdened by continual personal anxieties and mounting social insecurity.

STRESS AND CHRONIC ILLNESS

What are the effects of persistent emotional stress on human health?

Fifty years ago this question would have seemed irrelevant to the goals of medical research. The principal illnesses of the day were ascribed to the aging process, to a variety of "mechanical defects," such as blockages and ruptures, to a poor genetic endowment and to bacterial infection. Germs satisfied the need for precise explanations of disease. They entered the body in a limited number of ways; they could be isolated, cultured and tested on animals and human volunteers. With further knowledge, it was believed, all the effects produced by harmful bacteria would be understood and eventually controlled by some form of therapy. Emotional stress, on the other hand, was vague. It seemed to represent a generalized response on the part of the body to countless, often intangible stimuli. Although medicine was not unaware of the fact that emotional disturbances influenced the functioning of the heart and gastrointestinal tract, there seemed little reason to believe that stress played a causal role in the major diseases of man.

As chronic illnesses began to gain in importance, however, it became evident that the earlier approach was inadequate. Many arthritic conditions, for example, could not be explained by infection. Beginning slowly and insidiously, arthritis often produced in the end a hopelessly crippled, bedridden patient who faced a lifetime of pain and inactivity.

At the same time, such words as "strain" and "anxiety" began to acquire real physiological meaning, denoting conditions that involved glandular conditions, biochemical changes in tissues and involuntary activity of the nervous system. It was soon found that these physiological changes could produce or alleviate many of the symptoms associated with the common chronic diseases of our time.

A growing number of physicians now agree that emotional stress is a very important disease-promoting factor. It is safe to say that some disorders, such as peptic ulcers, arise primarily from anxiety and tension. During the latter part of the nineteenth century, peptic ulcers were regarded as a relatively uncommon disorder and there arose very confused explanations of what caused the illness. Physicians generally believed that it occurred more frequently in women than in men; it was looked upon as a disorder primarily of "chlorotic," or anemic, girls.

In the medical textbooks of the day, discussions of peptic ulcers were confined to descriptions of symptoms and dietary therapy. With the passing years, however, the disease became a widespread and serious problem. Today, peptic ulcers afflict about 2½ million Americans; each year nearly 400,000 are disabled for more than a week. Although a case of ulcers may often arouse a great deal of levity, the disease can reach grave proportions. About ten thousand Americans die of peptic ulcers every year. According to data compiled by the U. S. National Health Survey of 1957-9, the overwhelming majority of ulcer victims (73 per cent) are men. More cases appear in the thirty-five-to-forty-four age group—the years of greatest business and vocational activity—than in any other ten-year period of life.

Emotional stress is also deeply implicated in disorders of the blood vessels and the heart. "Physicians have long felt that the rapid pace of modern civilization might somehow be contributing to the development of heart disease," notes a report by the National Heart Institute. "The man who develops coronary artery disease is very frequently a hard-driving individual living in a state of more or less constant tension. In recent years evidence has accumulated that one way in which nervous tension may accelerate the development of coronary artery disease is through an elevation of the [blood] serum cholesterol level."

The evidence is impressive. In 1957, Friedman, Rosenman and Carroll, of Mount Zion Hospital in San Francisco, began a study of the serum cholesterol level and blood-clotting time in forty male accountants during and after the tax season—sharply contrasting periods of high and low occupational stress. Blood was taken from the accountants twice weekly from January to June and detailed records were kept of weight, diet and changing work loads. "When studied individually," the investigators report, "each subject's highest serum cholesterol consistently occurred during severe occupational or other stress and his lowest at times of minimal stress. The results could not be ascribed to any changes of weight, exercise, or diet. Marked acceleration of blood clotting time consistently occurred at the time of maximum occupational stress, in contrast to normal blood clotting during periods of respite."

Studies of a similar nature have been made of medical students during examination week. In 1958 a report of P. T. Wertlake at the College of Medical Evangelists in Los Angeles showed that the average serum cholesterol level of the students rose 11 per cent during the four-day period in which they took school tests. The investigators found that nearly half of the students responded to the stress situation with increases ranging from 16 to 137 milligram per cent over a mean control level of 213. The serum cholesterol level of one student rose from an average control level of 259 milligram per cent prior to the school examinations to a peak of 536 during one of the examination days—an increase of more than 100 percent.

It would be wrong to suppose, however, that our knowledge of the link between emotional stress and illness is based entirely on statistical findings. During the past two decades, researchers have discovered a number of the biochemical effects that persistent anxiety produces in the human body. Attention has focused primarily on the adrenal glands, which cap the kidneys. The surface layer, or cortex, of these glands produces a number of highly potent regulatory chemical substances, or hormones. The cortical hormones, or corticoids, help the body to ward off disease and resist the effects of physical damage.

A number of adrenal corticoids (aldosterone and DOC, for example) promote inflammation—the heat, swelling and redness with which tissues react to common injuries. Although inflammation protects the body from bacterial invasion by "walling off" an injured area, the inflammatory process would go too far if it were not for anti-inflammatory corticoids, such as cortisone, which limit the process and prevent it from becoming needlessly widespread. The output of cortisone, in turn, is stimulated by ACTH, a hormone produced by the pituitary gland, situated at the base of the skull. The control of inflammation requires a balanced secretion of ACTH, of the pro-inflammatory corticoids and of the anti-inflammatory corticoids. If the balance in the secretion of these three types of hormones is altered, the inflammatory process may damage parts of the body.

Secretions of ACTH and the corticoids are influenced by the emotional state of the individual as well as by physical injury. This discovery has aroused strong suspicions that the corticoids and, by inference, persistent nervous strain, anxiety and emotional conflicts play important roles in the occurrence of certain chronic disorders. In a review of the literature on rheumatoid arthritis and stress, Leon Hellman has suggested that "a more subtle form of stress in the guise of emotional conflicts is implicated in changes of the pituitary-adrenal system so as to render it less responsive or to alter the balance between various adrenal hormones secreted.

A patient with rheumatoid arthritis would cure himself if his hypothalamus [a nerve center in the forebrain] and pituitary would interlock to increase the secretion of ACTH." According to Hellman, it is quite possible that the production of ACTH is inhibited by a "neural block" arising from deep-seated emotional conflicts. Both ACTH and cortisone have been used with considerable success in treating arthritic disorders. The hormones alleviate rheumatoid symptoms so dramatically that hopelessly crippled, bedridden arthritics have been restored to almost complete use of their limbs.

The adrenal corticoids, however, influence more than the inflammatory process. They exercise extensive control over the level of minerals and sugar (glucose) in the blood. An imbalance in corticoid secretion is likely to have far-reaching effects on the body's metabolism and on organs that are commonly damaged by metabolic disorders, notably the heart and kidneys. By administering the pro-inflammatory hormone DOC to white Leghorn chicks, for example, Hans Selye and his co-workers at the University of Montreal were able to produce degenerative changes in the kidneys, with ensuing high blood pressure, hardening of the blood vessels and cardiac disease. During the course of the experiment, the DOCtreated chicks "began to drink much more water than the controls which were not given the hormone and gradually they developed a kind of dropsy.

Their bodies became enormously swollen with fluid accumulations under the skin and they began to breathe with difficulty, gasping for air, just like certain cardiac patients." By degrees, Selye's results and those of other researchers in the field began to include a large number of common chronic illnesses. Pro- and anti-inflammatory corticoids, it was found, seem to play roles of varying importance in diabetes, thyroid disorders, peptic ulcers and psychic disturbances. The anti-inflammatory corticoids have been very useful in combating many of these illnesses. Cortisone frequently produces striking though temporary remissions in cases of acute leukemia and the surgical removal of the adrenal glands often inhibits the growth of certain forms of cancer.

Selye has developed a general theory of stress from the data on the interplay of adrenal hormones. Stress consists of the physical changes within an organism which are caused by any environmental stimulus, whether it be heat, cold, infection, or a chemical irritant and by the emotional disturbances we encounter in man. All living things have an adaptive mechanism that produces changes in the organism in response to changes in its environment. The adrenal corticoids in man and higher animals are essentially chemical agents. that compel a living thing to respond internally to external stimuli. Every stimulus, desirable or harmful, produces a general stress reaction. Stress, in effect, is an important part of life.

But stress always results in a certain amount of "wear and tear" on the organism. "Many people believe that, after they have exposed themselves to very stressful activities, a rest can restore them to where they were before," Selye writes. "This is false. Experiments on animals have clearly shown that each exposure leaves an indelible scar, in that it uses up reserves of adaptability which cannot be replaced. It is true that immediately after some harassing experience, rest can restore us almost to the original level of fitness by eliminating acute fatigue. But the emphasis is on the word *almost*. Since we constantly go through periods of stress and rest during life, just a little deficit of adaptation energy every day adds up—it adds up to what we call aging."

No one, to be sure, can eliminate the "wear and tear" of life, but a reasonably clear distinction can be made between the "stress of life" and stress that results in ill health. Stress that results in ill health is severe, persistent and one-sided. Selye has demonstrated that if stress is too severe, the resistance and life span of the organism are drastically reduced.

An experimental rat may adapt itself for a time to a strong irritant, but the adaptation is made at a high price; longevity is decreased and general resistance is seriously impaired.

If the animal is exposed to even minor but persistent stress, comparable to the "low-grade" nervous tension and anxiety usually found in modern urban man, it pays a similar price for adaptation.

The animal is easily injured by irritants that ordinarily do not produce serious physical damage. The interplay of stress responses is so complex that the reader must turn to Selye's own work, *The Stress of Life*, for a detailed discussion. In nearly all cases of severe or persistent stress, Selye has found evidence of thickened arteries, heart abnormalities, kidney damage and increased blood pressure.

But Selye's work also demonstrates that stress need not be harmful, provided it is balanced and varied. A sheltered, sedentary life that lacks a variety of stimuli produces an undeveloped, often inadequate stress mechanism as well as an undeveloped personality.

A sheltered person has great difficulty in coping with many of the stimuli and irritants inevitably encountered in the normal course of life. If there is any notion that sums up Selye's "stress of life" theory, it is the "pre-scientific" intuition that variety and balance—emotional, physical and intellectual—are the bases not only for true individuality but for lasting health.

Selye's plea for variety in life, however, rests on a well-thought-out hypothesis. Man, as a complex, multicellular animal, is composed of many organs and systems, each of which bears a different amount of stress. The organs that compose his body do not "wear out" evenly.

Death invariably comes "because one vital part has worn out too early in proportion to the rest of the body. The lesson seems to be that, as far as man can regulate his life by voluntary actions, he should seek to equalize stress throughout his being, by what we have called *deviation*, the frequent shifting-over of work from one part to the other. The human body—like the tires on a car, or the rug on a floor—wears longest when it wears evenly.

We can do ourselves a great deal of good in this respect by just yielding to our natural cravings for variety in everyday life. We must not forget that the more we vary our actions the less any one part suffers from attrition."

Conceivably, an informed individual can try to cultivate a mature outlook that will lend distance to the petty irritations produced by the urban milieu. If circumstances permit, he can establish a personal regimen of after-work exercise and frequent excursions to the countryside. But on the whole, the metropolis exposes him to limited, intense occupational stimuli that produce an equally limited, intense stress response. A few organs continue to bear nearly the entire burden of daily life. Organs and systems that are not activated by modern forms of work and play are likely to be sheltered by the "conveniences" that the city affords.

"One might question whether stress is peculiarly characteristic of our sheltered civilization, with all its comforts and amenities," observe P. C. Constantinides and Niall Carey in a general discussion of Selye's work. "Yet these very protections—modern laborsaving devices, clothing, heating—have rendered us all the more vulnerable and sensitive to the slightest stress. What was a mild stress to our forebears now frequently represents a minor crisis. Moreover, the frustrations and repressions arising from emotional conflicts in the modern world, economic and political insecurity, the drudgery associated with many modern occupations—all these represent stresses as formidable as the most severe physical injuries."

THE PROBLEMS OF OVERURBANIZATION

A number of urban problems have arisen that no city dweller can hope to solve or even meliorate on his own; they can be solved only by the community as a whole. One such problem, urban air pollution, has become very widespread and constitutes a serious hazard to human health. "Millions of citizens are living in an air ocean that is, on good evidence, unhealthy to breathe," observes Herman E. Hilleboe, New York State Commissioner of Health. "Cities with the heaviest pollution load tend to rank high both in death and incidence rates for a number of diseases. This includes heart disease and cancer, the ranking killers and disablers of our time." Among the new pollutants that will soon be added to our environment, Hilleboe warns, are "by-products from petroleum and from synthetic materials spawned by our fastgrowing nuclear technology and from high-energy solid and liquid fuels. We are creating a new environment but we have not as yet done what is necessary to make this environment healthful and habitable for its people. Here again it is difficult to dramatize the matter of air pollution."

The problem has been dramatized by cases in which air pollution reached the proportions of an emergency, comparable in many ways to an epidemic. Until fairly recently, serious cases of air pollution usually occurred in highly industrialized river valleys. Two such cases-one in the Meuse Valley in Belgium in 1930, which claimed sixty lives and the other in Donora, Pennsylvania, in 1948, which killed twenty people—were due primarily to toxic fumes from metallurgical plants. To some degree, both could be regarded as industrial accidents, which could have been averted if suitable measures had been taken to control the effluents of local mills. A much greater respect for the potentially disastrous consequences of air pollution was created by the smog that descended upon London, a predominantly commercial city, during December 1952. Although the episode was brief, the daily death rate reached very high levels, comparable to those of London's cholera epidemic in 1854 and its influenza epidemic in 1918-19.

At dawn on Friday, December 5, the air in London began to thicken perceptibly. Unusual weather conditions caused a heavy smog of urban pollutants to linger over the city for four days. During the first twenty-four hours the death rate doubled, the total for the day reaching 400. The next day, Saturday, it rose to 600 and on each of the two following days, Sunday and Monday, it soared to 900, although business and industrial activity was suspended on Sunday. On Tuesday, when the smog had already begun to lift, the number of deaths was 800 and the death rate remained high for several weeks thereafter.

The London smog claimed at least 4,000 lives. The majority of deaths occurred among infants and elderly people, but William P. Dowie Logan, Britain's chief medical statistician, emphasizes that "it was by no means confined to the very young or the very old." The death rate in the fifteen-to-forty-four age group increased about 50 per cent. Deaths from coronary heart disease rose from 118 in the seven-day period immediately preceding the incident to 281 in the week that followed it, while deaths from bronchitis soared from 76 to 704, almost a tenfold increase.

The possibility that a lethal smog comparable to the one that descended on London, will develop somewhere in the United States cannot be excluded. If the word "smog" is defined as air pollution that produces haziness in the atmosphere and irritation of the eyes, nose and throat, then many American communities experience smog. The situation in Los Angeles is notoriously bad; the city is afflicted with fifty to seventy days of smog every year. Smog is found to a lesser extent in New York, Washington, Philadelphia, Boston and other coastal metropolitan areas of the United States. The differences between smog in England and smog in the United States are due primarily to the differences in the irritants that pervade the air of the two countries. Air pollution in London is caused mainly by the combustion of coal, whereas the principal irritants in Los Angeles are produced by the combustion of petroleum products.

Experts have emphasized, however, that "in the London episode the air pollutants, when considered in terms of their human effects, closely resembled those present in the air of many large urban areas. These pollutants were quite similar to those of many other urban areas in that they are irritating to the exposed living membranes (of the eyes, nose, throat and respiratory tract). For example, although Los Angeles air pollution is chemically different from that of London the two resemble each other in their effects on man since each causes irritation of exposed living membranes."

Ordinarily, smog is episodic and localized. In the long run, a more serious problem is posed by persistent, low-grade air pollution, which is often imperceptible to the senses and changes relatively little from day to day. This form of air pollution is very widespread in the United States. Nearly 10,000 communities, containing the overwhelming majority of the American people, have persistent air pollution problems. According to a recent report by the New York State Air Pollution Control Board: "Of the state's 40 communities with populations of more than 25,000, only one had negligible air pollution. The combined survey data show that approximately threefifths of the communities of 5,000 to 25,000 population and about one third of those with less than 5,000 people, had major or minor air pollution." A survey of Texas by the U. S. Public Health Service showed that three quarters of the state's communities with populations of more than 10,000 had "objectionable air pollution."

Although patterns of air pollution vary from one community to another, it is generally agreed that the air in nearly all American cities contains a number of highly toxic substances, most of which are waste products of industrial plants, motor vehicles and heating equipment. The solid particles in an urban atmosphere often include such highly toxic substances as lead, beryllium and arsenic. Common air-borne gases and vapors include sulfuric-acid mist, sulfur dioxide, carbon monoxide, formaldehyde, oxides of nitrogen, ammonia and scores of organic vapor contaminants. At least a hundred air pollutants have been identified and the interaction of gases, vapors and solid particles in the atmosphere produces many other compounds that have not been chemically analyzed. Several known toxicants that pollute the air are characterized by synergistic activity; they are more toxic together than when each is absorbed individually. For example, an effect that is more than additive is produced by the inhalation of carbon monoxide together with nitrogen oxide, two of the most common pollutants in the urban atmosphere.

The average individual breathes about 16,000 quarts of air daily. If he lives in an urban environment, his lungs receive about four times as many air contaminants as those of a rural dweller. John H. Ludwig, of the U. S. Public Health Service, suggests that repeated exposure to "relatively low levels of air pollution" may be involved in the development of chronic degenerative diseases, including skin and lung cancer, heart and vascular disorders and chronic bronchitis. During periods when urban air pollution is at its height, the contaminants may worsen existing chronic diseases, especially heart disorders, by interfering with the passage of oxygen through the membranes of the lungs into the blood stream. Certain air pollutants may combine with body proteins to form allergy-inducing, or allergenic, substances and lead to increasing sensitization and allergic reactions.

If the possible consequences of air pollution listed by Ludwig seem to be farfetched, let us enumerate some of the contaminants produced by the automobile, the principal source of air-borne toxicants in large American cities. Nearly 80 per cent of the pollutants that produce smog in Los Angeles come from motor vehicles. In burning 1,000 gallons of fuel, an automobile discharges 17 pounds of sulfur dioxide, about 18 pounds of aldehydes (estimated as formaldehyde), 25 to 75 pounds of oxides of nitrogen (estimated as nitrogen dioxide), 200 to 400 pounds of complex organic compounds and over 3,000 pounds of carbon monoxide.

Sulfur dioxide is both an irritant and a poison. It is probably a major contributor to the high incidence of chronic bronchitis in England. There is evidence to indicate that a fairly low level of sulfur dioxide—"a level not infrequently found in air"—is sufficient to produce temporary spasms of the smooth muscles in the lungs. In "somewhat higher concentrations," the compound produces severe inflammation and peeling of the respiratory membranes. Formaldehyde is a corrosive poison that not only irritates the respiratory membranes but also affects the central nervous system and nitrogen dioxide is a highly toxic gas that is extremely dangerous even in such relatively low quantities as 100 parts per million.

Several of the organic compounds produced by the combustion of gasoline and diesel oil are carcinogenic. This has been clearly established by Paul Kotin, of the University of California. When tarry material from the exhausts of motor vehicles was painted on laboratory mice, skin tumors appeared in 50 per cent of the animals. The largest amount of carcinogenic substances, according to Kotin's findings, is produced by slow-running and idling engines—that is, under conditions prevalent in areas with congested traffic.

A problem that has been largely ignored in the United States is the danger of chronic carbon monoxide poisoning. Until recently, conventional medical opinion held that carbon monoxide (CO) is rapidly removed from the blood stream. Few physicians regarded the enormous output of the gas by motor vehicles as a danger to public health. According to recent reports, however, carbon monoxide may be retained by the body for relatively long periods of time, perhaps as much as several weeks. The problem has aroused a great deal of concern in Europe, where the conviction is growing that chronic carbon monoxide poisoning is a serious hazard of the automobile era. In the United States, Richard Prindle, of the U. S. Public Health Service, emphasizes that "in a community in which carbon monoxide levels exist, 24 hours a day, seven days a week, for the lifetime of an individual, chronic CO poisoning is a distinct possibility." We need only consider the fact that smoking produces a definite level of carbon monoxide in the blood "to realize that coupling this with frequent, although fluctuating exposures to CO in the ambient air... might well lead to serious consequences in a large population."

Another problem that cannot be solved without the co-operation of the entire community is water pollution.

Water is a traditional medium for the transmission of germs and toxic substances. During the past three generations vigorous efforts on the part of medical and public health officials have enormously reduced the hazard created by water-borne infectious agents, but today old problems of pollution are beginning to recur and new ones to appear, especially in communities that obtain the greater part of their drinking water from rivers.

Although Americans tend to make a fetish of cleanliness, an appalling amount of untreated or inadequately treated urban sewage is discharged into river water—water which is often taken up again for public consumption by communities downstream.

Added to urban sewage are wastes from chemical factories, slaughterhouses and metallurgical plants. Although sewage and industrial wastes have produced local public health crises in the past, the postwar expansion of cities and metropolitan areas is turning water pollution into a grave national problem, comparable in many respects to that created by urban air pollution.

Attempts by federal, state and municipal authorities to control the contamination of our water are complicated by frequent changes in the composition of industrial and urban wastes.

Today drinking water may contain a wide variety of new bleaches, detergents, petrochemical and metallurgical wastes, insecticides, dyes and radioactive compounds.

Few if any of these contaminants are removed by ordinary methods of water purification. Rolf Eliassen, of the Massachusetts Institute of Technology, points out that the "exotic organic chemicals" discharged by petrochemical plants into streams "are not even detected by present conventional means of water analysis."

Neither industry nor pollution-control laboratories have been able to form a reliable picture of the long-range effects of the newer pollutants on public health. "Let us all be honest with ourselves," declares Robert A. Kehoe. "Specifications for human health and welfare, in relation to the common contaminants of many of our sources of water, do not exist and we shall not be able to deal effectively with this problem of public health until they can be formulated on sound physiological facts."

At the same time, the traditional problem of waterborne infections is gaining greater significance. Many cases of acute illnessess are being attributed to polluted has been lifted. Although Pittsburgh does not enjoy pure air, a reduction has been achieved in the more offensive pollutants that once filled the city's atmosphere. Air pollution programmes have gained ground primarily against the smoke and grime of the old Industrial Revolution, just as social reform has scored its greatest triumphs over illiteracy and child labour.

Since World War II, however, there has been a new industrial revolution and the problems of urban life have acquired new dimensions.

On the one hand, the sources of urban pollution have increased in number and variety; many pollutants, such as those produced by the automobile, are difficult to manage, even where everyone is willing to co-operate on the problem. On the other hand, metropolitan regions are being burdened beyond their capacity to cope with air pollutants and to meet the need for clean water.

Their waterways and atmosphere are expected to absorb a staggering quantity of waste products from industrial plants, homes and vehicles. Currently the United States must dispose of over 18 billion pounds of sewage solids every year, an increase of 70 per cent in the past two decades.

The water table in many areas of the United States is being lowered by the voracious demands of highly concentrated populations and expanding industries.

At the same time that the number of pollutants has increased, the ecological preconditions for wholesome air and plentiful water are being undermined. A major disequilibrium is arising between town and country, industry and the biotic environment and population and regional resources.

Rene Dubos, of the Rockefeller Institute for Medical Research, places smog among the major environmental factors that have unleashed the "Apocalyptic horsemen" of modern disease.

According to Dubos, St. John the Divine's vision on the isle of Patmos is symbolic of present-day urban and industrial life. The first horsemen of the Apocalypse to be seen by the saint were Famine and Pestilence.

"Then another, even more terrifying visitation was sent by the angered Deity," Dubos recalls. "After the fifth angel had sounded his trumpet he opened the bottomless pit and 'there arose a smoke out of the pit, as the smoke of a great furnace; and the sun and the air were darkened by reason of the smoke of the pit.'

And out of the bottomless pit came the scorpions that did not kill men but tormented them for five months before final destruction came 'by the fire and by the smoke and by the brimstone.' The time of fulfillment of the Apocalypse may not be far off."

Dubos is not being overly dramatic. We are producing a new spectrum of environmental hazards whose full effects still await the passage of time. The trends are not encouraging.

"Many diseases that are thought to be associated with, or caused by, air pollution have been increasing over the years," Prindle writes. "Included amongst these are the respiratory cancers, emphysema, chronic bronchitis and cor pulmonale. If air pollution continues to increase, one can only conjecture that this rising incidence of disease will continue and that the effect upon the health of the nation—and over the technologically-expanding world—may be severely augmented. The overall effect of air pollution on the economy, the health and the welfare of the people may become a disaster."

The effects of air pollution on public health will be difficult to judge for many years to come. A large number of adults straddle two worlds. They were born and raised in communities that have only recently acquired the features of metropolitan life. The early years of their lives were spent in the pre-nuclear age. But it is difficult to ignore the portents found in the high incidence of chronic diseases in all age groups of the population. Without a basic solution to the problems of urban life, Dubos's apprehension may prove to be amply justified.

5

Voluntary and Commercial Transactions: Paradigms of Health Tourism

The terms 'sex tourism' and 'prostitute' or 'sex worker' are self-evident, but it has also been shown that many different situations and interpretations exist. Hence, is there a single definition of these terms that encompasses all of these situations? It has also been argued that tourism presents an opportunity for people, male and female, to exploit their marginal status and their economic power to cross the line between the licit and illicit boundaries between the socially sanctioned and the 'socially suspect'. This blurring of the boundary needs to be examined more closely. The blurring or crossing of any boundary is not a neutral act. Nor are boundaries without importance. Simmel (1971:353) notes: 'The boundary, above and below, is our means for finding direction in the infinite space of our worlds.' Thus, the redrawing of boundaries means a redrawing of the frameworks of personal and societal knowledge and values. Boundaries are points of disjuncture and flux, and thus perversely, the existence of a boundary may actually act to ease the transmission of discourse just as, according to Porter (1997) they act as funnels for flows of trade, HIV and sex trafficking.

The crossing of such boundaries has the potential for the socially condemned, the apparent deviant, to enter the discourse of that which is normally socially sanctioned. The wider society must decide the basis upon which any penetration of the boundary with the 'illegitimate' is to be judged. The presence of, and interaction with, the illicit margin must be either denied or recognised. Various options exist. Either the illegitimate continues to be condemned, and those who interact with it are also subject to condemnation. Or, as is often the case with prostitution, the relationship between licit and illicit is left ambiguous, a grey area of hypocrisy, and as such subject to injustice. The ambiguity arises because of a wish to avoid punishment of the transgressor in the form of the client - a position that can only be possessed by one with power within the social framework, and whose transgression is thereby subject to varying degrees of toleration. Third, societal change may force a growing recognition of the injustices to which subordinate groups are subjected, and thus legal, political and social changes occur within which the mainstream society recognises those injustices and the conditions which created them. What causes this to occur? For any system both or either internal and external factors may force change.

In the case of sex tourism, as already noted, changing social norms within society as to sexuality may change views as to the roles that sex workers perform. It has been argued that within Western societies a greater recognition of the role gender plays, the separation of concepts of gender and sexuality, the growing tolerance of lesbian and homosexual communities and individuals, the changing roles of women and the expression of female aspirations through feminism have all had, as a by-product, a questioning of the role of sex workers. It is not a uniform discourse as has already been demonstrated, but it increasingly brings the role of sex workers, male and female, into a wider arena. The role of HIV/AIDS has also proven to be a catalyst in thinking. Evidence of this is provided through the personal experiences of those working with and on behalf of sex workers. Cheryl Overs, the NWSP (NetWork of Sex Projects) Coordinator and an organiser of the representation of sex workers at the 1995 Conference on Women in Beijing says:

Everything has changed. The women's movement is no longer the home of the sex workers' rights movement. The happiest time for me was the late eighties and early nineties when HIV/AIDS brought new links with gay men, and Madonna rose and rose. Our small band of sex worker rights activists suddenly had a new political family. Once a pro-sex feminist theory was articulated we even had new supporters from the women's movement who were listening to sex workers for the first time. Young feminists matured with the notion of sex workers rights as a fixed entry on the women's rights agenda. I enjoyed that because I felt exonerated. It had been hurtful, as well as frustrating, that for many years feminist puritans have said that our demands for recognition of sex work as valid work were a product of false consciousness which blurred our perceptions of our damaging experiences as victims of the sex industry.

The importance of HIV/AIDS cannot be over-estimated in affecting the attitudes and policies of non-Western governments. Notably, the Thai government has had to recognise the potential spread of AIDS not only through its sex industry, but in the transmission of AIDS to the rural communities of Thailand. In July 1994 the Thai Ministry of Health estimated that the number of HIV positive people in Thailand numbered 650,000. While this represents about 1 per cent of the total population, the figures for the rural areas of the north from which many of the sex workers come indicate that 7 per cent of the populations of those areas are HIV positive. Safe sex programmes are being initiated in the tourist bars (Hanson, 1998), but implementation appears to be uneven, and the problems go beyond the soi of Patpong to those areas which serve the need of local men. Safe sex programmes are also unlikely to have much impact on the traffickers of women. As will be described in, there does exist large-scale trafficking of women, much of it brutally exploitative, systematic and illustrative of a wider social ill within the body politic.

That it occurs at all implies that corruption exists in the highest levels of government. That corruption is a problem with economic and social consequences has all too often been demonstrated. It is not a problem isolated to non-democratic governments. The evidence of experiences in Italy has shown that even Prime Ministers have been allegedly involved in corrupt practices. Organised crime in countries like Russia are known to be involved in prostitution and drugs, and the commodification of women under such circumstances is no longer an academic conceptualisation of spreading consumerism, but a harsh, dangerous reality for many women. Even within what are generally deemed to be more enlightened countries like New Zealand where women can work in licensed massage parlours, and where working as a prostitute is not illegal, danger still exists.

Earlier reference was made to sex workers having, like any other worker, good days and bad. Unfortunately, as is known from past murders, the bad day might mean the loss of life.

This real danger is even more to the fore when women are in positions of being abused.Thus far, no definition of sex tourism has been undertaken apart from the notion that it involves interaction between liminal people. The point of any definition is to more clearly identify what is under discussion, but the very act of definition both focuses on and perhaps limits the nature of the problem.

For this, definition will be attempted, but by means of first identifying the parametres under which sex tourism operates. From this it appears that sex tourism operates under the following dichotomies from the perspectives of both parties:

- It is 'voluntary' or exploitative.
- It is commercial or non-commercial.
- It is enhancing or degrading for self-identity.

While Ryan (2000) uses these three sets of continua to analyse paradigms of sex tourism, in themselves they are arguably incomplete. What is evident in the literature is that a macro- and micro-perspective exists. As already alluded to when describing Turner's conceptualisation of liminoid people, such an analysis as that suggested by Ryan (2000) tends to work best at the individual psychological level. As many authors testify when discussing sex tourism in locations like Thailand, there exists too a macro-level of sociopolitical structures which create and perpetuate the infra-structures of sex tourism on a global level.

For O'Connell Davidson 'sex tourism must be recognised as first and foremost a form of economic exploitation' (1995:61), but one unlike other forms of exploitation in that no mutual set of dependencies exist. She argues that sex tourists, as a collective group, are not locked into a dialectical relationship with Thai sex workers, as prostitutes are unable to win concessions from their clients who are free to move on elsewhere. The maintenance of the flow of sex tourists is, she argues, one that is sustained by 'governments, international travel companies, hoteliers, local business people and so on, who have an economic interest in maintaining the flow of sex tourists'. Thus, in her view, programmes that direct action against sex tourists have but a marginal chance of improving the lot of the women involved. To what extent such dialectical relationships exist is debatable, and thus it is important to examine each of the three paradigms listed above, but to do so at a micro- and macro-perspective.

To undertake such a task is, however, not one conducted in a positivistic frame of enquiry. There are multiple truths, and the three paradigms are not independent of each other, but interactive. Equally, the distinction between macro- and micro-levels of analysis becomes increasingly difficult to sustain when looked at in detail. It also raises the question of to what extent is it possible to develop an explanatory model of sex tourism? At the micro-level the interactions between sex worker and client are individualistic, even while commonalities may be discerned. At the macro-level the different legal regimes in various countries, the miscellaneous social and ethical mores - all contribute to a series of case studies within national settings as well as illustrating generalities. Thus, of necessity, sex tourism is pluralistic, multivocal and multidimensional in its forms.

The question of how voluntary the work is from the viewpoint of the sex worker is a moot point. It may be argued that no sex worker enters the industry on a voluntary basis as it is a choice made generally out of economic necessity. This is not a new observation. Bell (1994:103) cites Parent-Duchatelet's study of Parisian prostitutes in 1831 and the conclusion that: 'Of all the causes of prostitution, particularly in Paris and probably in all large cities, none is more active than lack of work and the misery which is the inevitable result of insufficient wages.'

There is sufficient evidence that this continues to be the case from what has been published on prostitution to mention McLeod (1982), Boyle (1994), Jordan (1991) Kempadoo and Doezema (1998) among many such writers. It is seemingly a motive related to many forms of sex work. Ryan and Martin (2001) cite such a motive among many who enter the sex industry as strippers or exotic dancers. For example, one of their Australian respondents stated: 'If I was an unskilled man, no qualifications, left school early, I could still get $30 an hour by going on the building sites. What does a woman do in the same position - we can't do the same.'

Another, who had been an exotic dancer for ten years, described how she had left home, had initially had a job working in a retail store, had left that job because she had had a disagreement with a supervisor and thus:

There I was, no job, no money, so I started stripping. The only reason why you do it is the money. I know I can't keep doing this so at the end of this season I intend going back to school - I'd like to do psychology - you learn a lot in this job. Yet, while there is money to be made within the sex industry, few women will become rich, or even specifically well off from the industry. Prostitution may provide 'the bread', but the extra 'jam' is more noticeable by its absence rather than presence. Adult film actress, Nina Hartley, makes the point that 'while it's not a bad living, you ain't gonna get rich doing it', and points out that, as a film actress, you have to understand what it means to 'have a permanent record of you with a man's penis in your mouth'. The monetary expenses of working in the sex industry are high. Ryan and Martin (2001) describe the expenses involved in exotic dancing - the high cost of shoes which wear out quickly and the need to continually prepare costumes. It is of interest to note the different interpretations of the same act. What to the sex worker is a necessary investment is, for the moralist, a sign of decadence. To again cite Parent-Duchatelet, among the reasons cited for prostitution are 'vanity and the desire for the glitter of luxurious clothes is with idleness one of the most active causes of prostitution, particularly in Paris'.

While sex workers cite money as the reason for their work, like all workers, it is not so much money per se, but what money permits that is the reason for their work. Many motives and wants exist.

For some, money is the way in which a decent lifestyle is obtained. Sex work is the means by which single women provide food, a home and clothes for their families. For some older women, it is a means to bring in extra comforts. For others, as described by Nina Lopez Jones, it may be a passport to safety. Thus:

Having the money is also a way of avoiding a lot of other rape and violence in your life generally, whether from your family or not. It means you can afford to take a cab rather than waiting out on the street for a bus and running the risk of being attacked there. It means that you don't have to work necessarily in a job where either sex with your boss, or some kind of sexual work with your boss, is a requirement. It means you don't have to sleep with your landlord so that he doesn't evict you.

Plumridge's work in New Zealand seconds this as a motive. Reporting this research Ansley cites one respondent as saying:

I thought you got married, you'd be bright-eyed and bushy-tailed and rosy down the track. Instead there were 15 years of hell, beaten black and blue, raped ... I went through hell, broken windows, baseball batted. To him I was nothing but a sponging whore.

Yet Plumridge's work confirms that of other researchers that, in New Zealand, as elsewhere there exists a hierarchy of prostitution, and while parlour workers may prosper, those who work on the street continue to risk being beaten. The escape from violent marriages, for a minority, has so conditioned them to the prevalence of violence that the ever-present risk of danger for those working on the street continues to be less than that previously experienced.

But other motives also exist for continuing in the sex industry, either as prostitutes, strippers or workers in the pornographic industry. Ansley (2000) reports that the motive to work as a sex worker is not always born of a wish to escape financial marginality - it is a means by which women can prosper. It is a way of getting ahead, of getting a house. Nonetheless, such advancement does depend, as already noted, upon the management of the brothels where the women work. Bonds may be required, fines levied, and when business is slow, charges may be introduced for things like laundry bills - all of which reduces the money earned.

Yet several women do find it an interesting and reasonably lucrative lifestyle. In addition to money, the work brings several advantages of being an independent worker able to travel and work in many places of the world quite easily. Ryan et al. cite one of their respondents, an Australian worker in a Wellington, New Zealand, massage parlour, as saying:

At present I'm working here - I'll do it a for a few weeks, then I'll go down to see South Island and work in Christchurch - and that way I'll see South Island - I'll stay as long as I want. I've worked my way round lots of countries - it's a really good way to see places - you can stay as long as you want, people are nice - its better than most jobs.

Another sex worker said: 'It's a job - but it's not a bad job! I can work in a parlour or private. I've worked in Oz - had a good time there and spent longer and saw more than if I'd been in any other kind of work.'

In Ryan and Martin's (2001) paper on exotic dancing and the tourism industry one respondent, who had been dancing for eight years said:

I had been working in Woolworth's for a year and thought, I want to do more than this. I saw an advert for a club wanting bar work, so I phoned up, and it was quite open that it was a strip club, so I thought why not. Anyway I went for an interview and I walk in, it was the xxxx in Melbourne, and they have low tables for table dancing, and there was this women lap dancing and sticking her butt right in this guy's face and another dancing on the table and showing her pussy to this guy, no hands hiding it you know, just full on. I'd never seen this before. I was really naive, just 18, and I thought could I handle this? But I didn't want Woolworth's and so I got the job. At first I hated the girls, I thought all they wanted was just money. I didn't talk to them, but eventually I did and that's where I met xxx and I got to know just how nice they were. So eventually did a bit, you know never done any before, didn't know how to dance or handle the bar, and I got $2000 one week and thought 'wow'. Anyway, I decided to travel, hadn't been overseas before and went to London - that was great!

This statement confirms the motives for the need for money, but it also raises the issue of how women come to terms with the raw physical presence of sex work. O'Connell Davidson (1998) describes the ritualistic use of prostitutes by groups of men seeking to initiate one of their group into sexual experience. What is it like, she asks: to be taken to a total stranger by your friends or relatives and expected to immediately undress and engage in penetrative sex with this unknown person? What would it feel like to be expected to publicly and anonymously do that which you have been taught to believe is both private and intimate?

But it can be argued that the reality of the purchased sexual act for women is one of continually having to cope with this physical presence and question. What is it like to continually have to undress for a client whom you may not find attractive, for someone who by the power of the wallet alone has a perceived right to penetrate you, to fondle your private parts, to possibly enable them to live a fantasy that they would not otherwise talk about, much less do? And for the sex tourist, who in addition to the normal demands of a local client may bring a baggage of racist stereotypes of wild black women or demure oriental women, how does the woman cope with these demands not just occasionally, but perhaps every day of her working life? For O'Connell Davidson (1998:141) the answers partly lie in a process of commoditisation where the one creates of the other 'a function, an object' and where prostitution 'is valued because it strips women of the autonomy and separateness which clients find so very threatening'.

Yet, as has been already discussed, the very process of commodification permits the development of control, and of professionalism on the part of many sex workers. This process of commodification has numerous sides to it. First, it contains the danger of the sex worker perceiving him or herself as a separate commodity in order to survive in the job. In an interview with the first author, Jo said:

Why do women become engaged in sex work? It is the dressing up, looking good, being complimented, and it is the discovery of just how easy it is. Three minutes, and all that money.

But after a time the hanging around, the junk food, the continued routine just gets to you, and then it's the time to get out. There are a lot of women who are in it too long, they get hooked on the money, and they get hooked on drugs. The drugs are a recreational thing, and they help you get through the job. And there is a culture of drug taking - everyone is doing it.

From Jo's perspective, as a sex worker and in her role as an outreach worker, it is when you separate this commoditised role from yourself, and the role is the 'other', then it becomes necessary to leave the industry as this psychological distinction is but a short-term mode of coping and in the longer term is dangerous to the psyche. Michelle, another outreach worker and former prostitute stated:

Those who take on the role of the 'priestess' are so very few - they are a minority. Equally those being exploited by men in relationships are also a minority - they are extremes of a continuum, most fall in between. Each of us works out our own way - yet - I think I am a fully mature woman, able to cope with most things, but sometimes things come up from my past that are difficult to cope with - so what is it like for others?

Thus, if sex work is a commodity, it is also a job, and it is job within which women are able to, and do, take pride. The recognition of sex work as a job also means that the prostitute is no longer working at the margins of society, but can become a recognised tax payer and contributor to society through the normal ways in which any employee or employer does. Thus, for example, the New Zealand Prostitutes Collective has given advice to sex workers as to what job-related expenses can be claimed against taxation. However, what is applicable in New Zealand is not applicable in every country. Thus Phoenix (1995:66-67) argues that if the nature of prostitution is to be defined it must take into account:

- Place of work: where does the work take place?
- Mode of client contact: how do clients and workers get into contact with each other?
- Employment status: is the worker full-time, part-time, regular or casual?
- Peripheral activities: are there any other activities commercialised in the prostitution exchanges?
- Exchange practices: how are monies collected and distributed? What types of contracts exist?
- Formal relationships with others - what relationships exist with others apart from the client?
- Risks and protection: what risks to the worker are involved?

Thus, there is considerable difference between the girls and woman taken by force to work in backstreet brothels where she may be little more than a prisoner being raped by men who make payment only to her captors, to one who works independently, pays tax and who has considerable control over her clientele. Phoenix argues that significant differences exist between those who work on the streets, and those in massage parlours, escort agencies or from their homes.

There exists significant evidence that there are considerable differences between those who work in the same country as to working habits and patterns. For example, Plant (1997) argues that distinct differences exist between drug taking by sex workers in Glasgow and Edinburgh, noting very high levels of intravenous drug users in the former case whereas, in the capital, drug usage appeared to be of alcohol and cannabis. Pimping was much higher in Glasgow than in Edinburgh. The existence of pimping certainly seems to reduce any degree of voluntary work on the part of the sex worker. Silbert and Pines (1982) interviewed 200 sex workers in San Francisco. Seventy per cent reported that various forms of abuse affected their decision to become a prostitute and once on the streets, 70 per cent had been victimised by clients and pimps. Faugier (1994) argues that women in relationships with pimps are for the most part damaged both physically and psychologically. Milner and Milner (1972) quote one pimp as describing his relationship with a female prostitute as one where her personality is changed 'You create a different environment. It's a brainwashing process; the whole thing is creativity. When you turn a chick out, you take away every set of values and morality she had previously and create a different environment'.

The presentation of the pimp as an evil manipulator should not, argue Høigård and Finstad (1992), lead to 'easy' representations of the pimp as 'other' on the basis that it demarcates prostitution and its ills as a problem separate from wider society. Among many observations they make one might note their comment that: 'Many prostitutes have resources and personal qualities that make the average academic seem colourless and weak. Being in the position of a victim is a structural and relational attribute, separate from individual characteristics', and 'When the image of the outsider is not blocking our perception, we have to recognise that a number of young women today experience prostitution as the least of numerous evils. This says a good deal about their other alternatives'.

As seen from these examples and others previously discussed, there exists a considerable literature which has analysed the position of the prostitute as being the result of social structures that are male-dominated and possessing inequalities of economic wealth and power. It is argued that the sex worker is subordinate at both a personal and structural level because of male demand, and because males generally occupy the higher income levels. However, at least two different viewpoints exist. It should be noted that to argue different viewpoints exist is not to state that they are contrary perspectives, as the nature of prostitution and sex tourism is such that simultaneous differences can co-exist.

First, there is the issue that at an individual level prostitution does permit an expression of economic and pyschological independence. As already noted, it offers an occupation where women may decide their working hours to fit around their other roles as mother and care-giver to dependent others. While it may be argued that it is a structural problem that few well-paid jobs exist for women without high educational qualifications, it is true that sex work does provide such an occupation. Some feminists have argued that all that the prostitute does is to make explicit a truth about the female condition - that marriage itself is a contract whereby the woman exchanges sexual services for financial security. For Miles (1992) men get married only because they have to as a social obligation, and society rewards them to ensure their compliance by endowing them with power within the marriage.

Yet, she continues to argue, the state of marriage is such that it often ends up emasculating both parties. It is also a misrepresentation to argue that all sex workers have low levels of educational attainment. Equally, it is a falsehood to argue that all those students who do enter sex work to pay for tertiary education actually give up sex work upon graduation. Equally, it is false to maintain that all such students feel constrained in subsequent career choice because of a fear that their career will be prejudiced by their past sex work. Nonetheless, to argue that most sex workers are well educated would be an untenable position.

There are sex workers who admit to enjoying their work and their relationships with clients. Jordan (1991) interviews one such worker who claims to love all her clients. In interviews in Siren seven years later the same woman was still able to write:

To all those clients that I have loved over the past 18 years I say thank you for those stolen magic moments ... You have helped me understand the invisible thread between my being and yours, to know that sex is far more than just a physical act but a dance of our souls together, unique and precious.

However, the same issue contains another interview that began: 'Sex work sucks! Clients suck! (or hassle me to try and have a go at sucking), I wish I could tell the whole business to go suck! But, and it is a big BUT, I want the money! Who doesn't?'

Another former sex worker wrote:

I had a wonderful joyous time my first two years in this business. I gave each customer my full heart for that time I was with them. I loved each and every one of them. I had fun dressing up and felt light-hearted, happy and free and couldn't understand why the girls who had been in this business longer were so negative and depressed all the time.

Then after two years, it started to hit me too. I found myself being an actress more and more and not coming from the heart. Money became foremost and important. The fun was gone.

This need for 'time out' has been stated several times to the author by different women. To again quote Michelle, 'It is important to take time out, you can't keep doing it - you need time out to heal yourself.'

While being prepared to accept both versions ('I work because I like it' and 'I work for the money') as possessing truths for their respective respondents, the client would much rather accept the former than the latter.

The sex tourist wishes to engage in a belief that the act is a voluntary one, or if not voluntary, one that is permitted by local value systems. Thus those who comment upon the sex industry of Thailand note how often Western men (at least) argue that their relationship with Thai women is not a simple contractual one based upon an exchange of money for sexual services. Günther (1998) cites one sex tourist to Thailand who viewed the relationship as a romantic one, even though the woman concerned worked as a prostitute. 'R' is not a sex tourist because he lacked intent, he did not restrict his vacation to having sex with local women, he lacked promiscuity because he did not have sex with several women, he did not allow his sexual impulses to control his behaviour without constraint, and, according to Günther, for his respondent, the most telling argument is that he did not pay. Yet payments were paid, including bar fees. As is discussed by Cohen (1993), Seabrook (1996), O'Connell Davidson, Bishop and Robinson (1998) among other researchers, for many sex tourists there is a wish to deny their role as sex tourists. Equally, if that role is recognised, then it is matched by a wish to impute to the women those motivations that are simply mercenary, and furthermore, manipulative.

The attitude of the sex tourist has been variously identified as being exploitative and exploited, depending in part upon the writer. The contributions by sex tourists to the debate have been primarily through their discussions with academics (Høigård and Finstad, 1992; O'Connell Davidson, 1995; Seabrook, 1996; Ryan and Kinder, 1996b; Bishop and Robinson, 1998) or through publications generally aimed at other sex tourists, either in conventional paper form or on the World Wide Web. A possible intermediate level is expressed in fiction written by those with experience of the bar scene of places like Bangkok. An example of this latter is the novels of Christopher Moore (1991, 1993, 1995) with its insider references to 'HQ', 'termites' and other slang of the area. Many of Moore's characters reiterate the mantra of the Dexter-Horn video productions that Western women are demanding, ungiving, and hence the world of Patpong's bars is really the natural world where men can be men, and women are women who look after men. In A Haunting Smile, one of Moore's characters states that 'fucking a white woman is a step away from homosexuality' (1993:107).

This inability to deal with women as other than vaginas awaiting the thrust of the penis is a common feature of the interviews reported by O'Connell Davidson (1995) and Seabrook (1996). This comment also draws attention to the racial stereotyping that is prevalent in a number of the comments of clients that are reported by researchers. Cabezas (1999:111) reports that Dominican women reported 'that foreigners constructed them, both sexually and racially, in opposition to European women. Their amigos portrayed European women as cold, indifferent to sex, and like men at home.' Such portrayals reflect as already discussed, the mix of racial exoticism, the inability to cope with 'liberated women', and constructs of 'womanly women' and 'male men' by reference to norms derived from some perception of nineteenth-century values.

However, one problem with such reported conversations is that samples are usually small in number, and while it is not doubted that such views are expressed, it also needs to be recognised that the ontological expression of the research is that of critical reality. Guba (1990) defines this as research that is ideologically oriented enquiry. Its epistemology is subjectivist in the sense that values mediate the enquiry, and the methodological approach can be characterised as dialogic and transformative. The views of the sex tourist just enunciated are consistent with the view that 'sex tourists express a kind of misogynistic rage against women who have the power to demand anything at all, whether it is the right to have a say over who they have sex with and when, or the right to maintenance payments for their children'.

In an analysis of Christopher Moore's series of books set in the bars of Patpong, Bishop and Robinson (1998:171) discuss the 'Aging, alienation, and intimations of mortality' that characterise the 'hardcore' client. They note that the sex tourists, so caught up in their own world of the fantastical, argue that it is they, the clients, who are the victims, not the girls that they use. Such, argue Bishop and Robinson, is the extent of self-delusion and misplaced values that the sex tourist espouses.

As a result of his own research this author does not doubt the ability for self-deception that exists within human nature, and equally does not doubt the role of the researcher as a catalyst for sex tourists sometimes having to face these self-deceits. Yet, the rage, the inability to face truths, the disillusionment that is experienced when men realise that for Thai women sex work is but a means of economic support, little more, and thus the sought for affection may have been little more than a skilful play - the resulting mix of emotions may nonetheless be real.

Sex tourism for some males becomes like a drug. They repeat their visits, they spend their money, they repeat their cycles of disillusionment. From one perspective the irony is that in an attempt to continually enforce their concepts of masculinity though the roundabout of visits to bars and massage parlours, the men observed in this cycle continually re-state their weakness. For a writer like Schlessinger (1997), men are characterised by a 'stupid strength' and an inability to discuss things beyond a superficial level. Men, she writes, are uncomfortable with feeling weak, useless or rejected, and react by intimidation and use of force. Maleness is measured by sexual conquest. From this perspective the male sex tourist is little more than a man unable to come to terms with himself, and in that inability is running true to his being.

But if this is true of males, what of the female sex tourist? And, is all sex tourism like that of Patpong? The answer to the latter question is 'no' if one looks only at the sex business and the nature of its presentation. Also, as Hanson

(1998) reminds us, the sex tourism engaged in by the white farangs, high profile that it has in Western literature, is only but a mere fraction of the totality of prostitution, and, indeed, sex tourism in Thailand. For example, until the Malaysian government stopped the exchangeability of its currency in 1998, one of the main locations for sex tourism in Thailand was that of the Malay-Thailand border. The recognition of female sex tourists also raises a number of issues relating to the voluntary-involuntary nature of sex tourism. Albuquerque (1998) identifies four types of female sex tourist, namely:

- The first timers - the 'neophytes';
- The situational sex tourists, who do not travel with the specific intention of buying sex, but avail themselves of the opportunity when it arises;
- The 'veterans' who travel explicitly for anonymous sex and usually find multiple partners; and
- The 'returnee' who visits to be specifically with one man whom she has met on a previous visit.

For her part, Phillips (1999:190-191) identifies three types of female sex tourist, 'The Situationer' who emphasises romance, the 'Repeat Situationer' who too denies the remunerative nature of the relationship, and 'The One Nighters' who come for fun and to 'fuck a black man'. It is immediately obvious that such categorisations can apply to their male counterparts. If this is the case, do the same descriptions of male sex tourists as self-deluding, exploitative and weak apply to their female counterparts? Certainly, Albuquerque makes an explicit parallel in the case of the 'veterans', whom he compares with O'Connell Davidson's 'macho men' - in short, the transactions are explicit and focused, they 'find them, feed them, fuck them and forget them'. Likewise, the 'situational sex tourist' is akin to Günther's (1998) 'R'.

They do not intend to be sex tourists and she sees herself as a patron in terms of providing financial support, she tends to be loyal to the 'boy' for the duration for the holiday and sees the relationship as genuine and reciprocal. Companionship and a sense of romance are as important as the sex. Thus too with the 'returnee'. She has romantic sentiments, is loyal to the male, and brings back gifts. The Barbadian 'beach boys' who form part of Albuquerque's sample has the same behaviours as the Thai female sex workers described above. They work out schedules around visiting girl friends; they are not loyal to one foreigner. Indeed, it is observed that their local girl friends have to 'share' their boy friends with the visiting sex tourist. But Albuquerque observes that many of the women are just as promiscuous as their male friends and will abandon their beach boy if another takes their fancy.

However, one partial difference is played out, and that is with the possible exception of the 'veteran' it is the male who tends to initiate the procedure. Yet even the 'veterans' have to play by the rules, which are that too much public display of a sexual nature by female tourist (other than on the dance floor) is seen as being in bad taste. The role of fantasy is also evident. In the case of male sex tourists to Thailand it is seemingly the search for the compliant, submissive female. For women travelling to the West Indies, it is a case of stereotypical sexy black males who are active 'studs'. However, Hosein's (1995) work with young Caribbean women finds a local female opinion that Caribbean males are poor lovers, unskilled and simply interested in a 'slam, bam, approach'.

On the other hand, Phillips describes the specific strategies used by Caribbean beach boys. They tend to select women who are not tanned (thereby implying that they are recent arrivals). They seek women who may be a little overweight on the premise that they may not often attract men and so be more susceptible to their charms. Thus, like O'Connell Davidson's pictures of males who are balding, ageing and overweight, so too a similar picture might be painted of the female sex tourist. Just as Thai bar girls target their 'partners', so too do beach boys. The parallels and complexities of who is exploited and who exploits exist regardless of the gender of the sex tourist; and equally it may be said, any picture painted of these complexities says much of the researcher as well as the researched. Are, it may be asked, all sex tourists really so physically unappealing?

The Caribbean beach boys, the Palestinian shopkeepers, the Gambian males, Greek males and other groups of males around the world meet the needs of female tourists seeking sex and derive payments from it. But the nature of the market transaction is a veiled one. It is veiled because there is no payment of a previously agreed price. Through the money veil of payment for meals and drinks, through the giving of gifts, and in many cases through a sentimental attachment between both parties, however transient, similar needs are being met as discussed in the case of many of the male tourists to locations like Thailand. The processes of exploitation in the sense that one can afford the gift giving and the other requires the gift giving to sustain a desired lifestyle is still present, but exists within degrees acceptable to both parties.

If these sets of relationships are perceived as sex tourism, then does the money veil also come into play when neither party to the transaction is a veteran at the sex game? There are significant levels of evidence to suggest that many tourists, both male and female, are not adverse to sexual adventure if it happens during a holiday. Clark and Clift (1996) found within their sample of British tourists in Malta that 7.7 per cent admitted to having 'a romantic relationship' while on holiday.

Gillies and Slack (1996), in a sample of 541 holidaymakers, found that 5 per cent had had sexual relationships with other than their normal partner while on holiday. Ford and Eiser (1996) found that 24 per cent of their sample of 1,033 people under the age of 29 holidaying in Torquay had sexual intercourse with a new partner. Ryan and Robertson (1997) found that 12.5 per cent of their student sample of 400 had sexual intercourse with new partners while on holiday. Are all of these people sex tourists?

At one level, the answer has to be 'yes'. For many of them the possibility of sex while away from home had crossed their mind. Ryan and Robertson (1997) found that among the items taken on holiday about 10 per cent packed condoms along with the sun tan lotion. An intent existed. However, for younger people the patterns of behaviour exhibited on certain types of holidays that revolve around bars, clubs and partying was very similar to normal weekend activities undertaken in their home town. The activities, including sex, were the same, only the location differed. In this respect it is of interest to note that one Auckland massage parlour, in 1998, while advertising for new female staff, contained within its advertisement the message, 'think of it as a night out with the girls'.

At the micro-level of interpersonal relations it seems that while we concentrate on the icons of sex tourism that are evidenced in the bars of places like Patpong, we overlook the social structures that increasingly make such locations not a marginal place that is 'over there', but part of a multiplicity of sexual relationships that exist within wider society as a whole. Sex is increasingly more apparent, more discussed, more a part of advertising and of popular culture. Raw sex is part of a culture of self-expression, rebellion, acceptance and rejection. Skeggs (1994) quotes the lyrics of the pop song 'Two Minute Brother' sung by Bytches with Problems:

> Is this all you got?
> one minute and you go pop
> yous is a big disgrace ...
> I hate guys who talk a lot of shit
> how they last long and got good dicks
> talking shit and telling me lies ... the best lover?
> They all two minute brothers.

The challenge to male performance is explicit. Female black rappers may represent one extreme of a continuum between assertive and passive female roles, but they are representative of many females today of all ages in making distinctions between overtly expressing sexuality and being available for sexual usage. The role of the body, the expression of its sexuality and its relationship to identity are discussed, but it is worth also noting that the expression of sexuality and sex tourism of a new sort emerged in the latter part of the twentieth century and is becoming more important in the early part of the twenty-first century. These new forms of sex tourism relate to female demand and the emergence of gay and lesbian cultures in Western society, and their importance relates not only to the economic implications of such demands, but also to their impact upon the nature of the discourse about sex, sexuality and its recreational uses.

Before discussing these issues, it is perhaps pertinent to summarise the discussion thus far. Three dimensions have been suggested as being important in arriving at definitions of sex tourism. Thus far the discussion has concentrated on issues relating to problems of how voluntary participation in sex tourism by the sex worker (male and female) is and the level of commerciality involved in the transaction. This can be represented by a diagram in which one line represents a continuum between voluntary participation on the part of the sex worker at one extreme, and at the other, a position of total exploitation. A second axis represents a continuum between the purely commercial transaction and at the opposite an interaction not marked by set prices and menus of prices.

It then becomes possible to locate various forms of sexual interaction on these axes. The purpose is not to provide a definition of locations of various forms of sex tourists-sex worker interaction, but to show how fluid the actual conceptualisations are. While the holiday romance between two people, neither of whom is a sex worker, appears a clear example of a voluntary, non-commercial interaction, what is the situation when one takes into account the small proportion of people who have more than one partner on their holidays? An intent for sexual adventure thus exists, and it can be argued to be exploitative - indeed, more exploitative than is the case involving the sex worker. It can be exploitative because:

- No payment is made to the partner;
- There may be instances where the partner is perhaps not entirely happy about engaging in full sexual intercourse. This permits a range of scenarios from rape to one where, while consenting at the time, one partner may subsequently suffer feelings of guilt, remorse, or of 'being used'.

Ryan and Robertson (1997) draw attention to the role of alcohol in sexual encounters among young people while on holiday, and thus the degree of collusion between the 'non-commercial parties' is thus debatable.

Under these circumstances the location of the 'holiday romance' type of encounter must move to the right. The position of the 'Neophyte' is placed in a voluntary setting as it is the sex worker who initiates the 'chat up' process and selects the client. This can also happen in certain types of sex work settings. In some of the clubs in Darlinghurst, Sydney's red light district, while the club may be a strip club, women will circulate among customers and ask if 'extras' are wanted. The 'extra' may be a lap dance, but the nature of the interaction takes place away from the public arena. The sex worker has a degree of choice as to which client is selected for an invitation, and the nature of the invitation being made. If she does not want full sex, then the offer being made will be that consistent with the nature of the club being a striptease club. The 'returnee' occupies an ambiguous location. The nature of payments is non-commercial in the sense that there is no menu of prices and payments are in the way of gifts and daily purchases, and it is exploitative in the sense that the professional sex worker may take advantage of the client, even while the client is occupying the economic position of being able to purchase affection.

The 'returnee's' position illustrates the micro- and macro-dimensions of sex tourism, and the ambiguous nature of the boundary between these two aspects. At a micro-level the actual interaction may be psychologically fulfilling to both parties, and genuine affection may be present. Both parties enjoy each other's company, and the parting may be associated with genuine feelings of sorrow and joy about future meetings. Yet, at the macro-level, the personal interaction perpetuates a system of economic dependency on sex tourism, it may do little to offer the sex worker alternative ways of earning a living, it illustrates the economic domination-subordination inherent in different levels of income - in short, it reinforces the very global systems of which commentators like Seabrook (1996) and Bishop and Robinson (1998) complain. However, within this relationship it becomes very possible for the sex tourist to reject the term 'sex tourist' and to argue that compared to the philandering holidaymaker with several non-commercial sex partners, theirs is a less exploitative position.

Possibly the least problematic aspect of sex tourism, from a definitional viewpoint, is that associated with 'veterans', 'macho' clients and sex slavery. For the former two categories of sex tourism the whole transaction is one of a commercial transaction purchased through the possession of economic power. However, as will be discussed, whether it can be fully regarded as an exploitative transaction can still be questioned. The problem is that while it seeks to define paradigms of sex tourism, it does so by using ill-defined terms of 'commercial/ non-commercial' and 'voluntary/exploitative'. Can one be exploited if one does not feel as if one is exploited? For radical feminists like Dworkin, Barry and Marcovich the answer is that all sex workers by definition are exploited - every act of penetration is an abuse of power, whether the sex worker realises it or not. However, that is not a view shared by all, especially by many men and women who work in various roles in the sex industry.

'Sex slavery' seems to be an undoubted example of the worse kind of exploitative commercial relations. As such, and arguably it lies outside of the conceptualisation in that the very severity of degradation and abuse involved distinguishes it from the other situations being described.

Striptease is not often included in discussions of sex tourism, although Oppermann's (1998) book includes two chapters relating to striptease, but the discussion is more one of the exotic dance as a recreational activity. Ryan and Martin (2001) argue, based on an analysis on a six-month period in a club in the Northern Territory, that a significant part of the clientele are tourists, and this is even more true of locations like the Gold Coast in Eastern Australia or cities like Las Vegas. Equally, the dancers themselves are often travellers if not tourists, using their occupation to travel around their countries or overseas. In the case of Sydney's red light district, several of the Kings Cross exotic dancing venues prefer to hire trained dancers as they are able to provide a more interesting and sophisticated show to their audience which may keep them in the bars longer. Furthermore, such exotic dance venues are usually regarded by the dancers themselves as good, safe money which enables them to dance to an audience and keep fit.

Nevertheless, as a form of sex work it raises many of the same issues of identity, sexuality and roles as prostitution, and the boundaries between striptease and other forms of sex work are often easily infiltrated. The strength of these boundaries often lies in the self-perception of the dancer and what it is that she or he wishes to do. Yet exotic dancing does differ from other sexual interactions in the sense that it places the body as an aesthetic experience in a non-contact way and as being on show in a public arena in a manner arguably not associated with other forms of dance or sex work. It is difficult to locate within and has been located centrally but with an inclination to the commercial. It is commercial in the sense that it is an occupation engaged in for money. That very fact reflects the lack of opportunities for some young people, yet often strippers have an interest in dance as a valid form of artistic endeavour, and indeed in exotic dancing as having, even if rooted in burlesque, a long theatrical tradition that is not without honour.

Yet even in the case of exotic dancing, the boundaries are blurred. Thus in an interview with an exotic dancer, Dominque said:

An exotic dancer is one who knows how to dance - a stripper can just stand there and go (shakes her shoulders) just showing a great pair of tits and they can make money that way, but an exotic dancer can dance - its a show. When we do the 'fantasy room' that's just stripping, it's so small that you can't really dance. But you see the whole lot there, you know, full view of pussy. How much is a prostitute? I had this guy in and its $70 for a prostitute, and we get $50 for a 5-minute show - it's strange!

But lap dancing does involve contact and one stripper noted that:

What's the difference between stripping and prostitution? If I lap dance and a guy comes because I think what the hell, does it make any difference if I was doing a hand job or if I rub him with my body through his pants. It's all a question of degree, and the degrees can be pretty fine - but they exist and every girl determines her own boundaries.

Before discussing the third of the three dimensions previously identified, that of self-awareness and strength of identity, there remains another form of sex tourism not located in the diagram, and that is the sex tourism of cyberspace. Reference has been made to the expositions of sex tourists on the World Wide Web. Most commentators on this have referred to the web pages of the World Sex Guide and similar pages. Pages that have 'adult' themes are popular, but the listings possibly reflect patterns of access to the net as much as levels of interest by the general population. Bishop and Robinson (1998) and Kohm and Selwood (1998) are among the commentators who have noted this new form of sex tourism. For Bishop and Robinson their interest has lain in the way in which physical sex tourists report their sexual adventures and the attitudes that are being expressed. Writers engage in travelogues giving insights as to 'best places' and travellers' tips as to prices and practices. Many engage in forms of listing conquests and betraying stereotypical attitudes about women being 'great lays'. An example derived from the World Sex Guide dated 23 March 1997 describes a visit to an Auckland Massage Parlour thus:

At the top of the stairs, an older lady in a booth gets your agency fee ($55 NZ) which gets you in the door. The lounge is a swanky but small bar environment. The girls are all pretty hot compared to escorts in other countries, as a lot of really 'respectable' girls do this for extra cash on the side after their normal day jobs. I was immediately attracted to a blonde with very short hair, great legs, and ... well, she had porn star quality breasts, at least 40D and natural (as I found out later). Her name was Lee. We started with small talk and a drink, then migrated to a theme room [*i.e.* theme décor]. I had no idea what was coming next, as I had never been to an open, low stress place like this before. Lee ran some water into the Jacuzzi, and invited me to get in (I did). She slipped in behind me, but not before I saw how hot her body was.

And so it continues in the vein of judging women by sexual performance - but, as noted by Bishop and Robinson (1998), also accompanied by how good the correspondent was too. And if it wasn't good for him, then the fault lay elsewhere. Rarely is there a perception that it wasn't good for the women - if the woman is considered, then it is always 'good for her' because the correspondent is 'good'.

Sex on the Internet consists of both the passive and the interactive. In terms of the passive, the 'tourist' as voyeur is well catered for. It is a form of voyeurism that seemingly offers to the unwary the anonymity thought to be required as described by Ryan and Kinder (1996a). It permits apparent safety, an intimacy of privacy within which fantasy can be engaged, it is a form of relaxation, it offers like the travel brochure, the promise of being there, but without the risk of 'travel'. And, forgetting the trace left by the 'cookie' it all seems risk-free. This form of sex tourism has no risk of a sexually transmitted disease.

Of more interest as a sex tourism experience is the use of the 'chat rooms'. The anonymity is used by correspondents to be more direct and explicit than would be the case in normal society. Both men and women appear to feel removed from constraints and may be as direct as they would be in the case of their requests to sex workers. The publication generated a number of reviews and discussions in the popular press as to the authenticity of the experience. Internet reviews generally concur that, while dated, the experiences portrayed contained considerable truth, and indeed, if anything under-stated the nature of the references to sex. As such, the work contains many examples of men using the 'net to display a greater directness in sexual interest. For example, 'Charles Leslie' writes: 'I'll tell you right off the bat, I am a married man. This medium offers the possibility of connecting with persons of the opposite sex and engaging in sexually arousing conversations that benefit both parties without risking AIDS or the emotional and marital problems which might result from adultery'.

The female character in this book, Katherine Simmons (Kate), finds herself drawn into a series of relationships and is entranced by the power of the net. She writes:

I can confess this to you playing at being the temptress and the power it gives me over men is the real appeal computer relationships have for me (although, don't get me wrong, I enjoy the sexual titillation as well). I have been at the mercy of men all my life and have served them. I love turning the tables. It makes me feel invincible and young. In real life, I can't wield this power any more.

The parallels with both sex worker and sex tourist are obvious. As already cited, Kasl describes the 'power' felt by one prostitute as she dresses and 'men come running' (1989:154). But equally, like female sex tourists, Kate exercises and enjoys a sense of power over men as a means of feeling young. Like Wicken's 'Ravers' she takes time out from her daily reality to engage in the sense of being able to sexually want, and be sexually wanted. She wants to engage in telephone sex, she wants, eventually, to meet the men she converses with. She wishes for affection not gained from other sources. In the light of the previous discussions of motive she can be termed a sex tourist.

Thus we come to the third dimension of sex tourism, and that is the contribution to senses of self-identity. Kate's sexual life through cyberspace now begins to affect her sense of identity. She changes her hairstyle, she feels good about herself. But finally she has to address the question of the nature of the relationship with her computer lover, is it one of infatuation, an addiction, what and who is the 'real' Kate, and where is her home in a physical and spiritual sense? Thus, the question, what do the commercial sex relationships mean to people? How important are they?

6

Health Tourism: Identity and Development

SOCIAL DEVELOPMENT

The approach selected is an adaptation of what Turner (1982) has termed 'comparative symbology', that is, a comparative study and interpretation of symbols, but one within a wider socio-economic and political framework. It will be argued that both tourist and prostitute are symbols of, and actors seeking, needs generated by a wider social context formed by the modern era ushered in by the Industrial Revolution. Essential to this argument is the contention that both are marginal or liminal people. As marginal people, both tourists and prostitutes have had, at least in Western societies, their roles defined by hegemonies of power, and unless regard is paid to those structures, then at best any description of sex tourism remains but that - a description. Thus this first seeks to establish tourism and that part of tourism known as 'sex tourism' within a historical context and a specific discourse.

Within this explanation a number of themes are expounded, implied and hinted at, and in due course throughout this book, these facets will be elaborated and brought to the foreground. First, it will be argued that being a tourist is to occupy a liminal role within a temporal marginality. It will subsequently be argued that this is important in our understanding of sex tourism as in the western world the prostitute is also marginalised. The act of sex tourism can therefore be explained as an interaction between two sets of liminal people - but with a difference.

The one, the tourist, is enacting a socially sanctioned and economically empowered marginality, while the second, the prostitute, is stigmatised as a whore, a woman of the night, as the scarlet woman. Yet, as will be described, such stigmatisation is now being challenged, made ambiguous and respectability sought by emphasising the role of female labour within the terminology of being a sex worker. Additionally, any analysis which focuses on women alone as prostitutes is but partial as male strippers and prostitutes are an emerging sector of the sex industry, while homosexual and lesbian holiday markets utilising sex for reasons of relaxation and self-identification are also of growing importance.

Thus, a second theme will be hinted at within this historical review, and that is the process of the holiday as a source of self-identification. Thus, for MacCannell (1976:4) the tourist seeks to find the 'structures of modernity' and uses leisure, and holidays, as arenas in which the fragmented modern may recover his or her sense of structure.

But the question has to be asked, why is there a necessity in the modern world to use these demarcated periods for such purposes? A neo-Marxist analysis is provided which answers the question by noting the changing modes of production and the commodification of many things in our lives, and the emergence of the tourist as a consumer.

Again, links between tourism and prostitution will be noted in this introduction for later analysis. If our periods of escape from the role of worker are commodified, so too, it has been often argued by feminists, sex work is about the commodification (and degradation) of female sexuality. Both processes are thus linked to wider social change.

But, just as both forms of commodification are reactions to these wider processes of industrialisation - processes which incidentally devalue the non-paid work roles assumed by many in our society - notably those of house-bound women - so too both tourism and sex work contain potentialities to confirm the sense of self that Marx saw as being alienated by modernism. The third theme incorporated within this review attempts to include descriptions of sociopolitical order in terms of dominant hegemonies that have implications for the development of tourism in general and sex tourism in particular.

It will also be apparent from such a viewpoint that both tourism and prostitution possess dangerous forces; forces that, while subordinate to the mainstream of society, by their very presence challenge the norms of the dominant. Their existence continues to represent alternative lifestyles. From a positive stance, in the one case of non-work against work, and in the other, the unwillingness of some women to accept low incomes and thus use their sexuality as sources of income and self-image. However, it is readily recognised that these marginalities also represent the reinforcement of consumerism and the exploitation of women - but, then, ambiguity is inherent in the very nature of liminality.

It may, at first sight, seem strange to begin a book concerned with sex tourism with reference to, however briefly, the wider societal transition from pre-industrial patterns of leisure and work to contemporary situations. But the existing patterns of tourism and prostitution, and their inter-relationships, have common roots in the evolution of our society. It is true that the stigmatisation of prostitutes as fallen women existed before the Industrial Revolution, but it was this period of modernity that legalised, yet made ambivalent, the concept of the prostitute as a diseased woman - an attribution arguably made all the easier because the object vilified was female.

Yet, simultaneously it was this same period that created a discourse of sex that fantasised and objectified women - it is for example interesting to compare the works of a Zola with their social intensity and descriptions of courtesans or the anonymous Victorian English author of My Secret Life with the bawdy tales of a Geoffrey Chaucer, Rabelais or the adventures of a Moll Flanders or Tom Jones. Furthermore, the Industrial Revolution was also a period of empire building and a perceptual construction of an exotic other which engaged the sensual and sexual senses of Victorian England and the Anglo-Saxon world if not nineteenth-century Europe.

In short, many of the attitudes that exist today towards sex, tourism and sex tourism have their historical antecedents in movements of the last two hundred years, and to ignore these is to only partially understand how we have reached the current position and why within prostitution and tourism there lie responses of coping with and challenges to the status quo. It is a status quo born of complex socio-political-economic power structures, and thus any summary of a holistic over-view will be selective, incomplete, but hopefully sufficient to show that the themes of marginality, self-identity and economic-political hegemony are important in any analysis of sex tourism.As tourists and prostitutes are both real in themselves, but symbolic of the consequences of industrialisation and the later commodification of services and values associated with postmodernism, it may be advantageous to define some terms. As Turner (1982) notes, comparative symbology is narrower than semiotics but wider than symbolic anthropology. Semiotics incorporates three branches of study of the nature and relationships of signs in language, namely:

- Syntactics - the formal relationship and organisation of signs and labels within language, the syntax of language.
- Semantics - the relationship of signs and symbols to the things to which they refer.
- Pragmatics - the relationship of signs and symbols with their users.

The concern of this analysis is not with the technical aspects, the syntactics involved with symbology, but with the relationships between users of touristic and sexual services. Its concerns lie with the symbols they represent within a wider society, the way in which they are represented by power structures within that society and the ways in which interactions between prostitutes and tourists are played out within these relationships of power and symbolism. It has already been stated that sex tourism within this analysis is perceived as an interaction between two marginal groups, tourists and sex workers, and thus this analysis develops that commenced by Ryan and Kinde.

They concluded that conventional descriptions of deviancy were not sufficient to explain either the behaviour of the tourist who sought the services of prostitutes, and neither do such concepts fully explain the role of the prostitute in contemporary society.

What then is meant by liminal or marginal people? Liminal people are threshold people existing betwixt and between. They exist in an ambiguous position between 'positions assigned and arrayed by law, custom, convention, and ceremonial' (Turner, 1969:95). Turner notes that liminal entities may be disguised, wearing only a strip of clothing, or even going naked among preindustrial societies, thereby signing that they have no status, property, or insignia. How pertinent is it that the tourist sunbathes with little clothing, and the discerning symbol of the prostitute is the short, figure-hugging mini-skirt and low-cut dress? Boyle describes the 'work gear dictated by clients' demands and the environment'. Writing about 'Maria' she says:

If she is street walking, she opts for either a red leather mini-dress and thigh-length boots or black four-inch stiletto-heeled shoes, stockings and suspenders. They are carefully positioned to show just below the dress or a black stretch skirt which barely skims her thighs. Accompanying the skirt will be a lacy, gravity-defying basque which attempts to encompass her magnificent bosom.

In an earlier period Mayhew ([1851] 1999:416) draws our attention to the power of undress, dress and their significance as signifiers of the marginal. He cites one prostitute who says of herself, 'I have good feet too, and as I find they attract attention, I always parade them. And I've hooked many a man by showing my ankle on a wet day.' In the next paragraph Mayhew refers to 'black silk cloaks or light grey mantles - many with silk paletots and wide skirts, extended by an ample crinoline', but just as Odzer (1994) was to note a century and half later, a hierarchy existed wherein at the bottom in the Haymarket were 'wornout prostitutes or other degraded women, some of them married, yet equally degraded in character.

Lodge (1992), in his novel, Paradise News, describes tourists dressed in shell suits and shorts - signs of being a tourist. Both representations are concerned with a display of the body and nakedness or near nakedness are involved. Yet, the realism of the display is that it is not the appearance of glamourised bodies seen in pin-up calendars. The short, the fat, and the skinny are revealed and both tourists and prostitute have to come to the truth of their bodily appearance even while both hide and display the body at the same time. Annie Sprinkle's list of reasons as to why whores are heroes contains, at numbers 13 and 37, the reasons 'Whores wear exciting clothes' and 'Whores are not ashamed to be naked'. Thus again the ambiguity, the dialectical tension of opposites is evident within this marginal behaviour. In conversation with the first author, Michelle, a former sex worker in New Zealand, commented that there were many ambiguities in the dress worn by prostitutes. The point of dressing was to enhance the body, but one dresses to become naked, but naked in a flattering environment. There is, she commented, 'the sensuality of undressing - one dresses to undress'.

Within marginal groups, states Turner (1974), there exists a sense of communitas, of homogeneity and comradeship - they possess an area of common living. This is almost literally true for sex work. Areas of prostitution, termed 'red light' areas, offer mutual support systems for their inhabitants. Women on the street take down the number plates of cars that their fellow women get into in case there is any trouble. Clients, pimps, workers and drug pushers mark out territories so as to more easily sustain social relationships. It is consistent with the theories of liminality that the safety of such areas is fragile and what, at least for the client, they offer is the opportunity for anonymity. So too with tourism. As is noted below, tourists are found in purpose-built tourist spaces. It can be objected that these relate solely to mass tourism, but in response two viewpoints may be held. One may hold to the position of Boorstin (1963) that these are the epitome of tourism, and not to be present at such a place means that one is a traveller. Boorstin defines the modern experience of tourism thus: But the experience of going there, the experience of being there, and what is brought back from there are all very different. The experience has become diluted, contrived, prefabricated.

The modern American tourist now fills his experience with pseudo-events. He has come to expect both more strangeness and more familiarity than the world naturally offers. He has come to believe that he can have a lifetime of adventure in two weeks, and all the thrills of risking his life without any real risk at all.

For Boorstin these facts described the very character of modern tourism - from the perspective of an analysis of tourists as marginal people it seems to describe an essence of liminality. The tourist exists in an irregular world that is both strange and familiar. At the other extreme even Cohen's 'drifters' are notable by their style and by their tendency to drift towards certain roles and places. Travellers too are marginal persons, members in but not part of the crowd. For Bauman and the concept of tourist-traveller as flâneur, the tourist is one who goes for a stroll as one goes to the theatre (in the crowd but not of the crowd), taking in those strangers as 'surfaces' - so that 'what one sees' exhausts 'what they are', and above all seeing and knowing them episodically ... rehearsing human reality as a series of episodes, that is events without past and with no consequences.

Marginality assumes further importance by reason of temporality and transition. The tourist assumes the role of non-worker. The holiday trip is characterised by stages of preparation, absorption into the tourist role and then re-entry to the mainstream world. Each stage may be characterised by small rites - the process of checking in for flights, the purchase of holiday clothing, and the development of the photographs after the trip. The prostitute occupies other roles besides being a 'working woman'. She is mother, student, partner. As noted she dons the costume of the night - an act of ritual wherein the dress conveys power. Kasl (1989:154) writes '[the] addiction part is the ritual of getting dressed, putting on makeup, fantasising about the hunt, and the moment of capture. To know that you go out there and they would come running.

What power!' Thus Kasl demonstrates another paradox about the state of marginality, and that is the dialectic between powerlessness and power. The woman who is disdained is the woman with power over men. Likewise the tourist as hedonist, someone apart from the Puritan work ethnic, is pampered by an industry that recognises such hedonism as the reward of work. The non-worker, normally a position of powerlessness, possesses power over the worker. The reality, as Marx would have pointed out, is that such power is exercised by cash. But the differences of each respective marginality, sanctioned or condemned by society, again become evident.

The working girl exercises a power to earn cash; the tourist exercises a power due to the possession of money. Hence the possibility that the tourist may purchase the services of the prostitute or other sex workers. Therefore it is not surprising, given the hedonistic nature of tourism, that in many places the spatial areas of both tourist and sex worker overlap, and many hotel managers can bear witness to the fact that their premises might be regarded as both holiday accommodation and brothel. In some parts of the world the overlap becomes obvious and explicit. Amsterdam's red light district and the soi of Patpong are tourist attractions for clients and on-lookers alike.

To travel has been variously defined as an act of pilgrimage, escape, a search for adventure or for self. The rewards it offers are generally intangible, and those things that are purchased, as souvenirs, are mementoes designed to evoke memories. And arguably it is not so much the place that is evoked, but rather what was done at that place - the people one met, or the relationship between self and place through processes of evaluation - whether of the aesthetic values or events. In short, as humans, we can only experience place through the filter of our own selves. Urry (1990) has drawn attention to the role of the tourist gaze, but the perceptual is related to the corporeal. The role of the body is being recognised in studies of tourism. Our own bodily comfort or discomfort engages senses that also help to shape perception of place and activity. Describing the experiences of a student tourist group in Sarawak, Markwell describes how fatigue caused by climbing Mount Kinabalu the previous day, shaped activities and thus consequent memories and evaluations of a visit to an orangutan sanctuary. Thus one of his respondents, Jane stated:

I was really disappointed that we didn't get into it as much, like we'd really been looking forward to it, and I just remembered the day that we went there it was really hot and all we could think of was just getting to the cafeteria and like getting a drink and actually once we got there it was like, 'Oh, it's too hot to go back outside', and I really regret it because a lot of people went further up and they had contact with them [orangutans] and everything and we didn't and that's one thing I've really regretted.

Similarly, in an examination of eco-tourism in the heat and humidity of the 'Top End' of Australia, Ryan et al. (1999) contend that eco-tourism, like all forms of tourism, is concerned with spectacle. It is, they argue, designed to focus on culturally acceptable sights, but is done in such a way that the sight is elevated above the other bodily senses through the provision of shade in wind accessible places, thereby creating an experience of place that is a managed experience of raw nature offered by the climate. The elevation of the body as a source of pleasure is thus another theme that must be explored within tourism in general and sex tourism in particular.

Sun bathing brings not only the possibility of a suntan, but also the sense of sun upon the skin, a warmth and a pleasure. From sensuality to sexuality is a stepped procedure. And from sexuality to intercourse is but a further graduation based on payment. From the warmth of sun to the warmth of a massage to the body massage of Spalding Gray's bubbling lotions as described in his 1989 one-man show based on his text, Swimming to Cambodia (1985), to the act of intercourse - isolated to the context of the body, the relationships seem obvious. Gray describes this process with the Thai massage parlour as:

You go down into this small room and for a little bit of money you take off all your clothes and she stays dressed, and you get a mild, tweek-tweek massage ... A little more money and you get a hand job. A little bit more money and you get to fuck her. A little bit more money and you get the supremo-supremo ... the body-body massage ... And she gets on one side of the room and runs and hops on top of you and swiggle-swiggle-swiggle, body-body-body, and you slide together like two very wet bars of soap.

Yet even within this very narrow conceptualisation the role of sight has pre-eminence, at least in the early stages of any action. The sex industry is one of presenting images, and the choice of sex worker by the client is based upon sight as much as any other sense. Gray chooses his partner based on looks. 'Sarah' - a sex worker in Blenheim, New Zealand, describes the fact that escort work is easier than working in a massage parlour because there, in the parlour, one competes with other women for the custom of the 'gentleman'. Sensuality and sexuality - related but separate entities struggle for space in any understanding of tourism, prostitution and sex tourism. This issue of sensuousness versus sexuality is yet another theme to be disentangled within a conceptualisation of marginality.

Whether pleasant or unpleasant, whether uplifting, hedonistic or degrading, what remains of any tourist trip is an experience. Regardless of whether that experience fades with time as memories dim, or whether it remains real, re-interpreted and re-evaluated so that it may become a different thing, at some time it was thought to be important. It was sought out, or if it happened by chance, either prolonged or shortened. The tourist trip is full of encounters which involve us, the tourists, as actors and directors in the play that is the tourist trip - a play staged by a tourist industry that continually advertises the opportunities for 'experience'. That this is the case should not surprise. Experiences possess importance to people.

They form memories which help to pass time in the future, to help us survive hard times, and from memories we create expectations as to possible outcomes from future actions. But tourist memories are arguably a special category of memory, as holidays are specially demarcated special times. For Hollinshead (1999:11) 'the tourist gaze', as described by Urry, 'helps conduct people to all manner of new ecstacies in their travels and enjoyments'. The usual routine is set aside, and often travel to other places is involved. By this very fact they become marginal periods in our lives of potentially great importance. During these periods we live on the perimeter of our normal roles. They are not entirely divorced from those roles and we may carry into our holidays some of our normal roles, for example, as partners or parents. We carry into our holiday periods our skills, be they social skills or skills associated with our occupations. But primarily we leave behind occupational roles, social frameworks that guide or constrain our actions, and enter a period which society sanctions as a period of release from normal responsibilities.

From this perspective sex tourism is located firmly within the wider discourse of tourism. The sex industry presents spectacle in its portrayal of sexual adventure - the modes of dress as already noted are designed to appeal, to excite. Its literature promises ecstasy and finally, orgasm. Yet, within the sex industry lies ambivalence for the exotic dancers of striptease bars offer fantasy but no sexual intercourse, and dancers perform within circumscribed roles on the part of clients.

It is not for nothing that writers like Shields (1991), Rojek and Ryan have alluded to medieval periods of disorder when discussing holidays. During such periods settled order was set aside, the jester became king and hierarchies were challenged, albeit within a temporal framework where such disorder was temporary. But as Rojek and others emphasise, it was a specific form of disorder - it was the wantonness of carnival - lewd, rude, sexual - it was the farts and not the thoughts of radical rebellion against accepted order that characterised such periods. Thus the challenge to accepted order was made safe and earmarked as being an 'other'.

The very licentiousness of the form of assault upon normality undermines and thereby makes safe its challenge by de-politicising the nature of the challenge. This phenomenon continues today. Lawrence (1982) describes the Doo Dah Parade in Pasadena as a parade set up as a ritual of rebellion against the Rose Parade. This latter parade, which is organised, sponsored by business, possesses floats of flowers and innocuous smiling beauty queens. Doo Dah parodies it and its blandness.

Consequently Doo Dah is held by some residents to be tawdry, cheap and tasteless, but as a moment of misrule and disorder it is ambiguous in that it too is organised and became as successful a tourist attraction as that which it sought to parody. Yet it is of interest that within this context that the body, which was addressed previously in terms of sensuousness adopts another theme in this context - it is the body of orifice and lewdness. The symbolism of the body as caricature has also been noted in tourism. For Goldsmith, a female commentator of the political right, cites her objection to the homosexual displays of Sydney's Mardi Gras on the basis that:

Some drag queens are an undisguised and vicious parody of woman-hood: their grotesque make-up and clothing and their grossly exaggerated breasts and mannerisms turn women into a joke ... Again, some of the bondage in the Mardi Gras is a worry, when it displays, for example men leading women along by chokers around their necks. In a society where women are demonstrably less than equal and are subject to domestic and sexual violence, such images reinforce negative stereotypes and show violence against women as acceptable.

The carnival exists to defy and challenge 'normality'. So too, it can be argued, is the case with holiday periods, but in this case the defiance of normality has been tamed and commoditised. Holidays are periods of relaxation, and thus by their nature a statement that there exists a world other than work. Yet the lifestyle represented by holidaying is itself a de-politicised lifestyle - it is a reward for work and thus a creation of the process that created the discipline of work in the factories of the last century. The holiday is itself an invention of the modern world emerging from the industrial revolution. Rybczynski (1991) describes the history of 'The Weekend' as a response by the dominant classes in Victorian Britain to meet the needs of both God and Mammon. Describing 'Saint Monday', he writes:

Saint Monday may have started as an individual preference for staying away from work - whether to relax, to recover from drunkenness, or both - but its popularity during the 1850s and 1860s was ensured by the enterprise of the leisure industry. During that period sporting events, such as horse races and cricket matches, often took place on Mondays, since their organisers knew that many working-class customers would be prepared to take the day off. And, since many public events were prohibited on the Sabbath, Monday became the chief occasion for secular recreations.

A combination of industrialists and evangelicals combined to create the weekend where a half-day holiday was provided on the Saturday. Theories of social interaction between popular practice and the interests of the ruling classes also help to explain the emergence of the modern holiday. Cross notes reactions to legislation to paid vacation time in the United Kingdom thus:

Employers' reaction to the paid vacation was not nearly as hostile as it had been to the shorter workday. The vacation was a prerequisite which could raise work discipline (by denying it to workers who failed to remain on the job for at least a year or to workers with bad records of absenteeism). A paid vacation would 'implant in the minds of the employees that they were actually part of the business'.

Cross also argues that employers of that period also gained from being able to lay workers off during seasonally slow periods. They also benefited by conceding only forty hours of the working week for an extra week of holiday compared to 400 hours which would be lost by a movement from a forty-eight-hour week to a forty-hour week.

Ryan (1997) has described holidays as periods of potential re-discovery, of relaxation, of sanctioned escape but has omitted to assess the nature of the economic relationships within which the holiday emerged, even while describing its role as a continuation of carnival. Like Doo-Dah, the holiday has become an example of consumerism, not a challenge. While at the level of individuals holidays can be a source of cathartic experience, at a macro-social level holidays are conformist and themselves a source of further consumerism and industry creation.

To understand the nature of sex tourism requires an examination of the relationship between the body, sex and self-identity, the commoditisation of these periods of time and the liminal nature of these experiences, places and the tourist role. But in addition to these themes, and to make sense of how they become apparent, attention must be paid to the wider socio-economic-political context which determines how these forces shape holiday experiences. It should not be forgotten that tourism is big business - a whole industry, global in scope, exists to transport, feed, house and entertain tourists. But it is, arguably, an industry derived from, and shaped by other industries. It has been noted that holidays are a modern phenomenon. They are a necessity created by modes of production, which, from the 1880s, created the production conveyor belt, a system unknown to pre-industrial society. Industrialisation created a scenario where we work five or six days to relax, work free, on the remaining day(s) of the week, an apparent justification of the Marxian notion of man as the appendage to the machine. For Marx and Engels, the success of the bourgeoisie, meant that:

It has pitilessly torn asunder the motley feudal ties ... And has left no other bond between man and man than naked self-interest, than callous 'cash payment'. It has resolved personal work into exchange value and in place of the numberless indefeasible chartered freedoms, has set up that single, unconscionable freedom - Free Trade. In one word, for exploitation, veiled by religious and political illusions, it has substituted naked, shameless, direct, brutal exploitation.

Marx and Engels argued in the Economic and Philosophic Manuscripts of 1844 that the result was an estranged labour, by which man became objectified as a unit of labour. Thus man was turned into 'a being alien to him, into a means to his individual existence. It estranges man's own body from him, as it does eternal nature and his spiritual essence, his human being'. It further led to man being estranged from man and 'If a man is confronted by himself, he is confronted by the other man'.

The modernism of the Industrial Revolution created a need for and an ability to buy periods of sanctioned escape for purposes of relaxation. It commoditised relaxation in order to allow people to be better workers through a recognition of the fact that people cannot work continuously and thus, to be more productive, required holidays. By offering these periods of escape, by encouraging escape to other places, by validating such behaviour as being educational, it created an additional product - the holiday - which too could take its place in the portfolio of things to be purchased by a growing consumer class.

For Marx a sense of identity and the alienation of that identity were a consequence of an economic system wedded to capitalist systems that valued objects, and people, solely in terms of cash. The echoes of that process continue today. For Bishop and Robinson (1998) the capitalist system and the classifications of 'other' that are created by fragmentations based on hegemonies of European-American male-based cultures are important in explaining the emergence of sex tourism in Thailand. There is, they contend, a standard 'Objective' narrative about the Thai sex industry. As Phongpaichit and Baker note, it commences with: the decay of local communities leading to large-scale migration of rural girls (and later, also boys) to work in prostitution for the U.S. soldiers, for an increasingly prosperous urban market, later for the tourist trade, and finally as an export commodity.

This is, as far as it goes, an accurate summary, but it fails to ask a number of important questions that are both economic and socio-cultural in character. In 1971 Robert MacNamara, as head of the World Bank, visited Bangkok and initiated a series of subsequent meetings that generated plans whereby tourism was identified as a major component of the Thai economy. Truong (1990) noted that there existed a political motive for such plans. The unstable nature of the Indochina political structures of the time, that is the threats to American hegemony in the region in the late stages of and the post-Vietnam War period, meant that it was necessary to bolster Thailand's economy as that country was generally friendly to American aspirations in containing both communism and uncertainty in the region.

The structures created by RandR facilities, an important economic resource, would also fail without alternative sources of demand. Bishop and Robinson (1998:99) propose a thesis that a cynical rationality took place. Realising that because of then existing fare structures and resultant high costs of travel to Thailand, any tourism development was unlikely to attract family-based tourism, the World Bank and the Thai government colluded in a tourism policy whereby it was inevitable that a tourism based on prostitution could not but help occur. Thus was set in progress a chain of action whereby an economy was created based on sex tourism which continually re-confirmed the importance of massage parlours and bars - and in that re-confirmation failed to provide alternative forms of development, tourism based or otherwise.

It is possible to interpret this process as one whereby a marginal spatial location, Thailand, gained an importance because the economic interests of the United States required it to support a friendly country to stabilise a geo-political zone after a military defeat. Allied to these lay conceptualisations of an exotic other derived from a recent past born of popular literature and Hollywood. Bishop and Robinson (1998) argue the notions of Thai women as exotic, pliable, sexually innocent but fun-loving people emerge from a nineteenth-century conceptualisation of and fascination with harem life, especially as described by popular works like those written by Anna Leonowens The Romance of the Harem (1991). In 1862 Leonowens was employed by King Mongkut of Siam. Her early life, spent in India, and subsequent travels in the Middle East as the unchaperoned companion (at the age of 15) with a Reverend George Percy, had brought her into contact with the Muslim harem. Bishop and Robinson argue that these perceptions of the Muslim harem were applied by Leonowens to the Nang Harm or Royal Harem of the Siamese court. Through a series of reprints under different titles, The Romance of Siamese Harem Life; Siamese Harem Life; Siam and the Siamese, Leonowens represented the Siamese Harem as a location of the oppression of females, a place of slavery and of sexual purpose.

However, the messages of women's rights were submerged within a titillation of popular taste. Morgan (1991) argues that these messages were also lost due to the non-sanctioned source of the message (Leonowens was female, of mixed blood and not of the upper class). Of more importance was the interpretation of the book by its audience predisposed to a perception of the Far East as an exotic land with different norms of sexual behaviour. The significance of Morgan's comments is that, within the processes of hegemonies being established by a newly industrialising society, popular writing about harems, an exotic subject, transposed to a new and possibly even more exotic location by a woman who herself could be considered as an adventurer - all these factors conspired to reinforce notions that 'out there', beyond the boundaries of everyday society, there existed a different way of conducting male-female relationships; one where women were subordinated to male pleasure.

Furthermore, free from a Judaeo-Christian tradition, those women who were providing sexual services lived in a society where intercourse with other than a married partner was not seen, in itself, as immoral. It is possible to imagine that for the Victorian gentlemen personified by the author of My Secret Life (Anonymous, cited by Foucault, 1990), such revelations could not be other than attractive. Foucault ([1976] 1990) draws our attention to the fact that the Victorian period was not a period of sexual repression, but of sexual discourse in ways not previously undertaken - a discourse of detail, made moral and acceptable by scientific enquiry. Thus Foucault writes: 'A censorship of sex? Rather there was installed an apparatus for producing an even greater quantity of discourse about sex, capable of functioning and taking effect in its very economy' (1990:23).

Certainly, within nineteenth-century London, the economic implications of prostitution were significant. It was, for women, a major source of employment. Mayhew ([1851] 1999) estimated that in London, in the 1850s, there were approximately 80,000 prostitutes. By comparison Matthews (1997) estimated that in London, 635 women work 'off the street', 640 in private premises, 2,220 in massage parlours or sauna clubs, 1,260 as escorts and 500 in hostess clubs. He additionally estimated that weekly they entertain 80,240 clients for an annual turnover of£194 million. In short, prostitution was more embedded in London society in the nineteenth century than it is today if the criterion is solely that of numbers of both sex workers and clients.

For Bishop and Robinson, then, based on these foundations of Victorian sensuality, the elements of Leonowens' work that percolated through to Anna and the King of Siam, and the subsequent musical, The King and I, were those to which a wider populace were responsive. Allied with other sources of representation that are discussed by Bishop and Robinson, an exotic 'other' of friendly, relaxed, smiling people lay waiting for the tourist. They note 'Tomorrow will do, the Thais seem to say; relax, nothing is that serious, life is amusing, why not enjoy it?'. And of course, if nothing is that serious, neither is sex.

The exoticism of the Far East and South Pacific is commented upon by many writers. Thus Theweleit (1987) notes the derivation of the myths of the South Seas when the image of the South Sea Maiden 'began to construct the body that would constitute a mysterious goal for men whose desires were armed for an imminent voyage, a body that was more enticing than all the world put together' (1987:296) while Rose (1993:94) draws attention to the 'sexual, fertile, silent and mysterious Woman with a gorgeous, generous, lush Nature' painted by the artist Gauguin in his representation of Tahitian women.

For feminist writers like Rose, geographers have failed to understand or recognise the 'sensual topography of land and skin' which is, she argues, mapped by a mainly white male heterogeneous gaze. Given this historic context of industrialisation fragmenting the world-view into relationships of the particular in which the nineteenth-century Anglo-Saxon mind ascribed roles while secure in a confidence born of masculinity and economic power, it can be argued that it is of little surprise that because of the marginality of location, peoples and the exoticism ascribed to those people, sex tourism has become a sustainable force at the commencement of the twenty-first century. The historical shadows from the past are indeed long ones.

Those shadows, in the case of sex tourism in places like Thailand, are significant, argues Manderson, when the exoticised oriental female entity that Thailand became in the Western mind, itself becomes a scenario and a source of hedonistic self-discovery through sexual intercourse as displayed in the film Emmanuelle (1974). Manderson (1997) argues that the film was not about Thailand - she writes 'Thailand is simply the backdrop for a European pornographic fantasy' (1997:136), but 'the film fed into an emerging image of Thailand as sex-haven, and this was not accidental' (ibid.). In its messages of self-discovery by setting aside repression of sexual desire and experimentation, and siting that hedonistic sexual adventure in Thailand, the film reinforced notions of an erotic location and certainly did not harm the business interests of the emerging Thai sex tourism industry. Manderson goes on to trace an evolving sexual imagery of Thailand from the King and I, via Emmanuelle to the almost total commoditisation of Thai women as sexual objects in O'Rourke's film The Good Woman of Bangkok (1991).

By 1991, however, the designation of Patpong as a sex tourism destination was well known, and O'Rourke's film is a recognition of the ambiguity of both sex tourism and the director as sex tourist. As Manderson comments, its analysis is akin to those of published sociological works on prostitution in Thailand. It reveals the contradictions of modern complicities as being an inheritance of nineteenth-century certainties. The sequence from the King and I's representation of the governess as a civilising influence to the discourse of O'Rourke's film represents the dissolution of modern certainty into a postmodern recognition of multiple truths. To Manderson's text might be added the example of Ms Saigon, a further representation of Western perspectives of sexuality located in South-east Asia.

This analysis, a mixture of neo-Marxian, Freudian and Foucauldian thought, and incomplete though it may be in its contemporary interpretation of late capitalistic modes of production, begins to explain the growth of modern holiday taking and its relationship with the sex industry. To reiterate, first, as is evidenced from countless reports of the Poor Law Commissioners in the United Kingdom, and as described by Thomas Carlyle in Past and Present, ([1843] 1965), social life was divided and fragmented into periods and roles dominated by work and occupational status in the late nineteenth century and early twentieth century in Europe and Northern America. Fragmentation creates alien others, people not within specific social circles, activities that are not approved by the dominant mores in society and, with the growth of imperialism and the empires of the European nations in Africa and the East, exotic other places. It can be argued that this process of demarcation was tinged with the attributing of moral values which served to reinforce the superiority of those making judgements.

Such judgements extended to the discussion of gender, and the previous holistic assessments of sexuality and its role within the natural order of things were cast aside by many within the newly industrialising age. At its most extreme this was demonstrated by attitudes towards recently subjected indigenous peoples. Ann Cameron provides evidence of this from a recent past in quoting evidence from Indian women who belonged to a matriarchal, matrilineal society in Western Canada. Thus she writes: [T]he priests had to be content to take the girl children. Instead of being raised and educated by women who told them the truth about their bodies, the girls were taken from their villages and put in schools where they were taught to keep their breasts bound, to hide their arms and legs, to never look a brother openly in the eyes but to look down at the ground as if ashamed of something. Instead of learning that once a month their bodies would become sacred, they were taught they would become filthy. Instead of going to the waiting house to meditate, pray and celebrate the fullness of the moon and their own bodies, they were taught they were sick, and must bandage themselves and act as if they were sick. They were taught the waves and surgings of their bodies were sinful and must never be indulged in or enjoyed.

The industrial age sought to marginalise even further conceptualisations of the sacredness of female sexuality. In their work The Myth of the Goddess, Baring and Cashford (1991) argue that former civilizations recognised a sacredness in the duality of male and female, but it can be argued that the industrialisation of the nineteenth century reinforced Judaeo-Christian traditions of denying sacredness within the sexual act and the union of male and female. It did this, argues Foucault, by the adoption of a scientific de-aggregation of the whole by concentration upon the particular. As noted, Foucault argues that the nineteenth century offered a new discourse. He wrote: The family [became] as an agency of control and a point of sexual saturation: it was in the 'bourgeois' or 'aristocratic' family that the sexuality of children and adolescents was first problematised, and feminine sexuality medicalised; it was the first to be alerted to the potential pathology of sex, the urgent need to keep it under close watch and to devise a rational technology of correction.

Whereas for earlier generations sex was sacred, for the Victorian period sex was, according to Foucault, a pathological problem. However, it needs to be also noted that Thane (1999) refers to the slender evidence about the Victorian belief in the 'passive' woman and notes the diaries of Beatrice Webb as a counterpoint to such a view. Nonetheless, for London in 1894, the talking point was the state of the music hall, and its role as a venue for the meeting of prostitutes (Stokes, 1994). Thus, while within the societal fragmentations of the nineteenth century, just as there emerged the concept of holidays as periods of non-work as described above, additionally there also emerged the concept of the fallen woman as a source of disease and danger.

This was very specifically evidenced by the Contagious Diseases Acts of 1864, 1866 and the importance of such labelling and stigmatisation has long been clearly understood within the literature on deviancy. For example, Turner and Surace (1956) argued that in the case of 'Zootsuiters' in California, the hostility evoked by their behaviours became only actionable when labelled with a pejorative term so as to undermine the romantic and exciting images of being 'Mexican'. In passing it might be queried if this is but a further example of the racism implicit in Western representations of non-Occidental peoples failing to repress what are deemed as unsuitable behaviour.

Rock (1973:20) argues that the deviant role 'is given a recognised place in the social structure and those who assume it are led to expect that becoming deviant will be a fateful process'. To be deviant is to be a rule-breaker, and knowing oneself to be a rule-breaker predisposes one to certain actions, to certain roles and the acceptance of deviant personality. But Rock also recognises that the rules by which deviancy are defined are ambiguous, and often rest upon power relationships within society. It thus becomes possible to challenge these rules, the assumptions that lie behind them, and to take advantage of power shifts within society.

Thus, the assumptions of the recent past age of industrialisation are now being challenged by a prostitute voice which seeks recourse to an earlier discourse, that of the sacredness of the sexual act. This will be discussed in more detail subsequently, but it can be noted on the web pages of Annie Sprinkle, the feminist, performance artist and sex worker, and found in the pages of work expressing the prostitute voice. Veronica Vera - spokesperson of Prostitutes of New York (PONY) is quoted by Bell as saying:

Sex is a nourishing, life-giving force and as a consequence sex work is of benefit to humanity Sex workers are providing a very valuable service to be honoured. Sex work … is a good service, it is the best service that one individual can do for another individual.

By affirming sex as a nourishing, healing tool, by being tolerant of one another's sexual needs, by affirming sex workers as practitioners of a sacred craft, we accept and affirm our own humanity, an empowering act.

For a sex worker feminist writer like Susie Kruhse-MountBurton, who rejects Dworkin's position on prostitution as being too reductionist, 'Men hold most of the power in society and yet they are the sexual and emotional supplicants who depend upon women's bodies for nurture and reproduction' (1996:14). A middle way between the feminists who argue that women are manipulated and abused by men and those who reclaim the role of 'priestess' for prostitutes is represented by the view expressed by argument that the prostitute engages in strong boundary maintenance. Chapkis (1997) provides an illustration of this by citing the words of San Francisco sex worker Carol Queen, who argues:

We create sexual situations with very clear boundaries, for ourselves and for our clients. In fact, one of the things that people are paying us for is clear boundaries. It's like the person going to the massage therapist; you're paying to be touched without having to worry about intimacy, reciprocity, and long-term consequences.

As Chapkis (1997:76) observes, because sexuality and emotion are stripped from their presumed relationship with nature and self, it need not be assumed that subsequent alienation is destructive. The implication is that it is, in short, a job of work - one requiring skills that not everyone can do, but no more or less a job for all that.

It has been observed that the client has not suffered the same stigmatisation as the female, but this is not to deny that the client has not been criticised. For some researchers the habitual user of the services of prostitutes is a sorry sight. Thus:

The farther we look into this hard core of single habitual customers - those with the most prostitution experiences - the clearer the picture becomes of people who are 'on the outside.' They characteristically have difficulties holding down a job or managing their own finances, and they have a limited social network. Put bluntly: the more customer experiences a man has, the more different he is.

Similar expressions can be found in the literature relating to sex tourists. Very occasionally a 'happy story' can be found. Seabrook provides us with the story of 'Tony'. Tony's wife died when he was in his mid-forties, and for fourteen years he has sustained a relationship with Nok, a woman he met in a bar in Bangkok. Seabrook reports him as saying:

I won't take Nok to America. I have thought about it, but no. She has her family here. Her children are married - they are more accepting of me than my daughter is of Nok. To me Thailand is the place where I found some consolation for a loss I thought I could never bear.

Such stories are infrequent. The realities are commonly otherwise, and the problem with each such story is that it sustains the hope on the part of women like Nok for a man like Tony. In doing so it distracts from the economic and social realities of systems that sustain the form of sex tourism found in places like Bangkok, even while it reduces those social realities to the level of the individual.

Following Marx, it has been noted that the industrialisation process created a process of alienation. However, it can be argued that another process of fragmentation is also involved. Recognising claims for holidays reinforces a separation of work and non-work time. Haine notes that: 'The slow decay of the apprenticeship system and its rituals... during the first decades of the nineteenth century sundered the connection between work and play' (1992:469). Industrialisation separated these two worlds, but it went further. It emasculated the latent challenge of non-work lives as an alternative life-style. It commoditised periods of consumption of leisure in places other than home, and made safe such periods by the processes of consumption associated with the forms of capitalism common from the start of the twentieth century.

The period of holidays, being a consumer product, no longer represents embryonic alternative lifestyles. Rather, the worker- consumer needs to continue to work in order to afford the holiday period, and remnants of the Puritan work ethic continue as we declare that 'we have earned our holiday'. Additionally, by setting non-work periods as periods of less value, it ascribed to those who did not work, mothers and the elderly, a secondary social role. Yet, in spite of these processes, it could not entirely sweep aside the potential challenge posed by holiday periods as moments of escape.

The holiday retains a powerful potential for catharsis and identity confirmation or renewal. This is evidenced by popular literature, observation, personal experience and research.

For example, the novels of David Lodge illustrate the processes of renewal of self. At the commencement of Paradise News (1992) a description is given of garishly dressed tourists who, with varying degrees of anxiety, check in for their flights aided by world-weary couriers. Yet, by page 180 the main character is reviewing his past life, examining his religious beliefs and by the end of the novel a reborn life that comes complete with a booklet of the Hawaiian Folk Mass and a quotation from Miguel de Unamuno's The Tragic Sense of Life. Love, and sex, have entered our hero's life.

In Therapy - A Novel, the relationship between self-discovery, pilgrimage and tourism is made all the more explicit as the hero, Laurence Passmore who describes himself as 'I am fifty-eight years old, five feet nine-and-a-half inches tall and thirteen stone eight pounds in weight' and thus 'tubby', discovers lost love from forty years previously on a tourist holiday tracing the pilgrims steps to Santiago de Compostela in Spain. Similarly, Willy Russell's heroine, Shirley Valentine, discovers courage to be herself on holiday. This, as a windsurfing instructor in Greece (an example of acted out fantasy?) remembers a tourist who sold his business in Scotland to return to Greece to earn a living teaching holidaymakers to sail catamarans.

A nurse who was a tourist one year, returned the next as a windsurfing instructor, met a young man and was last heard of heading for the ski slopes with her new partner. In an article, 'Conversations in Majorca - the over 55s on holiday', Ryan (1995) recounts meeting a respondent who described herself as being a Shirley Valentine - being a tourist, returning home, divorcing her husband, returning to Majorca and eventually marrying, happily, a local Spaniard.

Wickens (1994) attributes the label 'Shirley Valentine' to a group of hedonistic tourists in Greece, and has one such describe herself as:

You are here to please yourself... As far as I can, I leave my everyday life behind. When I'm in England, I'm fitting into an appointed role of somebody's wife, somebody's secretary. Here, you can relax, and rub off some of the sharp corners. You are not restricted. Greeks are very tolerant of us... If you give yourself a chance, you can find out things about yourself that you did not know before ... I am less age-conscious here... I like sex but not with my husband ... I come to Greece for a bit of fun.

Holidays are thus the marginal periods with latent potential to change people's lives. Tourists live as liminal people caught in the between and betwixt worlds of their own homes, but not in the homes and worlds of their hosts. Sometimes their holiday homes are artificial homes, architecturally designed to encourage life by the side of the swimming pool, to gaze upon other tourists and cosseted so that daily tasks of making beds and washing dishes are no longer required. Spatially isolated from the world of home and the culture of the country within which they are located, resort complexes reside in a geographical marginality, often beside the liminality of the littoral zone - itself a place that is neither mainland nor sea.

This has begun to develop a thesis of sex tourism as an interaction between two groups of liminal people, people who occupy spaces between different worlds. The tourist engages in a temporary escape from the world of work, but returns to it. The prostitute exists more permanently on the edges of society, but also engages in processes of departure and return as she, or he, resumes non-prostitute roles. For both, as will be developed more fully in later issues of self-identity arise.

However, our conceptualisation of these roles has its antecedents in the development of the processes of industrialisation ushered in by the Industrial Revolution in the latter half of the nineteenth century. While, in the tourism literature, such an analysis has become subsumed in a move towards postmodernism and concepts of de-differentiation, it is thought important not to lose sight of the conditions of the Industrial Revolution and the powerful influences they had upon patterns of life and subsequent thinking. Durkheim's book The Division of Labour in Society, while written in 1893 was only translated into English in 1933 and thus today we are further removed from the period when Durkheim's analysis entered the consciousness of Anglo-Saxon scholars than Durkheim himself was distant from the processes he described. Yet these were indeed revolutionary forces and they should not be under-estimated.

Carlyle, writing in 1843 described the consequences of industrialisation thus:

So many hundred thousands sit in workhouses: and other hundred thousands have not yet got even work houses; and in thrifty Scotland itself, in

Glasgow or Edinburgh City, in their dark lanes, hidden from all but the eye of God, and of rare Benevolence the minister of God, there are such scenes of woe and destitution and desolation, such as, one may hope, the Sun never saw before in the most barbarous regions where men dwelt.

The age created such fragmentations of society that their echoes still persist today. The processes of industry commenced then have given rise to the multinational corporations of today, and the inequalities of wealth are still perpetuated, between and within nations. As will be described, some women are exploited due to the poverty of their families, a poverty located within global systems of wealth and power. Some women turn to prostitution to deny the poverty that might otherwise be ascribed to them.

For a nineteenth-century female activist like Emma Goldman, the cause of the trade in women was: the merciless Moloch of capitalism that fattens on underpaid labour, thus driving thousands of women and girls into prostitution ... these girls feel, 'Why waste your life working for a few shillings a week in a scullery, eighteen hours a day'.

Many still echo this sentiment today. In their turn, workers turn to tourism as an escape, a relief from patterns of work that increasingly make demands upon time and their families, and as part of that process seek relief from prostitutes. Such relief is symbolic of both processes of exploitation and succour. The processes of the Industrial Revolution, it has been argued, created the antecedents of the modern holiday by creating a demand for, and a supply of the tours offered by Mr Thomas Cook and his European counterparts. It has created a dichotomisation of women - the Madonna/harlot which fascinated and appalled the Victorian mind.

The imperialism of the period also extended this classification of womanhood into an exotic other - of eastern women alluring, sensuous and equally dangerous. Sex tourism combines all of these historic connotations which are continually made explicit and implicit every time the client asks, 'How much?'. Yet, while this has been based on Turner's use of comparative symbology but selecting symbols of past and present, such an analysis can only be partial. The 'Social Dramas' described by Turner (1974) have their symbolic value because of the functions they perform. The functional and pragmatic must too be assessed, and thus the question as to why prostitution and tourism go so closely hand in hand in the modern era needs to be asked.

7

Social Milieu — Alcohol and Drugs

INDIVIDUAL AND SOCIAL ASPECTS OF HEALTH

A new Approach is likely to gain easier acceptance if it involves individual rather than social action. The majority of people tend to look for immediate, practical solutions that they can adopt without having to face major social and environmental problems. They search for personal recipes and formulas for physical well-being. This attitude is understandable. Health and illness are intimate problems, involving the ability to survive and enjoy full lives. Health is enjoyed by the individual, not by such abstractions as "man" and "the community." Any discussion of health usually evokes the query: "What can I do right now to remove hazards to my health and assure my physical well-being?"

This question has been answered, to a great extent, by authorities cited in the previous chapters—implicitly if not always directly. Diet should be highly varied. If at all possible, it should be based on foods that receive minimal or no treatment by processors, such as whole-wheat breads, fresh meat, vegetables and fruit. Weight control is desirable in all stages of life, not only in middle age. Urban man should put his body to frequent use, with an emphasis on mild daily exercise, such as walking, rather than on sporadic sessions of competitive sports. Certainly smoking is utterly incompatible with good health and should be reduced or eliminated.

There is a good deal of evidence to indicate that a high intake of starches, sugars and polysaturated fats predisposes the individual to coronary heart disease. At any rate, a diet that is ordinarily regarded as suitable for active growing children seems to be very undesirable for adults. The food intake of the individual should be carefully scaled to his age, to his work load and to his activities during leisure hours.

The individual should attempt to cultivate a serene attitude towards the surrounding world, an outlook based not on a psychoanalytic accommodation to the ills of society, but rather on a critical sense of values that places the trivia of daily life in a manageable perspective. To seek an uncritical, brainless state of euphoria is selfdebasing. On the other hand, to respond with equal sensitivity to every disquieting aspect of daily life is spiritually paralysing and physically harmful. In trying to reduce the tensions that an overly urbanized, bitterly competitive society engenders in the individual, there is no substitute for a truly humanistic philosophy that helps us to discriminate between problems that warrant a strong emotional response and those that should be dismissed as inconsequential. To live a life without intense feeling is as dehumanising as to live one that is filled with ill-defined, persistent agitation.

Health is the result of a lifelong process. It cannot be acquired by a pill or by a "magic" food. Physical wellbeing presupposes a rounded mode of life and a comprehensive diet geared to the needs of the body. Any attempt to prescribe a single "health-giving" recipe that fails to encompass the totality of the individual—his past as well as his present—is irresponsible. Neither "royal jelly" at one extreme nor a "miracle drug" at the other will provide an individual with health if his environment and manner of life are deteriorating. Attempts to resolve health into a single formula may be well-meaning, but they are woefully incomplete.

The need for a comprehensive approach to health is stressed in Iago Galdston's critique of modern medicine and his argument for social medicine. Modern medicine has failed, in Galdston's opinion, not because it has "no cure for cancer, for essential hypertension, or for multiple sclerosis. Were it to achieve these and other cures besides, it still would have failed." Its failure is due to the fact that "modern medicine is almost entirely preoccupied with diseases and with their treatment and very little, if at all, with health. It is obvious that an individual sick with pneumococcus pneumonia can be effectively treated by chemo-therapeutic agents, or by antibiotics. But such an individual, though cured of his pneumonia, may and most likely will, remain a sick man unless, in addition, efforts are made to help him regain his health." Galdston advocates more than convalescent care. He proposes a change in medical education, medical outlook and medical methods.

A physician trained according to the principles of social medicine "would not be moved to enquire 'what's he got and what's good for it,' but, confronted by an ailing individual, he would attempt to determine the nature and extent of the disability as it is manifest, not merely in the presenting symptoms, but in the over-all performance of the individual according to his position in life; that is, in the light of his age, educational, vocational, social and other prerogatives and obligations. He would not affirm 'this man has a peptic ulcer,' and undertake to treat the ulcer, but would by the presence of the ulcer recognize that the individual is sick and seek to determine and to correct, or amend, what ails the individual; what, in other words, impedes the individual in the fulfillment of his adventure in living."

Galdston's remarks constitute a much-needed attempt to widen the contemporary medical outlook. Efforts to expand prevailing notions of illness, treatment and health beyond the germ theory and the emphasis on specific cures for specific diseases were thwarted at the turn of the century. This defeat culminated in tragedy when Max von Pettenkofer, the great German sanitarian, took his life in 1901 in despair over the rejection of his viewpoint. Pettenkofer had never denied the germ theory of disease, regardless of popularizations of medical history to the contrary. The controversy in his time centered around whether germs alone caused disease or whether environmental conditions and the constitution of the individual should also be considered in the study of individual illness and epidemics. As John Shaw Billings, the great American authority on public health, put it in 1883: "It is important to remember that the mere introduction of germs into the living organism does not ensure their multiplication, or the production of disease. The condition of the organism itself has much influence on the result. Pasteur has certainly made a hasty generalization in declaring that the only condition which determines an epidemic is the greater or less abundance of germs."

Today, three generations later, the issue is being raised again—and in what appears to be a much broader sense than even Galdston has suggested. Many of the biological problems created by poor sanitation and slums have been resolved, at least in the Western world. We are no longer as deeply concerned with killing epidemics of communicable diseases as were Pasteur, Pettenkofer and Billings. But we are very much concerned with harmful environmental influences on some of the most intimate aspects of individual life. The necessities of life, even its pleasures, are now being manufactured for the millions. As a nation of urban dwellers in a mass society, we are becoming increasingly dependent upon the decisions of others for the quality of our food, clothing and shelter. These decisions affect not only our diet and our private lives; they affect the water we drink and the air we breathe. To speak of an environmental "influence" on health is an understatement; there is a distinct environmental and social dimension to every aspect of human biology. Man today is more domesticated than he has ever been in the long course of his history.

It is here that we encounter the limits of the individual's ability to attain health on his own. The average man finds it extremely difficult to reorganize his mode of life along lines that favour well-being and fitness. If he lives in the city, he cannot possibly avoid exposure to air pollutants. Similarly, there are hardly any rural areas in America where the individual is not exposed to the assortment of pesticides that are currently employed in agriculture. Any serious attempt to limit the diet to pure foods, free of pesticide residues, artificial colouring and flavouring matter and synthetic preservatives, is well beyond the financial means of the average person. But even if the individual can afford it, he will find that untreated foods are difficult to obtain, for relatively few pure foods are grown in the United States and those that reach urban centers are rarely sold in large retail markets.

The layout of the modern city and its routine demands on the urban dweller tend to discourage a physically active way of life. Movement in the large city is organized around the automobile and public means of transportation. Most of our occupations and responsibilities demand mental dexterity, a routine of limited physical work, or rapid communication. It requires a heroic effort to walk instead of ride, to do instead of see, to move instead of sit. Although a few exceptional individuals may succeed in modifying their mode of life in a way that promotes health, the overwhelming majority of urban dwellers can be expected to go along with things as they are.

Does this mean that modern man will never attain optimal health, that it is, in fact, a "mirage"? Rene Dubos has argued rather persuasively that health is a relative concept. Man's criteria of health change with the economic, cultural and political goals of each social period. "Clearly, health and disease cannot be defined merely in terms of anatomical, physiological, or mental attributes," Dubos writes. "Their real measure is the ability of the individual to function in a manner acceptable to himself and to the group of which he is part. For several centuries the Western world has pretended to find a unifying concept of health in the Greek ideal of a proper balance between body and mind. But in reality this ideal is more and more difficult to convert into practice. Poets, philosophers and creative scientists are rarely found among Olympic laureates. It is not easy to discover a formula of health broad enough to fit Voltaire and Jack Dempsey, to encompass the requirements of a stevedore, a New York City bus driver and a contemplative monk."

Perhaps so. But the truth is not exhausted by the limited notions men form of a given event or situation. That which individuals, classes, or communities really believe to be health in a given historical period—all pretensions aside—does not tell us what health *could* be or what it *should* be in a broader biological and social perspective. It is one thing to say that historical notions of health have been limited; it is quite another to contend that they will always be limited. Although Dubos may be correct in describing life as a series of ideals for which men can be expected to sacrifice their health and even their lives, there is no reason to believe that health, defined primarily "in terms of anatomical, physiological, or mental attributes," is incompatible with a rational manner of life. On the contrary, a manner of life that promotes health is likely to be more satisfying culturally and socially than one that militates against the attainment of fitness and well-being. Health is nourished by all the environmental and social factors that advance thought, creative effort and a rounded personality. The social factors that promote health also promote the adventure of life.

On the other hand, the more cloistered the man, the more cloistered the mind. The more one-sided the way of life, however "challenging" or "adventurous" it may seem on the surface, the more limited the range of thought and art. Voltaire was a brilliant writer but a superficial thinker. His life, spent for the most part at the château of Cirey and in his "lairs" on the Franco-Swiss border, shows in his work. One is entitled to wonder whether he would have acquired greater depth had he been exposed, like his more profound contemporary, Diderot, to an earthier life in the streets of Paris. Similarly, Olympic laureates seldom become poets and philosophers because their limited notions of "adventure" are focused entirely on physical activity for its own sake. Far from challenging the "Greek ideal of a proper balance between body and mind," the very incompleteness of their lives and thought is evidence of its validity.

Dubos, in effect, tends to equate health with adaptation. The environments to which men are expected to adapt are conceived of as dynamic, emergent phenomena —a rather ambiguous approach that seems to take the environment too much for granted. Unlike other animals, man can consciously remake his environment, within certain limits and the real issue to be faced is whether it is man or his unsatisfactory environment that should be changed. Viewed from this standpoint, the problem becomes much clearer. One can conceive of many circumstances in which health is not an end in itself and even of circumstances in which the achievement of certain ends is worth the loss of health. By and large, however, a health-promoting environment encourages social and cultural progress. There need be no conflict between health and a truly creative, rational civilization.

On the whole, however, Dubos has performed a notable service in focusing attention on the relationship between human fitness and social development. We cannot conceive of progress in the field of public health without advances in society. Management of the soil has always depended upon the prevailing forms of land tenure. The quality of today's food is partly determined by whether the interests of food manufacturers or the interests of consumers determine technological changes in the industry. The form and direction taken by urban life are guided by the kind of social relations men establish in the management of their affairs. Any attempt to preserve the health of individuals which does not also aim at creating social patterns that will favour the health of mankind as a whole may result in limited improvement but not long-range solutions. The majority of individuals who seek optimal health as soloists in a deteriorating environment have far too much to cope with in attaining their ends.

At the same time, today, more than at any other time in history, every social change has deep-seated biological consequences. Man has developed extremely effective methods for changing the world around him. The results of his activity over the face of the earth are far-reaching. The natural world can no longer successfully oppose dense forests, vast bodies of water and climatic rigors to his penetration. The developments of modern technology have deprived nature of its old defences against the invasion of man. But the natural world can strike back in the form of disease, exhaustion of the soil and desiccation of the land. The importance of caution and the need for exercising reason in changing the world around us can hardly be given too much emphasis. "What is new is not necessarily good," Dubos observes, "and all changes, even those apparently the most desirable, are always fraught with unpredictable consequences. The scientist must beware of having to admit, like Captain Ahab in Melville *Moby Dick*, 'All my means are sane; my motives and objects mad.' "

THE PROBLEMS OF REMEDIAL LEGISLATION

How much progress can we expect from attempts to improve the health of the American public by means of legislation? More, certainly, than we can expect from isolated individual efforts. The United States has by no means exhausted all the possibilities of welfare legislation; it has lagged behind many European nations in fulfilling its responsibilities to the sick and the infirm. Its national health programmes consist of *ad hoc* aid and a patchwork of laboratories and clinics to meet the mounting needs of research and therapy. Food and drug laws have not kept pace with the rapid changes in food technology and the operations of federal agencies responsible for administering them leave much to be desired. An account of the advances, conflicts and retreats in the field of food and drug control offers a valuable perspective on what remedial legislation can and cannot be expected to do.

The problems of food and drug control have been surrounded by such a dense fog of official overstatement that almost any criticism of existing laws and agencies invites countercharges of "quackery" and "faddism." Consider the following blurb, made up in part of official statements, which the public is expected to accept as good coin:

"When the American housewife pushes her shopping cart through the supermarket, she can select attractively packaged foods and drinks with the confidence that they are honestly labeled, pure and wholesome. Her confidence is based on the existence of good laws that are vigilantly enforced. Most American food manufacturers today have the will and the know-how to produce the pure foods that she wants.

They accept the *Food, Drug and Cosmetic Act* as a blueprint of their obligations to the Nation's consumers. The additives that go into food are there to improve the food and bring it to the housewife in better condition and in a more convenient form. Reliable food processors have not reduced the nutritional quality of our foods or created inferior products through the use of chemical additives. Actually, the quality and sanitary characteristics of our food have been improving."

Most of these complacent remarks can be dismissed as rubbish. Without doing any injustice to the facts, the blurb might be rewritten as follows: "When the American housewife pushes her shopping cart through the supermarket, she encounters many products whose packaging often misleads her concerning the quality, quantity and nutritive value of their contents. Generally, the enforcement of food-labeling laws and regulations has been handled in a very slovenly fashion by federal and state authorities. Most processed foods are certainly not 'pure,' if by a pure product is meant one that does not contain chemical additives. Food and drug control is far from satisfactory and it has often been necessary to prod federal agencies into discharging their responsibilities to the consumer.

The F.D.A. has shown an unusual susceptibility to influence from the food industry; the agency's performance has been distinguished by its leniency and patience with food manufacturers. More often than not, food processors and drug manufacturers have bitterly opposed improvements in regulatory legislation. Although some of the chemicals that are added to food may possibly improve them, the safety of many food additives is very doubtful. Finally, reliable food manufacturers have definitely reduced the nutritive value of certain common foods and additives have often served to conceal inferior products."

The first statement attempts to evade the problems of modern food control; the second, to face them. It is almost begging the question to claim that producers of food accept the Food, Drug and Cosmetic Act as "a blueprint of their obligations to the Nation's consumers" when the law is not as demanding as it should be and those who administer it are satisfied with a second-rate achievement. Nor is the case for the law strengthened by smuggling the housewife's "wants" into the issue. The wants of many consumers are created by high-pressure advertising and salesmanship. The average consumer knows far too little about nutrition to evaluate advertising claims. Food purchases are guided partly by sales technique, partly by the appearance of the food. Thus, the food industry tends to generate the very wants it professes to satisfy and conventional books and articles on nutrition tend to equate the satisfaction of these industry-created wants with improvements in the quality and purity of our food.

The truth is that federal food and drug legislation has always been a poor, unstable compromise between the interests of the food industry and the demands of an aroused public opinion. More than a quarter of a century separates the first unsuccessful attempts to enact a general anti-adulteration law (1879) and the adoption of the basic *Food and Drug Law of 1906*. The story behind these and later conflicts in the field of pure-food legislation indicates the amount of effort that has been required to preserve the integrity of our food supply. The needs of industry were consistently given priority over those of the public; during this entire period, Congress was quick to favour special interests. It put an end to the export of adulterated products only when the reputation of American food began to decline on the world market. It enacted legislation against oleomargarine in behalf of domestic dairy interests.

On the whole, the public interest was served only indirectly. At the turn of the century, the most flagrant cases of adulteration were the work of small-scale producers, whose adulterated goods placed major producers at a competitive disadvantage. In these cases, both Congress and most of the food manufacturers responded readily to the need for specific anti-adulteration legislation, but the food industry's support for a general food law was, at best, hesitant and in the halls of Congress support for a pure-food law gathered very slowly.

The publication of *The Jungle* in book form, however, had aroused widespread public indignation against the meat-packing industry. The scales were tipped in favour of the law when President Theodoure Roosevelt released part of a report by a federal investigating commission which fully corroborated the details in Sinclair's novel. The national uproar that followed these disclosures threw the industry into retreat and on June 30, 1906, the first federal Pure Food and Drug Act was signed into law. Its administration was placed largely in the hands of Wiley and his Bureau of Chemistry. Although the law had many shortcomings, some of which were corrected in later years, the high standards of food and drug control which Wiley sought to establish during his tenure in office have never been equaled by his successors. The history of the fight for pure food after Wiley's departure from government service reads like an anticlimax to the vigilance and dedication that marked earlier policies.

These policies were guided by two basic principles. The first was that the consumer should know precisely what he is getting and that he should get precisely what he wants. Wiley bitterly opposed labels or claims that misrepresented a product to the buyer, even if the use of a spurious description was harmless to public health. He stubbornly fought attempts by food manufacturers to describe glucose as "corn syrup" or to represent whiskey made partly of neutral grain spirits as "blended whiskey," a name that generally denoted a blend of several genuine whiskeys. For Wiley, a label had to be complete and truthful. He expected the food manufacturer to disclose an the artificial ingredients added to a product. The name on a package, can, or bottle had to convey the nature of the product without any ambiguity or misrepresentation.

Wiley's second principle was that if any doubt exists about the toxicity of a chemical additive, the doubt should be resolved in favour of the consumer. As it is impossible to prove a negative such as "harmlessness," Wiley argued, it is not permissible to use any questionable additive that is not indispensable to the production, storage, or distribution of food. If an additive contributed nothing to health or to the availability of a food and if its use might conceivably prove harmful, the Bureau of Chemistry sought to have it removed. Wiley seldom wavered on this score; his decisions almost invariably favoured the public interest.

Many people in the food and chemical industries felt differently, however and their complaints evoked a sympathetic response from the government. By 1912, Wiley's attempts to execute his policies were being frustrated to such an extent that he left government service. With his departure, the law underwent steady reinterpretation. An increasing number of doubts about the toxicity of new chemical additives were resolved in favour of food growers and food processors. The Bureau of Chemistry and its successor in the enforcement of the law, the Food and Drug Administration, began to exhibit undue sensitivity to the financial welfare of industry. The improvement of food was equated with lower costs, attractive packaging and sales-promotion devices. Wiley had combined the zeal of a crusader with the knowledge of a physician; with his departure, the policies of the federal regulatory agencies were guided increasingly by lawyers and professional administrators who began to give priority to legal considerations instead of problems of public health.

The consumer could ill afford this development. Although an overhaul of the food and drug law was made in 1938, the situation began to deteriorate to an appalling extent. After the end of World War II, the American food supply was deluged with an unprecedented variety of new chemical additives. DDT and other organic insecticides, unknown in 1938, were being used extensively in agriculture and the home. The responsibility for proving that a chemical additive was harmful to the consumer rested with the F.D.A. Food growers and food processors were free to use what they chose until such time as the government could establish that the additives involved were toxic substances. Testing standards in many laboratories were inadequate; experimental work on new additives was often limited to sixty- and ninety-day feeding trials on one or two species of rodents.

In September 1958, Congress changed the law drastically; it made the manufacturer responsible for establishing the safety of a food additive and inserted the Delaney anti-cancer clause, a provision that flatly prohibits the use of additives "found to induce cancer when ingested by man or animal..." Although the anti-cancer clause was strongly supported by the American Cancer Society and by leading cancer specialists, it was opposed by the F.D.A. Testifying in April 1958 before a House committee studying pending revisions of the law, F.D.A. Commissioner George P. Larrick observed: "Two of the bills before you make specific mention of cancer." The F. D.A. -supported bill, H.R. 6747, does "not mention it specifically... This bill bars the use of an additive unless it is established that it is without hazard to health. Thus, the bill would prohibit the addition of any chemical additive to the food supply until adequate evidence, acceptable to competent scientists, shows that it will not produce cancer in man under the conditions of use proposed." Although Larrick endorsed the goal of "seeing that cancer-producing foods are not on the American market," Congressman Delaney reminded the National Health Federation that "in 1956 an FDA ruling permitted, at a certain concentration, residues of a pesticide to remain on marketed fruits and vegetables, even though it had been shown to induce cancer in test animals. Later tests showed this chemical to be even more injurious than the earlier tests demonstrated and the FDA has now taken action to prohibit any of its residues on raw agricultural commodities."

The credit for finally adding an anti-cancer clause to the 1958 law must be given to Delaney, who saw to its enactment despite strong opposition from the food industry and the F.D.A. By 1960, the F.D.A. had reversed its position and, at the hearings on food colours conducted by the House Committee on Interstate and Foreign Commerce, expressed its fervent support for the Delaney clause. Presumably all is well that ends well, but the F.D.A. refuses to let the clause remain as it is. At the food-colour hearings, the Secretary of Health, Education and Welfare, Arthur S. Flemming, began to nibble at the Delaney clause by suggesting that it "should be modified to provide that additives used in animal feed which leave no residue either in the animal after slaughter or in any food product obtained from the living animal be exempt from the provisions of the clause. A comparable amendment to the anti-cancer clause in the colour additive legislation under consideration would be appropriate." Experience with Yellow OB and Yellow AB suggests that such standards of purity are impossible to achieve.

The sweeping legislative revisions of 1958 were not gained without a sacrifice. For all its shortcomings, the 1938 law had one redeeming feature: It flatly prohibited the use of any toxic chemical additives in food other than those that were clearly indispensable to food production. Although the burden of proof rested with the F.D.A. instead of the manufacturers, the 1938 law set a new functional standard for chemical additives in food. This criterion was dropped in the 1958 revisions of the law, largely on the urging of the food industry and the F.D.A. The burden of proving that the additives are safe has been shifted to the manufacturers, but toxic chemicals can now be added to food provided they are used in amounts that are deemed to be "harmless" to consumers.

Thus, after the passage of a half century, the law makes no attempt to resolve Wiley's original problem: Does an additive contribute to the nutritive value and availability of a food or does it merely function as a dispensable technological aid? Modern refrigeration and canning techniques have eliminated the need for many artificial preservatives in our food supply. Hardly anyone will contend that colouring and flavouring matter are indispensable to food production. If consumers really desired artificial colours and flavours, they could be marketed as independent products and the public could use them at its own discretion. The food industry could modify its production methods so as to operate with a minimum number of chemical additives and with a view towards retaining many nutrients that are now lost because of an overemphasis on mass production and highly processed foods. Many synthetic additives that have no nutritive function could easily be replaced with valuable nutrients. For example, ascorbic acid (vitamin C) is a good antioxidant and an excellent flour bleach, but as it is relatively costly, it would be unprofitable to use it.

The food industry has demanded complete freedom in determining the function of chemical additives in food. The following remarks by the National Association of Frozen Food Packers are fairly typical: "We join with other segments of the food industry in fundamental opposition to provisions which would permit the Food and Drug Administration to determine the composition of food products upon the basis of its conception of functional value or utility of food ingredients." This seems to be a matter of principle, not a lack of confidence in the F.D.A. After asserting that the chances are "rather remote" that a food processor would engage in costly tests of a toxic additive, the association adds: "In any case, the question of usefulness of an ingredient shown to be safe is one which the manufacturer of a food is entitled to resolve upon the basis of his own experience and is not properly a matter of the opinion of the Food and Drug Administration."

The F.D.A.'s superficial approach to food and drug legislation has largely been exhausted. The next overhaul of the law must return to the principles that guided Wiley a half century ago. Moreover, we require not only a better food and drug law but comprehensive national legislation that will confront the problems raised by urban and industrial pollution, radioactive contaminants, the misuse of X radiation and industrial carcinogens. Water pollution can be appreciably reduced if all sizable communities are required to treat their sewage and if an effective national programme is developed to reclaim and re-use water to meet industrial needs.

The highest-quality water, that which requires a minimum of chemical treatment, should be reserved for drinking purposes. The problem of air pollution should be met resolutely, without qualms about cost and without fear of offending industrialists, motorists, or homeowners. Recently developed catalytic and non-catalytic burners, for example, can remove many harmful agents from automobile exhausts. "Automobile engineers know now that for perhaps $10 per car they can eliminate 50 per cent of the hydrocarbons; for something over $300 they can eliminate them almost totally," observes George A. W. Boehm, of *Fortune* magazine. "Any city or state that decides to apply air-pollution regulations to cars will have to decide how much the motorist can be made to pay for how much purity and how far it is prepared to go in enforcing purity regulations."

But let us not deceive ourselves; an environment based on mammoth, expanding cities will never be a healthy one. In the United States, the ecological and nutritional problems created by monoculture and the land factory are likely to grow worse and many chemical additives will be required in the mass production of our food. Insecticidal residues will undoubtedly continue to pervade our food staples. The substitution of nuclear energy for mineral sources of fuel will be accelerated in the years to come and more radioactive substances can be expected to enter man's environment. Urban life will undoubtedly become increasingly one-sided as cities expand and occupations become more sedentary. The improvements that our technicians, sanitarians and city planners have projected for the "world of tomorrow" may meliorate some of these problems, but they are not likely to eliminate them if our society continues to develop in the pattern of the giant metropolis. We can no more expect engineering devices to give us a healthful environment than we can expect the therapeutic agents of modern medicine to create a healthy individual.

DECENTRALIZATION

Without having read any books or articles on human ecology, millions of Americans have sensed the over-all deterioration of modern urban life. They have turned to the suburbs and "exurbs" as a refuge from the burdens of the metropolitan milieu. From all accounts of suburban life, many of these burdens have followed them into the countryside. Suburbanites have not adapted to the land; they have merely adapted a metropolitan manner of life to semi-rural surroundings. The metropolis remains the axis around which their lives turn. It is the source of their livelihood, their food staples and, in large part, their tensions. The suburbs have branched away from the city, but they still belong to the metropolitan tree.

It would be wise, however, to stop ridiculing the exodus to the suburbs and to try to understand what lies behind this phenomenon. The modern city has reached its limits. Megalopolitan life is breaking down—psychically, economically and biologically. Millions of people have acknowledged this breakdown by "voting with their feet"; they have picked up their belongings and left. If they have not been able to sever their connections with the metropolis, at least they have tried. As a social symptom, the effort is significant. The reconciliation of man with the natural world is no longer merely desirable; it has become a necessity. It is a compelling need that is sending millions of people into the countryside.

The need has created a new interest in camping, handicrafts and horticulture. In ever-increasing numbers, Americans are acquiring a passionate interest in their national parks and forests, in their rural landscape and in their small-town agrarian heritage. Despite its many shortcomings, this trend reflects a basically sound orientation. The average American is making an attempt, however confusedly, to reduce his environment to a human scale. He is trying to re-create a world that he can cope with as an individual, a world that he correctly identifies with the freedom, gentler rhythms and quietude of rural surroundings. His attempts at gardening, landscaping, carpentry, home maintenance and other so-called suburban "vices" reflect a need to function within an intelligible, manipulatable and individually creative sphere of human activity.

The suburbanite, like the camper, senses that he is working with basic, abiding things that have slipped from his control in the metropolitan world—shelter, the handiwork that enters into daily life, vegetation and the land. He is fortunate, to be sure, if these activities do not descend to the level of caricature. Nevertheless, they are important, not only because they reflect basic needs of man but because they also reflect basic needs of the things with which he is working. The human scale is also the natural scale. The soil, the land, the living things on which man depends for his nutriment and recreation are direly in need of individual care.

For one thing, proper maintenance of the soil not only depends upon advances in our knowledge of soil chemistry and soil fertility; it also requires a more personalized approach to agriculture. Thus far, the trend has been the other way; agriculture has become depersonalized and over-industrialized. Modern farming is suffering from gigantism. The average agricultural unit is getting so big that the finer aspects of soil performance and soil needs are being overlooked. If differences in the quality and performance of various kinds of soil are to receive more attention, American farming must be reduced to a more human scale. It will become necessary to bring agriculture within the scope of the individual, so that the farmer and the soil can develop together, each responding as fully as possible to the needs of the other.

The same is true for the management of livestock. Today our food animals are being manipulated like a lifeless industrial resource. Normally, large numbers of animals are collected in the smallest possible area and are allowed only as much movement as is necessary for mere survival. Our meat animals have been placed on a diet composed for the most part of medicated feed high in carbohydrates. Before they are slaughtered, these obese, rapidly matured creatures seldom spend more than six months on the range and six months on farms, where they are kept on concentrated rations and gain about two pounds daily. Our dairy herds are handled like machines; our poultry flocks, like hothouse tomatoes. The need to restore the time-honoured intimacy between man and his livestock is just as pronounced as the need to bring agriculture within the horizon of the individual farmer.

Although modern technology has enlarged the elements that enter into the agricultural situation, giving each man a wider area of sovereignty and control, machines have not lessened the importance of personal familiarity with the land, its vegetation and the living things it supports. Unless principles of good land use permit otherwise, a farm should not become smaller or larger than the individual farmer can command. If it is smaller, agriculture will become inefficient; if larger, it will become depersonalized.

With the decline in the quality of urban life, on the one hand and the growing imbalance in agriculture, on the other, our times are beginning to witness a remarkable confluence of human interests with the needs of the natural world. Men of the nineteenth century assumed a posture of defiance towards the forests, plains and mountains. Their applause was reserved for the engineer, the technician, the inventor, at times even the robber baron and the railroader, who seemed to offer the promise of a more abundant material life. Today we are filled with a vague nostalgia for the past. To a large degree this nostalgia reflects the insecurity and uncertainty of our times, in contrast with the echoes of a more optimistic and perhaps more tranquil era.

But it also reflects a deep sense of loss, a longing for the free, unblemished land that lay before the eyes of the frontiersman and early settler. We are seeking out the mountains they tried to avoid and we are trying to recover fragments of the forests they removed. Our nostalgia springs neither from a greater sensitivity nor from the wilder depths of human instinct. It springs from a growing need to restore the normal, balanced and manageable rhythms of human life—that is, an environment that meets our requirements as individuals and biological beings.

Modern man can never return to the primitive life he so often idealizes, but the point is that he doesn't have to. The use of farm machinery as such does not conflict with sound agricultural practices; nor are industry and an urbanized community incompatible with a more agrarian, more natural environment. Ironically, advances in technology itself have largely overcome the industrial problems that once justified the huge concentrations of people and facilities in a few urban areas. Automobiles, aircraft, electric power and electronic devices have eliminated nearly all the problems of transportation, communication and social isolation that burdened man in past eras. We can now communicate with one another over a distance of thousands of miles in a matter of seconds and we can travel to the most remote areas of the world in a few hours.

The obstacles created by space and time are essentially gone. Similarly, size need no longer be a problem. Technologists have developed remarkable small-scale alternatives to many of the giant facilities that still dominate modern industry. The smoky steel town, for example, is an anachronism. Excellent steel can be made and rolled with installations that occupy about two or three city blocks. Many of the latest machines are highly versatile and compact. They lend themselves to a large variety of manufacturing and finishing operations. Today the more modern plant, with its clean, quiet, versatile and largely automated facilities, contrasts sharply with the huge, ugly, congested factories inherited from an earlier industrial era.

Thus, almost without realising it, we have been preparing the material conditions for a new type of human community—one which constitutes neither a complete return to the past nor a suburban accommodation to the present. It is no longer fanciful to think of man's future environment in terms of a decentralized, moderate-sized city that combines industry with agriculture, not only in the same civic entity but in the occupational activities of the same individual. The "urbanized farmer" or the "agrarianized townsman" need not be a contradiction in terms. This way of life was achieved for a time by the Greek polis, by early republican Rome and by the Renaissance commune. The urban centers that became the wellsprings of Western civilization were not strictly cities, in the modern sense of the term. Rather, they brought agriculture together with urban life, synthesising both into a rounded human, cultural and social development.

Whether modern man manages to reach this point or travels only part of the way, some kind of decentralization will be necessary to achieve a lasting equilibrium between society and nature. Urban decentralization underlies any hope of achieving ecological control of pest infestations in agriculture. Only a community well integrated with the resources of the surrounding region can promote agricultural and biological diversity. With careful planning, man could use plants and animals not only as a source of food but also, by pitting one species of life against another, as a means of controlling pests, thus eliminating much of his need for chemical methods. What is equally important, a decentralized community holds the greatest promise for conserving natural resources, particularly as it would promote the use of local sources of energy. Instead of relying primarily on concentrated sources of fuel in distant regions of the continent, the community could make maximum use of its own energy resources, such as wind power, solar energy and hydroelectric power.

These sources of energy, so often overlooked because of an almost exclusive reliance on a national division of labour, would help greatly to conserve the remaining supply of high-grade petroleum and coal. They would almost certainly postpone, if not eliminate, the need for turning to radioactive substances and nuclear reactors as major sources of industrial energy. With more time at his disposal for intensive research, man might learn either to employ solar energy and wind power as the principal sources of energy or to eliminate the hazard of radioactive contamination from nuclear reactors.

It is true, of course, that our life lines would become more complex and, from a technological point of view, less "efficient." There would be many duplications of effort. Instead of being concentrated in two or three areas of the country, steel plants would be spread out, with many communities employing small-scale facilities to meet regional or local needs. But the word "efficiency," like the word, "pest," is a relative term. Although a duplication of facilities would be somewhat costly, many local mineral sources that are not used today because they are too widely scattered or too small for the purposes of large-scale production, would become economical for the purposes of a smaller community. Thus, in the long run, a more localized or regional form of industrial activity is likely to promote a more efficient use of resources than our prevailing methods of production.

It is true that we will never entirely eliminate the need for a national and international division of labour in agriculture and industry. The Midwest will always remain the best source of our grains; the East and Far West, the best sources of lumber and certain field crops. Our petroleum, high-grade coal and certain minerals will still have to be supplied, in large part, by a few regions of the country. But there is no reason why we cannot reduce the burden that our national division of labour currently places on these areas by spreading the agricultural and industrial loads over wider areas of the country. This seems to be the only approach to the task of creating a long-range balance between man and the natural world and of remaking man's synthetic environment in a form that will promote human health and fitness.

An emphasis on agriculture and urban regionalism is somewhat disconcerting to the average city dweller. It conjures up an image of cultural isolation and social stagnation, of a journey backward in history to the agrarian societies of the medieval and ancient worlds. Actually, the urban dweller today is more isolated in the big city than his ancestors were in the countryside. The city man in the modern metropolis has reached a degree of anonymity, social atomization and spiritual isolation that is virtually unprecedented in human history. Today man's alienation from man is almost absolute. His standards of co-operation, mutual aid, simple human hospitality and decency have suffered an appalling amount of erosion in the urban milieu. Man's civic institutions have become cold, impersonal agencies for the manipulation of his destiny and his culture has increasingly accommodated itself to the least common denominator of intelligence and taste. He has nothing to lose even by a backward glance; indeed, in this way he is likely to place his present-day world and its limitations in a clearer perspective.

But why should an emphasis on agriculture and urban regionalism be regarded as an attempt to return to the past? Can we not develop our environment more selectively, more subtly and more rationally than we have thus far, combining the best of the past and present and bringing forth a new synthesis of man and nature, nation and region, town and country? Life would indeed cease to be an adventure if we merely elaborated the present by extending urban sprawl and by expanding civic life until it completely escapes from the control of its individual human elements. To continue along these lines would serve not to promote social evolution but rather to "fatten" the social organism to a point where it could no longer move. Our purpose should be to make individual life a more rounded experience and this we can hope to accomplish at the present stage of our development only by restoring the complexity of man's environment and by reducing the community to a human scale.

Is there any evidence that reason will prevail in the management of our affairs? It is difficult to give a direct answer. Certainly we are beginning to look for qualitative improvements in many aspects of life; we are getting weary and resentful of the shoddiness in our goods and services. We are gaining a new appreciation of the land and its problems and a greater realization of the social promise offered by a more manageable human community. More and more is being written about our synthetic environment and the criticism is more pointed than it has been in almost half a century. Perhaps we can still hope, as Mumford did more than two decades ago in the closing lines of *The Culture of Cities:*

"We have much to unbuild and much more to build: but the foundations are ready: the machines are set in place and the tools are bright and keen: the architects, the engineers and the workmen are assembled. None of us may live to see the complete building and perhaps in the nature of things the building can never be completed: but some of us will see the flag or the fir tree that the workers will plant aloft in ancient ritual when they cap the topmost story."

ALCOHOL AND DRUG USE

Since early times prostitution has frequently been associated with drinking and with other forms of drug use. Indeed, the locales in which sex is available for sale are often also places wherein alcohol or other psychoactive drugs may be imbibed, legally or illicitly. In many cultures pleasure-seeking and risk-taking commonly involve both sex and various forms of drug use. Moreover, there is an extensive literature linking sexual behaviour with the use of alcohol and other substances. In recent years the advent of HIV/AIDS has provided a stimuli's to studies concerned with the possible connection between drinking or illicit drug use and high-risk sex. A number of these studies have focused on prostitutes and their clients as potentially being at special risk in this respect. This examines some of the available evidence on this topic, with special reference to the situation in Britain. This evidence is placed in the general context of patterns of alcohol and drug use in society and of evidence on the connection between drinking and drug use in relation to high-risk sexual behaviour and the transmission of HIV/AIDS.

Humanity has long exhibited a great propensity to use psychoactive (mind-altering) drugs. Virtually every known society has tolerated, if not actively sanctioned or revered, some forms of recreational drug use. In addition, drugs are often also integrated into religious rites and major social events. Most adolescents and adults in Britain consume alcohol and an increasingly large proportion have also used illicit drugs such as cannabis. Tobacco use, though declining, continues to be widespread, especially amongst those in lower socioeconomic positions.

The role of alcohol in British culture is so deeply entrenched that the invitation to 'have a drink' is frequently assumed to indicate an alcoholic beverage. Evidence indicates that even young children begin to develop strong impressions about alcohol and that by adolescence, most people regard drinking as a hallmark of sociability and maturity. Surveys further indicate that amongst British teenagers and young adults, the overwhelming majority have begun to drink by the ages of 15 and 16. In England and Scotland as a whole only a small minority, 3-4 per cent appear to be abstainers at this age. Even so it appears that in some areas, such as Northern Ireland and the Western Isles of Scotland, a substantial proportion of teenagers do not drink. This probably reflects a number of cultural factors, including religion.

The normality of alcohol consumption is emphasized by the findings of Foster et al. (1990) that 93 per cent of adult males and 88 per cent of females in Britain were classified as drinkers. Surveys suggest that the heaviest drinking sections of the community include young single males and females in their late teens and early 20s. Males generally drink more heavily than females and males are also more likely than females to experience adverse consequences (problems) because of their drinking. Most of those who drink do so in moderation and without evident harm. Even so, some people drink in ways that cause problems. The harm associated with heavy or inappropriate drinking includes medical, social and public disorder problems. There are occupational and regional variations in the levels of such problems. These reflect, amongst other factors, long-standing social and cultural differences in drinking habits and in the social pressures to drink.

The use of other psychoactive drugs is generally far more restricted than that of alcohol. Even so a substantial minority of people do use such substances. Tobacco smoking has been declining in the United Kingdom, as in a number of other countries. In 1974 it was reported that 45 per cent of those over the age of 16 in Britain smoked. By 1988 this proportion had fallen to 32 per cent. The prevalence of smoking varies by region, with the highest levels in Scotland, Wales and the North of England. Smoking is much more commonplace amongst those in lower socioeconomic positions than those in higher positions.

A number of studies also indicate that smoking amongst teenagers in Britain is more prevalent amongst females than amongst males. Tobacco use, like alcohol consumption patterns, varies according to occupational group. This fact has considerable relevance to the subject of this, as will be elaborated below. In contrast to the decline in smoking, the use of illicit drugs has been increasingly markedly. Surveys suggest that in many areas of Britain at least a quarter of those in the age range 16-18 have at some time used such substances and that in some areas illicit drug use is far more widespread.

One study, for example, indicated that 51 per cent of a study group of teenagers in the Manchester area had used illicit drugs. Most illicit drug use is confined to cannabis, although other substances are also used. Surveys of teenagers and young adults suggest that the majority of those who have used illicit substances have done so in only a very limited and often temporary way. Drug use is rare, but by no means uncommon, amongst pre-adolescents. Some studies have noted the use of glues and solvents by such individuals. Moreover, a number of drug workers and other commentators have reported some evidence of the increasing use of other drugs by children in London and other, mainly urban, areas. It is clear that there has been an increase in the use of substances such as heroin, cocaine, MDMA (ecstasy) and a variety of so called 'dance drugs'.

Moreover drugs such as amphetamines, benzodiazepines and LSD have been in illicit circulation for over two decades and continue to be used recreationally by some individuals. There has been a steady rise in 'problem drug use', as indicted by statistics recording the numbers of 'addicts' notified by doctors. These have risen from 1,426 in 1970 to 33,952 in 1994. Convictions for drug offences have also risen. In 1979 14,339 persons were found guilty of drug offences. In 1993 75,122 people were dealt with for drug offences.

Alcohol, Drugs And High-Risk Sex

There is a rich folklore connecting sex and the use of alcohol or drugs. In Shakespeare's Macbeth it was stated that alcohol consumption 'provokes the desire but it takes away the performance'. Moreover, drinking, illicit drug use and sexuality have been linked for a variety of social, psychological reasons.

It is a well-established belief that consuming alcohol or using drugs such as cannabis, cocaine or amphetamines might lead to 'disinhibition' and thereby encourage potentially risky behaviours. 'Disinhibition' has been defined in several ways, but basically means the release of inclinations or behaviours that would otherwise be restrained or held in check. In many societies it is assumed that drinking alcohol, for example, leads to relaxation and makes it more likely that an individual will act in a carefree manner. Drinking has often been used as an excuse for behaviour that later provokes shame or regret: 'I would not have done it if I had been sober.' Available scientific evidence suggests that the role of alcohol in relation to disinhibition is complex. In fact the effects of any drug depend upon the chemistry of the substance, the characteristics of the user and the environment in which use occurs. Social setting and expectations are influential, even if they are very often difficult to assess.

Clearly, the assumption that psychoactive drug use and sexual behaviour might be connected is long-standing. In spite of this, scientific interest in this topic has been greatly stimulated by concerns about the spread of HIV infection. From very early in the recorded history of HIV transmission, it was evident that the sharing of infected injecting equipment by intravenous drug users was an important factor.

A very influential study concluded that US gay men who had combined sex with drinking or the use of drugs such as cannabis were particularly likely to report having engaged in 'high-risk' behaviours. These findings prompted a flurry of research activity into the possible connection between drinking and the use of non-injected drugs and sexual risk-taking. These have been reviewed in detail elsewhere. Available evidence on this topic has been reported from the USA, Britain. Australia and Norway. This indicates that amongst young adult heterosexuals those individuals who drink heavily are more inclined to engage in high-risk sex and a number of other potentially dangerous activities.

The latter include smoking and illicit drug use. Some individuals clearly take more risks than do others. Studies of gay men have produced rather more inconsistent results in this respect, with only some concluding that heavier drinkers take more risks. One of the largest studies, from Britain, concluded that drinking was unrelated to sexual behaviour, examining results from two surveys of young adults, concluded that risk-taking was neither general nor specific. A number of types of risk-taking were evident. These included illicit drug use, heavy drinking and sexual risk-taking. Different patterns of association were evident amongst different sub-groups of people. The most striking feature of research into this topic is that not a single study of which this author is aware has demonstrated that consuming alcohol on a specific occasion does foster high-risk sex. Many people appear to believe, or at least to report, that there is such a connection, but it has not been born out empirically.

Alcohol, Drugs And Prostitution

Prostitution is a world-wide activity involving enormous numbers of people. For the purposes of this, 'prostitution' is defined as the provision of sexual services in exchange for some form of payment. Many of the men and women who work as prostitutes drink alcohol, smoke and use illicit drugs. In part this is simply a reflection of general social habits, especially those that relate to young adults. As noted above, both drinking and illicit drug use are commonplace amongst many social groups in Britain, and in many other countries. The relationship between drinking, drug-taking and prostitution is not straightforward. As noted above, different sub-groups of people use legal and illicit drugs in different ways. Habits vary between localities and even different groups within a single locality. This is true of both alcohol, the most widely used drug, and of tobacco and illicit drugs.

Moreover, the links between drinking and drug use and prostitution are further influenced and complicated by the ways in which the sex industry is organized in specific localities and the ways in which services for problem drug users are arranged (Plant 1990). These influences are reflected by major differences between even neighbouring cities, such as Edinburgh and Glasgow. In Edinburgh there is relatively little street prostitution, while this is commonplace and extensive in Glasgow. If 'saunas' and 'massage parlours' are permitted in a town, this may provide relatively unobtrusive, safe and congenial working conditions for men and women who might otherwise meet clients by working around bars or on the streets. If a town has an efficient drug prescribing service this may reduce the necessity for 'problem drug users' or drug-dependent individuals to engage in prostitution in order to purchase drug supplies. In some localities, police policy simply does not permit widespread street prostitution. The latter is, in fact, illegal in the United Kingdom and in a number of other countries.

A series of studies have examined the connection between prostitution, alcohol consumption and illicit drug use. As noted above, such investigations have been greatly encouraged by the advent of HIV/AIDS and by its obvious link in some areas with intravenous drug use. A convincing body of evidence supports the conclusion that the occupational culture of the sex industry actively fosters the relatively heavy use of alcohol, tobacco and illicit drugs. The evidence supporting this view is now briefly presented.

An Edinburgh study elicited information from both male and female prostitutes. This investigation collected information by interviewing a non-random study group of 102 males and 103 females. The mean age of the females was 26 and that of the males was 23. Only 4 per cent had stayed on at school beyond the age of 16, in comparison with 39 per cent of Scottish school pupils in general. This investigation showed that many of these mainly young working class men and women contacted clients in licensed premises and that many were very heavy drinkers. In addition, illicit drug use was commonplace. Even so, only a fifth of those interviewed reported ever having used drugs by injection. Females were more likely than the male prostitutes or 'rent-boys' to report intravenous drug use. A number of people commented that drug-dependent females are more likely than drug-dependent males to engage in prostitution to pay for drug supplies; males are more likely to engage in theft. The overall levels of psychoactive drug use reported by the Edinburgh prostitutes were high. A total of 87 per cent of females and 73 per cent of the males interviewed reported that they smoked.

This is in contrast with only a third of adults in Britain as a whole, though the level of smoking is highest amongst manual/blue-collar workers (Foster et al. 1990). As noted above, heavy drinking was commonplace amongst this study group. Only eight females and six males indicated that they did not drink. Approximately two-thirds of the study group reported having been intoxicated during the week preceding interview. Amongst those who had drunk in the past week, the mean alcohol consumption for the females was 48.1 units and that for males was 63.8 units. A 'unit' is equivalent to half a pint of normal strength beer, lager, cider or stout or to a single bar-room measure of spirits or to a glass of wine.

Respondents were also asked how much they had consumed on their most recent drinking occasion, not necessarily in the past week. Female drinkers reported a mean consumption of 13.9 units and males a mean of 17.7 units. In comparison with studies of both the general population and of other young adults, these people included many very heavy drinkers. It should be noted that Edinburgh does not have a major 'red-light area' and that most prostitute-client contacts are conducted indoors. Many initial contacts are made in bars, discos and other similar venues in which drinking is a prominent, if often only a secondary, social activity. Under such circumstances, drinking and smoking were strongly encouraged. The vast majority of respondents also reported having used cannabis: 90 per cent of males and 83 per cent of females had smoked cannabis and more than half had done so in the month before interview. In addition a minority had used other substances such as amphetamines, LSD, benzodiazepines, glues and solvents. Only a minority, it should be noted, had used drugs other than cannabis in the past month. A third of the females and eleven males had at some time used heroin. Cocaine had been used by 48 females and 28 males. Females were also more likely than males to report having used benzodiazepines.

Forty-one individuals, roughly 20 per cent of those interviewed, stated that they had used drugs by injection. Fewer than a third of 'those who reported being current injectors stated that they had never shared injecting equipment with other people. All of the injectors noted that they had shared equipment in the past. Morgan Thomas (1990:100) concluded: The remaining seventeen respondents who currently used intravenous drugs and who still shared their injecting equipment were asked about the frequency with which they did so. The five males reported sharing equipment on average five times per month with an average of 2.3 people. The twelve females reported sharing on average 7.5 times per month with an average of 6.3 people. Their sharing was not confined to Edinburgh. Three males and nine females reported sharing in other parts of the UK.

This Edinburgh study indicated that approximately half of the male and female prostitutes interviewed reported having experienced some form of adverse consequences because of their drinking or illicit drug use. Most commonly these related to financial, domestic or legal problems. In addition 26 per cent of females and 22 per cent of males with such problems reported adverse consequences associated with their health. Smaller proportions also reported having encountered social or work-related difficulties.

The male and female prostitutes in this Edinburgh study were far from homogeneous. Some regarded themselves as full-time professionals, some of whom clearly disdained those who worked 'on the beat' (on the streets) or who used drugs intravenously. In spite of this, many of those who were included in this study had worked as prostitutes in a number of different settings. Some of those who currently worked in saunas and massage parlours had earlier worked for escort agencies, in bars or on the streets and there was clearly some movement between these different modes of operation. Overall, the results of this study, like the evidence reviewed in the previous, failed to support the conclusion that alcohol consumption or illicit drug use per se did foster 'unsafe sex'. It was apparent that high-risk sex was influenced by a considerable number of factors. In Edinburgh in particular, and in much of Scotland, it appears that very few prostitutes have 'pimps'.

The latter are important in some other areas and have been noted to be an important source of sexually transmitted diseases for the prostitutes with whom they have contact and over whom they exert control. Nevertheless, this study showed that many prostitutes report being asked by clients to engage in sex without condoms and that some did consent to this for extra payments. Moreover, most of the Edinburgh prostitutes reported having had recent sexual contact with lovers or other non-paying partners. Most of those who had regular non-paying partners rarely, if ever, used condoms with these individuals. Approximately 60 per cent of the men and women in this study reported having had an HIV test, though not necessarily a recent one. Twelve females and five males reported that they were HIV infected. All of these males had used drugs intravenously and had shared injecting equipment. Nine of the females also had such a background.

The remaining three females attributed their HIV infection to sexual transmission. One reported that her regular partner was a seropositive intravenous drug user. The other two reported that their former partners included people whom they knew were HIV seropositive. Both women also reported having had hepatitis B at least once. It is therefore probable that their sero-conversions were also related to intravenous drug use by their partners.

It is clear that levels of illicit drug use vary markedly amongst different groups of men and women who work in the sex industry. This has been emphasized by De Graaf et al. (1994), commenting on their findings in the Netherlands.

These authors concluded that street working male prostitutes were more likely to use 'hard' drugs (such as heroin) than those who worked at home. Moreover, it was concluded that street working prostitutes were also more likely to be heterosexual, to have no other job, to have more clients, but fewer 'steady' ones and to have a 'more negative working attitude'. De Graaf and his colleagues noted that homosexual prostitution brings together gay men and injecting drug users. They further commented that both of these sub-groups have high rates of HIV infection. This Dutch study indicated that most of the male prostitutes who were intravenous drug users had been drug dependent before beginning to work in the sex industry:

While they did use their earnings from prostitution to pay for their addiction, only very few ever felt compelled to recruit customers while 'sick', *i.e.* in acute need of drugs. When that did happen, they were seldom particular about their choice of client.

De Graaf et al. also commented that of the men they interviewed who consumed alcohol while contacting clients: 'Alcohol use was highest among those who recruited clients in bars: they took, on average, 12 glasses when they worked, compared to eight glasses for the whole group of alcohol drinkers'. (1994:279). De Graaf et al. concluded that men already using 'hard drugs' became prostitutes in order to finance their drug dependence and as an alternative to crime. They also noted: 'drug users were caught in a vicious circle out of which they knew no way' (1994:281).

Another Dutch report concluded that drinking and illicit drug use by heterosexual and homosexual prostitutes was common. The authors noted that consumption patterns varied amongst different subgroups of people:

Those meeting their clients in clubs or bars reported the highest consumption of alcohol; hard drugs were used predominantly by street prostitutes. It appears that the main effects of alcohol and drug use are on how the individual experiences working as, or calling on, a prostitute, the social interaction between the two parties and the sexual contact itself. The common assumption that drinking has negative effects on condom use was not borne out; though female prostitutes under the influence of drugs were significantly more likely to report unsafe sex.

Studies from Glasgow, only 60 kilometres west of Edinburgh, have shown a very different pattern from that evident in the Scottish capital. It has been reported that street prostitution, often involving intravenous drug users, is extremely widespread in Glasgow. For example, McKeganey et al. (1990) reported that roughly 300 women worked as street prostitutes in Glasgow's red-light area and that 60 per cent of those were intravenous drug users. McKeganey et al. (1992) further reported that of a study group of 206 street working females, 71 per cent were injecting drug users. Of those in this investigation who were HIV tested, 2.5 per cent were found to be HIV infected. Taylor et al. (1993) have described fifty-one female drug-injecting prostitutes in Glasgow.

These authors reported that 45 per cent of these women had injected with used needles and syringes in the previous month. It was also noted that condom use with clients was 'almost universal', but was low with non-paying partners. Another Glasgow study examined HIV prevalence amongst female street prostitutes attending a health care drop-in centre. This indicated that 4.7 per cent of the intravenous drug users tested were HIV infected. All infected individuals were intravenous injectors. Another Glasgow study elicited HIV test information from female prostitutes who were intravenous drug users.

Different methods were used to study subjects. HIV prevalence rates ranged from 1.2 per cent to 4.7 per cent. Green et al. (1993:1581) have reported that some female prostitutes attending a Glasgow drop-in centre were engaging in a practice known as 'frontloading':

Frontloading is used by two or more injectors to share out drugs. The injector draws up the drug solution from a preparatory vessel ('cooker') into his/her own syringe and then injects ('spouts') a proportion of the solution directly into the barrel of his/her colleague's syringe.

Gossop et al. (1993) have reported that, amongst London heroin users, the severity of drug dependence was positively associated with the frequency with which they had engaged in sex for either money or drugs. These authors commented that this connection applied to females as well as to men who had sex with men. Generally low levels of condom use were higher in contacts involving payment than in those with non-paying partners. This disparity has also been reported by other commentators (*e.g.* Morgan Thomas 1990; Morgan Thomas et al. 1990b; Taylor et al. 1993). The fact that prostitutes are less likely to use condoms with lovers than with paying clients is not surprising. For many people, using a condom is not only a public health measure. It is a barrier to intimacy and trust. Rhodes et al. (1994) examined female drug injectors in London, some of whom were engaged in prostitution.

The latter were significantly more likely to be in contact with drug treatment agencies and to have had an HIV test than were the non-prostitutes. There were no significant differences between prostitutes and non-prostitutes in levels of HIV infection (12.9 per cent and 14.2 per cent respectively). These findings lend support to the conclusion that the major HIV risk for British prostitutes appear to come from intravenous drug use, rather than through prostitution in itself.

Gossop et al. (1994) have also stated that there were high levels of alcohol intoxication amongst prostitutes in south London. Matthews (1990) had commented upon high levels of alcohol and illicit drug use amongst female street working prostitutes in Liverpool. Morrison et al. (1994) reported that 10.5 per cent of a study group of female prostitutes in Liverpool had consumed more than 30 units of alcohol per week. This group had a mean week's consumption of over 200 units. The majority of Liverpool prostitutes surveyed, 67 per cent, reported working under the influence of alcohol. Half had used drugs intravenously.

The possible role of alcohol and illicit drugs has been discussed by Morrison et al. (1995). These commentators noted:

The most inebriated prostitutes on the street appear to be the most successful in attracting clients. Women who appear entirely powerless and incapable of setting the boundaries of sexual activity to take place will attract men who may wish to legitimate an act of sexual abuse by the payment of cash.

We feel that a distinction must be made between escort prostitution and street prostitution. A contract between a sex trade client and an escort prostitute may be one of equal partners and she will have the choice to decline business unacceptable to her. In street prostitutes, who are funding their dependence on alcohol or drugs, the power is with clients who have the money to set the agenda for the type of sex they want.

Drug use by prostitutes has periodically been noted as having clear health risks. Bloor et al. (1991) have speculated that an increase in Temazepam use by prostitutes might reduce levels of condom use with their clients. Syphilis has been associated with drug use amongst female prostitutes in Connecticut and amongst both male and female prostitutes in Amsterdam. Intravenous drug use has been found to be associated with HIV infection amongst male prostitutes in the USA. This study also found that the use of 'crack' in the past month had been reported by 54.9 per cent of those studied, while 35 per cent had histories of intravenous drug use. Another US study supported the conclusion that crack smokers in three cities were more likely than non-smokers to engage in both prostitution and high-risk sex.

A Dutch study of male drug users supported the conclusion that duration of intravenous drug use was positively associated with HIV infection. A fifth of the men in this study had worked as prostitutes. An Australian study of female prostitutes and other women at the Sydney STD centre indicated that cannabis was the most widely used illicit drug by both groups. Other substances used were sleeping pills, amphetamines, cocaine and heroin. The prostitutes were more likely than the other women to smoke tobacco. In contrast, however, the prostitutes were less likely to drink, but were more likely to do so at a harmful level if they did consume alcohol.

Sex Industry Clients

As part of the Edinburgh study noted above, information was obtained about alcohol and drug use by clients, those who purchased sexual services. These details were elicited in two ways. First, the male and female prostitutes who were interviewed were asked to comment upon the proportions of their own clients who, in their view, appeared to be under the influence of alcohol or illicit drugs at the time of contact. These individuals indicated that approximately two-thirds of their clients appeared or were believed to have been drinking and that roughly a third appeared to have been using illicit drugs such as cannabis. It is emphasized that such reports were purely subjective.

They did not necessarily imply intoxication nor even heavy alcohol/drug use by clients, simply perceived or apparent use. The second approach to clients involved direct interviews with a non-randomly contacted study group of 206 males and three females who had obtained sex in exchange for some form of payment (Morgan Thomas et al. 1990a). Most of the clients interviewed were men who had contacted prostitutes through saunas and massage parlours. Twenty-six of these men had contacted male prostitutes, five had contacted both males and females. One of the female clients had paid for sex with both men and women. Two had paid for sex with males.

Twenty-six of the male clients reported having at some time used drugs intravenously, of whom twenty-two also stated that they had at some time shared injecting equipment. Seven men reported that they were HIV infected. All of these had histories of intravenous drug use. Most of the men interviewed, 78 per cent, reported that drinking was sometimes a feature of their contacts with prostitutes. In addition 12 per cent stated that they 'usually' or 'always' used illicit drugs while in contact with prostitutes.

A further 17 per cent indicated that they 'sometimes' used drugs while in contact with prostitutes.

Only ten clients reported being non-drinkers. The mean alcohol consumption of the male clients who did drink was 10.6 units of alcohol. Twenty-five men (12 per cent) had consumed more than 50 units of alcohol in the past week. Consistent with the relatively heavy drinking of these clients, 71 per cent also smoked tobacco and 71 per cent also reported that they had smoked cannabis. Following a parallel procedure to that used in the survey of Edinburgh prostitutes, respondents were asked to assess the proportion of prostitutes with whom they had been in contact who were 'under the influence' of alcohol or illicit drugs at the time.

The responses thus produced indicated that 69 per cent of male prostitutes and 38 per cent of females were judged to have been under the effects of alcohol. The corresponding proportions for perceived illicit drug effects were 40 per cent and 32 per cent. It should be noted that clients came from all socioeconomic strata. These ranged from affluent and senior professionals to the unskilled, low paid or unemployed. No escort agency clients were, however, included in this study group. These clients, largely due to the way in which field-work was organized, were heavily skewed to emphasize men who visited massage parlours and saunas. Even so, a considerable proportion of those interviewed had contacted prostitutes in other ways, such as in hotels, bars, brothels, escort agencies or on the streets. Consistent with the results of this Edinburgh study, De Graaf et al. (1995), commenting on the situation in the Netherlands, concluded that alcohol use by sex industry clients was common, though less so than amongst the prostitutes with whom they had contact.

Discussion

Not surprisingly, the evidence reviewed in this supports the conclusion that the vast number of men and women in the sex industry do not conform to a single stereotype. These individuals come from a wide range of social backgrounds and work in a variety of different settings. Even so, it is also clear that the sex industry does sometimes attract alcohol- and drug-dependent people and that a high proportion of those in the sex industry are heavy users of alcohol, tobacco and illicit drugs. This certainly reflects many different factors: first, in some localities men and women work as prostitutes, most probably as street prostitutes, in order to pay for alcohol or drug supplies. Second, the working conditions and social milieu surrounding prostitution commonly foster the use of both licit and illicit psychoactive drugs. This reflects the fact that many prostitute-client contacts are made in and around bars, clubs and other licensed premises. It also probably reflects the fact that there is a strong occupational ethos of regular and heavy drinking, smoking and illicit drug use. Such a tradition is evident in a number of occupational groups.

On the basis of the evidence reviewed above, it can reasonably be concluded that many of the prostitutes studied were heavy drinkers, and used both tobacco and illicit drugs, especially cannabis. A high proportion of street working prostitutes are clearly opiate users, intravenous drug users and drug dependants. Such findings are certainly distorted by the difficulty of obtaining a 'representative' sample of those engaged in an occupation that is, in most contexts, socially stigmatized and which often operates with some degree of secrecy.

In spite of the obvious methodological problems of conducting research into the sex industry, there is persuasive evidence to confirm the view that several areas of the sex industry do actively attract heavy drinkers or drug users, or foster such behaviour. Most, but not all, prostitutes are young. Most, but not all, come from working-class families. Many of those engaged in prostitution have little formal education and many are unmarried or without long-term partnerships. These demographic characteristics-youth, being unmarried and from working-class backgrounds-by themselves are consistent with relatively high levels of tobacco smoking and illicit drug use. The working environments of many of those in the sex industry also promote the social and convivial use of both legal and illicit drugs.

Some of the individuals in the sex industry are professional prostitutes who work indoors in 'saunas', 'massage parlours' or brothels. Others work for escort agencies and often visit expensive hotels. Such individuals are clearly often very different from intravenous drug users who may engage in prostitution on a temporary basis to pay for their drug supplies. Heavy or problematic drinking or drug use are incompatible with some forms of sex work, such as for escort agencies and a number of indoor establishments. The managements of some agencies actively attempt to screen out and exclude individuals who are intravenous drug users or whose alcohol or drug use impedes work performance.

The use of alcohol, tobacco and illicit drugs is widespread amongst post-adolescents in most cultures. Sex, drinking, smoking, drug use and leisure are connected for a host of psychological and social reasons. The sex industry is not unique in its ability to bring these behaviours together. Most people use some form of psychoactive drug. What is striking about those engaged in the sex industry, either as prostitutes or as clients, is their variety, rather than their uniformity.

RETHINKING PROSTITUTION

One of the principal motivations for this was to occasion and assist a rethinking of the institution of prostitution in Britain. It is apparent from recent discussions in the public sphere-involving not only academics, intellectuals and sex workers themselves, but politicians, the police, social and health workers and bodies like the Mothers' Union-that there is profound and wide-spread unease at the existing state of affairs. This is perhaps most obvious in relation to the law. It is clear that the anti-prostitution laws of the 1950s penalized women sex workers, especially street workers, while either proving ineffective against or ignoring other key participants in the sex industry, such as pimps, exploitative landlord and clients. Moreover, this legislation has now been exposed as unacceptably sexist. It was gender-biased even in conception: there was a High Court ruling on 5 May 1994, for example, that only women can be charged with loitering under the Street Offences Act of 1959.

As Shrage (1994:82) notes, feminists who disagree markedly on the morality and symbolism of prostitution nevertheless tend to agree that 'the legal and political instruments available to control prostitution are problematic. In general, feminists who entertain the hope of eliminating sex commerce, and those who do not, all favour removing existing legal prohibitions against it.'

The fact of unease in the face of current legislation need not, then, imply a consensus around a programme of change. Debates about the rights and wrongs of prostitution, and what form of regulation-if any-it warrants, go back centuries. It is not possible to do justice to these debates here; but we want to close by briefly addressing some of the social and moral issues raised by current dissensus and dispute. It will be expedient to consider first, selected philosophical reflections on these issues; second, to precis some feminist critiques; and finally, to comment on certain pragmatic considerations of policy and practice in Britain.

Philosophical Reflections

There have been several attempts recently to marshal philosophical arguments either for or against sex work. A paper by Ericsson (1980), which outlines and challenges the major arguments against sex work, has proved a particularly potent catalyst, eliciting a number of uncompromising responses. Ericsson points out that almost all extant philosophical treatments of prostitution seem to take it for granted that prostitution is undesirable, and he goes on to identify seven common 'charges' made against it. The first is that sex work is intrinsically immoral. Having considered possible historical and social antecedents for this conviction, Ericsson offers a personal response: 'If two adults voluntarily consent to an economic arrangement concerning sexual activity and this activity takes place in private, it seem plainly absurd to maintain that there is something intrinsically wrong with it.' Moreover, any claim that prostitution is 'intrinsically wrong' would seem to rule out any possibility of rational discussion.

The second charge, which Ericsson describes as sentimentalist, is that sex between prostitute and client is 'impoverished, cold and impersonal'. Ericsson's retort is that much sex, including intramarital sex, can share these same characteristics (*i.e.* is far from the sentimentalist's putative ideal); and he adds that sex without love is not necessarily 'bad' sex. He stresses too that the sex worker does not sell her body or vagina, but rather sexual services.

The third or paternalist charge is that sex workers are so vulnerable to assault and prone to physical and mental disorders associated with their work that steps should be taken to discourage recruitment to the industry and to aid rehabilitation thereafter. They are, in short, acting against their own interests. Ericsson (1980:344) remarks that other occupations are no less hazardous, and that most of the problems experienced by sex workers are a function of 'the social anathema attached to their way of life'. We might, he suggests, take steps to minimize the risks of sex work rather than try to rehabilitate those who run them. And in what sense can voluntary adult sex workers be said to be acting against interests pre-defined for them by others?

The fourth charge, labelled Marxist, eschews moralism and instead sees the sex worker as the most degraded and miserable representative of an exploited class. Ericsson's rejoinder is that this analysis, purely derivative of Marx's critique of capitalism, is too general: not only has the institution of prostitution existed in primitive and feudal as well as capitalist societies, but, since it is not exclusively the product of 'economic factors', a transition to socialism would prove no panacea.

The fifth or feminist charge can, as we have intimated, take a multiplicity of forms. Crucial, however, is the contention that 'the relation between hooker and "John" is one of object to subject-the prostitute being reified into a mere object, a thing for the male's pleasure, lust and contempt...a piece of merchandise'. Moreover, prostitution is an unequal institution: 'it represents a way out of misère sexuel only for men'. Having noted in passing the existence of substantial numbers of male prostitutes in most modern urban centres, Ericsson reiterates his view that sex workers sell not themselves but sexual services. He continues:

Since when does the fact that we, when visiting a professional, are not interested in him or her as a person, but only in his or her professional performance, constitute a ground for saying that the professional is dehumanized, turned into an object?

And if the sex worker is treated as a means to an end, is the client any less so? We might, Ericsson suggests, look upon sex and sexuality with: the same naturalness as upon our cravings for food and drink. And, contrary to popular belief, we may have something to learn from prostitution in this respect, namely, that coition resembles nourishment in that if it can not be obtained in any other way it can always be bought. And bought meals are not always the worst.

Commercialization is the sixth charge. At the core of this charge is the contention that prostitution encourages the growing commercialization of lifestyle. Ericsson's counter is that the sex industry is in this respect a symptom not a cause: 'Capitalism is perfectly able to create commercialistic dystopias on its own. It hardly needs the aid of prostitution in the process.'

The final charge considered is that of a disturbed emotional life. Ericsson admits that some sex workers might well meet with emotional problems due to their work, but he insists that the prime source of such problems is the stigma and public antagonism heaped upon the industry. The salient concept here is that of 'secondary deviation'.

Some of the stronger rejoinders to Ericsson have come from feminists, whose arguments we shall sample next; but before we do so it should be recorded that while Ericsson is at pains to dispute the rarely contested claim that 'prostitution is undesirable', he is not concerned to defend the counter-claim that 'prostitution is desirable'.

Feminist Critiques

Prostitution raises difficult issues for feminists. On the one hand, many feminists want to abolish discriminatory criminal statutes that are mostly used to harass and penalize prostitutes, and rarely to punish johns and pimps-laws which, for the most part, render prostitutes more vulnerable to exploitation by their male associates. On the other hand, most feminists find the prostitute's work morally and politically objectionable. In their view, women who provide sexual services for a fee submit to sexual domination by men, and suffer degradation by being treated as sexual commodities.

Perhaps it is not unreasonable to characterize the standpoint of a number of feminists by the slogan 'Against prostitution.

For prostitutes' (although the subtlety of this position has undoubtedly been lost on many sex workers:it is difficult for them to see as allies those apparently campaigning to render them redundant).

Shrage's (1989:348) own strategy is to show that the sex industry, like others of our social institutions, is 'structured by deeply ingrained attitudes and values which are oppressive to women'. While Ericsson at least seems aware of this type of feminist claim, Pateman (1983) insists that what she terms his 'liberal contractarianism' necessarily denies him any effective means of rebuttal. Her stance differs from his in several important respects. For example, she maintains that prostitution is not simply the selling of sexual services; rather, 'when sex becomes a commodity in the capitalist market so, necessarily, do bodies and selves.... In prostitution, because of the relation between the commodity being marketed and the body, it is the body that is up for sale'.

She also disagrees with Ericsson's notion that sex work is like 'sex without love or mutual affection', arguing that the difference between sex without love and prostitution is not the difference between cooking at home and buying food in restaurants; the difference is that between the reciprocal expression of desire and unilateral subjection to sexual acts with the consolation of payment: it is the difference for women between freedom and subjection.

Pateman argues that Ericsson 'stands firmly in the patriarchal tradition' in that he discusses prostitution 'as a problem about the women who are prostitutes, and our attitudes to them, not a problem about the men who demand to buy them'. She rejects the view that prostitution is an example of a free contract between equal individuals in the market, insisting that for feminists it is not possible to separate sex from power. Indeed, 'prostitution is the public recognition of men as sexual masters; it puts submission on sale as a commodity in the market'. Ericsson is in error, according to Pateman, in assuming that the (sexual) selves of women and men are interchangeable. 'This may appear radical', Pateman remarks, 'but it is a purely abstract radicalism that reduces differentiated, gendered individuality to the seemingly natural, undifferentiated, and universal figure of the "individual"-which is an implicit generalizatisn of the masculine self.'

Pragmatic Considerations

Alongside philosophical reflections on and feminist critiques of the sex industry are more pragmatic concerns about what should be done. And such concerns have of necessity to be tailored to the possibilities afforded for change in contemporary-patriarchal and capitalist-Britain. It does not in our view follow that too many punches should be pulled. In discussing how best to meet the health needs of sex workers, we have elsewhere distinguished between three 'levels' of change: operational, political and structural.

We used the term operational change to refer to formal health promotion or service initiatives overseen by health workers and allied experts which neither challenge nor threaten core social institutions. Political change refers to initiatives which bear on health but are beyond the conventional spheres of influence and authority of health workers to accomplish. Such change, typically requiring government action, increases awareness of core social institutions and may indirectly pose a challenge or threat to them. Structural change refers to fundamental revisions within core social institutions which have a bearing on health but are beyond the capacities of both health workers and government to deliver. Structural change typically requires a mobilization of mass public support which, in turn, typically requires sustained and organized extra-parliamentary political action.

We used these distinctions to argue that operational change, from outreach health promotion programmes to more user-friendly clinics, necessarily adds up to little more than an exercise in damage limitation; and that this is a function of the social marginalization of women sex workers in communities and the law, and their resultant suspicion of all branches of 'officialdom'. We went on to advocate political change, on health and other grounds, in the form of a decriminalization of the sex industry, which would both remove the anomaly of a gender-biased body of legislation exclusive to a particular area of work and prepare the ground for de-marginalising women sex workers and restoring basic citizenship and other rights to them. Finally, we noted that the elimination of one set of gender-biased laws would leave much else intact, and made a case for structural change to address the systematic disadvantages facing women, and especially lone mothers, in the British labour and housing markets, maintaining that relative poverty and limited opportunity are necessary elements of any sociology of the sex industry.

Axiomatically, these distinctions have applicability beyond issues of health, and the case for further consideration of the potential for political and structural change pertinent to the British sex industry towards the close of the twentieth century seems unanswerable. Arguments around political change tend to focus on the law. While there is a consensus that the current law is untenable, opinions on appropriate reform are much more fragmented, and not only among philosophers and feminists. There has been some experimentation with 'tolerance zones', or designated areas where sex workers can work set hours under conditions laid down by local authorities (*e.g.* in Birmingham and Nottingham); but the two modes of reform most often discussed are legalization and decriminalization.

Legalization is generally accompanied by a system of registration for women sex workers, who have also to submit to 'rules' designed to protect public health and decency. This usually means that women are required to have regular health checks to retain their licences to work in specified houses or localities.

Legalization has attracted some support recently and there is evidence of public receptiveness. In a much-publicized report in 1992 the Mothers' Union watered down its opposition to the legalization of brothels. Publics, if not necessarily clients, tend to be more tolerant of forms of sex work which are perceived to be clean, safe and invisible. However, many sex workers, including the International Committee for Prostitutes' Rights (ICPR) and the English Collective of Prostitutes (ECP), argue that legalization merely represents an alternative, and in some ways more blatant, male mode of control of female sexuality than exists under present statutes. Moreover in countries where legalization has been introduced (*e.g.* Germany) it has on the whole not proved 'successful', since many women are unwilling to provide assembly-line sex for taxed pay in a state brothel and prefer to work illegally. Some women barred from working legally because of sexually transmitted diseases or other sickness also continue outside the law. Most women working illegally are vulnerable, at risk of exploitation and abuse and beyond the reach and influence of health workers and other agencies.

Decriminalization, or the total abolition of laws and sentences which discriminate against women sex workers, has been the subject of sex worker campaigns in Britain-notably by the ECP-and elsewhere since the mid-1980s. The ICPR has supplemented its (global) call for the decriminalization of 'voluntary adult sex work' with demands also for appropriate regulation of third parties; the impartial enforcement of extant legislation against fraud, coercion, rape, child abuse and so on; the granting of human and civil rights for sex workers; the extension of the taxation and benefits system to sex workers; and help and support for women electing to leave the sex industry. These are among the key demands articulated in the ICPR's 'World Charter'.

The decriminalization of adult sex work freely entered into would not put sex workers beyond the law; but it would eliminate the anomaly of an essentially sexist body of law exclusive to a particular area of work. Nor would decriminalization in this country solve the growing global problem of 'stolen lives' due to 'sexual trafficking'; but it would perhaps help loosen the grip of more or less organized crime syndicates and other criminals. It should be noted, however, that Matthews (1986) has taken a contrary view, namely, that decriminalization would in all likelihood increase the level of exploitation of prostitutes.

Citing Wilson's (1983:224) statement that 'wholesale de-criminalization would simply mean a free for all for men', he (1986:199) suggests 'the removal of legal constraints would give a free hand to entrepreneurs to organize prostitution as a legitimate business. The criminalising of prostitution by reducing its legitimacy also reduces the potential profit and thus the overall rate of exploitation.'

In preference to either legalization or de-criminalization, Matthews (1986:204) advocates a 'radical regulationism'. This involves: (a) a clear commitment to general deterrence; (b) the reduction of annoyance, harassment and disturbance; (c) protection from coercion and exploitation; and (d) the reduction of the commercialization of prostitution. Shrage (1994) is sympathetic to Matthews' fourfold strategy, although she notes his lack of comment on the means for its effective implementation. She (1994:159) expounds her own version as follows:

It would be a system where prostitutes would not be 'registered' and brothels would not be 'licensed', but where prostitutes themselves would be licensed, much like other professionals and semi-professional. Since in the sex industry the primary productive assets are the bodies of sex providers, and the primary trade secrets are contained in their personal skills, knowledge, charm and talent, sex providers should be given as much control as possible over the operation and use of these talents.

The standards for licensing should be established by 'public boards or commissions made up of service providers, community leaders, educators and legal and public health experts'.

Shrage sees a number of advantages in licensing individual sex workers: it would allow sex workers to work for themselves or form cooperatives, which would leave them less vulnerable to large commercial interests; by controlling how their services were offered, it would render them less vulnerable too to clients, small-scale entrepreneurs, pimps and public officials; it would afford them semi-professional status, which would give them the authority to 'lead certain kinds of business and sexual transactions'; by engaging in sex work profitably, they might challenge the cultural association between sex and harm to women; by involving sex workers in designing and monitoring the procedures for licensing, it would empower those likely to protect sex workers' legal rights; and, finally, it would both give clients reassurance that certain standards would be met and 'provide the public with a vehicle for addressing possible hazards that might result from the industry'.

Legalization, decriminalization and regulationism have been introduced here as exemplars of political change and as ideal types; other-and 'mixed'-reform packages are possible. Our concern has been to trigger further debate in the public sphere on what almost all commentators agree is an unacceptable set of prostitution laws presently in force (in England and Wales). We have only been able in the confines of this Afterword to give a flavour of the pros and cons of select recipes for reform.

It is perhaps fitting to close with another reference to structural change. British women's continuing economic and hierarchic heterosexual dependencies are part and parcel of a comprehensive system of patriarchal institutions, norms and relationships, as are the constrained, marginal and often hazardous and health-exacting lives of contemporary women sex workers. Structural change towards the elimination of gender disadvantages in material and ideological circumstance, is in our view a precondition for the effectiveness of legal reform and for the reconstruction or 'displacement' of the flawed British sex industry of the 1990s via the empowerment through full citizenship of all its current sex workers.

8

Bodies on the Margin: Other form of Health and Sex Tourism

The idea of the sex tourist and sex tourism occupying liminal space has been central to the development of this book. The notion of Turner (1974) that liminal entities are neither here or there, that they are betwixt and between the positions assigned and arrayed by law, custom, convention and ceremony has been utilised to help partly explain the cultural space that sex tourism fills. As has been discussed, the tourist is therefore a marginal person, with the extent to which tourism is sanctioned varying from society to society and the nature of such marginality changes over time. For example, Lea noted that in the early 1960s 'the advent of young westerners and their casual attitudes to sex and drugs had a severe impact on the predominantly Roman Catholic Christian Goan community'. Writing several years later Wilson noted that there is 'little evidence of hostility and resentment among local people against the majority of such tourists', and argued that this is because, in part, such low-budget, low-income tourism in Goa has spread the economic benefits of tourism more widely through the local community than five-star hotel development. Wilson quotes an interview by Anderson with one villager in north Goa who stated:

The villagers were devout Catholics and they had been offended by hippies bathing naked in front of their homes. But that had now stopped. [They were] not bothered by the hippies' lifestyle. The village as a whole were happy to augment their incomes by renting out rooms in their houses to budget travellers and running little cafés and bars which fell well short of overwhelming village life.

In 2000 Goa actively promotes itself as a tourism destination to the West, often with reference to the image established by the 'hippie' period and is now a major location for the hosting of rave dance parties on the beach.

A range of lifestyles and activities may occupy this liminal space; Beddoe (1998) mentioned it in association with beach boy related tourism in Sri Lanka. Similarly, Lett (1983) in investigating the sexual behaviour of individuals on yacht charter in the British Virgin Islands, found that the customary courting relationships were abandoned during the holiday period and individuals were more apt to engage in sexual relationships with strangers. Based on Turner's (1974) work, Lett conceptualised 'liminoid' as having liminal qualities without a ritual component, 'Liminoid activities, in short, are those socially accepted and approved activities which seem to deny or ignore the legitimacy of the institutionalised statuses, roles, norms, values, and rules of everyday, 'ordinary' life.' In Lett's study, charter tourists were engaged in a liminoid experience, with an altered point of reference, which allowed then to behave almost opposite from their normal behaviours in their home environment, including their sexual behaviour. Nevertheless, as Currie noted, 'Given the opportunities and resources of a destination or the particular needs of individuals, this sexual inversion may not be possible or desirable for individuals.'

Graburn argued that such reversals or inversions of behaviour are a necessary part of life and imply that, 'certain meanings and rules of 'ordinary behaviour' are changed, held in abeyance or even reversed'. Graburn depicted inversions as polar opposites that reside on a continuum that allows individuals to determine the degree to which behaviours are reversed or inverted from their lifestyles in their home environment, with each kind of tourism being 'characterised by the selection of only a few key reversals'. Wagner (1977), in reference to male prostitution in the Gambia for the predominantly female Scandinavian market, argued that the 'inversion' brought about by such relationships, was perverting the norms ruling gender relations in many societies. Wagner argued that there was a destructive potential in these relationships:

What to the tourist is a pleasant and refreshing interlude where the disregarding of norms in no way threatens the structures pervading in their home society, could result in the destruction of one of the very foundations of local social structure, that of ordering social life according to age and generation differences.

Nevertheless, such inversions are not a given, as Graburn noted: reversals are bi-directional, that a number of the polarities are related to each other; that rarely are tourists motivated by only one kind of behaviour reversal; and that tourists only choose to switch a few of their behavioural parametres at any one time, while retaining the vast majority of normal repertories.

If, sex tourism has occupied a marginal position in tourism research, so issues of homosexual roles are even more marginalised. Indeed, the position of women, ethnic minorities and homosexuals in tourism is almost as marginalised in the tourism academy as it is in the articulation and representation of heritage, identity and tourism. Nevertheless, in recent years a number of significant attempts have been made to redress the imbalance in studies of gay tourism. In this, the expression 'gay', generally understood as the historically specific US slang term from the 1970s, now often internationalised, travelling globally via gay politics, gay culture and gay tourism is used in preference to 'homosexual' or 'homosexualities', the attempt at a universal, pluralistic (but uneasily, is it only male?) term, which deliberately situates and re-situates the medico-legal discourses of the late nineteenth century to the present day.

In the year 2000 gay tourism as an expression of gay lifestyle is marked by stereotypes, homophobia, significant misunderstandings and, often deliberate misrepresentations. Right-wing church and religious groups in particular often seek to portray homosexuality as some sort of crime against God and typically seek to deny the gay community the rights which are assigned to most individuals in society. In particular, the expressions of gay pride at community events and festivals that often represent, to some, portrayals of indecent and lewd behaviour, are often represented as the 'norm' to the mainstream community and 'dangerous' to society.

Indeed, certain homophobic groups often equate the homosexual community with the actions of paedophiles in terms of being sexual predators or engaging in 'public orgies'. Such representations clearly match certain portrayals of sex tourism in terms of its potential to 'undermine' or 'affect' society. However, as in the case of sex tourism there is a multiple layering of meaning in the expression of gay lifestyle through travel and community celebrations, as there is in any group in society. Indeed, we recognise that there is a danger in sectioning out in a book on sex tourism a specific discussion on gay travel as it may reinforce the representation that the expression of gay love is somehow deviant. That is not our intention at all. Instead we want to illustrate the marginal space of liminality through a range of different settings and how they may be read and interpreted. Indeed, in examining aspects of tourism in relation to gay and lesbian travel we also want to highlight the manner in which the tensions of marginality may actually contribute to greater understanding and tolerance in society.

One of the great myths of gay lifestyles represented in some of the mass media is that it is full of single gays and lesbians who are seeking casual sex. As with all myths it is based on truth. However, within an examination of homosexual lifestyles there is no reason to believe that there is more casual sex than in the expression of heterosexual behaviours. For example, Clift and Forrest (1999) in a study of gay travel motivations, noted that 'opportunities for sex' ranked substantially lower than many other motivations.

Despite the stereotyped image of homosexuals as people seeking loveless sex it is not unusual for gays to be in monogamous relationships. For example, a Canadian report indicates that most gays and lesbians would rather be in a stable relationship or married and are not just interested in casual sex. A poll of 1,700 gays and lesbians for Fugues, a Canadian gay magazine, indicated that

55 per cent of the respondents were in a stable couple and 69 per cent wanted to get married. According to Michael Hendricks of Operation couple, a group that wants to demystify the social and sexual lives of gays:

It breaks the stereotype that we are lonely men going around looking for other lonely men ... We buy candy and flowers for each other at this time of the year and everyone that's alone is hoping that Cupid will strike. Rejean Barbeau, who was helping launch Operation couple, said, 'People have the impression there's no stability in the gay community when there is ... But that impression distorts the reality. There are couples who are together as well as singles'.

While many myths abound regarding gay lifestyles, it can be noted that travel and holidays constitute an important part of gay identity in Western society. As Hughes (1997:6) observed, 'Tourism and being gay are inextricably linked. Because of social disapproval of homosexuality many gay men are forced to find gay space ... Gay space is limited ... and gays find it necessary to travel in order to enter that space.' The extent to which gays travel has made them a lucrative travel market. According to the 1999 report on the gay and lesbian travel industry by Community Marketing (1999) the gay and lesbian travel sector is worth approximately US$47.3 billion, or about 10 per cent of the US travel industry total. Gays and lesbians have a higher propensity to travel than the non-gay population. According to the report, 85 per cent of gays and lesbians surveyed took a vacation in the previous twelve months, compared to a 64 per cent national average.

Thirty-six per cent took three or more vacations, while 45 per cent went overseas, compared to just 9 per cent of the national average. Gay and lesbian income demographics reported in this travel survey are similar to those of other studies (*e.g.*, Pritchard et al., 1998). Many gays and lesbians have a higher household income level. Some 75 per cent have incomes of more than $40,000 per annum, and 23 per cent have an income over $100,000 per annum (compared to 9 per cent of mainstream American travellers). Though one of the most significant indicators of the gay markets propensity to travel was the result that of the survey population 78 per cent held a valid passport, compared to just 29 per cent of the mainstream. Similarly, in Australia, Campaign magazine's research shows that gay men earn and spend much more than the population average. The study also revealed that companies who had marketed themselves towards the gay spending dollar were already reaping large profits. Conducted by Significant Others Marketing Consultants, the survey results have gay men earning significantly above the national average with almost 40 per cent travelling overseas the previous year, more than half eating in a restaurant at least once a week and 23.6 per cent dining out two or more times a week. The survey also noted that more than half would change banks if offered a gay credit card.

In the American survey sea cruises were particularly attractive to the gay and lesbian travel population with the survey finding that 15 per cent had taken a cruise in the previous twelve months. By comparison, only about 2 per cent of the mainstream population cruised in the same period. In this market gays and lesbians were choosing mainstream though 'gay friendly' cruise options rather than exclusive tours. To date, only Carnival and Windstar cruise lines have openly sought the gay and lesbian market with advertising and promotions. In terms of airlines, the survey reported that among domestic carriers, American Airlines was rated 'favourite' for the fifth year in a row, primarily because of the airline's visibility in the gay community, sponsoring charities and gay travel-related promotions. In fact, according to Community Marketing's research results, 'giving back' to the gay community - in the form of donations and other support - was an important factor for 89 per cent of survey respondents when choosing among travel supplier and agent options.

Given the degree of homophobia in certain sections of society, 'many gays will choose to travel in search of an anonymous or safe environment in which to be gay'. Therefore, perhaps unsurprisingly, being a gay friendly location acts as a significant factor in travel planning. Among American urban destinations, San Francisco rates first, with 49 per cent having visited in the past three years. Resorts such as Palm Springs and Key West also remained significant destinations. Activity- and event-related trips are also very popular among the gay community. In the previous three years, 50 per cent went to a gay pride event, 13 per cent travelled to attend a circuit party, and 4 per cent participated in a 'gay ski week' event.

Where destinations are overtly unfriendly to gays, then their tourism industry may suffer. For example, in light of a number of concerns raised by gay and lesbian tourist interests, the Jamaica Forum of Lesbians, All-sexuals and Gays (J-FLAG) called on government and tourism interests to make Jamaica more appealing to the international gay and lesbian tourist market with the organisation being concerned that Jamaica's international image of not being welcoming to gays and lesbians will damage the country's already fragile tourist industry. J-FLAG (1999) notes that Jamaica's internationally known homophobia will alienate it from markets in countries that have no sanctions against sexual practices between consenting adults. They observe that Jamaica may also come under increasing pressure from international gay and lesbian organisations, such as the International Gay and Lesbian Travel Association (IGLTA), whose Executive Director Augustin Merlo on 30 December 1998 stated that his organisation strongly condemns Jamaican authorities: for failing to ensure the safety, welfare and comfort of gays and lesbians living on and visiting the island nation. The island nation appears to be a leader in the region's emerging homophobia that has already shown its ugly face in the Cayman Islands and Costa Rica. That is a tragedy … If Jamaica is unwilling or unprepared to welcome gay and lesbian tourists to [its] shores, then IGLTA is prepared to warn all of our member companies and associations that our tourist dollars are no longer welcome in that country.

J-FLAG believe that significant fallout in the tourist market could result from the IGLTA statement, noting that if Jamaica continues to be seen as a destination that discriminates against gay and lesbian tourists, it will lose out on the multi-billion dollar international gay and lesbian tourist market, which South Africa, with its non-discriminatory policies, has aggressively begun to court. Therefore, J-FLAG was calling on the Jamaican government and tourism interests to put in place measures aimed at welcoming all tourists regardless of their sexual orientation, including repealing the nation's buggery law and a change in the interpretation of the gross indecency law.

Despite the positive tourism image of Australia in the gay travel community because of the success of the Sydney Gay and Lesbian Mardi Gras, Australia has a long history of homophobic attitudes and laws, many of which are still in place (Brother Sister, 1996c). In the mid-1990s, the State of Tasmania in Australia introduced a series of anti-gay laws (since overturned), which Tasmanian gay activists claim were costing the State valuable tourist dollars. For example, at a tourism conference in Hobart, the state capital, the General Manager of a tourism promotions company, Landmark South Pacific, Judy Ashton, said that Tasmania was missing out on the lucrative gay travel market because of the perception overseas that it was illegal for two men to book a room together. Tasmanian Gay and Lesbian Rights Group spokesperson, Rodney Croome, also confirmed that visiting gay couples reported being denied accommodation on the basis that homosexual activity was still illegal in Tasmania. According to Croome:

If we are to have any chance of tapping into the gay and lesbian travel market our anti-gay laws must either be completely repealed by the Parliament or conclusively invalidated by the High Court ... For this reason we call on those members of the Upper House who oppose gay law reform to put their personal prejudices to one side in the interest of job creation.

In contrast to the Tasmanian situation, the State Government of New South Wales began to openly support gay tourism in 1995. Opening the 1995 NSW Tourism Conference, which for the first time included a workshop on the niche market of gay and lesbian travel, State Premier Bob Carr cited the Gay and Lesbian Mardi Gras Festival as an important factor in boosting Sydney's international profile as a tourist destination and announced that Sydney had been voted the world's best city for tourists in a survey conducted by the magazine publishers, Condé Nast.

In contrast to the previous conservative state government which ordered the state tourism organisation to remove reference to the Mardi Gras in its promotion, Premier Carr made specific mention of the significance of the Mardi

Gras Festival to the state's tourism industry, not only in dollar terms but also its celebration of arts and culture.

In addition, Lynne Hocking, founder of the travel group Destination DownUnder whose company organises holidays for more than 1,500 gays and lesbians a year, speaking at the conference, said that mainstream travel agents were increasingly educating their staff to meet the needs of gay and lesbian travellers in a bid to be regarded as gay friendly, concluding that professionalism without prejudice was the key to being part of this growing market. Further signs of change in the Australian mainstream tourism industry with respect to gay travel were the decision in 1995 of the national tourism promotion organisation, the Australian Tourism Commission (ATC) to part-fund a brochure aimed specifically at the gay and lesbian market, representing the first time that the ATC has targeted the gay niche market. The brochure was produced with the state tourism offices of Victoria, NSW and Queensland, after the ATC pledged to match other contributions dollar for dollar.

Sydney's Gay and Lesbian Mardi Gras has a substantial spin-off effect across Australia. For example, international visitors to Mardi Gras spent an average of $347.25 per day and stayed for about twenty-one days, outstripping general tourist spend by 30 per cent. In relation to the effects of the 25th Mardi Gras held in 1999 the corporate manager at F.O.D. Travel, Greg Miller, stated:

The US market is always huge, but this year they have really strong buying power... One of the things people forget is that these tourists come back every year. There is very strong repeat business and when they're here, they spend ... Nine out of 10 Americans include Cairns in their trip.

Nevertheless, despite such financial success gay tourists are not always welcome. For example, in February 1999 the Australian Gay and Lesbian Tourism Association hit out at claims by Opposition Tourism spokesman Graham Healy that holiday resorts marketing gay and lesbian holidays in Queensland after the Sydney Mardi Gras was not in the best interests of Queensland.

Mr Healy said that he would not like to see Queensland holiday resorts targeting only certain sections of the community and noted that he is only concerned that Noosa's up-market French Quarter resort may be tagged with a reputation for attracting one type of customer. Thus he stated:

It would, I think, be unreasonable to suggest that the whole area surrounding that particular resort could be classed as something that it certainly is not. In Queensland we have a reputation for attracting tourists from all walks of life, and certainly national and international tourists, and I think that to specifically say that a particular area could become a particular individualistic area for a particular market is something that I think is unreasonable and not in the best interests of tourism in Queensland.

Opposition to gay tourism and events is also seen across the Tasman in New Zealand. The Hero Parade and associated festival, New Zealand's equivalent of the Mardi Gras has been held every year since 1991, except 2000, when funding problems caused the cancellation of the parade though other events went on. Described as 'Auckland's favourite free event', Hero was set up in 1991 as a pride event for gay men and has developed into a two-week gay and lesbian festival, which incorporates the parade and the party and a host of other cultural events. Its mission was to raise awareness and money for HIV/ AIDS organisations, which at the time received very little funding. Hero Project Director Steve Berry-Smith described Hero as an umbrella organisation for the gay community.

It's an umbrella organisation that provides a forum for all kinds of organisations and individuals to express themselves ... For a lot of people, particularly in small towns, coming out can be very difficult. The Hero event can give them something to identify with, a beacon if you like.

Indeed, Hero attracts participants from all over New Zealand while gays from overseas also participate on their way to or from Sydney's Mardi Gras celebrations. In 1999 publicity regarding Hero's poor funding situation assisted in raising its profile in the corporate sector and increasing sponsorship. According to Berry-Smith:

Interest and awareness are definitely up from the business side and the public. It's one of the biggest events in the country now and Hero is pretty much a household name. We've received increased support from large corporate sponsors this year, which indicates how the acceptance level for Hero has grown.

However, not all public comment was positive. The Christian Heritage Party called for a boycott of sponsors of the Hero Parade, saying the procession is nothing more than a 'public orgy'. Christian Heritage Party leader, Graham Capill said that it was 'sickening in the extreme to see companies sell their corporate souls' to attract more custom. Graham Capill wanted 'every decent New Zealander to send a message to Qantas by flying Air New Zealand, to Pepsi - by buying Coke, and to Metro - by reading North and South'.

More overt homophobia was an advert placed in the New Zealand Herald of 12 February 1999, featuring photographs of Dame Whina Cooper (a Maori rights activist), Mahatma Gandhi, Mother Teresa and Martin Luther King junior, stating it 'takes more than a parade to make a hero'. Readers who endorsed 'traditional family values enough to oppose the promotion of destructive sexuality' were invited to post a coupon to a group called Stop Promoting Homosexuality International (NZ). The Rev. Bruce Patrick of the Auckland Baptist Tabernacle Church said the group, which was newly established in New Zealand, was trying to raise money to help pay for the advertisement from a 'silent majority': 'You get the feeling that it is very, very hard to present any view that isn't "politically correct" through the media, that the media has a party line, and views that don't fit with that are very difficult to present'.

Complaints about the advertisement were lodged immediately with the New Zealand Human Rights Commission and the Advertising Standards Complaints Board. Kevin Hague, executive director of the Aids Foundation, said the advertisement was offensive:

I wonder if it had been about Maori people or Jewish people, or one of the minority groups that those four people pictured had belonged to... There's no mention of the churches they are involved with, which is very deliberate, and no mention of anyone who is actually involved with this organisation.

Chief Human Rights Commissioner Pamela Jefferies said that the advertisement was unfortunate noting that the New Zealand Human Rights Act protected a wide range of different groups from unlawful discrimination, including gay and lesbian people: 'Attempts to stir up ill feeling against any of those groups are destructive. Such behaviour is inconsistent with the spirit of a tolerant and inclusive society'. As events turned out, the 1999 Hero Parade, opened by the Prime Minister, attracted the biggest-ever spectator crowd in its nine-year history with about 200,000 people flocking to the event to see more than fifty floats moved down Ponsonby Road, featuring everything from a chorus of male Marilyn Monroe lookalikes to gay garden displays.

FROM LOCK-UP TO FROCK-UP

The first Sydney Mardi Gras was organised in 1978 in solidarity with gays and lesbians in San Francisco who were fighting against a homophobic bill proposed by Republican Senator John Briggs. Activists in a range of community and political organisations, including the Active Defence of Homosexuals on Campus, the Gay Task Force and Campaign Against Moral Persecution (CAMP), formed a committee to organise a rally. On 24 June 1978 a daytime rally was held, followed by a night-time carnival. According to Ken Davis:

City shoppers and workers saw an unprecedentedly large lesbian-led street march. The march passed without incident, everyone exhilarated by the turnout and the vehemence of our demands against discrimination, the law and violence. For many, it was their first demonstration, their first coming out.

However, the night-time carnival was marred by conflict with police who prevented a march by demonstrators into Kings Cross, Sydney's red light district with fifty-three people being arrested.

In response to the police actions a protest rally was held the following 15 July, with more than 2,000 people marching to demand that the NSW Labour government drop the charges. At the time it was the largest lesbian and gay rally ever held in Australia. After marching through Kings Cross, the demonstrators stopped in front of Darlinghurst Police Station and laid wreaths of pansies. In response, the police arrested eleven more people. The police actions provoked national outrage with rallies in support of the marchers also being organised in Melbourne, Adelaide and Brisbane. A commemorative rally held the following year attracted 3,000 demonstrators. Mardi Gras had become an annual celebration of gay and lesbian pride which marks broader changes in Australian and New South Wales society. As Bucknell records:

There are Mardi Gras regulars who weren't born when the first parade, a demonstration for gay and lesbian rights, was held in June 1978. 'Out of the bars and into the streets,' the protesters chanted along Darlinghurst's Oxford Street. Many were bashed and arrested as they tried to escape a police blockade. How far we've come. For a decent spot to view the parade along the Golden Mile these days you need to set up several hours early with a milk crate (street price: A$25) to beat the 500,000 others. The police work with Mardi Gras marshals along the route.

However, from the 1980s on there have been sharp debates within Sydney's gay and lesbian community over the direction of the Mardi Gras and the extent to which it should reflect political actions against its more commercial, party emphasis. For example, lesbians, although always present from the first Mardi Gras, were secondary players up until the late 1980s. Fierce internal debate accompanied the proposal to incorporate the word 'lesbian' into Mardi Gras' name in 1988. This commitment to 'coalition politics' reflected a growing interest from lesbians in the celebration of sexuality that Mardi Gras had become during the 1980s.

The AIDS epidemic has also added another dimension to the Mardi Gras with the significance being recognised not only of a safe sex message but also remembering those who have died from AIDS. According to Begg (1999), those who wanted to make Mardi Gras more of a party and less of a demonstration gained the upper hand. In 1982 Mardi Gras was moved to a summer schedule and Brian McGahen, on behalf of the organising committee, declared 'we are keen on having maximum commercial participation'. To justify the shift in emphasis in Mardi Gras, the 1983 organising committee explained, 'We do not see politics in any narrow sense. Our right to lead our chosen lifestyle is a major political demand' (in Begg, 1999). Raising lesbian and gay visibility has become a focus of Mardi Gras, rather than just using the march to campaign for equal rights. Nevertheless, as activist Craig Johnston observed, the transformation from political movement to mainstream consumer event may have been inevitable. 'Same politics of dignity and rights, different style. Gay liberation's ideological sharpness was defused as it diffused into the scene queen's body'.

Today, more than 500,000 people participate in the Mardi Gras parade whether as participants or spectators. In addition, many people watch the parade on television. In 1985 the media were inflammatory. The Sydney Morning Herald, which now produces its own Mardi Gras lift-out, was far from supportive.

In the 1985 Herald report on the parade a journalist invented quotes she attributed to the then Mardi Gras director. To his horror he read, on the Monday after the parade, references he was supposed to have made to people with AIDS as 'freaks' and 'Elephant Men'. The Herald was forced to publish an apology.

Research by the Australian Graduate School of Management (AGSM) in 1998 found that Mardi Gras contributed more than $40 million to the Sydney economy. There were more than 5,000 international visitors to Sydney during the 1998 festivities, 3,600 of whom came specifically for the event. Of the 7,300 interstate tourists, 4,800 had Mardi Gras in mind, and AGSM also recorded 2,400 'holidays at home'. According to Begg (1999), Qantas earned $1.5 million from international visitors, and the Mardi Gras attracts more international and interstate visitors than any other cultural festival in Sydney, Melbourne, Perth or Adelaide with the festival guide carrying advertising from Hahn Ice, Qantas, Telstra, Foxtel, Land Rover and other large corporations.

The pink dollar is now a significant attraction to companies. In 1999 the 25th Sydney Gay and Lesbian Mardi Gras attracted a record A$800,000 worth of corporate sponsorship. Telstra, Qantas, Coca-Cola, Lion Nathan and Southcorp Wines were among the blue chip business names that have lined up to support and cash in on the annual celebration of gay and lesbian sexuality. For example, Telstra launched a commemorative Mardi Gras phone card featuring its official Drag Queen spokeswoman, Ms Candee. Coca-Cola used the festival to promote its Mount Franklin Bottled Water with full page advertisements in the gay press featuring a Sydney Drag Queen, Verushka Darling. Stolichnaya Vodka sold its Lemon Ruski bottles across Sydney with tiny pink feather boas wrapped around their necks. However, the degree of commercialism and corporate involvement attached to Mardi Gras has served to heighten tensions surrounding the meaning of the event within the gay community. For example, Ian Johnson, principal of Significant Others, a marketing consultantcy specialising in targeting gays and lesbians stated:

Corporate sponsorship is necessarily a bad thing. However, I think that by it's very nature whatever deals are struck have to be handled very sensitively and strategically… At the end of the day the interests of the gay and lesbian community must be paramount otherwise they [the sponsors] risk the support of Mardi Gras's own membership base.

More vociferous were the comments of Anthony Yeo, in response to the prevention of a gay group collecting donations at a Mardi Gras Fair Day, in a mailing to several gay and lesbian news lists:

What on earth has gotten into the very swelled heads that permeate Mardi Gras? First The Rainbow Party, now this insanity. Rebel people rebel, against a commercially driven organisation that has completely lost all touch with reality and the community it is supposed to serve. It comes as no surprise no-one from the Erskineville bunker will comment, far too afraid of the backlash?

The same message also contained a previous mailing from Norrie in relation to the same issue:

That's just MAD! Does anyone think these people haven't gone too far? Stop giving them your money! Stop supporting their fascism with your cash! Don't buy a ticket to the Mardi Gras party! Next year, if you've already forked out!

Starve the bastards! The community festival will live on, and the parade, with or without the sponsorship dollars! This gig started as a community driven event, and it may need to again for the sake of the community!

Although corporate sponsorship is now an important part of the Mardi Gras, the extent to which such commitment extends is perhaps debatable. For example, the front page Column 8 of the Sydney Morning Herald (1999) reported one reader's comments:

Qantas has acknowledged that the Sydney Gay and Lesbian Mardi Gras is a major event by mentioning it in its in-flight magazine. But although Qantas is a sponsor and official carrier, there is no mention of it being a gay and lesbian event. It's described thus: OOH LA LA, IT'S MARDI GRAS - Sydney's wildest, brightest and most fabulous festival turns 21 this year ... Some tourists might get a bit of a surprise.

The tensions surrounding the meaning of Mardi Gras, however, are well recognised by the festival's organisers. At the official opening of the 1999 Gay and Lesbian Mardi Gras on the Sydney Opera House forecourt in front of an audience of more than 20,000 people, Festival President David McLachlan used a wide-ranging speech to acknowledge the Aboriginal traditional owners of Sydney, applaud the character of French tennis player Emily Mauresmo, criticise the conservative nature of all politicians on social reform, and criticise the Opera House Trust, which had withdrawn permission for the Sisters of Perpetual Indulgence to conduct tours of the site during the festival. According to Mclaughlin, the festival marked a special time. '... when we celebrate and illuminate and share our lives, not only with each other, but with the whole bloody world'. The chief executive officer of the AIDS Council of New South Wales, Robert Griew, said at the opening that the Mardi Gras is also important as a reminder of how much remains to be done:

It started as a political struggle, and it means we think about all the people we've lost with HIV, and the fact that the struggle keeps going on... It's not over, it continues, and it's a time to remember that, but to celebrate the strength of the community, and the base that is for the struggle with HIV.

David McLachlan's reflections on Mardi Gras in an article with a sub-heading, 'Fairy stories do come true', provide an opportunity to witness his own observations of the meaning of Mardi Gras in a manner that reflected the various meanings associated with the annual festival. As with many Australian gays and lesbians the Mardi Gras was, and continues to be, an important defining moment in life, providing an opportunity to come out publicly and be able to celebrate their sexuality in an accepting environment. The ritual nature of carnivals and festivals, such as the Mardi Gras, as liminal space is highlighted in McLachlan's (1999) observation: 'For many it is the ritual of Mardi Gras which is its most defining quality. It is the annual cycle of anticipation, mounting excitement, repeated we-do-it-every-year events, the big day itself and then the letdown which is an important part of the ebb and flow of their lives.' McLachan's comment on the Sydney Mardi Gras provides an opportunity for meaningful inversion, in the same way as carnival does in Latin and South America, the nature of that meaning is complex and multilayed even seen from within the gay and lesbian community.

For many it is Mardi Gras as an arts, cultural and community festival which is most valued and most important. The festival is now one of the major arts festivals in Australia with an international reputation. It is an opportunity to experience the best of artistic expression as part of a curated lesbian and gay arts festival. For others it is Mardi Gras as a community cultural arts festival that is most important. It is an opportunity for our various and often quite disparate communities to come together to share, inform, entertain and engage with each other and with a wider community with artists and performers from those communities providing the lead and the focus. Many will say to you that it is the public scale and dimension of the festival and in particular the parade that is most important.

The notion of taking to the streets is seen as empowering. The launch occurs in the very centre of one of Sydney's prime civic spaces. Our parade for the best part of a day overwhelms central Sydney. For much of the final week most of inner and central Sydney (and increasingly further afield) is a buzz with queer tribes from everywhere publicly and loudly celebrating the spirit of Mardi Gras. For others the absolute core of Mardi Gras is its political purpose. It grew from a time when taking to the streets was an intensely political act. It has allowed us more effectively than any other means to deliver a message about homophobia, intolerance and legal equality. Above all it is about visibility which in 1999 is still capable of informing, affirming and challenging.

Many say that Mardi Gras is increasingly about money. More and more it is seen as having economic importance for the Sydney and Australian economy as a whole rather than just for Oxford Street businesses. At the same time it remains the most important fund-raising opportunity for many of our community organisations. The economic benefits that flow to businesses within and outside our community are likely to continue to grow. Some see this as Mardi Gras' greatest challenge: to remain true to its community and political purpose in the face of its increasing attraction to commercial interests. Others see this as the ultimate path to real change and real acceptance in a city where money talks and opens doors and can ultimately deliver real social and political change.

However, McLachlan (1999) concludes by noting that for him Mardi Gras is primarily a deep personal significance:

It still stimulates in me that childlike excitement which has me counting down the days and leaves my stomach fluttering with anticipation. Often times it exceeds my highest expectations. Sometimes it must be said it disappoints me. Invariably it leaves me drained and exhausted and sad that it is over.

The hosting of 21st Mardi Gras in 1999 provided an opportunity for much reflection on the meaning of Mardi Gras. A series of responses to the question of meaning is extremely revealing. To political satirist Pauline Pantsdown, Mardi Gras is 'A big chance to broaden the definition of mainstream Australia and of the gay and lesbian scene itself.' According to Sister Salome of the 9th Mystic Rhinestone of the Order of Perpetual Indulgence, 'For the sisters, it means hard work, high visibility and, more often than not, wimple rash.' For Peter Baldwin President of Gay and Married Men's Association and a father of three, Mardi Gras has a wider meaning, 'Reflection on the fact that society still practises discrimination, not just against gays and lesbians but a lot of minority groups', while for Janet Carter, workshop artist for Mardi Gras, it represents, 'A chance for me to have my politics with a bit of icing on top. You can make big statements about homosexual issues such as equal rights and HIV in a really fabulous way.' This integration of politics and party is also seen in the comments of writer and historian Garry Witherspoon, 'Hedonism and optimism. It means summer in Sydney. But it also still means politics ... we need equality in same-sex relationships, equal age of consent'.

The Sydney Mardi Gras, described as a 'sequinned revolution', has undoubtedly provided a space within which many different levels of meaning occur. It is also a space of belonging and identity as well in which some gays may feel more at home than in their normal home environments. Nevertheless, representation and control of this space remain contested, not only by conservative elements in society, but also within the gay and lesbian community. Begg (1999) posed the question as to whether visibility was enough. Visibility is undoubtedly important. Mardi Gras is a powerful 'in your face' reminder that there are hundreds of thousands of people who refuse to be silenced by homophobic attitudes. As the 1999 programme stated, 'We won't stand for any infringement of our basic right to be who we want to be and love who we want to love'. For Begg along with others, visibility is not enough:

Although it may be 'OK to be gay' for the one night of Mardi Gras, when the party is over discrimination against gays and lesbians remains. As the 1999 festival guide points out, gay sex is still illegal in 40 per cent of countries around the world. In Australia, there are a myriad of laws which discriminate against gays and lesbians. Today, Mardi Gras is part of establishment culture. It is an 'outrageous' night which shocks the shockable (Fred Nile maintains his vigil against the sin of it all), but simultaneously makes private businesses millions of dollars and provides a platform for hypocrites such as Kim Beazley, Bob Carr and Peter Collins. It is one big queer night during which everyone is expected to wear as much (or little) leather, sequins and latex as possible, so long as they come down after the party and go home. To achieve real equality for lesbians and gays, much more is required. The radical movement which sparked the first Mardi Gras provides the clues as to what is required.

Begg's comments will strike a chord for many who are seeking equal rights for gays and lesbians. However, they represent just one strand of several in attaching meaning and identity to the Mardi Gras. The Mardi Gras, as with other forms of gay travel, is significant for the relationship between sexuality and tourism in its broadest sense. It demonstrates the wide variety of meaning and association attached to the event by a number of members of the community, it also indicates the difficulty that some members of mainstream society may have in accepting such expressions of sexuality and, therefore, identity, in relation to travel.

The complexities of understanding the relationship between sex and tourism in the context of gay travel are therefore no different from heterosexual expressions of this relationship, except that, perhaps, from the viewpoint of some in Western society, the gay and lesbian community lies at the margins of the margin. Nevertheless, the tensions created in the liminal space by the Mardi Gras and other gay events and travel products may have created opportunities for better understanding of gay and lesbian issues. Visibility may therefore be a precursor to understanding and eventually equality.

Hopefully, the myths associated with gay tourism and its relationship to paedophilia and child sex tourism may eventually be dispelled. The marginal space of gay tourism is therefore very similar in structure to the marginal spaces of heterosexual tourism. In both cases issues of identity and meaning occur. However, it is possible that because of homophobic elements in Western society tourism may be more important for identity for gays than for heterosexuals. If this is the case, then Mardi Gras is as much a cause for celebration of tolerance and understanding in a multi-cultural, multi-lifestyle and diverse society than it is protest. To conclude this with a life-affirming comment from Bucknell's (1999) review of Wherrett's (1999) book on twenty-one years of Mardi Gras:

One of my favourite stories is from Greg Logan who, in 1996, walked alone in the parade carrying a placard saying 'Mum... there's something I've got to tell you'. He warned his parents to watch the telecast, choosing this unconventional way to break their silence, and it worked.

9

South-East Asia: A Hub of Health Tourism

TOURISM AND PROSTITUTION

In the Asian region, tourism has been promoted actively since the United Nations' declaration of 1967 as 'The Year of the Tourist'. Korea, for example, started to develop Chejudo, a small island off the south-west coast, as a resort in the early 1970s, the Philippines established its Department of Tourism in 1973 and Thailand set up the Tourism Authority of Thailand in 1979. The promotion of tourism also brought about a massive growth in female prostitution in the region. Since 1964, when overseas travel was liberalized in Japan, many package tours have been organized to popularize overseas trips among the Japanese.

However, many package tours were marketed exclusively to men, particularly those to South-East Asian countries, which were promoted as a male paradise. Japanese male tourists' behaviour was severely criticized by such organizations as the Christian Women's Federation of Korea, which organized vigorous protests against sex tourism. These campaigns were subsequently internationally coordinated by feminists and pressure groups in South-East Asian countries, including Japan.

The protest movements made a significant impact on Japanese Prime Minister Suzuki when he visited the ASEAN countries in 1981 and met massive demonstrations at the airport in each country. Japanese men started to hesitate about visiting these countries.

The result seems to have been a shift in prostitution which, while still widespread in tourist destination countries, is increasingly prevalent in tourist origin countries.

Since the early 1980s, increasing numbers of women from South-East Asian countries have started to work in the leisure industry in Japan, mainly as bar hostesses, dancers and prostitutes. Those women working in Japan have experienced abuse and exploitation, physical coercion, threats, confinement and economic deprivation.

This aims to analyse the effects of tourism on women from South-East Asia working in Japan. First, we will discuss the growth of tourism and prostitution in South-East Asia and the increase in Japanese tourism in these countries. The subsequent decline in Japanese sex tourism abroad and the background issues which persuade women to come to Japan will be considered in the context of the economic and social situations in both their countries and Japan. The 'double standard' which divides Japanese wives from women who work as prostitutes will be examined and we will show that there are also important differences between the Asian women who work in prostitution-related activities in Japan. Some of the Asian women's experiences in Japan and their responses to them will be discussed, based on interviews with them. Finally, we will consider some possible ways of improving these women's situations.

The issue of prostitution and tourism has been discussed by a number of authors, for example, Awanohara (1975), Takazato (1983), Phongpaichit (1982), Truong (1983), Handley (1989), Lee (1991), Hiebert and Ladd (1993). Prostitution has, for a long time, been a means by which the governments of a range of developing countries have obtained increasing amounts of foreign income from relatively rich tourists from industrialized countries. The process by which the government of the Philippines instituted a policy of tourism promotion and expansion is discussed in several papers, and the conditions of the women who are employed in the sector are examined in Sylvia Chant's chapter in this book. Richter (1980, 1981) considered President Marcos' policies towards tourism, including the 1973 Presidential Decree for the Promotion of Tourism, and the ways in which the policies were formulated and implemented by his government. Wood (1981) describes the way in which loans from international organizations were spent on the construction of infrastructure for tourism as part of a strategy for achieving economic growth via tourism. However, these tourismoriented policies generated large-scale prostitution.

It is not easy to identify when the first criticisms of sex tourism took place, since women's groups in both developing and industrialized countries have a history of campaigning to improve the status of prostitutes. Many of the authors who have been concerned with the issue have described conditions in the prostitution industry and the profiles of the women who work in it. ISIS (Inter-Cultural Studies Information Service, 1979) published a special edition on Tourism and Prostitution, focusing on the tourism industry in Asia and depicting the conditions in Korea, the Philippines and Thailand. Villariba (1993) tells of the situation of Filipino women and the forces which impel them to industrialized countries. The Ecumenical Coalition on Third World Tourism, a Bangkok-based organization, provides a wide range of information about tourism and prostitution, describing the background context and current situation, as well as proposing campaigns and measures against sex tourism; for example, Srisang et al. (1991) and O'Grady (1994) have highlighted the issue of child prostitution in Asia.

Besides the papers written by pressure groups, many academics have published articles and books on prostitution. Hall (1992) provides a review of prostitution in South-East Asia, examining Korea, the Philippines, Taiwan, Thailand, and Australia as a sex tourist generating country. He concluded that sex tourism performs a function of commodifying people and that the sexual relationship between prostitute and client is a mirror image of the dependency of South-east Asian nations on the developed world' (1992:74). In Thai girls and farang men', Cohen (1982) provides information about the short- and long-term relationships between prostitutes and tourists, based on interviews with Thai women, and shows how the economic gains made by the women are offset by significant social and psychological costs.

Heyzer (1986) discussed the control of female sexuality as a local and international business, as well as the personal characteristics and contexts of the women and children who are involved in it. Academic arguments and empirical research were interrelated by Phongpaichit (1982), who obtained detailed information about the economic backgrounds of prostitutes during her meetings with them.

Further analytical work on the economic aspects of prostitution in the tourism industry was undertaken by Truong (1983). It is the economic aspect of tourism which has been a major reason why the governments of South-East Asian countries have encouraged the growth of the sector.

Promoting Prostitution Tourism

In Asian countries, tourism is an important means of earning foreign currency. In Korea, the government's plan to develop Chejudo, an island near to Japan, as a tourist resort aimed to attract 0.6 million tourists with the construction of hotels, casinos and kisaeng (prostitution) houses (Yamaguchi, 1980). In the case of the Philippines, from 1973 to 1980 tourists to the country increased by about 26 per cent and total foreign income from tourism reached $320 million in 1980.

During this period, the government received large loans from such international organizations as the World Bank and Asian Development Bank for the construction of its tourism-related infrastructure, including luxury hotels and paved roads in sightseeing areas. One of the important advantages of tourism is that it creates jobs.

However, as Wood (1981:7) has pointed out, There is some evidence that hotels run by multinational corporations tend to generate less employment than locally-managed hotels', whereas 'the largest single such "spin-off" occupation is often left politely unmentioned: prostitution. It has been estimated that tourism has helped create 100,000 prostitutes in Manila alone.'

Matsui (1993a) claims that the governments of the South-East Asian countries increased their promotion of tourism to compensate for a decrease in exports in the late 1980s since, even in the first half of the decade, earnings from tourism sometimes exceeded those from the staple commodity, rice. The tourism campaigns of 'Visit Thailand Year' in 1987 stimulated a large increase in foreign tourists visiting the country. The number of Japanese travellers to the country rose from 108,500 in 1985 to 162,000 in 1987, a 49 per cent increase. Prostitution tourism in South-East Asian countries had, however, developed long before the 1980s. It is argued that prostitution spread over South-East Asia to provide the US army with relaxation and recreation after the Vietnam War broke out in the 1960s. O'Grady (1992) argues that the end of the Vietnam War, in 1975, left a huge prostitution industry in these countries, and describes how two types of prostitution occurred in Thailand: first, cheap prostitution for local people and, second, large-scale prostitution tourism. O'Grady (1981) also pointed out that many of the fivestar hotels in Manila, which were built according to the Presidential Decree to promote tourism, were occupied by Japanese male tourists.

In the late 1970s and 1980s, many governments failed to act against sex tours because of the large amounts of profit generated by them. For example, even when Thailand was referred to as the 'brothel of Asia', high government officials introduced legislation which underpinned prostitution tourism. More recently, some high ranking officials have begun to question the promotion of tourism. Mechai Viravaidhya, Minister of Industry in Thailand, was the 'first minister to look not only at the financial benefits of tourism but also at its impact on the environment and society' and proposed a 'Women Visit Thailand Year' campaign. Public statements by representatives of government and business have changed in the context of the many protests and criticisms which have been levelled at prostitution tours and in view of the spread of AIDS. The next examines the changes in Japanese tourism to South-East Asian countries which have occurred in the light of such protests.

JAPANESE TOURISM AND PROSTITUTION

The 1960s — Liberalization of Travel Abroad

Japanese prostitution tours to South-East Asia are said to have started in the 1960s, along with the 1964 liberalization of travel abroad and the growth of the country's economy (Japan Travel Bureau, 1991). Although travel abroad was just a dream for most Japanese and was initially limited to a few rich people, overseas travel approximately quadrupled between 1964 and 1970. Tourism was promoted in the form of package tours. 'JALPAK' tours, marketed by Japan Airlines, first appeared in 1965 and their all inclusive nature and tour guides enabled lower income Japanese, with little knowledge of foreign languages, to travel abroad.

The numbers of Japanese travelling abroad were originally dominated by business tourists. In 1964, approximately 37,600 Japanese visited foreign countries for business purposes and just under 19,000 were holiday makers. However, as early as 1965, for the first time, the number of tourists travelling abroad for vacations exceeded those taking business trips and the disparity continued to increase in subsequent years. During the 1960s, Japanese tourists tended to travel to geographically proximate countries, particularly Taiwan and Korea, and the numbers of Japanese visiting these countries, as well as the Philippines and Thailand, increased considerably during the latter part of the decade. It has Geographically proximate destinations of Japanese tourists been argued that the main beneficiaries of this boom were middleaged men, many of whom were participating in prostitution tours.

The 1970s — Japanese Tourists to South-East Asia

During the 1970s, the numbers of Japanese tourists continued to increase greatly and the main destinations were countries within the South-East Asia region. Arrivals were dominated by men, who constituted 80-90 per cent of all travellers from Japan in 1979, in contrast to tourism to West European countries and the USA, where men were 50-60 per cent of the total.

In the case of Korea, for example, the number of tourists from Japan rose from just over 45,000 in 1970 to over 411,000 in 1973 and to over 526,000 in 1979, over 90 per cent of whom were men. Many men visited the newly developed resort of Chejudo, whose kisaeng tours had become well-known after their promotion by the mass media. One subsidiary of a large-scale car manufacturing company was reported to provide overseas trips for workers who made high profits for the firm, the destinations always being countries in the South-East Asia region, including Korea, Taiwan and Thailand. 'Mr Ogawa', who joined a tour as a reward for his sales profit, described how he bought a girl in Thailand and how, another time, three Japanese men from the same company brought Thai girls (prostitutes) to their hotel in Bangkok. It was argued that: this company has been making use of sex tours as a reward to sales workers for more than ten years.... Although they do not attract them as before, since workers have got used to them and their wives are against them, the company cannot find better rewards than giving an opportunity to go on sex tours. However, he also mentioned that the company's policy has been changing in recent years.

The 1980s — the Era of the 'Japayuki-san'

Following the boom of the 1970s, the structure of Japanese prostitution tourism changed in the 1980s. From 1980 to 1987, there was lower growth in the numbers of men travelling to Korea, the Philippines, Taiwan and Thailand. Traditionally, the number of men who were tourists had exceeded the number of women, but from 1981 onwards, the rate of growth in the number of Japanese women who travelled to most of the countries exceeded that for men. Women became the object of increasing attention from the viewpoint of marketing tourism. In 1987, the JALPAK 'AVA' cheap tour was produced, targeted at young women office workers. The company also introduced a female marketing group, 'VIE', to collect information about women's needs in tourism, which were reflected in product planning by women involved in tourism marketing.

As the growth in the number of male tourists to South-East Asian countries declined during the 1980s and that of Japanese women tourists increased, the number of women coming to Japan from South-East Asia rose dramatically. The figures for Koreans and Taiwanese are relatively high, as they have a long history of living in Japan. In the case of Thai immigrants between the ages of 15 and 24 years, the numbers of women exceed those of men. The data for Filipinos demonstrate that, between the ages of 15 and 29, there are considerably more women immigrants than men and, in 1982, the numbers of women were almost eight times those of men. Most of these women received entertainer visas to work in Japan and the number of 'Japayuki-san'-foreign girls coming to Japan to work as prostitutes-increased dramatically.

The background to the increase in immigration into Japan by girls and women from South-East Asia is one of resistance to sex tourism. In 1972, for example, the Christian Women's Federation of Korea formulated and publicized a declaration opposing sex tours and, in 1973, university students of Korea organized a large demonstration, at Kimpo Airport, against Japanese coming on kisaeng tours. Women's groups in Japan also organized a demonstration at Haneda Airport in 1974. These demonstrations are argued to be one reason why tourism by male Japanese shifted from Korea to SouthEast Asian countries, where sex tours flourished in the late 1970s and early 1980s. However, the protest campaigns also spread to the Philippines and Thailand and male tourists from Japan subsequently met criticisms and protests throughout South-East Asia. Within the month of January 1981, when Prime Minister Suzuki paid an official visit to the ASEAN countries, Asahi Shimbun, one of the leading newspapers in Japan, published a range of articles which reported on the protest movement against sex tours to these countries. Many demonstrations and meetings were organized and letters and declarations of protest were sent to Prime Minister Suzuki.

A number of protests by Filipino women took place in Manila and were coordinated with action by Japanese women (Matsui, 1991). Sixteen groups organized a forum to protest against Japanese prostitution tours in Asia and received messages of support from Japanese women's groups. In the same period, Asahi Shimbun reported that a human rights group was planning protest actions in Bangkok, and the newspaper Thai Rat stated its appreciation for the movement in Manila. The paper also reported that five women's groups from the national University, the 'Friends of Women' group and seven organizations involved in issues concerned with women and religion, had sent letters of protest to the deputy prime minister of Thailand and Prime Minister Suzuki. On the same day, a demonstration was organized by Thai people in front of the Japanese Embassy in Bangkok.

These actions put effective pressure on the government of Japan and, in the same month, the Department of Tourism of the Ministry of Transportation in Japan took action against a travel agency which had organized prostitution tours. The criticisms and protests which had greeted Japanese male tourists during the 1970s and 1980s had the effect of decreasing the numbers of sex tours to South-East Asia and, instead, women from the region started to come to Japan.

Migrant Workers

People migrate for various reasons. Migrant workers abroad aim to earn foreign currency, of which a large proportion is remitted to their countries of origin. Migration also increases employment opportunities for the people who remain in the country. In addition, ex-migrant workers can transfer technologies from more industrialized countries. It has been pointed out that more women migrate for economic reasons than for individual or social motives (United Nations Population Fund, 1993:25):

Although women are often thought of as 'passive movers', migrating only to join or follow family members, research has found that economic rather than personal or social considerations predominate.

The United Nations Population Fund also refers to Findley and Williams' (1991) finding that 50-70 per cent of migrant women in South-East Asia, Latin America and the Caribbean move to search for jobs. In Latin America, the Philippines and the South Pacific, young women migrate to aid their families and send money to their families more often than men, although their earnings are usually lower.

Various reports and articles about women from South-East Asia support Findley and Williams' findings. Miyoshi (1986), for example, cites a girl from Davao who came to Manila to earn money to send to her family. She also refers to the fact that 70 per cent of girls and women working in the hospitality sector in Manila are elder sisters. Ogawa (1985) explains how japayuki-san at a city in Shikoku Island came to Japan for the sake of their families. The rest of this discusses the economic reasons why Asian women work as prostitutes.

The Size of the Economy: Urban and Rural Areas in Thailand

Migrant workers from rural areas usually enter urban areas of their own country before moving to richer countries. People move to the places where they hope to get jobs. Taking the example of Thailand, the huge difference in economic wealth between urban and rural areas is often described as the reason for migrating. In 1988, the economic structures of the three regions of the north-east, north and south differed considerably from that of Bangkok. The agricultural sector accounted for between 32 per cent and 37 per cent of gross domestic product in the three regions while, in Bangkok, it was only 3 per cent compared with the 47 per cent and 50 per cent shares of industry and services respectively. There was a considerable gap between the economic wealth of Bangkok and that of the remaining regions, with the exception of the Central region; while 16 per cent of the total population of Thailand resided in Bangkok, it accounted for half of total gross domestic product.

It is clear that workers migrate to urban areas to look for better lives. Phongpaichit (1982), for example, explained how, although the ratio of earnings outside Bangkok to those in the city increased during the 1960s and 1970s, earnings in Bangkok remained considerably greater than those in the other regions. It is clear that Bangkok has grown in economic terms, leaving the other regions behind, and this induces people to migrate from rural areas in search of a better standard of living.

This does not explain why many girls chose prostitution as their jobs. Examination of monthly pay by different occupations at the end of the 1970s, shows at least one of the reasons; compared with other jobs, women who work as prostitutes or masseuses gain far higher earnings. This is a major factor inducing girls to move from their local area to work in the urban service sector, including the tourism industry.

Many people migrate to obtain jobs and to support their families. They also migrate to earn more money to purchase consumer goods. The change of lifestyle in Thai villages is considered by Takigawa (1985), who describes the changes brought about by the introduction of a money economy. People who used to weave their clothes at home now buy goods made in factories. The commercialization of products by the mass media, and the spread of a credit system, lead to an increase in expenditure by farmers and causes the migration of village people to the urban area in search of jobs. Women work as prostitutes in order to obtain money, for motives ranging from the desire to help their families to survive in conditions of extreme poverty, to gaining additional earnings for spending on commercial products.

Size of Economy: Japan and South-East Asia

The value of gross national product (GNP) can be used as a measure of the differences in wealth between countries. The economic power of Japan far exceeds that of other South-East Asian countries. Even Korea, which is counted as one of the newly industrialized economies (NIEs), and which accomplished dramatic growth during the 1980s, is still far behind Japan; in 1991, for example, the per capita GNP of Japan was about four times greater than that of Korea.

Although Thailand also grew rapidly in the late 1980s, its GNP is small compared with that of Japan and that of the Philippines is even lower. People migrate for the purpose of getting jobs and money, and migration between Japan and the South-East Asian countries is argued to be due to the economic imbalance between them. However, migration is also caused by circumstances specific to different individuals, as is illustrated by the motives which three Thai women gave for working in Japan:

- 'I wanted to renovate a house for my child, as we lived in a miserable house which might fall down just because of a strong wind.'
- 'We needed money as my father was sick. My mother could not work in farming as she had a problem with her waist. I decided to come to Japan as a debt only kept on increasing.'
- 'I just wanted to be free from a poor life in a house with no toilet and kitchen. I also wanted to get electrical appliances.'

National Policy: Sending Workers Abroad the Philippines

The Philippines has a history of sending workers abroad. The Statistics Office of the Republic of the Philippines (1989:660) says that, There are two mainstreams of manpower outflow; first is permanent migration, wherein the workers leave on a more or less permanent basis; the second, contract or temporary migration.'

It describes how the first category of migration started in the early 1900s. After the USA took over the country as a colony, the country sent about 110,000 workers to Hawaii to provide cheap labour for pineapple plantations. The second category of migrant labour commenced after World War II, when the country sent many labourers to American strongholds to work on the rehabilitation and reconstruction of these areas. From the end of the 1960s to the early 1970s, many doctors and nurses were employed abroad. When the Middle East was enjoying a construction boom, a large number of Filipinos went to work in Arab countries.

In 1974, the government of the Philippines organized the Overseas Employment Development Board and, in 1982, it established the Philippines Overseas Employment Agency to help Filipinos to work abroad. The Philippines National Statistics Office estimates that workers remitted a total of $856.8 million in foreign earnings in 1988, equal to about 10 per cent of the country's export earnings in that year. In 1993, approximately $2.5 billion was sent to the country by migrant workers, through the national bank. The total amount, when remittances via private channels are included, was around four times greater, accounting for just under 20 per cent of the country's GDP in the same year.

During the 1980s, the majority of Filipinos who worked abroad were employed in the construction sector. However, the number of workers in the service sector, in which many women were employed, increased considerably during the decade and just exceeded the number of production process, transport workers and labourers in 1987. Many women worked as maids in Hong Kong and Europe and some were employed as teachers in Africa. While 13,400 Filipinos were employed as 'entertainers' overseas in 1982, by 1987 the number had risen dramatically, to just under 40,000. This increase appears to be related to the decrease in the number of Japanese tourists to the Philippines in the 1980s, along with the protests against prostitution tourism in the country. In 1988, President Aquino's government announced that the country was to stop sending Filipino maids to foreign countries because of the vulnerable situations in which many found themselves and stated that the controls would only be removed for host countries which provided acceptable working conditions. This measure resulted in a decrease in the number of Filipino women of 15 to 29 years who entered Japan in 1989. However, the numbers entering Japan increased considerably between 1990 and 1991 and although the figure for 1992 was lower than that of the previous year, it remained far higher than the numbers of women who had entered Japan during the previous decades.

Thailand

Whereas the Philippines has a long tradition of sending its workers to foreign countries, Thailand has a relatively short history. Thai labourers began to go to the Middle East to work in the construction sector in the early 1970s, and there was a boom in out-migration during the late 1970s (Sasaki, 1991; Yanaihara and Yamagata, 1992). These workers had originally been employed building US bases in Thailand during the Vietnam War. Before 1982, the Thai government did not have a clear policy on overseas migration. The Fifth National Economic and Social Development Plan (1982-86) included four guidelines: first, the promotion of overseas employment and the establishment of a labour office in recipient countries; second, the establishment of labour protection rules and controls over out-migration; third, skill training for workers; and fourth, the promotion of foreign currency remittances through the branches of Thai banks.

The Sixth Development Plan revealed ten new policies: the promotion of good relations with recipient countries, effective administration of overseas labour, the extension of out-migration to areas other than the Middle East, skills development for workers; skill examination and certification for workers, removal of obstacles to working abroad, reduction in the cost of out-migration, protection of workers and the punishment of illegal intermediaries, provision of information about overseas labour and intermediaries, and reception measures for workers returning to Thailand. Because Thailand started to send workers abroad relatively late, the government's measures were introduced only in recent years. Although the Thai government seems to be optimistic about its migrant workers, information about adverse working conditions in foreign countries has become available to the public, notably the case of the Thai hostesses who were arrested for murdering their boss, in a drinking bar in Japan, in order to gain their freedom.

The Double Standard

Many Asian women enter Japan to work as prostitutes for economic reasons, in the context of their countries' policies for sending workers abroad. However, they would not come to Japan if there were no 'pull factors'. The demand for prostitution can be examined from both economic and social viewpoints. From an economic perspective, for example, middlemen earn considerable profits by sending South-East Asian women to work as prostitutes in Japan and Japanese men pay Asian women less than Japanese prostitutes.

It is impossible to examine this issue adequately without touching on social and cultural features of Japan. Why do men buy women? Are there any specific reasons? It is difficult to answer these questions since the explanations are complex. However, it is clear than many men buy women because they think it is normal for men to do so; at least, many men do not feel guilty about doing so. This is argued to be caused by the double standard. This will review, historically, the creation of the double standard in Japan, focusing on prostitutes and the past and present status of Japanese women.

The Muromachi and Edo Periods

One of the first official acknowledgements of prostitution in Japan occurred during the Muromachi Period of the fifteenth and sixteenth centuries, when the Shogun government started to tax prostitution houses in Kyoto to ease its troubled financial situation. In 1590, a prostitution area was established in Kyoto by the ruler, Toyotomi, who also permitted prostitution in part of Osaka, in order to provide his followers with 'recreation and comfort'.

Japanese conservative society is said to have been established during the Edo Period (1603-1868). During this time, women's position in the family became highly vulnerable, as they lost the right to keep their own property and money. There was great pressure to maintain ie, the Japanese family system, and women were expected to give birth to a boy, who would become the head of a family. Men were allowed to have several wives under the pretext that families must be sustained and women were expected to be loyal to their husband so as to maintain the family blood line. Farmers' wives were subject to particular pressure as farmers were a key source of tax revenue for the Edo government, so that farmers' wives were expected to labour on the land as well as to give birth to a boy.

During the Edo Period, prostitution became more widespread. In 1617, prostitution houses were officially opened in Edo (Old Tokyo), as one of the strategies by which the government attempted to maintain its hold on power after a long period of warfare throughout Japan. The feudal lords were made to stay in Edo and encouraged to spend large sums of money in the prostitution houses, which made available prostitutes with a wide range of regional cultures. Over time, as the warrier class became less wealthy relative to the growing merchant class, the customers of the prostitution houses changed and private prostitution houses spread throughout Japan.

The Meiji Period

The Meiji government which succeeded the Edo regime introduced, in 1898, a new civil law which gave more power to the head of the household, normally a man. The law was reinforced by the education system, which taught girl students that their role was to become good housewives. Women were expected to obey the head of the household, married women were to change their name to that of their husband and were not allowed to engage in economic activities without their husband's permission and a husband was allowed to divorce his wife if she had extra-marital affairs while a wife could only do so if the husband's lover was married to another man who took legal action against the husband. In spite of the fact that the law only permitted monogamy, children born out of wedlock were allowed to inherit the house of their father, so that the keeping of mistresses by husbands was informally accepted. Thus, the double standard, which allows men to have sexual relations outside marriage but does not permit women to do so, developed during the Edo and Meiji eras.

Divided Women

The double standard also divided women into two types: women who are expected to be loyal to their husands and to be good mothers, and other women. It is not only men who accept the double standard; many women do too. Women's acceptance of the double standard has been discussed by a number of authors. For example, Usuki cites two women; one, a university student, commented 'A man who cannot have an amour is not attractive. I do not care if my boyfriend buys a girl abroad' and a wife said 'As my husband works very hard to build a new house for us and he is good to us, I allow him to have affairs'.

A conversation between two wives living in Tokyo is referred to in Kishimoto's paper:

A: My husband went on a sex tour with members of...cooperatives yesterday. He said that it was for socialization with other members, but I cannot stand it!

B: Well, my husband has been three times already...I had an argument with him in the beginning but I have already given up trying to persuade him. Men are always like that. I tolerate it so long as he doesn't get venereal diseases.

A further example of housewives who do not consider their husbands' buying prostitutes as having affairs is that of a 38-year-old wife who wrote about her husband's behaviour: the writer noted that Nokyo (Agricultural Cooperative) has been sending what she is convinced are sex-buying group tours to Taiwan for ten years. Although she requested her husband not to join this year's tour, as a staff member of Nokyo, he felt obliged to participate. If he did not attend, he said, he would be ostracized and made to feel ashamed for giving in to his wife's demand.

Japanese women, therefore, accept the double standard, some willingly and others unwillingly. Some were led to believe that having extra-marital affairs is natural for men and that wise women do not complain about it. Even if women doubt this norm, it is sometimes difficult for them to persuade their husbands to refrain from such behaviour.

Japanese society is changing and women of the younger generation are becoming more powerful. Some think that women, like men, should be allowed to have extra-marital affairs. It is difficult to deny that the wives mentioned above are victims of the double standard in the sense that they are expected to tolerate their husband's behaviour. However, they may also be victimising other women by allowing men to buy other women's sexualities. Women are divided by the double standard, which allows only men to have affairs outside marriage and which classifies women into good wives and other women. Many women who are in the category of good wives find it easy to accept the norm that women who sell their bodies are a different type of woman, in a category of 'whores', racial difference making this division visible with ease.

Differences Among Women from South-East Asia

Entering the 1980s, we have seen a gradual shift of prostitution away from tourist destination countries to tourists' countries of origin. As the number of sex tours has decreased, so the number of women coming to Japan from Korea, Taiwan, the Philippines and Thailand has increased. These women enter Japan with the hope of getting a better job, but in many cases they end up engaging in prostitution, often abused and exploited. However, what we should recognize is that the women from the four different countries do not have the same working conditions, nor do they engage in the same kind of jobs. It seems that their situations in Japan differ according to their nationalities.

Korean and Taiwanese women find themselves in similar situations in Japan. The number of Korean and Taiwanese women who come to Japan every year is high. In particular, the total number of Taiwanese women entering Japan every year is between 6 per cent and 25 per cent greater than the number of Taiwanese male entrants. However, not much evidence can be found to conclude that most Korean and Taiwanese women are working as prostitutes in Japan. The statistical material 'Illegal Activities and Overstay cum Illegal Activities' published by the Japan Immigration Association indicates that some Korean and Taiwanese women work as prostitutes. For example, in 1987, 43 Korean and 196 Chinese women (including women from Taiwan, Hong Kong and mainland China) were apprehended and deported under the charge of illegally working as bar hostesses.

It is often the case that bar hostesses are expected to serve as prostitutes. These numbers are rather small compared with the 5,103 Filipino and 702 Thai women apprehended during the same year under the same charge. In addition, the number of Korean and Taiwanese women going to refuges for protection is much less than that of Filipino and Thai women. A report issued by the Asian Women's Shelter HELP (House in Emergency of Love and Peace founded in 1986) informed us that they aided four Korean and five Taiwanese women from 1986 to 1993, whilst they provided support for 312 Filipino and 1103 Thai women during the same period (HELP, 1994). Although Korea and Taiwan have been two of the destination countries for Japanese sex tourism, it can be concluded that Korean and Taiwanese women do not make up the main workforce of prostitutes in Japan and if any of them are engaged in prostitution, they have relatively secure working conditions.

What are the reasons for the differences between Korean and Taiwanese women on the one hand, and Filipino and Thai women on the other? They occur primarily because Korean and Taiwanese women started to come to Japan before Filipino and Thai women. Japan has had a longer relationship with both Korea and Taiwan, especially through occupying these countries before World War II and many Koreans and Taiwanese have already lived in Japan, so that women from these two countries have had easy access to Japan through their relatives or acquaintances. This entry time gap has allowed some Korean and Taiwanese women to establish some kind of status in Japanese society such as becoming a bar owner rather than a hostess or taking up permanent residence through marriage.

Moreover, considering the rapidly developing economies of both Korea and Taiwan, it is reasonable to assume that not many Korean and Taiwanese women are desperate for money and willing to come to Japan as prostitutes or for a job with poor working conditions. In terms of visa status, more Koreans and Taiwanese now come to Japan on student visas than Filipinos and Thais. Nowadays, we see many young Koreans and Taiwanese studying in language schools, vocational schools and universities in Japan. Their student visas allow them to work up to four hours a day and their minimum hourly wage is guaranteed by Japanese labour law. It seems that Koreans and Taiwanese come to Japan for diverse purposes, including employment, study, vocational training and visiting relatives.

Filipino and Thai women, who have made up the main force of prostitutes working in Japan since the 1980s, are in a different situation from Korean and Taiwanese women, and many of them have suffered severe ordeals. However, although both Filipino and Thai women have been exploited as prostitutes, the degree to which they have been abused differs. It seems that Thai women have a weaker and less secure position in Japan than Filipino women. What are the reasons for this difference? The following comparative chart of the recruitment process between Filipino and Thai women sheds some light on this issue.

The first point to consider is that Thai women go through many levels of brokers in their recruitment process and Yakuza gangsters are deeply involved in recruiting women to come to Japan and placing them in the entertainment industry. The Yakuza is a Japanese underworld criminal syndicate which either overtly or covertly controls the management of bars and clubs in most of the entertainment districts of Japan. In the case of Filipino women, they must sign a contract through entertainment promotion agencies in the Philippines in order to apply for a visa. At first, the agencies were run by local Filipino people but soon Yakuza gangsters started to join in the process of choosing women at audition times. Then, the gangsters took the women to Japan and earned commission by placing them in bars and clubs in the entertainment districts of big cities or spa resorts in the countryside. They sometimes let the women work in bars which they or their common-law wives run. Apart from their legitimate jobs as show dancers or singers, the Filipino women are often forced by the bar or club owners to become involved in prostitution. If a woman spends the night with a client, she can earn 100,000 yen whilst the bar owner receives 200,000 yen from the client.

Soon, the Yakuza gangsters found another target for exploitation. They discovered that they could easily make a larger amount of profit from Thai women. Although we see many Filipino dancers in the entertainment districts of Japan, they are not so visible as prostitutes nowadays. Instead, we see many Thai women working as prostitutes in bars, clubs and on the streets. Judging from the statistics issued by the refuge centre, HELP, the shift happened sometime around 1988. Is it a coincidence that the Thai government launched a campaign called 'Visit Thailand Year' in order to promote tourism in its country that year? The statistics published by HELP indicate that the majority of women coming to the refuge for protection were Filipino women up until 1987, but from the next year their numbers decreased considerably. Conversely, the number of Thai women seeking protection rose from nine in 1987 to 144 in 1988 and the number has continued to increase during the 1990s. Statistics issued by a refuge called Women's House Sala show a similar tendency; two Filipino women and 54 Thai women had used the refuge out of the total 56 women during the period from September 1992 to April 1993. These women are, of course, a tiny minority of the women who work as prostitutes in Japan.

It is reported that two different underworld criminal syndicates are involved in sending Thai women to Japan, Chinese syndicates on the side of Thailand and Yakuza syndicates on the Japanese side. The syndicates in Thailand have already established the means of recruiting young women from poor farming areas and sending them overseas. They use local people as recruitment agents to collect women, and then members of the syndicates forge passports, make all the necessary arrangements, take the women to Japan and hand them over to Japanese brokers, mostly Yakuza gangsters, who pay between 1.5 and 1.8 million yen per woman as commission to a Thai broker.

The Japanese brokers place the women in bars and clubs all over Japan and charge 3 to 3.5 million yen as commission for the women. The bar/club owners add some extra money to the commission and tell the woman that they have a 'debt' of 3.5 to 4 million yen to repay. It is the women who have to bear the entire cost. The Thai women are burdened with an enormous debt which they work to repay, although there are no legal grounds on which they have to repay it. The system of recruiting Thai women for Japanese bars and clubs can be identified as human trafficking and the women are confined and exploited within the system. It is obvious that the recruiters, brokers and bar owners are making huge profits by sending Thai women to Japan.

The second point to consider is the visa status of the women. The Philippines government's policy of encouraging people to get jobs overseas as a means of expanding employment opportunities and gaining foreign currency to accelerate the growth of the economy was discussed above. Filipino women are not the exception under this policy. When they try to look for jobs in Japan, they face a big obstacle: closed labour markets for overseas workers in Japan. Japan follows the policy of accepting only specialists from overseas, not simple manual labourers such as factory or construction site workers, waiters or waitresses and shop clerks.

The entertainer's visa seems to be the only legitimate working visa which most young Filipino women can obtain without much trouble. The entertainer's visa at least guarantees their security to some extent. Obtaining an entertainer's visa requires a proper contract which stipulates wage and accommodation conditions, the name of the responsible agent and so on. It also allows the holder to stay in Japan legally for up to 180 days. As a contracted worker, she is entitled to appeal for legal protection or bring an action against her employer in the case of contractual violation. However, in practice, such prosecutions are not always easy to undertake because of the difficulty in obtaining enough evidence.

For example, women who run away from their employers usually do not carry their contract with them, so that it is hard for them to prove the name of their employers or the place where they worked. On the other hand, the majority of Thai women come to Japan on short stay visas. A short stay visa is the easiest type to obtain for entry from overseas but does not allow the holder to work or stay in Japan for more than 90 days. Hence, those women entering Japan on tourist visas have no means of looking for a job openly by themselves and if they do something for money, they fall into the category of illegal workers so that they cannot rely on any legal protection and rather try to hide themselves from the public sphere due to the fear of deportation. Taking advantage of the Thai women's insecure status in Japan, Yakuza gangsters and bar owners make use of the women, who usually work in particularly adverse conditions, to gain an easy profit.

The third point to consider is the degree of their self-help. Both Filipino and Thai women do not usually speak Japanese, so they do not easily understand what is happening around them. However, most Filipino women speak English, in which they can communicate with the local Japanese when necessary. Thai women often only speak their own language so they tend to be more isolated and have less access to information. Moreover, compared with Filipino women, Thai women are more restricted in their daily behaviour. For example, they are not allowed to go anywhere by themselves, even to a nearby shop. They are always under close watch of their employers. Therefore, even in times of emergency, it is difficult for them to contact someone for help. Filipino women have a further advantage over Thai women. Because they are usually Catholics, they tend to go to church regularly, which enables them to make friends, exchange information and set up support groups if they wish, or to obtain help from church officials and local churchgoers.

Women's Experiences: The Case of Thai Women

Women engaging in prostitution have a wide range of different experiences. Some are successful in saving up large amounts of money to take back home and others run away from their owners and come to a refuge for protection or end up in terrible hardship. What is common among them is that they have little power to negotiate their working conditions with their brokers or bar/club owners. The following is a typical example of a Thai woman's experience of coming to Japan and engaging in sex work. The story is based on one of the interviews I conducted in 1993 with the help of an interpreter. The Thai woman, called 'M', was 26 years old and started working in a bar in Tokyo in December 1991. She wanted to remain anonymous because she was afraid of the consequences that might occur because of the interview.

M decided to come to Japan after being invited by a woman living next door. She went from a small village near Chiang Mai in the north of Thailand to Bangkok and worked as a shop clerk after graduating from a vocational school. At the time when M heard about the job opportunity in Japan, she was very depressed after losing her boyfriend and wanted to go somewhere far away. Although her parents disagreed with her decision and she was told she would have a debt of 3.6 million yen to pay off in Japan, she did not change her mind. She was worried at first that 3.6 million yen was a lot of money, but was told that it would only take 3 months to pay back. Someone arranged to get hold of a passport for her, which was a forgery. She came to Japan on a tourist visa escorted by a Thai man who took her from Bangkok to a bar in Tokyo. M was told by the Mama-san who ran the bar to start working from the next day, also that she was indeed 3.8 million yen in debt. The Mama-san was Taiwanese.

When she first started working, there were 20 other women working in the bar as hostesses and at the same time as prostitutes but in 1994 eleven women (nine from Thailand, one from Hong Kong and one from Taiwan) were working there. All the women working in the bar had to live above the bar, until they became free by paying off their debt. It took five months for her to repay the debt including an extra 20 thousand yen for moving to a new apartment. Her clients were mostly in their 40s and she felt some of them treated her very badly. After she became free, she continued to work for the bar on an unpaid basis but was allowed to receive the full charge for her sexual service and kept working in the same bar to save money for her parents and herself. Her parents, sister and her sister's husband built a new house with the money she sent them and are now living there together. She said that she does not want to go back to Thailand because Tokyo is more exciting and there are a lot more things to do and see than in Bangkok. Some of her clients took her for day excursions or trips of a few days, and the most impressive trip for her was going to Sapporo for the Snow Festival. She now has a Japanese boyfriend, a sugar daddy, who gives her some money so that she has not engaged in prostitution for the last three months.

Until they finish paying off their debt, Thai women receive no money from the work they do. Only a tip from their clients makes up the income at their disposal. They are provided with food and a place to live by the bar owners but in many cases the owners do so to prevent the women from going out freely. Sometimes bar owners calculate the daily expenses of a woman and add them to her debt. Another Thai woman, called 'S', said that she was told to pay 50 thousand yen as a housing fee every month on top of her debt after she had worked for five months. If a woman takes a day off, she is usually fined 10 thousand yen, which is added to her debt. It is said that it costs 15-20 thousand yen for a few hours or 25-30 thousand yen to stay overnight with a prostitute on average. M worked off the debt in five months, which means she had a client nearly every day during that period. S has not yet paid off the debt of 3.9 million yen, even though she has worked for about ten months.

In contrast to Filipino women who sometimes take tourists as clients because they work as show dancers at hotels in resorts, Thai women usually work for local bars and therefore most of their clients are local men living in the vicinity, aged 'mainly from 30 to 50 years old and married', according to a bar owner whom I interviewed. There are cities and towns in Japan which have entertainment districts where many Thai women work. Big factory compounds, large construction sites or an army post of the selfdefence force are often located there. Hence, these cities and towns have many unmarried men or married men separated from their families, gathered together for work, and prostitutes accommodate their demands. In cities like Tokyo, entertainment districts are scattered in several different areas and it is rare to see Thai women working in bars and clubs in such a top area as 'Ginza' where high class company executives entertain their important business customers and Japanese bar hostesses predominate. Thai women said that some clients were nice and gave them a lot of money and others were cruel. For example, S spent a night with a client who terrified her by putting a 'long knife' near the bed and saying that he was always ready to use it if she did not obey him.

When women have finished working off their debt and become independent, they rarely go back home straight away. Instead, they try their best to earn and save money for themselves or their families through working for the same bars independently, moving to other bars with better conditions or becoming streetwalkers. As streetwalkers, they can work as freelance prostitutes but inevitably take the risk of being easy targets for police discipline and Yakuza gangsters' demands to act as pimps. On the whole, the future of women without debts is to go back home with some money saved, to stay in Japan continuing to work as a prostitute, to become the mistress of, or get married to, a Japanese man, or to become agents or brokers who recruit women to Japan.

Women's Responses

Prostitution is often criticized at both personal and institutional levels as an immoral and anti-social activity. The South-East Asian countries from which the women come often have Buddhist, Catholic or Confucian faiths that condemn prostitution as a shameful form of behaviour. The women are, therefore, constantly under psychological pressure. An activist of a support group said that about onethird of the women coming to Japan knew, beforehand, that they would be working as prostitutes in Japan. The rest of the women had no choice but to accept the work even though they found out after arriving in Japan that they had been deceived. S said 'One of my acquaintances invited me to work in Japan as a waitress. When I was told to work as a prostitute, I didn't know what to do and where to go, so I accepted the work. I had already come to Japan, so what could I do?' Most of the women accept prostitution as a means of survival; survival for themselves and their families back home. Even though they cannot escape feelings of shame, they have pride in the fact that they support themselves and contribute to the sustenance of their families.

On the other hand, there are many women whose lives have been devastated by their experience. Some have risked their lives by running away from their bar owners and have gone to a refuge for protection or to their embassy for help. It is reported that the Thai Embassy in Tokyo dealt with about 3,000 Thai women who sought help in 1991 and with 3,000-3,500 every month in 1992. The non-governmental refuge HELP provided a refuge for 1,170 Thai and Filipino women from 1987 to 1992, Sala helped 56 women during nine months in 1993, and Mizura aided 67 Thai women between 1992 and 1993. Criminal offences in which Thai women are either the offender or victim are increasing, too. Between January and September, 1992, there were 57 criminal offences involving Thai women and 397 Thai women were arrested or placed under police protection. Amongst the offences, three murder cases stand out and highlight the plight of South-East Asian women working in Japan.

The first case is that of three women on trial for killing their Thai female boss in Shimodate, Ibaragi Prefecture. The second is that of six women, including a 15-year-old girl, accused of killing their bar owner, a Taiwanese woman, in Shinkoiwa, Tokyo. The third is that of five women on trial for killing their bar owner, a Singapore woman, in Mobara, Chiba Prefecture. According to the women's testimony and letters to their support groups, they committed the killings because they wanted to escape from the bars. They had believed they were going to work in factories or restaurants until they came to Japan but in reality they were forced to engage in prostitution.

On their arrival, they were told to pay back 3.8 million yen and their passports were taken away. Some were told that if they ran away or did not do what they were told, their parents would be killed. Others were stripped of their clothes, photographed and told that the photographs would be sent to Thai newspapers if they misbehaved. They were fined for speaking in their own language, smoking, not smiling and not giving adequate service to customers in the bars. The women in the Mobara case were told to do everything that their clients wanted. For example, an overnight engagement of sexual services means having sexual intercourse several times and having to massage the clients until morning, and the women are not allowed to sleep during the night. They were like prisoners, having no freedom to go out by themselves. One of the women wrote a letter from a Detention Centre saying:

There was no factory where I could work in Japan, but only pubs and bars. There were only men who thought about nothing more than getting drunk and having sex with strangers. For me every day was suffering. I had to sleep with men whom I did not know at all. If I did not obey the orders of the manager of the bar I was beaten. For the Japanese masters, women from Thailand are considered to be lower than animals.

Prostitution tourism is a product which has evolved from the interplay between political, social, cultural and economic factors. Since the 1960s, tourism has been promoted under government leadership as an important part of the development of the nations in the SouthEast Asian region. This policy of promoting tourism induced a massive growth of prostitution, with large numbers of men coming from industrialized countries across the world. Because of the vicinity and economic power of Japan, together with their cultural expectations that women be submissive, Japanese men were among the most dominant tourists in search of sexual pleasure in those countries.

Campaigns against prostitution tourism were stimulated by the criticisms voiced by the Christian Women's Federation of Korea in 1973 and gained further momentum when the National Christian Council (NCC), its branch organization the Japan Women's Christian Temperance Union (JWCTU) and other women's groups joined together in publishing research papers, visiting travel companies, making slides to reveal the activities of Japanese sex tour groups and protesting to the Ministry of Transportation. They also developed a campaign to coordinate with women's groups in the Philippines and Thailand and, as a result, when Prime Minister Suzuki visited ASEAN countries in 1981, he met large demonstrations in each country. However, as travel companies started refraining from organising sex tour groups after facing considerable protest movements in the 1970s, prostitution spread from the tourist destination countries to tourist origin countries, including Japan, and has spread widely over the country. Why was this shift possible? What are the reasons and factors underpinning the phenomenon and what are some of the possible ways of improving the women's situations?

First of all, the focus should be on the great material differences in wealth between the nations. Japan is extremely wealthy compared with the other four countries in terms of income per capita. The strong economic power of Japan is also reflected in the exchange rate of Japanese currency. Since 1985, the exchange rate of the Japanese yen against other currencies has appreciated dramatically, providing workers paid in yen with a huge increase in their purchasing power. As a result, Japan has attracted migrant workers from many developing countries in South-East Asia, the Middle East and South America. The flow of women from South-East Asian countries is, thus, not an isolated phenomenon in the context of the world economy. On the other hand, taking advantage of their affluent economic status, Japanese go to luxurious resorts for rest and leisure and sometimes associate with prostitutes. In the case of prostitution involving South-East Asian women, it is clear that international disparities in power and wealth determine who is doing the buying and who is selling.

Second, we should consider the interrelationships between material interests and political power. In the cases of both Filipino and Thai women who come to Japan, most work for their own sustenance and that of their families and wish to obtain a better standard of living. Thus, the number of women who want to work in Japan will not decrease so long as poverty is not irradicated in their home countries. For example, expensive houses stand in the middle of some poor farming villages in Thailand and the owners of these houses have daughters working in Japan. It is possible for women to earn a large amount of money in a relatively short period through prostitution in Japan. In fact, they can earn much more in Japan than they would earn by doing the same job in their home countries. However, it is the intermediaries who benefit most by using the women and have real power to control the situation. In the case of Thai women, in particular, recruiters, brokers, agents and bar owners make extremely high amounts of commission through the process of transporting women. In the end, women are told to pay off about 3.5-4 million yen, which is equivalent to £20,000- £22,800. Until they work off the debt, they are resigned to their powerless position and receive no wages for the job they do.

In addition, clients benefit from South-East Asian women prostitutes because the majority seem to charge less for their sexual services than Japanese women. The district and the types of establishment in which they work are different. For example, we can see only Japanese women working in bars and clubs in Tokyo's most expensive neighbourhood, demonstrating both racist and class overtones in the demand for prostitution. The women from South-East Asian countries can be found in less expensive areas of Tokyo and local cities which are full of cheaper drinking places. This means that Japanese men, as clients, spend less for their sexual pleasure.

Third, we should address socio-cultural factors in Japanese society, where many women have been accepted as prostitutes. Historically, prostitution has been used to satisfy and control male sexuality. Japanese society has been tolerant towards, or sometimes praised, men's promiscuity in so far as they keep households secure. On the other hand, women are divided into two categories: virtuous daughters and wives, and 'whores'. Women in the former category are required to give their absolute loyalty to their fathers and husbands after marriage. Women in the latter category are regarded as outcasts of society, segregated into special quarters for the sake of protecting public morality and accommodating men's sexual needs. This tradition allowed the establishment of a series of prostitution systems in the past such as the state-regulated prostitution system inherited from the late sixteenth century and abolished as late as 1946 by the disuse of the Regulation of the Control of Shougi (a kind of Geisha), the comfort women drafted into sexual slavery by the Imperial Army during World War II, and the Recreation and Amusement Association (RAA) established to accommodate the sexual needs of the soldiers in the Occupation Army. In the same way, South-East Asian women are accepted into Japanese society as a means of controlling and satisfying male sexuality, and yet they are shunned by mainstream society and treated as outcasts.

Traditions persist. To some extent, both Japanese men and women cannot be free from traditional values. Under the remaining influence of the absolute power traditionally given to the head of the family, there are still many Japanese men who hold traditional ideas about women's submissiveness and obedience towards them and South-East Asian women are often told to satisfy those demands. The women accept the demands without being able to protest because of their powerless situation. The ambivalent attitude taken by Japanese wives also reveals the fact that they are still confined by tradition in wondering on what basis they can complain about their husbands' conduct in so far as their husbands fulfill their roles in the family as heads of households and breadwinners. Tradition tells us to be tolerant of men's promiscuity. Many Japanese wives would conclude that buying prostitutes is just temporary, after all, because prostitutes belong to a different group of women and it is pointless to risk the family's security and stability by complaining too much about their husband's unfaithful behaviour. However, this attitude emphasizes the material aspect of the couple's relationship and diminishes the spiritual aspect. Mutual trust and respect are also important components in maintaining the couple's relationship but tend to be forgotten. Such a materialistic ideology and double standard allows people to be blind to the fact that prostitutes have their own families at home and engage in sex work on behalf of their families.

The legal approach towards prostitution in Japan prescribed in the current Prostitution Prevention Law should be re-examined. The Law was enacted in 1956 and consists of two components. One is concerned with penalization of acts. The name of the Law states 'prevention' and not 'prohibition' and the objective of the Law is not to penalize the act of prostitution itself but to impose a penalty on any acts which encourage and promote prostitution, such as soliciting in public and procuring women for prostitution. The second component is concerned with establishing facilities for counselling and the rehabilitation of prostitutes. However, the Law has three main defects in the administration of justice for women working as prostitutes.

First, it lacks effective measures for penalising procurers operating today, particularly regarding procurement of women from South-East Asia. Under the Law, it is possible to prosecute bar owners in charge of procurement for prostitution but, in practice, such prosecution is hard to undertake because the women do not wish to get involved in law suits due to their illegal status in Japan. Besides, even if a woman running away from her bar owner wishes to make a prosecution with the help of a lawyer, the attempt is usually in vain because she cannot prove where she worked and the name of the bar owner for whom she worked. The primary problem in prostitution within Japan itself is the serious degree of exploitation by bar owners as procurers of women. It is urgent that effective measures are taken to punish procurers.

Second, making soliciting an offence works against women. It is always prostitutes who are arrested and charged and men's kerbcrawling or looking for a prostitute goes unquestioned. Nowadays, the main target of police operations are Thai women who become free from their procurers and work on the streets for themselves. In order to end this one-sided administration of the Law, there are two points to be considered: one is the question of establishing some measures to impose a penalty on men's kerb-crawling and the other is to rethink the necessity of Article 5 of the Law, which states that soliciting should be penalized.

Third, although the counselling and rehabilitation scheme is an important component of the Law and could provide good opportu- nities for indicating alternative options to prostitutes, women from South-East Asia have no chance of benefiting from the scheme unless they hold a legally valid visa, otherwise they will be sent to the Bureau of Immigration Control for deportation. Language is also a big barrier to women's ability to make use of the opportunities. Furthermore, facilities for the scheme are in danger of being run down because of the government's limited financial support. We should pressurize the government to provide more finance to revitalize such schemes and, at the same time, it is important to ensure that the rehabilitation programmes truly respond to women's needs today.

In addition to the above three defects, it is necessary to re-examine the effect of the conventional approach towards prostitution. The anti-prostitution movement in Japan was launched more than a hundred years ago under the leadership of Christian organizations such as the JWCTU, founded in 1886, and the Salvation Army, founded in 1895. The movement has made a significant contribution towards abolishing state-regulated prostitution, providing relief and rehabilitation facilities for prostitutes and formulating government policies on prostitution. Their activities have been conducted with the aim of the total abolition of prostitution, presuming that prostitution is offensive and exploitative towards women. It is clear that they have condemned not the individual prostitutes, but the practice of prostitution as an institution. However, their stance entails a rather negative attitude towards prostitutes, regarding them as passive victims who should be guided and saved. How far is this approach consistent with the reality of South-East Asian women working as prostitutes in Japan? Prostitution enables the women to obtain a large amount of money which is necessary for their livelihood and that of their families and, despite all the exploitative working conditions, many women still choose to work as prostitutes. Therefore, it is important to investigate the possibility of a form of prostitution permitted by society, in which the prostitutes' human rights are not violated.

The issues of prostitution tourism cannot be solved by a domestic solution alone, but require internationally coordinated action. As we have seen, the expansion of tourism has brought about the proliferation of prostitution in South-East Asia. Such a social change in the region seems to be interlocked with the increasing entry of SouthEast Asian women into Japan and their resulting powerless situation. The national development strategies currently taken in the region need to be reconsidered not only in the light of the enrichment of the nations but also in the light of reducing the economic disparity within the nations. A microeconomic perspective is more relevant in alleviating the hardship that South-East Asian women are facing than a macroeconomic approach. It is important that overseas development aid from Japan to the developing countries in the region should be coordinated towards empowering individuals.

BANGKOK'S SEX TOURISM INDUSTRY

Maps do not only serve interests by contributing to the social production of tourism spaces; they work in conjunction with the process of identity construction. Furthermore, maps do not merely make present what is distant in space and time, they are intertextually linked with the spaces, identities, experiences, and other texts of and about tourism that might not be revealed in a cursory reading of a map. As we argue in the Introduction to this, maps work because people use them in their experience of places. Tourism maps are not simply objects, but parts of the places to which people travel. They are thus inextricably linked to everyday experience. In addition, maps reference, or make present, a host of existing representations of tourism space. Any critical perspective of mapping must therefore investigate the multiple historical and spatial referents that are part and parcel of any tourism map. This compilation of referents comes together and constitutes what we call a map space.

In this, we present an example of how to read the map spaces of tourism in a manner that recognizes a map's complex intertextuality. Bangkok Stadtplan für Männer Presents the Nightlife, a 1991 German sex tourism map of Bangkok, "works, " in part through its linkages to a long history of producing Thailand as a feminized and sexualized space for Western tourists. Given the complex intertextual linkages between this map and the spaces and identities it represents and reproduces, our reading cannot be a simple investigation of how the social power inscribed on the map during production serves to reproduce existing social norms and values. As Sparke (1995) so eloquently puts it, we do not simply want to demythologize the map; rather, we want to interrogate the multiple and unequally contested meanings that are present within any map space. This demands the recognition that map spaces are much broader than the paper on which they are printed. They include the margins of the map and the various representations that it calls upon in its construction of tourism spaces and identities. It also demands that we recognize that a map space is an open and never completed process. Thus, any reading of a map, just like the map space itself, is always partial and incomplete.

Map Spaces as Texts

Most critical readings of maps, like recent readings of landscapes in cultural geography (Cosgrove 1984; Cosgrove and Daniels 1988; Duncan and Duncan 1988, 1992; Mitchell 1994; Nash 1996), rely on treating maps as social texts. Pickles (1992: 193), for example, argues that maps are textual "in that they have words associated with them, that they employ a system of symbols with their own syntax, that they function as a form of writing ..., and that they are discursively embedded within broader contexts of social action and power." He employs hermeneutics to unpack the complex relationships between propaganda maps as texts and the "object-worlds" they portray. Harley (1988, 1989, 1990) calls for a deconstruction of maps and relies on Foucault and, to a lesser extent, Derrida to uncover the power relationships behind the map that ensure that it reproduces the sociospatial status quo.

Unfortunately, Harley and others who employ this formulation of deconstruction tend to produce readings that effectively close off a map's meaning. "Truths" about the social space reproduced through the map are revealed once and for all by the deconstructionist. Returning to Derrida (1972, 1988b), however, suggests that Harley's methodology is much more a "historicization and a Foucauldian sensibility towards the power relations underpinning, and expressed in, maps". Sparke calls this "demythologising the map" and argues for critical readings that open up rather than reduce the complex interrelationships between map and space.

Critics of deconstruction may argue that such a call invites a total retreat from the political nature of Harley's project. But, as many authors have argued, deconstruction is a political project intended to subvert the foundational nature of Western philosophies. In Sparke's formulation of a critical cartography, elements of Derridean deconstruction are added to demythologization in order both to recognize the hegemonic nature of most maps and to keep open the possibility of other readings. We would argue that one such element is the destabilization of the oppositional binaries that underlie seemingly natural categories.

This argument is paralleled by developments in identity theory. Over the past two decades challenges to essentialist identity politics in cultural studies, postcolonial and poststructuralist literary theory, and later in geography have posited that identities based on race, gender, sexuality, and/or class are not inherent or natural, but are constructed as categories through hegemonic discourses. In other words, identity categories are themselves representations. As can be seen in the constitution of tourism identities, an other—the working nontourist for example—is constructed in opposition to leisured tourists. Because the sites of leisure for the tourist depend directly on the work of nontourists, however, tourism spaces always contain within them both the dominant identity, the tourist, and its submerged other, the tourism worker. Such constructions are articulated through hegemony: the employment of social power to make categories appear to be naturalized and fixed in space.

The identity categories constructed through these representations are always partial, however. They never capture the complex differences that constitute a particular social actor. This allows, and is caused by, individuals who perform their identity within and beyond these categories. In tourism spaces, tourism workers perform as part of the site and thus reproduce the tourism space and their identity as "host" through their actions. As individuals, they are to "become" the site, thus hiding what is, for them, work. At the same time, their performances can expose the partiality of the representational action through, for example, their resistance to the acts themselves. Their adlibbing rewrites scripts and regulated work norms. Thus, identity categories only imperfectly capture the identities of social actors performing within and beyond these categories, making the relationship between the category and any actor ambiguous and open to contestation.

The resultant tourism map spaces are thus tension-filled because they exist at a set of constructed boundaries between the exotic and the everyday, between resistance and regulation. Thus, while the maps and other representations deployed in tourism by entrepreneurs and government officials appear to fix and demarcate the boundaries between such dualisms, their ambiguous relationships to social actors performing their identities in tourism spaces ensure that these representations both legitimate and destabilize identity categories. Destabilizations of apparently authorial representations are thus possible because no one is merely a "tourist" or "tourism worker, " but is instead a multiple subject constituted of many discourses and identities. Each actor exists in a variety of social spaces simultaneously—at the "centre" of one category designation and at the "margins" of another.

Reading Identities in Tourism Map Spaces

In the simplest sense, we can examine the tourism map as a product of hegemonic discourses, as Harley does. We can analyze it for the way it incorporates texts, drawings, or photographs to fix the identities of both tourism spaces and social actors in those spaces. These attempts, however, never fully inscribe the map with meaning, because the map is not limited by the boundaries set on it through production. Maps do not just fix meaning at the moment of production, but (re)present the ambiguities and partiality of space and identity categories. Thus, following Sparke, we do not simply demythologize a map. Instead, we examine the complex sets of social relationships that produce and reproduce the map and the space it is a part of as an ambiguous site of identity construction.

Reading maps not just for the "exclusions" that Harley sought to expose, but for the intertextuality of the map, tourism space, and the identities of social actors, demonstrates the multiple meanings that are part of any identity category.

Therefore, we read maps not just as texts but as spaces. As such, a map space is not bound by the margins of the paper on which it is printed, but is inscribed with meaning through its intertextual linkages with other texts and spaces. In addition, map spaces are sites through which we can examine the processes of identity construction, and the historically and spatially contingent social relationships that constitute identity categories. To do this, we follow other identity theorists by arguing that all social actors perform within and beyond identity categories.

Map spaces, which represent these performed identities, similarly reproduce the traces of the ambiguities that are part of all categorical designations. Hegemonic discourses that seek to fix oppositional markers—leisure and work or the exotic and the everyday, for example—expose the intertextuality of any set of oppositions. Thus, it is important to examine how identities are disciplined within map spaces. At the same time, because traces of the other are always hidden within any category, we must examine how these disciplinary representations expose the presence of exclusions, margins, and other ambiguities. It is our contention that this process is readable in any map space.

This definition of map space presents some methodological challenges. It is not enough to write a history of representing Thailand to provide context or background before claiming that the map, in this case Bangkok, Stadtplan, contains the same tropes we identify in the history. A map space does not contain meanings as much as it "makes present" images, memories, spaces, and other representations that readers use to interpret it (Wood 1992). Therefore, we employ a less linear method to trace some of the many intertextual connections through which Bangkok, Stadtplan contributes to the reproduction of spaces and identities. Beginning with the symbols or icons that make up the map itself, we identify the oppositional categories that this map attempts to fix by reading through the map to other well-known representations, both past and present, which are structured around the same dualisms. At the same time, we note how the map space—composed of Bangkok, Stadtplan and the other texts and spaces it recalls—reproduces the tensions and ambiguities between and within these oppositions. Further, we illustrate how these work to undermine the categories of space and identity that this map space is intended to fix and reproduce.

Ambiguous Identities in Tourism Map Spaces of Thailand

Using the theoretical framework and methods already outlined, we now explore the reproduction of tourism identities and spaces in Bangkok, Stadtplan für Männer Presents the Nightlife, a 1991 map produced to guide German sex tourists to and through the thoroughly sexualized city of Bangkok. This map of sex-tourism spaces, identities, and performances is cartoonish, off-colour, and potentially offensive, making it a perfect example of the type of map dismissed or ignored by most cartographers and geographers of tourism. We believe, however, that reading this map as an unbounded space offers critical insights into the always partial attempts to fix the spaces and identities of tourism through the employments of oppositional categories.

Although this is, of course, only one of many different map spaces constructing Thailand and Bangkok as tourist destinations, we demonstrate how this representation of Bangkok is interconnected with some of these other markers of Thai tourism identities, both past and present. Produced by tourism capital and the Thai government, these images are re-presented on the map, helping to define Bangkok, and to a certain extent all of Thailand, as a tourism space and to identify Thai people as the perfect exotic hosts for Western tourists. We do not claim to capture the totality of Thailand's representational history, however. Instead, we explore some of the common tropes that are deployed throughout the history of writing Thailand as a place and identifying it as a tourism site. These are made explicit by our reading "through" map icons and across the map's boundaries to these other representations. At the same time, we note how this map space fails to fully fix the categories it recalls and reproduces, creating ambiguities and the potential for alternative interpretations, contestations, and other performances of resistance.

The set of images presented in this map is only one piece in a larger series of guidebooks, videos, and maps designed to guide the tourist through the sex-tourism spaces of the Southeast Asian region. The map itself is a white-on-gray road grid overlaid and overwhelmed by a colour-coordinated icon system designating the different forms of sexual entertainment. The map also has, on the back, a brief introduction to Bangkok, an advertisement for various videos on Southeast Asian sexual entertainment sites, and the names and descriptions of various forms of "entertainment." The map's cover is a reproduction of three women wearing tank tops and bikini bottoms working in a go-go bar. In essence this map is supposed to normalize Bangkok's function for exotic sex and demonstrate the safety of the space for the sex tourist. At the same time, the map images fix the tourist—normalising the practices of the tourist as "free from his everyday constraints"—and ease his movement from one form of entertainment to another.

Bangkok, Stadtplan's effectiveness in fixing the everyday/exotic and discipline/freedom oppositions onto Thai spaces and identities is dependent on its explicit and implicit references to other popularly known representations employing these and other dualisms to reproduce Thailand's image for tourists. For example, the guidebook Nightlife in Thailand (1988) deploys a common trope of urban areas as spaces of sexual availability. It is intended to highlight what is and what is not "open" for tourists seeking nighttime pleasures. Just as Bangkok, Stadtplan is intended to ease the tourist's movements to and through certain districts in Thailand's capital city, this representation of the guidebook's geography situates for the reader five major urban areas in Thailand where active "nightlife" is available. In addition, both maps normalize these sites as distinct from those found in the everyday lives of tourists. Nightlife in Thailand speaks to a wide audience, from those interested in five-star restaurants to go-go bars, allnight discos, and massage parlors, but seeks to make some experiences common to all who travel through Thailand's nightlife sites. For example, the authors of Nightlife argue that it is the go-go bars that most visitors to the city [Bangkok] really want to see. The name Patpong [a district in the downtown area] has become known the world over, so much so that coming to Bangkok and not seeing Patpong would be like going to Rome and ignoring the Coliseum. Thus, sex tourism has become a "normal" function of the everyday in Bangkok, and in other cities, as both Bangkok, Stadtplan and Nightlife in Thailand describe in detail. At the same time, the identity of these major urban tourism areas is constructed in opposition to an other, the rural. The rural exists as those spaces "ignored" in the Nightlife and Bangkok, Stadtplan maps, everything in between these major cities. The maps thus reproduce the tensions of a developing country actively engaged in opening up its urban areas to development, while demonstrating the lack of concern for the rural. It is only in the urban map spaces of nightlife, such as Bangkok, Stadtplan, that a tourist can find leisured cosmopolitan comforts in the site of an exotic other.

Bangkok, Stadtplan and other contemporary tourism map spaces of Thailand do not just reference each other. Ultimately, they become intelligible in the presence of a long history of disguising the tensions within the everyday/ exotic, rural/urban, and other dualisms by fixing them as oppositions. G. William Skinner notes that as early as the fifteenth century Southeast Asia was constructed as a sexualized space for foreign visitors:

Both Ma Huen and Fei Hsin [part of Chinese admiral Cheng Ho's mission throughout Southeast Asia during his famous 1405–33 expeditions] were greatly impressed by the independent status of Siamese women, and above all their predilection for Chinese men. According to Fei, "whenever meets a Chinese man, she is greatly pleased with him, and will invariably prepare wine to entertain and show respect to him, merrily singing and keeping him overnight." The husband in such a case, according to Ma, is not perturbed but flattered that his wife should be beautiful enough to please the Chinese. From this idyllic account, it would appear that the Chinese had other reasons than trade for resorting to Siam. In any case, the fabulous stories told by the expeditionaries after their return to China greatly stimulated trade and emigration to Nan-yang.

The sexual availability of Thai women for the Chinese marks this space as an other within their geographical imagination. It is not just Thailand, but all of Southeast Asia, that becomes a place that draws Chinese men to the region for "resorting." One can argue that this same myth motivates the large number of Chinese Malaysians and Singaporeans who today travel to southern Thailand for weekend vacations in the cocktail bars and cabaret lounges of Hat Yai, the largest urban centre in the southern part of the country. It is also possible that the early myths of the sexual availability of Thai woman spread through the trade routes between Europe, Africa, India, and China and reproduced Thailand's sexualized identity for both Chinese and non-Chinese men alike.

Thus, it is not surprising that Western representations of the nineteenth and twentieth centuries also rely on and reproduce many of the same dualisms, as they imagine Thailand as an exotic leisure paradise and identify Thai people as sensual, beautiful, erotic, and sexually available. J. Antonio's Guide to Bangkok and Siam (1904), for example, paints an image of a land and people sitting at the margins of civilization. He positions Thailand's unique exotic nature between the modern and the traditional, the West and the East. "In Siam to-day one sees a country emerging from the darkness of an ancient barbarism and rapidly assimilating those western methods which alone can assure it a permanent existence as a political entity".

The emergence of Thailand as a "modern" political entity is tempered by the iconography of this "barbarous" society. This tension is reproduced in the representations deployed to identify Thailand. As an example, photographs of Thai costumes highlight the multiple identities and class structure of urban and rural Thai peoples in Antonio's text. The use of women as models for these various fashions attaches Thailand to Western notions of femininity and sexuality. Additionally, the image captions categorize the styles as "traditional, " "modern, " and "hill tribe." "Traditional" denotes the clothing of the dominant central Thai people, while modern dress incorporates the European styles worn in Bangkok by wealthy elites, both royal and bourgeois. This latter fashion statement signals that this country, or at least parts of it, is available and "safe" for Western travellers, whereas the traditional garb is a reminder of Siam's exotic nature and the hill tribe "costume" represents its barbaric side.

Although tensions between the modern and the traditional are not as overt in Bangkok, Stadtplan, some of the map's entertainment icons call upon the East/West dualism directly to assure tourists that they can enjoy Western safety and comfort in the midst of Eastern exoticism. For example, the "nightclub and disco" icon represents for the tourist a comfortable and safe environment of simple leisured practices, practices that ironically can be had most anywhere. Because this is now in the tourism map space of Bangkok, however, it becomes an exotic, unique space of leisure apparently opposed to the leisure spaces of the West.

The "coffee-shop" icon in Bangkok, Stadtplan also reproduces the tensions between East and West, the everyday and the exotic. It appears to mimic an idyllic 1950s Western soda shop, and is therefore a "safe" and comfortable space in exotic "Oriental" Bangkok. The two men, both Caucasian, are engaged in conversation, as the third person, a "Thai" woman with Western features and clothing but "almond-shaped eyes, " sits on the side staring at the two men. This reactionary moment represents the reason some Western men travel to Thailand: to reassert a position of dominance in a relationship with a women, to have a companion who is "seen and not heard." The map thus contains within it traces of Western feminism that, for the reactionary male tourist identified in this map space, mark Western women as "less available" and thus less exotic. Such traces of an imperfectly excluded other—Western feminism—ensure that this map space contains more than just the leisured activities of a Western masculine fundamentalism.

These icons' negotiations between the exotic and the everyday and East and West "make present" images used in other contemporary promotions of Thailand produced by the tourism industry. As an advertisement for the Siam International Hotel titled "Rudyard Kipling Never Stayed Here" states:

Mr. Kipling never stayed with us at the Siam International Bangkok, because our hotel hadn't been built in his day. And as far as we know, he didn't venture as far East as Thailand. But if he had, we feel sure he would have had second thoughts about his immortal line: "East is East and West is West and never the twain shall meet."

Because at the Siam International we've combined the best of the East with the best of the West. Our building is of spectacular Thai design. And our service is wholly Thai. So we do everything possible to make you comfortable and we do it all with a smile. Yet we offer you the very best of western comfort, cuisine, and entertainment. When in Bangkok you owe it to yourself to stay at the Siam International.

Thus, it is through the map's icons that the map space of Bangkok is a part of other representations and spaces of Thailand's tourism sites. In effect, these icons represent the disciplining of leisure through its confi nement to particular places and specific tourist rituals.

The "nightclub and disco" icon, therefore, fixes the identity of the tourist as a "rednosed drunk, " yet passive observer of the performances of particular acts designed to attract his attention. He engages in the regulated map spaces of tourism and acts within the bounds of an identity constructed out of its opposition to his "everyday."

The use of the exotic/everyday and East/West dualisms to fix the spaces of tourism in Thailand is practiced not only by Western tour companies and Thai capitalists, but by Thai government agencies and officials as well. At the suggestion of the World Bank, the Thai government embarked on a campaign in the 1960s to actively promote tourism as a form of sustainable development. First through the Tourism Organization of Thailand (TOT) and later through the Tourism Authority of Thailand (TAT), the Thai government produced texts and images that portrayed Thailand as both a site of exotic natural human and physical beauty and of ancient traditions, all of which are safely placed within a modern booming economy, a democratic society, and an anticommunist stronghold. These official representations of Thai spaces and identities for the purpose of tourism lend meaning to Bangkok, Stadtplan.

Thailand Illustrated, a magazine that was published by the Department of Public Relations in Thailand beginning in the 1960s and through the 1970s, is an example of official attempts to fix Thailand as a tourism space. An examination of the magazine for the period 1967 to 1974 reveals some interesting representational consistencies and demonstrates that several ideological motivations lay behind the design of the magazine. Using representations of the royal family, archaeological sites, traditional customs, and beauty contest winners, the magazine supports tourism growth and promotes nationalism while demonstrating how these two projects are intertwined. Dignitaries, such as British royalty and California governors, are ushered through the pages of this text and place Thailand at the centre of a developing Southeast Asian region.

The linkage between tourism and nationalism, developed discursively through representation, is materially produced in government-sanctioned festivals, markets, entertainment districts, and particular cultural practices demonstrating the safe and accessible contexts for tourism travel. Protests and other transgressive practices against the government are hidden by this celebration of nationalism through tourism. Bangkok, Stadtplan has similar erasures. Hidden behind the cartoon icons are slums and other establishments not related to the sex-tourism industry, thus promising a hassle-free environment for the tourist.

More obviously connected to the Bangkok, Stadtplan map space is Thailand Illustrated's construction of Thailand as site of natural human beauty and sexual availability. Beauty contest winners and other Thai women are represented on 44 per cent of the magazine's covers from 1967 to 1974. This is not surprising considering the economic importance of the developing sex-tourism industry at this time and the role that feminine identities have played in the development of national identities.

In addition, although the government has never officially sanctioned sex tourism, its long-term benign neglect of the industry coupled with its representations of Thailand, especially of Thai women, helps reproduce the country as a unique site for leisure activities and defines it as a space of sexual openness far away from the disciplining mores of Western society. ("A farmhouse in the central region of Thailand" and "A northern belle at Mae Klang Waterfalls, Chiang Mai") demonstrate the central role of Thai women in the Illustrated's production of Thailand for tourists. The covers and the advertisements and photographs inside the magazine often depicted women in traditional roles and rural settings, but sacrificed accuracy for beauty by replacing farm attire with the finest sarongs. The romanticized view of the land and of farming in particular, is also transferred directly to the female figure. Instead, a woman is placed in the physical landscape: tropical beauty and human beauty are fused. Unlike the first image, the women are removed from any form of economic or ritual activity, such as farming, and are juxtaposed with the landscape. Her wrap, a Thai bathing cloth, is as close to nude as one can get in this context: in the village no adult is ever seen without a wrap when bathing.

The tourism-development literature produced by the Thai government thus draws on images of a sexualized past and a set of ephemeral qualities—beauty, serenity, peacefulness, and exoticism—to mark Thailand as an exotic and erotic site. This process of representing Thailand through the image of women can also be noted in an advertisement for Thai International Airlines from 1971, which positions the following text above the smiling face of a young Thai woman:

What could she learn in Sweden? Every one of Thai International's hostesses is taught the trade in Sweden. That means getting to grips with the technical details involved in serving over 100 people in the confines of today's big jets. It's a complicated business and they go to the best air hostess training centre in the world to learn it. Their side of the business you see is a different matter. To a Thai girl friendliness, courtesy and willingness-to-please are second nature. It's something they are born to have. Other airlines talk about girls trained to be friendly and helpful. To our girls any other way of doing things would be unthinkable.

The Thai flight attendant is trained in the European tradition but embodies a pure Thai sexuality that is exemplified by "friendliness, courtesy and willingness-to-please." It is an attempt to naturalize this identity and fix it for the tourist.

Returning to the "coffee-shop" icon, we can see how Bangkok, Stadtplan reproduces this supposed sexual availability of Thai women. In Bangkok, the coffee shop is a commonly accepted place to meet freelance commercial sex workers. Thus, the passive woman depicted in this "innocent" scene is not just a 1950s throwback, but is available for sex as well. The almond eyes confirm her Thai identity, further assuring Western male readers that she is friendly, courteous, and willing to please. Nevertheless, women may transform this reactionary moment into a positive net effect for themselves. Playing a "role" for tourists allows them to earn income, for example, from men who may feel that they have "fallen in love." They are therefore not simply victims but agents performing identities.

In this way, a tension is created within the most fundamental set of oppositional categories in tourism: work and leisure. The coffee shop, an apparently safe and readable leisure space for the tourist, is also a space of work for women, bartenders, and others performing identities. Leisure thus depends on its opposite, work, to sustain its meaning for tourists and nontourists alike. The map space is intended to annihilate work from its image, but the very production of any leisure space is dependent on its other, work, for its identity. The map space, and the material spaces it is tied to, are both leisure and work spaces simultaneously. Thus, attempts to fix the boundaries between the exotic and the everyday, leisure and work, expose the hegemonic discourses that seek to define and maintain these differences and reveal the ambiguous and blurry natures of these mutually constituting identity categories. This is brought forth even more strongly in the icon of the go-go dancer. Her face maintains an obvious grimace. It demonstrates the outward reality of this industry and the difficulty that such a job brings to someone who must sell her body and emotions on a daily basis. Work, monotonous and sometimes depressing, is brought to the fore.

Also recalled in Bangkok, Stadtplan are some of its more immediate representational precursors. An informal set of writings that began to popularize the Thai sex-tourism industry in the 1960s highlights further the tensions existing within the dualisms—everyday/exotic and work/leisure—that are produced when these oppositions are employed to fix the identities of Thai tourism

For example, Andrew Harris's (1968) underground classic Bangkok after Dark became a fantasy guide for incoming European and North American sex tourists throughout the 1970s and served to reinscribe Thailand as a unique, yet safe, sexualized space. Harris echoes the sentiments of the Thai International advertisement in his opening chapter:

But even while the plane was still in the air, there were indications of what lay ahead… The two hostesses brought a continual procession of drinks and food… they were coffee-coloured creatures with almond shaped eyes who moved with a grace I had never seen before…. And the girls were continually smiling—not the usual smiles of airline hostesses, but warm smiles that seemed to transform the cold airplane cabin. (Harris 1968: 9)

Like the comforts of modern air travel and the "procession of drinks and food" mixed with the exotic "coffee-coloured creatures with almond shaped eyes" provided by the Thai flight attendant, the map space examined here exhibits similar tensions and demonstrates the intertextual linkages between this space and other spaces.

The Thai flight attendants are both the exotic and the everyday. On the map, Thai women are represented with Caucasian-image icons that constitute their bodies as sites of tension between "Eastern" and "Western" sexuality.

The poses, clothes, and hairstyles assert the comfortable—the safeties of the everyday in a Western context—but the "almond-shaped" eyes identify and maintain the idea of the exotic. The performance of go-go and the deployment of Caucasian-image icons demonstrates that these are acts designed to fit into a particular set of preconceived notions of sexuality.

The icons therefore represent neither authentic nor inauthentic acts, but instead demonstrate that the practices of social actors are within (and perhaps beyond) particular category designations. Similar processes of identity formation occur on the plane and in the map space. The performances of these social actors also appear to "naturalize" Thai female sexuality as exotic and other and expose the identification of a space of leisure as a space of work as well.

Thailand is safe, not only because of the traces of a familiar West, but also because it is a space outside the everyday routines of tourists. Thus acts that might be deemed inappropriate are more manifest in this unique and socially distant place. It is thus not surprising that this map space, which claims to be distant and exotic, represents multiple ways in which tourists can engage in activities not consistent with their everyday lives. Further, as a leisure space Thailand is available for a variety of transgressions from the heterosexualized norms present in everyday Western—and Thai—society. The image of the "transvestite" illustrates further how this map space represents the tensions present in any identity construction.

Present in the Bangkok sex-tourism landscape are the possibilities to act outside heterosexualized spaces and within those spaces designed for "third" genders. This icon signals alternatives to heterosexual experiences for the tourist. It is not a Thai man in drag, but a German man, goatee and all, who stands in for the image of the transvestite. At the same time, this emancipatory moment demonstrates that sexuality is not only performed but also regulated through the confinement of particular practices to specific sites in the urban landscape. This moment of emancipation cannot exist outside of its other, regulation. They are mutually constituted.

The collision of the dualisms—exotic/everyday, authentic/inauthentic, emancipation/regulation, gay/straight—within the map spaces of tourism illustrates the mutual constitution of these oppositional pairs. The exotic icons are dependent on everyday images of leisure. This is necessary so that the tourist can read and act within a set of temporarily fixed identity markers. Similarly, the staged acts of the tourism workers highlight the performative nature of identity and demonstrate that these acts are neither authentic nor inauthentic.

They are instead the result of the temporary suturing of particular performances to particular identity categories in a map space. Thus the representations that are intended to stand in their place are also constitutive of the temporary and performed identities of both tourists and nontourists in Thailand and represent the ambiguity of these spaces.

The ambiguous identities present in the map space also mean that the map itself is open to multiple interpretations and uses that reference alternative representations of Thailand that have always existed. Despite the power of the Thai government and capitalists (both international and national) to promote Thailand as site of tourism bliss, their images are called upon to attract the outrage of an international audience of activists and scholars as well. Thus, maps such as Bangkok, Stadtplan document and open up this space to both local and global criticism and to alternative uses (such as this essay).

The map space's production and existence create their own negations and their own opposition. Women's groups speak out against sex tourism and Buddhist monks contest what they see as the growing commodification of Thai society and a loss of moral ethics. For example, the Asia Watch Women's Rights Project (1993) has published a scathing exposé on the trafficking of Burmese women, who are literally sold in Burma to Thai entrepreneurs and corrupt border police who sell these women to brothel owners in the southern and western parts of the country. In addition, groups in Thailand such as Empower and Friends of Women have gained international recognition for their efforts to improve the position of women in Thailand and challenge the power of the sex-tourism industry. These challenges demonstrate that, once produced, any attempt to inscribe the map with meaning will be completely contingent on the reader himself or herself and how he or she chooses to deploy the embedded images.

The international attention garnered through such critical responses to the sexualized and commodified tourism spaces of Bangkok, Stadtplan and other representations has helped activists in Thailand continue to combat the uneven relationships between men and women, rich and poor. It, along with internal attention drawn to Thailand's AIDS epidemic, has helped force the Thai government to address commercial sex work and some of the economic inequalities that promote such an industry. The Thai government has reevaluated tourism and diversified its tourism economy, a trend that is evident in the tourism map spaces of Thailand. As an example, the shift in cover representation on Nelles Verlag's Thailand map from the image of a woman on the 1994 edition to that of a Buddhist monk on the 1998 edition illustrates how Thailand is being represented less as an exotic, overtly feminine site to one that is more focused on the "traditional" cultural attractions that Buddhist icons represent.

One has to be careful, however, not to read counterhegemonic discussions as wholly "outside" the systems that inform dominant discourses. Through the reliance on models of colonialism, markers of wealth and poverty, and/or biological reductions of sexual difference, such counterhegemonic discourses reinscribe, to a certain extent, the dominant discourses and identity categories that often hide the voices of those peoples that they are hoping to illuminate. Groups, represented as an individual identity designation, such as "Thai female prostitutes, " for example, can become the stand-in for a much more complex, dynamic, and individual experience of commercial sex work that varies across space, class, and ethnicity. We can recognize, therefore, the ambiguities that exist in any set of representations and read such representations for both the absences they produce and those notions that are, perhaps, most present.

Further, as representations proliferate and sectors of the global tourism industry fight for a share of the market, these representations and the spaces they claim to represent are reinscribed with new meanings and juxtaposed with new spaces and images in order to maintain themselves as tourist sites. A quick look at Patpong, one of the most famous sextourism sites in Thailand and found as an inset on Bangkok, Stadtplan, illustrates these changes.

By the late 1980s, the Thai government began efforts to shift its image as a sexualized space and diversify its tourist economy. Investments throughout the 1980s in beach resorts, ecotourism, trekking, and shopping districts have altered the arrangement of the industry.

Patpong has changed as well, masking its sex-tourism persona behind a government-sanctioned night market. Today, the entire site is covered with this market and serves as one of the major attractions for men, women, and couples in Thailand.

The once exclusively sex-tourism space of Bangkok is now a tourism shopping mecca, with hundreds of stalls fronting the neon signs of the go-go bars and sex-show shops.

Only Thanon Thaniya, an area that sits next to Patpong and is designated euphemistically as "Little Tokyo, " escapes this masquerade. Its less visible members clubs, many located on second-floor shops, are not as overt a demonstration of Thailand's sextourism history.

It may have not been Bangkok, Stadtplan für Männer Presents the Nightlife per se that anchored the challenges that led to the covering of this space, but its existence and complex interrelationships to other representations, spaces, and identities made this shift possible.

It is no secret that Thailand depends heavily on tourism and tourism dollars to sustain its economy (Ulack and Del Casino 2000).

That dependence has given rise to an enormous representational infrastructure, both within and beyond Thailand, through which some social actors, particularly entrepreneurs and governmental tourism officials, struggle to maintain Thailand's "exotic" appeal.

This process of constructing Thailand as a tourism destination, both materially and socially, involves the isolation and deployment of key dualisms: the exotic is positioned against the everyday and leisure is negotiated as an opposite of work, for example.

The representational practices of tourism entrepreneurs and government officials are intended to reify and naturalize these dualisms by drawing on a reconstructed history of Thailand's lands and peoples. Exoticism and leisure are thus "transferred" to social actors who are meant to perform a particular set of scripted practices as they work in and through tourism spaces.

Through an examination of Bangkok, Stadtplan we have explored some of the ways in which such apparently fixed dualisms may be destabilized and (re)presented through a critical cartographic framework. We have "chipped away" at the rigidly constructed and hegemonic representation of Thailand and

Thai sexuality as fetishized objects and exposed the ways in which the categories of Thainess, Thai femininity, and Western and Asian masculinity are socially and spatially constructed through representational practices.

In addition, our reading of Bangkok, Stadtplan is intended as an illustration of both a theoretical framework for understanding the relationships among maps, spaces, and identities and a methodological approach for examining any tourism map.

Thus, we argue that neither a tourism space nor the map that claims to represent that space are final products; rather, both are processes through which social and spatial identities are constructed and contested.

The complex intertextual linkages that make the maps, spaces, and the identities of tourism "work" actually make any tourism map an integral part of identity formation and the production of space. The boundaries between maps and spaces are, therefore, erased, resulting in what we call the map spaces of tourism.

Because a tourism map space is always an ongoing process as people simultaneously use and experience it as they practice tourism, it follows that no single reading can ever reveal a final and complete set of intertextual moments within a map space that enable it to work. Furthermore, all map users will approach the map from different directions and will bring with them their own sets of knowledges and experiences.

In other words, different people will focus on different map icons and will make different intertextual connections with these symbols. Because of this, we choose not to simply place an entire map in a linear history of the production of tourism spaces and identities through representation.

Instead, we employ a nonlinear reading method in which we trace out possible connections between a map icon and the representational field constructing tourism space and identities and then return to the map to trace another set of connections.

We do not do this, however, to argue that representational strategies serving dominant interests are any less likely to succeed in reproducing hegemonic categorizations of space and identity. Rather, we argue that the precise ways that both hegemonic and resistant texts are invoked in the map spaces of tourism are always subject to change.

Indian Sex Tourism

Sex tourism in India has assumed "serious dimensions" because of lack of open protest by citizens and slender chances that the abusers will be caught or punished.

While Goa has been the "sex destination" of foreign tourists for a long time, a growing number of cases have been reported from the beaches of Kovalam in Kerala, Puri in Orissa and Digha in West Bengal.

In India, the abuse by tourists of both male and female children has assumed serious dimensions. Unlike Sri Lanka and Thailand, this problem has not been seriously tackled or discussed openly and has remained more or less shrouded in secrecy.

The likelihood of child abusers being caught and punished is low and the silence of the community and its unwillingness to speak out and openly discuss the issue has further complicated the problem. In Puri, for example, the local people depend on tourists for survival and so they do not protest, even though they know enough about what is happening.

Ever increasing number of sex offenders from Western countries are shifting their operations to developing countries because of increasing vigilance and action against paedophilia in their own land and the fact that many of these nations are turning a blind eye to the problem with a view to encouraging tourism.

Bibliography

A.K. Sarkar.: *Action Plan and Priorities in Tourism Development*, Kanishka Publication, Delhi, 2010.

A.K. Sarkar.: *Indian Tourism, Management, Motivation and Mobility*, Rajat Publications, Delhi, 2003

A.S. Dileep, T. Rajesh.: *Ayurvedic Tourism*, Sonali Publications, Delhi, 2012.

Amrita Bhagnani: *Handbook of Tourism*, Abhijeet Publications, Delhi, 2012.

Anjali Verma.: *Dictionary of Tourism*, Radha Publication, Delhi, 2006.

Annamalai Murugan.: *Hospitality and Tourism Laws With Conventions*, Abhijeet Publications, Delhi, 2012,

Srivastava and Keya Pandey.: *Anthropology and Tourism*, Serials Publications, Delhi, 2012.

Anupama Srivastava and Keya Pandey.: *Anthropology and Tourism*, Serials Publications, Delhi, 2012.

Arvind Gautam.: *Critical Analysis of Hospitality and Tourism Industry*, Axis Publication, Delhi, 2010.

B S Badan, Harish Bhatt.: *Hospitality and Tourism*, Commonwealth Publications, Delhi, 2007.

Dilip Das.: *Critical Issues in Tourism*, Murari Lal and Sons, Delhi, 2011.

Graham Dodgshun, Michel Peters.: *Cookery for the Hospitality Industry*, Cambridge University Press, New York, 2001.

Gulshan Soni.: *Consumer Protection in Hospitality Travel and Tourism*, Aman Publication, Delhi, 2011.

Hemant Sharma.: *HRM in Hospitality Industry*, ABD Publication, Delhi, 2006.

Jitendra K. Sharma.: *Contemporary Tourism and Hospitality Management*, Kanishka Publication, Delhi, 2006.

K. Sharma.: *Contemporary Tourism and Hospitality Management*, Kanishka Publication, Delhi, 2006.

M. Sarngadharan, V.S. Sunanda.: *Health Tourism in India*, New Century Publications, Delhi, 2009.

Madhusoodan Tripathi, Nishant Singh.: *Indian Tourism Industry*, A Blueprint to Success, Radha Publications, Delhi, 2007.

Mahadev Kertwal.: *Advertising in Leisure and Tourism*, Cyber Tech, New Delhi, 2012.

Nepal, Ramesh Raj Kunwar: *Anthropology of Tourism: A Case Study of Chitwan-Sauraha*, Adroit Publication, Delhi, 2002.

Nirmal Dubey.: *Hospitality Tourism and Hotel Management*, Sonali Publications, Delhi, 2011.

P C Sinha: *International Encyclopaedia of Tourism Ethics (3 Vols- Set)*, Anmol Publications, Delhi, 2006.

P.K. Bal.: *A Text Book of Hospitality Tourism and Aviation*, Cyber Tech Publication, New Delhi, 2011.

K. Bal: *A Text Book of Hospitality Tourism and Aviation*, Cyber Tech Publication, Delhi, 2011.

Ramesh Raj Kunwar: *Anthropology of Tourism: A Case Study of Chitwan-Sauraha*, Nepal, Adroit Publication, New Delhi, 2002.

Sunil Sharma.: *Hospitality and Tourism Marketing*, Akansha Publications, Delhi, 2005.

Varinder Singh Rana.: *Catering Hospitality and Tourism*, Centrum Press, Delhi, 2012.

Singh Rana.: *Catering Hospitality and Tourism*, Centrum Press, Delhi, 2012.

Index